The Emergence of Pentecostalism in Wales

A Historical, Theological Evaluation of the Early Development of the
Assemblies of God Denomination in South East Wales

With Special Reference to Crosskeys and Newbridge

by Dr Chris Palmer

ΑΠΟΣΤΟΛΟΣ

APOSTOLOS PUBLISHING LTD

The Emergence of Pentecostalism in Wales by Dr Chris Palmer

First Published in Great Britain in 2016

Apostolos Publishing Ltd,

3rd Floor, 207 Regent Street,

London W1B 3HH

www.apostolos-publishing.com

Copyright © 2016 Chris Palmer

British Library Cataloguing-in-Publication Data

A catalogue record for this book is available from the British Library

ISBN: 978-1-910942-31-4

Cover Design by Blitz Media, Pontypool, Torfaen

Cover Image © Dmytro Tolmachov | Dreamstime.com

Printed and bound in Great Britain by Marston Book Services Limited, Oxfordshire.

Foreword

In this book Chris Palmer gives us the first detailed and wide-ranging account of the emergence of Pentecostalism in Wales at the start of the 20th century. He uncovers links that have been unknown to previous historians and shows the crucial importance of Welsh congregations not only to Wales itself but to the whole of Pentecostalism in the UK. Set against a broad social background and supported by careful research there is much here to interest the academic historian and inspire ordinary churchgoers interested in understanding their faith.

William Kay, Professor of Theology at Glyndwr University, Wales and Professor of Pentecostal Studies at the University of Chester, England.

Preface by the Author

The roots of this book reach back to my Master's Degree studies at Mattersey Hall, the AoG GB&I training college, in 1998–99. I was sat through the immensely entertaining lectures of Dr David Allen on Pentecostal Church history. During his lectures a brief mention was made of some correspondence between a few men in Crosskeys, Wales, and the AoG in America in 1923. This led me to think about the roots of my own spiritual heritage in the valleys of SE Wales; for I knew that the assembly at Crosskeys had commenced life around 1912; much earlier than the lectures suggested. What should I do? I decided to research and discover the truth about my spiritual AoG forefathers; who as I have subsequently discovered were pioneers in the area of Pentecostal experience well before the AoG GB&I was formed in 1924.

This research led me to Wales Evangelical School of Theology (WEST) Bridgend and the pursuit of a PhD under the supervision of Rev. Dr D. Eryl Davies and Lampeter University's Professor D. Densil Morgan. These two men helped, guided, supported, corrected, and challenged my thinking during the period of research and writing. I am extremely grateful to them for their encouragement and guidance. This book is an edited version of my PhD dissertation which was accepted in 2013.

I am also indebted to a number of other people; firstly to One Mission Society—my employers—who allowed me the time to dedicate to research and writing. The benefits now being seen in my ability to travel widely and teach at OMS related Bible Colleges. Secondly my parents David & Susan for the introduction to AoG teaching from childhood and a godly example throughout my life.

Also to the members of Crosskeys Pentecostal Church who for a period of 3 years allowed me the privilege to lead, preach, and teach from their pulpit following in the footsteps of some significant AoG figures. And to allow me the opportunity to learn more of the early developments of that key assembly. Finally to Jayne & Thomas who have endured hours of me being locked away in my study, the constant book buying and a lack of quality family time over the 5 years of research – thank you! - Newbridge 2015

Dedicated to my father David and Uncles John and Peter; Pentecostals who have been influential in my spiritual and theological formation.

Abstract

British Pentecostalism is linked to the Azusa Street Revival in Los Angeles through T. B. Barratt and Anglican vicar Alexander A. Boddy at Sunderland. Boddy's experience and subsequent ministry set the foundation in Britain for the rise of the Apostolic Church, the Elim Church and the Assemblies of God. Each of these Pentecostal denominations had their roots in Wales.

Following the Welsh Revival of 1904–05 some, enthused by their experience, sought a deeper relationship with God; and this search ultimately led them to Pentecostalism. A group of eager believers emerged around the town of Crosskeys in South East Wales. By 1912 they had established the Crosskeys Full Gospel Mission, which soon became a centre for Pentecostal activity. The central role of the Crosskeys group is seen in the development of the Assemblies of God in Wales and Monmouthshire denomination which was in existence by 1921. The Crosskeys based group had been in correspondence with the American Assemblies of God (AG) regarding joining that denomination as an official presbytery. It was this action that caused a group of like-minded English Pentecostals to pursue the establishment of the Assemblies of God in Great Britain and Ireland in 1924. This British denomination incorporated some thirty eight Welsh Pentecostal assemblies.

This book considers some of the important theological, political and social influences which shaped these embryonic Welsh Pentecostals. I hope to demonstrate that belief in premillennial eschatology, divine healing, an aggressive missiology which was fuelled by Pentecostalism's distinctive pneumatology, were the distinctive factors which moulded the brand of Pentecostalism that emerged in South East Wales in the early twentieth century—a movement which was to have a wide ranging influence on subsequent Pentecostal history far beyond the borders of Wales.

Contents

Chapter 1 Introduction

Between 1921 and 1924 a group of Christian men representing disparate Welsh Pentecostal assemblies was in correspondence with the American Assemblies of God to investigate the possibility of becoming a 'Welsh Presbytery' attached to that denomination.[1] This action is understood by AoG historians David Allen and William Kay as being one of the catalysts in the eventual formation of the Assemblies of God denomination in Great Britain & Ireland.[2] Leaders of similar disparate English Pentecostal groups—such as John Nelson Parr, Thomas Myerscough, Howard Carter and John Carter—began proceedings to unify their respective assemblies into a new denomination, and invited their Welsh counterparts to join an exploratory meeting for this purpose. Two representatives from Wales, Tom Mercy of Crosskeys and George Vale of Gorseinon, joined the discussions. This initial meeting of British Christian leaders who held to the teachings now associated with the Assemblies of God took place at Sheffield, England, on 23 and 24 May 1922.[3] Ten men signed a declaration that contained recommendations regarding the structure, fundamental truths and ordinances of a movement that was to become the Assemblies of God (AoG) in Great Britain & Ireland (GB&I). This meeting, however, failed in its purpose of forming a new denomination.

Consequently, the Welsh assemblies continued to correspond with the American representatives and were well advanced in the process of being accepted as an official presbytery. This stung the English Pentecostal leaders into action and they revived their earlier discussions. On 1 February 1924, the majority of the original leaders and representatives from the May 1922

---

[1] Cited in David Allen, 'Signs and Wonders: The Origins, Growth, Development and Significance of the Assemblies of God in Great Britain and Ireland 1900–1980' (PhD Dissertation, University of London, unpublished, 1990), 110–11. For American AoG see Edith L. Blumhofer, *The Assemblies of God: A Chapter in the story of American Pentecostalism, Volume 1 - to 1941* (Springfield, MO: G.P.H., 1989). See Appendix 1 for copies of correspondence between Wales and America. I am indebted to Mr Desmond Cartwright for making copies of these letters available to me.

[2] Allen, 'Signs and Wonders', 110–11. William K. Kay, *Inside Story: A History of British Assemblies of God.* (Mattersey: Mattersey Hall, 1990), 78.

[3] Taken from a copy of the original/proposed Constitution of the General Council of the Assemblies of God in Great Britain and Ireland, held in Sheffield 23–24 May 1922. Donald Gee Centre for Pentecostal & Charismatic Research, Mattersey Hall, Nottinghamshire <www.matterseyhall.com>

meetings reconvened and held discussions that led to a ratification of the earlier proposals. This action paved the way for the official formation of the AoG GB&I. The inaugural meeting took place on 31 May 1924 in Birmingham when 38 of the 76 Assemblies in agreement with the proposals were from Wales. Of the 38 Welsh assemblies represented, 17 were from South East Wales. There were two Welsh representatives on the original executive presbytery, T. L. Hicks (who had replaced T. Mercy) of Crosskeys and W. Davies (who had replaced George Vale) of Caerau.[4] It will be necessary to chart the developments prior to 1924 that led to the emergence of these Pentecostal groups In South East Wales. Reference will also be made to the theological influences on the emergent Pentecostals during this period within South East Wales, and any possible effects these may have had upon the emerging Pentecostalism, but specifically the AoG.

Aims

1. The first aim of this book is to investigate the origins and development of AoG within the social, economic, political and theological context of South East Wales. The period 1901–1924 will serve as its focus, since 1901 is the accepted date for the commencement of Pentecostal teaching in America, and 1924 is the official date of the origins of AoG in Britain. In respect to South East Wales, 1914 is the year some Welsh Pentecostal pioneers travelled to All Saints parish church, Monkwearmouth, Sunderland, in order to observe and experience the ministry of Rev. A. A. Boddy, an Anglican rector.[5] The founders of the Crosskeys Pentecostal Church—which is viewed by AoG historian Alfred Missen as the mother church of South East Wales Pentecostalism—made this initial visit to Sunderland and brought back the Pentecostal message to the eastern valleys.[6]

---

[4] Minutes of the General Presbytery of the Assemblies of God in Great Britain and Ireland, Birmingham, 1 February 1924.

[5] Gavin Wakefield, *Alexander Boddy: Pentecostal Anglican Pioneer* (London: Paternoster, 2007), Neil Hudson, 'The Earliest Days of British Pentecostalism', *JEPTA* 21 (2001), 49–67, William, K. Kay, 'Sunderland's Legacy in New Denominations,' *JEPTA* 28/2 (2008), 183–99, Gavin Wakefield, 'The Human Face of Pentecostalism: Why the British Pentecostal Movement began in the Sunderland Parish of the Church of England Vicar Alexander Boddy,' *JEPTA* 28/ 2 (2008), 158–68.

[6] Alfred F. Missen, *The Sound Of A Going,* (Nottingham: AoG, 1973) 47.

During these early years of Pentecostal fervour, some who had received 'the baptism in the Holy Spirit' returned to their traditional denominational churches. Their desire was to share their new experience and theological stance with their own congregations. This, however, led mostly to friction and eventually the formation of independent Pentecostal groups. In Crosskeys the critical theological disputes initially focused on Premillennialism and healing; from 1914 onwards Pentecostal issues moved to the forefront of the debate. I will return to these theological developments later. However it was these Welsh pioneers who were responsible for the correspondence with the American AG.

According to Donald Gee, there was particular concern over the issue of theological accountability and the possibility of erroneous teachings within the independent Pentecostal groups.[7] Gaining the support of the larger and well-structured American denomination would allow for such accountability and theological support. The importance of the correspondence between Wales and America should not be overlooked, as it contains valuable information regarding the emergence of AoG in South Wales. A careful reading of it reveals a significant group, some 31 assemblies, in South Wales and Monmouthshire that had adopted the title Assemblies of God. This was three years before the official GB&I denomination came into existence. The names T. L. Hicks, H. Crook, R. Anthony, W. Attwood, Price Davis and T. Mercy were included in the letters to America as officers and executive members of the Assemblies of God in Wales and Monmouthshire pre 1924.[8] Hicks and Mercy subsequently served on the full GB&I Executive of AoG. The intention of this study is to explore the significance of this Welsh group of assemblies in relation to the development of the British AoG generally, a fact which is more significant than AoG historians have previously suggested.[9] How these early figures influenced the theological thinking of the denomination is an aspect of research which

---

[7] Donald Gee, *Wind and Flame* (Croydon: AoG, 1967), 122–30. Here Gee relates the general situation within the small assemblies that had emerged throughout Britain.

[8] Letter to E. N. Bell American AG dated 6 Feb. 1922—signed by H. Crook of Pontnewydd, Cwmbran, Mon. (See Appendix 1).

[9] Both David Allen and William Kay refer to a single letter but neither gives this issue the necessary attention I deem it deserves.

will be pursued. Were these Welsh leaders influential in the formation of Pentecostal doctrine on a national scale? Or did they submit to, and agree with, the English leaders who dominated the higher positions of leadership within the denomination?

In highlighting and evaluating the salient features of the complex theological and religious scene in Wales during this period, the aim will be to ascertain whether a root of Pentecostalism emerge at this time. One prominent figure in South East Wales was Pastor Thomas Madog Jeffreys of Waunlwyd, Ebbw Vale. Jeffreys was the pastor of the English Congregational Church in Waunlwyd and had been affected by the 1904–05 Welsh Revival. In his attempts to continue the effects of the revival he turned to the emerging Pentecostals. In 1907 A. Moncur Niblock, a Pentecostal from London who had contact with both A. A. Boddy and Cecil Polhill, conducted a mission at Waunlwyd in which he proclaimed the Pentecostal message.[10] Jeffreys had by now been introduced to, and was supportive of, the Pentecostal message; having come into contact with Boddy through the latter's involvement in Wales.[11]

Traditional chapel life in South Wales was in no way Pentecostal; although a number of the early members of the movement emerged from local chapels they had no previous knowledge of any Pentecostal-type doctrine. The prevailing evangelicalism within Wales would certainly have promoted the person and work of the Holy Spirit, but would have done so without reference to an Acts 2 type experience as defining Spirit baptism. In the Crosskeys locality, some were drawn from the Methodist chapel at Ponty-waun, some two miles from the site of the current Pentecostal assembly. Hence for some the link with the holiness movement with its distinctive 'second blessing' teaching

---

[10] Gee, *Wind and Flame*, 34–37, 60–66. Colin Whittaker, *Seven Pentecostal Pioneers* (Basingstoke: Marshalls, 1983), 49. T. M. Jeffreys was involved with the PMU and at various times during his ministry taught at its newly formed Pentecostal London Training Home, which had been established under the leadership of A. Moncur Niblock, he also had a great interest in missions. There are many missionary articles penned by him in Confidence magazine.

[11] Tony Cauchi, *Confidence Magazine 1908–1926, on CD Rom* (Bishop's Waltham: Revival Library, 2004), April 1908, 13. All researchers into Pentecostalism are indebted to Tony Cauchi and the Revival Library staff for their diligence in collecting and collating much primary documentation and producing it in easily available format.

was strong.[12] Another more significant group emerged from the Congregational churches at Ponty-waun and Wattsville a few miles from Crosskeys. It was here that a group of miners was challenged by teaching on the imminent premillennial Second Coming of Christ; a message which prompted them to urgent evangelism and to seek after a greater holiness of life. With such teachings being given prominence, the theological differences soon became apparent and the embryonic Pentecostal groups began to be ostracised with the result that many of them left their denominations. The result of their departure was the appearance of small cottage meetings that developed eventually into Pentecostal groups and some eventually into AoG churches. From 1912 the Pentecostals in Crosskeys met in a house at Hafod Tudor Terrace, Wattsville, and by 1914 there was a group regularly worshipping at the site still used today in Crosskeys. In Newbridge, a house meeting commenced on North Road and then at Tynywedd Farm on the High Street from 1918 or, possibly, as early as 1916. By 1923 they were established at their current location. Within this context it will be necessary to trace, if possible, any effect alienation may have had on the development of AoG. Establishing and assessing the constituents of the congregations of the embryonic AoG in South East Wales is an important aim of this research. South East Wales was a key region of heavy industry in early twentieth century Britain. Coal mines and steel works provided the livelihoods of the majority of the population. Some of these industrial workers, often with little formal education, became local leaders in both the established denominations and the emergent Pentecostal denominations. Examining the sociological make up of fledgling Pentecostal congregations will inform our understanding of how these groups developed, and help us assess the impact they had upon society in general. The Pentecostals were forthright in denouncing the 'ills of the age' such as alcohol abuse, gambling, and attending the cinema. The South Wales

---

[12] The Holiness movement emerged from Methodism especially in America and its British counterpart was promoted through the Keswick Convention for the Promotion of Practical Holiness. Steven Barabas, *So Great Salvation: The History and Message of the Keswick Convention* (Eugene, OR: Wipf & Stock, 1952); Donald W. Dayton, *The Theological Roots of Pentecostalism* (Metuchen, NJ: Hendrickson and Scarecrow Press, 1987); Vinson Synan, *The Holiness-Pentecostal Tradition* (Grand Rapids, MI: Eerdmans, 1997); C.E. Jones, 'Holiness Movement', in Stanley M. Burgess, *New International Dictionary of Pentecostal and Charismatic Movements* (Grand Rapids, MI: Zondervan, 2003), 726–9, (*NIDPCM*).

industrial workers were men and women who knew how to both work and play hard. Due to the social ills and with urgency born of a belief in the imminent Parousia of Christ, the Pentecostal groups were actively involved in the evangelisation of their communities.

2. The second aim of this book is to identify the theological influences on the early leaders of the AoG in South East Wales. This will be a two-fold investigation, firstly concerning the internal influences within Wales and secondly the more external factors of influence. The years 1901–24 will be examined in an attempt to explore if any traces of Pentecostalism within the traditional Welsh theological and denominational environment can be identified. Coupled with this, the Revival of 1904–05 casts its formidable shadow over this period and must be considered in terms of its possible influence; especially since important leaders within Pentecostalism were affected by the Revival especially those who came to faith during that earlier period. William Kay remarks that, 'the connection between the Welsh Revival and the Pentecostal movement is to be seen in terms of people rather than doctrine.'[13]

This may be an over simplification in respect to the fact that these 'Children of the Revival' would have been affected by the theological melting pot that was Welsh evangelicalism during this period. So it will be vital to discover the ways in which these people were affected by the theological and experiential issues surrounding the revival before we analyse their own impact on Pentecostalism. Many individuals, who were important in this period of Welsh religious history, became specifically linked to initial Pentecostal teaching; among them George and Stephen Jeffreys and Pastor D. P. Williams.[14] The role of the Forward Movement in the Presbyterian Church of Wales, and characters such as Seth and Frank Joshua, will also be highlighted for their possible

---

[13] Kay, *Inside Story*, 11.

[14] Desmond W. Cartwright, *The Great Evangelists: The Remarkable Lives of George and Stephen Jeffreys* (Basingstoke: Marshall Pickering, 1986); Edward Jeffreys, *Stephen Jeffreys – The Beloved Evangelist* (London: Elim, 1946); B. Jones, *The King's Champions 1863-1933* (Cwmbran: CLP, 1986); William K. Kay, *Pentecostals in Britain* (Carlisle: Paternoster, 2000), 18–20; Walter Hollenweger, *The Pentecostals* (London: SCM Press, 1972), 191-3 and W. K. Kay, 'Apostolic Church', *NIDPCM,* 322–3.

influence.[15] As part of the wider 'holiness' movement, the Keswick conferences and teaching also contributed in some degree to the rise of Pentecostalism within South East Wales; some of the pioneers of the new movement such as Sidney Mercy of Trinity Congregational Church, Pontywaun, Crosskeys visited the Llandrindod conventions.[16]

Looking beyond the borders of Wales, two significant issues must be mentioned. The first was the event commonly described as the 'Pentecostal revival' in Azusa Street, Los Angeles, USA. This event—led by holiness preacher William J. Seymour, who promoted the teachings of Charles Fox Parham—is recognised by AoG historians as the 'birthplace' of the denomination and hence cannot be ignored.[17] The second was Rev. A. A. Boddy and his ministry in Sunderland, England. Boddy's pneumatology and involvement with the Pentecostal Missionary Union (PMU) is vital to understand early AoG history in Wales. Some of the men from Crosskeys visited Sunderland and received the teaching and experience of these new Pentecostals. Hence Boddy's role is pivotal in British Pentecostalism and certainly affected South East Wales.

3. The third aim of this research is to evaluate the nature and development of AoG theology in the area during this formative period, and especially its understanding of pneumatology, eschatology and healing. Exploring links between AoG eschatology, experiential pneumatology, and aggressive missiology is a key issue; from an early Pentecostal interpretation of Acts 1 and

---

[15] Geraint Fielder, *Grace, Grit and Gumption: The Exploits of Evangelists John Pugh, Frank and Seth Joshua* (Fearn: Christian Focus, 2004) provides an informative and easy to read overview of the Forward Movement in Wales at this time.

[16] Brynmor Pierce Jones, *The Spiritual History of Keswick in Wales 1903–1983* (Cwmbran: C.L.P. 1989). Though valuable, Jones' material should be read with care as he does tend to write in a style that focuses on the positives without giving due consideration to some of the difficulties raised by some of the figures researched.

[17] Cecil M. Robeck, Jr. *The Azusa Street Mission and Revival* (Nashville, TN.: Thomas Nelson, 2006). See also Dayton, *Theological Roots;* Frank Bartleman, *Azusa Street: An Eyewitness Account* (Gainesville, FL: Bridge-Logos, 1980) and Aaron Friesen, 'The Called Out of the Called Out: Charles Parham's Doctrine of Spirit Baptism,' *JEPTA* 19/1 (2009), 43–55; Roberts Liardon, *The Azusa Street Revival When The Fire Fell* (Shippensburg, PA: Destiny Image, 2006); Wilmington Group, *The Great Azusa Street Revival: the Life and Sermons of William Seymour* (Fort Lauderdale, FL: Wilmington Group Publishing, 2006).

2, Christians are expected to be engaged in mission rather than focusing on charismatic or ecstatic speech. In the words of Allan Anderson:

> Pentecostalism has probably been the fastest growing religious movement in the twentieth century and it is now found in almost every country in the world. One of the reasons for this must surely be because it has always had a strong emphasis on mission and evangelism. From the beginning Pentecostals and Charismatics have been involved in these activities, but this has always issued from their strong pneumatology.[18]

The evidence, however, is that for these early pioneers mission was the responsibility of all believers and the Pentecostal experience was viewed primarily to empower evangelisation in light of the Parousia. However, for some, tongues and other charismatic gifts were the goal of their spiritual quest.[19] As a result of the threatened imbalance, one issue that arose was the need for accountability between the disparate groups that had emerged. The main reason for this was a desire to protect the new movement from erroneous teaching and extremes of experience. It was largely due to this desire for corporate accountability that AoG eventually emerged, uniting small but relatively successful house groups and missions into a fledgling denomination. The early pioneers appeared genuine in their interpretation and application of scripture and their stated desire was to experience the same God they read of as being at work in the Book of Acts. Indeed, the early Pentecostals emphasised the importance of Acts as their blueprint for church development, experience, and practice; and so how their interpretation of Acts and especially chapters 1 and 2 influenced the development of the Welsh AoG is a point which must be explored.

---

[18] Allan Anderson, *An Introduction to Pentecostalism* (Cambridge: C.U.P. 2004), 206. Although these may be the significant theological reasons it is also vital to assess the sociological reasons that helped the Pentecostal denominations grow.

[19] Gary B. McGee, ed., *Initial Evidence: Historical and Biblical Perspectives on the Pentecostal Doctrine of Spirit Baptism* (Eugene, OR: Wipf & Stock, 2007).

Another aspect relating to early Pentecostal pneumatology/missiology is that of the contrast in understanding between 'glossolalia' and 'xenolalia'.[20] These contrasting interpretations of the gift and use of tongues is relevant within this developmental period. A false understanding of xenolalia led some missionaries to leave home with no language skills, believing the Holy Spirit would enable them to preach in foreign languages. Needless to say, this interpretation brought disappointment and these missionaries soon became disillusioned, and were made to rethink their pneumatology before embarking upon further missionary activity.[21] Within the context of Welsh Pentecostalism, an interest in mission was apparent in the formative years. Donald Gee records that in 1911:

> The missionary work of the Pentecostal Missionary Union soon gained a specially warm place in the hearts of the Welsh Pentecostal Friends. The offerings of the Welsh Assemblies for foreign missionary work have sometimes been heart-moving in their generosity during times of deep poverty throughout the Valleys.[22]

What motivated the financially poor believers in Wales to support missionary work overseas financially was closely related to the areas of eschatological pneumatology and mission which were at the core of early AoG teaching and practice. This missionary interest is illustrated in the early life of the Crosskeys assembly; the relevance and significance of the teaching received through the Crosskeys leaders inspired their spiritual daughter churches to continue the interest in missions. An example of the specific interest in mission and the particular links with Congo Evangelistic Mission at Crosskeys will be discussed later. An evaluation of this significant link between theology and practice will be vital in our understanding of the impact which South East Wales made on the religious world of the early 1920s. I will return to the connection between

---

[20] Glossolalia is the belief in tongues for the use of glorifying God and personal edification whereas xenolalia is the belief that the baptism of the Holy Spirit was a supernatural ability to preach the gospel in foreign languages so that the missionary need not gain any language skills for their intended field of ministry.

[21] Gary B. McGee, 'Historical Background', in Stanley M. Horton, ed., *Systematic Theology* (Springfield, MO: Logion Press, 1995), 9–37.

[22] Gee, *Wind and Flame,* 67.

these theological disciplines later in order to evaluate their place in Pentecostal theology.

4. The final aim of this book is to suggest ways in which this research may have pastoral and theological application today. The author comes from an AoG background and has been involved with the assembly at Newbridge since childhood and until recently served as the pastor of Crosskeys assembly. Within the changing nature of modern society the local church must be relevant to the needs of those with whom it has contact. In the history of Welsh Pentecostalism this relevance arose from the close knit nature of society and in particular the brotherhood of workers who faced the harshness of industrial labour. Today the socio-political scene in the eastern valleys is far removed from the early twentieth century. However the need remains for the church to be relevant to a changing society, to preach a gospel that connects with a modern generation whilst avoiding the extremes that can be associated with some of the charismatic groups that have emerged in the late twentieth century. How does a balanced Pentecostal theology find a relevant message in the twenty first century? The history of Welsh Pentecostalism helped to shape the reality of today, but to what extent is this relevant to a society that has distanced itself from chapel, the gospel and the particular brand of Pentecostal theology available in Wales?

Definitions

Having outlined the 4 major aims of this book, the key terms used in this study are defined thus.

South East Wales

The term South East Wales (SE Wales) in this book describes a geographical area stretching from the border with England in the east, commencing at the Severn Bridge, following a westerly direction as far as the city of Newport. Then the area extends northwards from Newport passing through Machen, Bedwas, Caerphilly and then returning eastwards to Ebbw Vale and eventually to the border at Monmouth. In 1924 that area was a part of the greater region within AoG, known as Wales and Monmouthshire. The original assemblies that had emerged in the region were: Aberbeeg, Aber-Bargoed, Bedwas, Crosskeys, Cwmfelin(fach), Cwmbran, Caerphilly, Earlswood, Machen,

Maesycwmmer (sic), Newport, Newbridge, Pontnewydd, Pontllanfraith, Risca and Rogerstone.[23] The region also contained one affiliated assembly that was situated in Lydney, which is no longer in existence. In addition, due to council reorganisation, Lydney is now situated in Gloucestershire, England. Although the details of its origins are outside the remit of this book it may be necessary to refer to any issues that could have included key individuals from the Lydney assembly. This geographical region may appear small; however it contains two vital centres for Pentecostalism that affected the growth of the movement not only Wales, but also across the British Isles.

Crosskeys and Newbridge

Crosskeys is a former mining village approximately eight miles north of Newport in the Ebbw Valley, and Newbridge another former important mining town is a further five miles along the same valley. The assembly that emerged at Crosskeys will serve as a case study since it was highly influential in the initial formation of AoG congregations in SE Wales; its influence spread throughout the valleys of eastern Wales and affected other emergent groups. Crosskeys, as previously indicated, is believed to be the first proto-AoG work to be established in this area. It commenced worship on 6 October 1912.[24] The initial adherents of these churches can be viewed as the pioneers of the AoG strain of Pentecostalism in SE Wales. Alfred Missen, AoG pastor and historian, writes of the influence of the Crosskeys assembly:

> Under the ministry of Tom Mercy, the work at Crosskeys grew quickly and attracted visitors from all over South Wales. Before long T. L. Hicks was pastoring a work at Cwmfelinfach and Leonard Jenkins an assembly at Newbridge. In 1934, when the present spacious premises at Crosskeys were opened, it was claimed that no less than forty assemblies owed their existence directly or indirectly to this "mother" assembly.[25]

---

[23] Minutes of the General Presbytery of Assemblies of God of Great Britain and Ireland, August 1924, Donald Gee Centre, Mattersey Hall, Doncaster.

[24] The original financial records of the church in the author's possession stating this date to be the commencement of the congregation.

[25] Missen, *Sound Of A Going*, 47.

The impact of Crosskeys deserves detailed examination as will be seen later. The ongoing effects of that early witness in Crosskeys are still in evidence today. Although Crosskeys has now withdrawn from membership of the AoG, its importance in the development of the AoG must not be overlooked.[26] Newbridge has also served as an important centre for Pentecostal testimony in the region, and has had close links to Crosskeys since its beginnings in 1918. The first pastor, A. L. (Leonard) Jenkins, initially an elder at Crosskeys, served the Newbridge congregation from 1922 (some two years prior to the AoG GB&I coming into existence) until 1967. He was a well-respected member of the executive committee of AoG for many years, and as such attracted many of the leaders of the new denomination to Newbridge. Both Crosskeys and Newbridge have, since their earliest days, emphasised biblical preaching and teaching as well as Pentecostal theology and experience. As a result, both assemblies have seen numerous men and women called into Christian ministry both home and overseas. That two small Welsh mining towns have had such influence and success in terms of the AoG work is remarkable. The following study will examine the development of both Crosskeys and Newbridge, identifying the more significant individuals and developments of these groups into local assemblies embracing AoG teaching. Some individuals were prominent in the establishment of several new assemblies; for example, the assembly at Newbridge grew out of a house meeting visited and encouraged by a Mr Terrell, an elder in the Crosskeys assembly. Of the sixteen initial assemblies who joined AoG from SE Wales, those in Aberbeeg, Cwmbran, Maesycwmmer, Cwmfelinfach and Pontnewydd, are no longer in existence.

Methodology

This book adopts a historical approach while interacting theologically with the teachings of the early AoG. The AoG in SE Wales will be considered in its wider historical and theological context with special reference to evangelical Christianity. However, the paucity of material on the early period of AoG in SE Wales poses a challenge. Assessing the available literature specific to AoG in SE Wales has led me to the various general AoG historical works and a few references in other religious histories.

---

[26] The Crosskeys assembly withdrew from the AoG denomination in 2008.

Since the formation of the AoG GB&I in 1924, there have been some significant histories written on the subject. Chronologically, there is the benchmark publication of Donald Gee entitled *The Pentecostal Movement* published in 1941 and revised in 1967 under the title *Wind and Flame*.[27] Although a key source, due to the fact that Gee was a pioneer pastor, teacher and leader of the new denomination, a major weakness of this work is its lack of referencing and corroboration. Gee was able to write from his vast personal experience and knowledge of the worldwide Pentecostal movement to supply a general overview of the developing global Pentecostal phenomenon up to the early 1960s. This wide coverage leads to another weakness, however, for there is little room for important historical detail. Wales is mentioned only briefly. Gee refers to the Welsh Revival of 1904 and to those he labels as 'Children of the Welsh Revival' but he does endorse the importance of the Crosskeys assembly that emerged 'about 1912.'[28] Particular mention is made of the leading figures who established that new assembly, namely, Sydney Mercy, Tom Mercy, Tom Hicks and Leonard Jenkins.[29] According to Gee, the Crosskeys assembly became prominent not so much as a result of its pneumatology but because of its prominent eschatological emphasis. This early emphasis upon eschatology shaped the ministry of Crosskeys and those emergent assemblies upon which it was very influential. It is accepted that premillennial eschatology was the major theological teaching that led to the establishing of the Crosskeys assembly, and this is a subject to which I will return later. In respect to the theological foundations of Pentecostalism eschatology requires greater investigation especially as to the link with its Pneumatology. Gee makes reference to the correspondence between the 'Welsh Assemblies' and the American AG and states it was this action that 'stung the English brethren into action' that is, the preliminary meetings leading to the eventual formation of the AoG GB&I.[30] The formation and early work of the Pentecostal Missionary Union also receives treatment from Gee in which he

---

[27] Gee, *Wind and Flame* and Richard Massey, *Another Springtime: The Life of Donald Gee Pentecostal Leader and Teacher* (Guildford: Highland Books, 1992).

[28] Gee, *Wind and Flame,* 5–6, 34–37, 66–68.

[29] Gee, *Wind and Flame,* 77–78

[30] Gee, *Wind and Flame,* 126–7.

briefly charts its rise and development until the PMU merged with AoG in 1925.[31] Gee's work is an invaluable source of information, despite the afore mentioned weaknesses.

Another AoG insider who tackled its history was executive council member Alfred Missen. His work *The Sound of a Going* is a much shorter record than Gee's but continues the story to the early 1970s.[32] Missen's publication, like that of Gee's, suffers from a lack of referencing (not to mention a dubious index) yet he succeeds in capturing both the fervour of the AoG from its inception and its work on the national and international stage. Missen devotes a whole chapter to the 'Sons of Wales',[33] and despite the brevity of his book, highlights the early contributors in Crosskeys and Newbridge,[34] as well as the fact that a group of Welsh assemblies had applied to the United States AG for affiliation.[35]

Swiss theologian Walter Hollenweger also produced an extensive work entitled *The Pentecostals.*[36] This broad overview of the whole Pentecostal phenomenon remains a major academic work on the subject. Supplying insight into Pentecostalism worldwide, his treatment of AoG GB&I is succinct yet he does consider links with the Welsh Revival of 1904.[37] A whole chapter is dedicated to Donald Gee and his significant involvement with the international Pentecostal situation.[38] While Hollenweger's work is extensive and valuable for the serious student of Pentecostalism, it lacks information regarding AoG in SE Wales.

Other AoG historians specialising in the denomination are David Allen and William Kay; both are accredited AoG ministers and have served on the staff at Mattersey Hall, the AoG Bible College. David Allen researched the history of AoG 1900 to 1980 for a doctoral thesis at London University; this remains

---

[31] Gee, *Wind and Flame,* 131-2.

[32] Missen, *Sound Of A Going.*

[33] Missen, *Sound Of A Going,* 46-52. It must be noted here that the contents page and index are numerically incorrect.

[34] Missen, *Sound Of A Going,* 47.

[35] Missen, *Sound Of A Going,* 11.

[36] Hollenweger, *Pentecostals* see also Walter J. Hollenweger, *Pentecostalism: Origins and Developments Worldwide* (Peabody, MA: Hendrickson, 1997).

[37] Hollenweger, *Pentecostals,* 176-87, 191-3.

[38] Hollenweger, *Pentecostals,* 206-16.

unpublished but serves as a valuable source of information.[39] The situation and outcomes of the Welsh Revival 1904–05 are considered briefly by Allen and he draws the conclusion that its greatest effect on the formation of the AoG was in the conversion of significant individuals who later joined the Pentecostal groups.[40] Specific to the AoG, reference is made to the conversion of Donald Gee under the ministry of Seth Joshua during the latter's preaching at a north London Congregational church.[41] As with Gee and Missen, Allen mentions the important correspondence between Wales and America around 1923, but pays little attention to other developments within Wales during these formative years.[42]

William Kay's research led to the publication of his work, *Inside Story* in which he brings the AoG history up to1990.[43] The situation in Wales is not dealt with in any depth and, as mentioned above, Kay suggests the Revival was linked to Pentecostal personnel and not doctrine.[44] The statement is questionable, or at best ambiguous, but since it is a theme also noted by Allen it will require serious attention; for discovering who these individuals were and what their theological influence was will help clarify our understanding of the Welsh situation. Kay also mentions the correspondence between the Welsh group and America but does not enlarge upon its importance.[45] Kay's other significant contribution is his *Pentecostals in Britain*, which contains a wider survey of the main Pentecostal groups in Great Britain.[46] Dealing with the four main denominations, the AoG and its roots are only briefly highlighted.[47] This publication contains much statistical data collected by means of questionnaires distributed to pastors and leaders of their respective denominations and

---

[39]Allen, 'Signs and Wonders'.

[40] Allen, 'Signs and Wonders', 38–43.

[41] Allen, 'Signs and Wonders', 43, Gee affirms that fact in, Gee, *Wind and Flame*, 34.

[42] Allen, 'Signs and Wonders', 110–11, here Allen records how the English brethren represented by (John Nelson) Parr were 'stung into action'.

[43] Based on a Nottingham PhD thesis, Kay, *Inside Story*, 7.

[44] Kay, *Inside Story*, 11.

[45] Kay, *Inside Story*, 78.

[46] Kay, *Pentecostals in Britain*.

[47] The four major Pentecostal denominations addressed by Kay are: The Apostolic Church, Elim, AoG and The Church of God; Kay, *Pentecostals in Britain*, 18–36.

collated into various graphs and charts. But it does offer some important issues regarding the formation of AoG.[48] There is also the work of Richard Massey who researched the origins of AoG in Britain and also produced a biography of Donald Gee.[49] Within the scope of these Pentecostal/AoG histories one is confronted by a stark reality, namely, the lack of information regarding the rise of AoG in Wales.

The general Pentecostal and specific AoG histories do not deal at any length with the situation within Wales in the formative years of the movement. This has made the task of researching more difficult. However, two invaluable primary sources are W. G. Attwood, *How Pentecost came to Crosskeys,* written by a founder member of Crosskeys and later pastor at Risca assembly; and Price Davis's *A Testimony and a Brief Record of the Beginnings of the Pentecostal Movement in the Merthyr Borough, Bedlinog and the Aberdare Valley.*[50] Both of these sources have been helpful in investigating the original characters and events within South East Wales. Despite their lack of corroboration, they do support Gee's understanding of the situation in Crosskeys and the surrounding area. These are further supported by a more homily type series of articles by Paul Mercy that appeared in *Redemption Tidings* as 'Mercy Drops'. Mercy, an AoG minister, commits to writing his personal recollections of his family's involvement in the founding of the Crosskeys assembly.[51] Although lacking any academic structure, these articles do agree in principle with Attwood and Gee's view of the Crosskeys group.

Books dealing with Welsh religious history also lack information relating to the development of AoG. D. Densil Morgan's work, *The Span of the Cross,* pays scant regard to Pentecostalism.[52] References are reserved to a generalisation as to the impact of the Wales Revival 1904–05 upon Pentecostalism and in

---

[48] Kay, *Pentecostals in Britain,* 1–36, here Kay briefly traces the development of Pentecostalism in Britain.

[49] Richard Massey, 'A Sound and Scriptural Union: an examination of the origins of Assemblies of God in Great Britain and Ireland during the years 1920–25', (PhD Dissertation, University of Birmingham, 1987) and Massey, *Another Springtime.*

[50] W. G. Attwood, *How Pentecost Came to Crosskeys,* (c. 1940) and Price Davis, *A Testimony and a Brief Record of the Beginnings of the Pentecostal Movement in the Merthyr Borough, Bedlinog and the Aberdare Valley* (c. 1961) <www.dustandashes.com/624.htm>

[51] Paul Mercy kindly made available to me the original articles written during the 1980s.

[52] D. Densil Morgan, *The Span of the Cross Christian Religion and Society in Wales 1914–2000, revised edition* (Cardiff: University of Wales Press, 2011).

particular the rise of the Apostolic Church; the AoG are reserved for a brief mention post-1960. Morgan does, however, state that the spread of Pentecostalism in Wales was 'one result of the 1904–05 Revival'.[53]

R. Tudur Jones also reviewed Welsh religious history in his *Faith and the Crisis of a Nation Wales 1890–1914*.[54] This detailed survey of the religious scene in Wales concentrates on the main denominations, especially the Nonconformist ones, and Jones only makes a reference to Pentecostalism when he refers to: 'Donald Gee, a Welshman and one of the most respected leaders of the Pentecostal movement.'[55] However, while Gee was a respected leader yet he was not Welsh, for he was born in London in 1891;[56] however, the Welsh link was that Gee was converted through the preaching of Seth Joshua, a South Wales Presbyterian evangelist, during a campaign in North London in 1906. Jones appears to disregard Pentecostalism and his short treatment of it is somewhat inaccurate.

Noel Gibbard, in evaluating the effects of the 1904–05 Welsh Revival, gives Welsh Pentecostalism more serious, if brief, consideration. His book *On the Wings of the Dove* not only charts the missionary effects of the revival, but also assesses its theological impact, particularly in relation to the rise of Pentecostalism.[57] Gibbard claims that 'The Welsh Revival made a marked contribution to Pentecostalism.'[58] Specifically referring here to the rise of the Apostolic Church, Gibbard proceeds to deal with other aspects of early Pentecostalism in Wales. Alexander Boddy and the PMU are mentioned along with T. M. Jeffreys of Waunlwyd, Ebbw Vale and Tom Mercy of Wattsville, Crosskeys.[59] Gibbard's other major work *Fire on the Altar* also gives attention to Pentecostalism although much of the material is the same as in *On the*

---

[53] Morgan, *Span,* 13–14, for Apostolic Church in Britain see James E. Worsfold, *The Origins of the Apostolic Church in Great Britain; with a Breviate of its Early Missionary Endeavours.* (Wellington, NZ: Julian Literature Trust, 1991).

[54] R. Tudur Jones, *Faith and the Crisis of a Nation Wales 1890–1914,* Robert Pope, ed., translated by Sylvia Prys Jones, (Cardiff: University of Wales Press, 2004).

[55] Jones, *Faith and the Crisis,* 348.

[56] Massey, *Another Springtime,* 7.

[57] Noel Gibbard, *On the Wings of the Dove* (Bridgend: Bryntirion Press, 2002).

[58] Gibbard, *On the Wings,* 179.

[59] Gibbard, *On the Wings,* 203–7.

Wings of the Dove.[60] Gibbard's treatment of Pentecostalism is a brief but refreshing change from the otherwise negligent evangelical assessments of this small, but significant movement.

Robert Pope also contributes to the arena of Welsh religious history with his *Building Jerusalem: Nonconformity, Labour and the Social Question in Wales, 1906–1939.* This highly socio-political investigation of those troubled times in Wales is an excellent work; yet it too lacks any significant reference to Pentecostalism.[61] Pope's analysis of the political, social and theological web highlights the fact that the early Pentecostals did not become embroiled in these social issues and so were left free to promote their teaching.

Continuing to identify and asses the materials available for the researcher into the AoG in SE Wales, there are original copies of minutes and correspondence between key figures within the fledgling AoG movement (available in The Donald Gee Centre for Pentecostal and Charismatic Research at Mattersey Hall). There is also the denominational magazine, *Redemption Tidings*[62] which was the official means of disseminating information and theological teaching to AoG followers in the early years. From the first issue in July 1924, mention is made of an interest in missions and those associated with overseas ministry. For information pre-1924 it will be necessary to refer to *Confidence* Magazine published by A. A. Boddy 1908–26 which contains valuable primary source material on the events within the new British Pentecostal scene.[63] Another useful tool will be the *Flames of Fire* magazine published 1911–17 which contains information on the Pentecostal Missionary Union.[64] Additional information on the early years of British Pentecostalism can be found through

[60] Noel Gibbard, *Fire on the Altar: A History and Evaluation of the 1904–05 Revival in Wales,* (Bridgend: Bryntirion Press, 2005), 181–4, see also Tony Cauchi, *The Welsh Revival Library: Centenary Edition 1904–2004, On CD ROM* (Bishop's Waltham: King's Centre, 2004).

[61] Robert Pope, *Building Jerusalem: Nonconformity, Labour and the Social Question in Wales, 1906–1939* (Cardiff: University of Wales Press, 1998). See also Robert Pope, *Seeking God's Kingdom: The Nonconformist Social Gospel in Wales 1906–1939* (Cardiff: University of Wales Press, 1999).

[62] Tony Cauchi, *Redemption Tidings 1924–1939 on CD-ROM* (Bishop's Waltham: Revival Library, 2005).

[63] Tony Cauchi, *Confidence Magazine 1908–1926 on CD-ROM* (Bishop's Waltham: Revival Library, 2004). See also Mark Cartledge, 'The Early Pentecostal Theology of *Confidence* Magazine (1908–1926): A Version of the Five-Fold Gospel?' *JEPTA* 28/2 (2008), 117–30.

[64] Tony Cauchi, *Flames of Fire 1911–1917 on CD-ROM* (Bishop's Waltham: Revival Library, 2004).

the writings of A. A. Boddy.[65] In addition, it will also be necessary to consult relevant newspaper articles published between 1901 and 1924 in SE Wales and elsewhere. Making use of local chapel records has also been necessary, though this has brought problems of its own as some of these churches in SE Wales no longer exist and consequently many records have been lost. Moreover, as the earliest AoG groups generally met in unofficial house groups and cottage meetings, documentation is scarce.

Who are the Pentecostals?

In defining this complex term 'Pentecostals', it is necessary to differentiate between the general descriptive term 'Pentecostals' and the narrower denominational signature 'The Assemblies of God'. To its adherents, the Pentecostal movement claims to have its roots in New Testament teaching and practice so that F. D. Bruner notes that the term Pentecostal, 'could appear to stretch from the enthusiastic Corinthians (1 Cor 12–14) or even the Old Testament anointed and ecstatic (e.g. Num 11; 1 Sam 10).'[66]

The alleged claim that Pentecostals are achieving the restoration of 'Apostolic Christianity'[67] is largely based on a distinctive interpretation of the apostles' experiences in Acts 2, as Gee observes:

> The designation "Pentecostal" arises from its emphasis upon a baptism in the Holy Spirit such as recorded in Acts ii. that occurred on the Day of Pentecost. The Pentecostal Movement shares with most sections of the Holiness movement and some others in the Church, the conviction

---

[65] Tony Cauchi, *The Works of Alexander Boddy 1854–1930 on CD ROM* (Bishop's Waltham: Revival Library, 2010).

[66] Fredrick Dale Bruner, *A Theology of the Holy Spirit: The Pentecostal Experience and the New Testament Witness* (Grand Rapids: Eerdmans, 1970), 35. In this work, Bruner gives a valuable potted history of the Pentecostal movement, 35–55. See also Max Turner, *The Holy Spirit and Spiritual Gifts Then and Now* (London: Paternoster, 1996, second ed. 2008), 3–20; also Michael A. Eaton, *Baptism with the Spirit: The Teaching of Dr. Martyn Lloyd-Jones* (Leicester: I.V.P. 1989). Eaton provides an interesting overview of the historical position on Spirit baptism by some major theologians.

[67] J. Rodman Williams, *Renewal Theology: Systematic Theology from a Charismatic Perspective Three Volumes in One* (Grand Rapids: Zondervan 1996) volume 2, 181–321, in this section Williams gives comprehensive support for the traditional Pentecostal view and especially emphasises the Acts model. See also Carl Brumback, *What Meaneth This?* (London: Elim, 1947) 191–233.

that such a baptism in the Holy Spirit remains as a separate individual experience possible for all Christians, irrespective of time or place (Acts ii. 38, 39).[68]

There was a strong emphasis on Acts 2 by the early Pentecostal pioneers and this has remained an essential part of Pentecostal teaching. In order to provide a general introduction to Pentecostalism, Gee employs the term 'Pentecostal Movement', linking it to the various 'revivals' that occurred world-wide in the first quarter of the twentieth-century.[69]

We must acknowledge that the umbrella term 'Pentecostal' is difficult to define as there are differing views on what constitutes a 'true' Pentecostal doctrine and experience. Melvin Hodges, for example, claims:

> Pentecostals are so called because they believe that the Holy Spirit will come to believers today as He came to the waiting disciples on the Day of Pentecost. They recognise the Holy Spirit as the divine Agent of the Deity in the earth, without whom God's work of redemption through Jesus Christ cannot be realized.[70]

Hodges here places emphasis upon an expectancy resulting from a belief that God reproduces biblical patterns throughout history which he regards as an emphasis of Pentecostalism. Hodges does not refer here to the controversial subject of Spirit baptism but simply reinforces the Pentecostal belief in the necessity of a greater engagement with the Holy Spirit in the life of individual Christians. Walter Hollenweger offers a more specific definition in relation to the baptism of the Holy Spirit: 'Most Pentecostals would say the distinguishing feature is the experience of the baptism in the Holy Spirit with the 'initial sign of speaking in tongues'.[71] Interestingly, Hollenweger uses the word 'most' in his definition and thereby implies the complexity of this subject and

---

[68] Gee, *Wind and Flame*, 7. Gee also gives reference to the biblical texts that were the emphasis for the early Pentecostals in support of their teaching, 6–8.

[69] Gee, *Wind and Flame*, 3–12, highlights revivals in Wales, America, Sunderland, Scandinavia, India, South China, Chile, Europe, S. Africa and Australia as being important within the context of world Pentecostalism. See also Stanley Frodsham, *With Signs Following* (Springfield, MO: GPH, 1946), 19–228. A guide to the overall picture of Pentecostalism, Charismatic groups and theology is found in *NIDPCM*.

[70] Melvin L. Hodges, 'A Pentecostal's View of Mission Strategy', in Grant McClung, ed., *Azusa Street and Beyond* (Gainesville, FL: Bridge-Logos, 2006), 157.

[71] Hollenweger, *Pentecostals*, xix.

differences amongst some Pentecostals themselves. He then modifies his definition by identifying two main issues that were the focus of his research into groups forming the Pentecostal movement. He states:

> all the groups who profess at least two religious crisis experiences (1. baptism or rebirth; 2. The baptism of the Spirit), the second being subsequent to and different from the first one, and the second usually, but not always, being associated with speaking in tongues.[72]

An experience subsequent to salvation/rebirth/conversion involving a personal encounter with the Holy Spirit can be seen as a distinctive teaching and feature of the Pentecostal movement. James D. G. Dunn continues this theme by commenting that according to the Pentecostal movement, 'in apostolic times, the speaking in tongues were considered to be the initial physical evidence of a person's having received the baptism in the Holy Spirit'.[73] Dunn's summary of the doctrinal origins of the Pentecostal movements continues:

> As a result of their own experience the early pioneers of this movement came to believe that the baptism in the Holy Spirit is a second (Pentecostal) experience distinct from and subsequent to conversion which gives power for witness (Acts 1:8), that speaking in tongues, as in Acts 2:4, is the necessary and inevitable evidence of the 'baptism', and that the spiritual gifts listed in 1 Cor 12:8–10 may and should be manifested when Pentecostal Christians meet for worship.[74]

Dunn states that evidential tongues are a distinctive tenet of belief within the Pentecostal movement, although Hollenweger questions its universal acceptance. Even within this wide range of opinions, there are further differences adding to the difficulty in defining the term 'Pentecostals'. Keith Warrington provides an interesting summary of the situation:

> That which most distinguishes Pentecostalism is the doctrine relating to the baptism in the Spirit. However, even the baptism in the Spirit has

---

[72] Hollenweger, *Pentecostals*, xix.

[73] James D. G. Dunn, *Baptism in the Holy Spirit* (Philadelphia, PA: The Westminster Press, 1970), 2

[74] Dunn, *Baptism in the Holy Spirit*, 2.

received varied comment by Pentecostals. For example, although many anticipate that a consequence of the baptism in the Spirit will be power, this has various nuances and expectations for different Pentecostals. Many expect to manifest this power in their lives specifically with regard to evangelism. In practice, however, this power has been mainly associated with charismatic gifts. [75]

Warrington here highlights the difficulty in attempting to offer a simple definition of Pentecostalism, yet recognises baptism in the Spirit as the distinctive aspect within its theology and experience. Warrington continues his search for a definition of Pentecostalism by asserting:

Thus, the baptism in the Spirit is not simply to be recognized as a distinctive doctrinal feature of Pentecostal theology but to be understood as reflecting that which is central to Pentecostalism, namely encounter and experience. [76]

The emphasis on experiencing the power of the Spirit in a personal manner ranks high in the expectations of Pentecostals. How this 'encounter and experience' manifests itself may well be one of the secrets to understanding the plethora of Pentecostal/Charismatic denominations that have developed. Roberts Liardon emphasises this aspect of experience within Pentecostalism, when he writes:

Experience, rather than doctrine, has often been noted as the principal reality and heart of Pentecostalism. Although the Pentecostals are conservative in their theology, they are passionate in their spiritual experiences. The emphasis on the Holy Spirit is essential to Pentecostal reality, and almost all Pentecostal denominations believe that the "initial evidence" of Spirit baptism is the manifestation of glossolalia or what is commonly referred to as "speaking in tongues". [77]

Liardon here encapsulates the kernel of Pentecostalism; the prominence of the personality, deity and essential ministry of the Holy Spirit. But Liardon goes further, adding that Pentecostals are characterised by 'dynamic worship, and

---

[75] Keith Warrington, *Pentecostal Theology: A Theology of Encounter* (London: T&T Clark, 2008), 19.

[76] Warrington, *Pentecostal Theology,* 22.

[77] Liardon, *Azusa Street,* 11.

evangelistic fervour.'[78] However, no matter how difficult it is to define the term Pentecostal and identify its core teaching, the AoG which is within the Pentecostal movement embraces the teaching of 'initial evidence', even though as Hollenweger correctly states, not all Pentecostals do so. D. W. Bebbington observes, when examining differences within the main Pentecostal denominations, that for the AoG 'speaking in tongues is always the initial evidence of the baptism in the Holy Spirit.'[79] When AoG was formed in GB&I in 1924, the emphasis for those leaders was on the baptism in the Holy Spirit with the 'initial evidence of speaking in other tongues'; this experience was intended primarily to empower the individual for witness and service. Kay confirms this characteristic of AoG teaching when he writes that, 'The core distinctive was the belief that the baptism in the Holy Spirit is accompanied by evidential tongues. All other distinctives were auxiliary.'[80]

Stanley M. Horton adds to the debate but in so doing highlights a significant factor within Pentecostalism:

> The recognition that we are not self-sufficient, but totally dependent on Christ and the Holy Spirit to do anything that pleases God, and the willingness to give Him all the praise, is the secret of the success of the Pentecostal Movement today.[81]

Horton accepts that reliance upon the Holy Spirit is crucial to the Pentecostal movement, but he also adds the importance of recognising Christ as the source of the gift of the Holy Spirit. Without this recognition and desire to please God, the Pentecostal movement loses the 'secret' of its success. Any debate about the definition of Pentecostalism must recognise the basic element that the foundation for their experience is Christ, the saviour, healer, baptiser in the Spirit and coming king. Hence any overemphasis upon spiritual gifts should be

---

[78] Liardon, *Azusa Street*, 11.

[79] D. W. Bebbington, *Evangelicalism in Modern Britain: A History From the 1730s to the 1980s* (London: Routledge, 1993), 197.

[80] William Kay, 'Assemblies of God: Distinctive Continuity and Distinctive Change', in Keith Warrington, ed., *Pentecostal Perspectives* (Carlisle: Paternoster, 1998), 51.

[81] Stanley M. Horton, *What The Bible Says About The Holy Spirit* (Springfield, MO: G.P.H. 1995), 13.

regarded as a questionable perspective even within Pentecostalism.[82] Veli-Matti Karkkainen suggests that one should be studying Pentecostalisms (plural), as there is such a diversity of theological thinking and experience within the Pentecostal movement. There is a need, therefore, to assess the term Pentecostalism from a wider theological scope whilst at the same time recognising that emphasis upon the Holy Spirit is the key to understanding its origins and progress. This is especially true in our examination of Pentecostalism in SE Wales, where the early emphasis was not on gifts but on eschatology—an emphasis which led to a vibrant hope and a necessity to 'preach the gospel to every creature'—a task that required a total reliance upon the empowerment of the Holy Spirit.[83] Hence the label 'Second Comers' became applied to many of the embryonic Pentecostal groups in SE Wales. It can therefore be suggested that although there are differences of opinion over the theological understanding and practice of Spirit baptism among Pentecostals, the underlying theme of Pentecostalism is an eschatology that focuses on spiritual empowerment and gifts which help facilitate an urgent missiology. I will return later to the debate over theological distinctives and especially the influence of eschatology. The doctrinal position on tongues differentiates the main Pentecostal denominations but this is not the only difference, for the structure and government of these denominations provides an additional layer of complexity.

Before proceeding to an in-depth analysis of the AoG in SE Wales, a summary of the other two major Pentecostal denominations will be necessary, particularly as they both have their roots in Wales. Along with AoG the other two major 'classical' denominations, are, Elim Pentecostal Church and The Apostolic Church.[84] Both Elim and Apostolic denominations owe their origin

---

[82] Veli-Matti Karkkainen, 'Encountering Christ in the Full Gospel Way: An Incarnational Pentecostal Spirituality.' *JEPTA* 27/1 (2007), 5–19.

[83] Frank D. Macchia, *Baptized In The Spirit: A Global Pentecostal Theology* (Grand Rapids, MI: Zondervan, 2006). See also Amos Yong, *The Spirit Poured Out On All Flesh: Pentecostalism and the Possibility of Global Theology* (Grand Rapids, MI: Baker Academic, 2005).

[84] A wider introduction to these denominations can be found in Kay, *Pentecostals in Britain*. I employ the term 'classical' in relation to the original major denominations and in order to differentiate between them and the more recent Charismatic groups to emerge. Allen, 'Signs and Wonders', 79–90. For a wider discussion on the roots of Pentecostalism see David Allen, *There is a River* (Mattersey: Authentic, 2004), 74–143 and Dayton, *Theological Roots*. For an Apostolic view of Pentecostal theology see Ian Macpherson, *The Faith Once Delivered* (Milton Keynes: Word Publishing, 1988). Warrington, *Pentecostal Theology*, writes from an Elim perspective.

directly to 'sons' of the Welsh Revival of 1904–05. Some early Pentecostal groups survived for up to ten years before seeking denominational security and these became the AoG in South Wales and later in GB&I.

The first official Pentecostal denomination to be established in Britain was The Apostolic Faith Church founded in 1908 by W. O. Hutchinson of Bournemouth.[85] This denomination was small but by no means insignificant especially as it gave rise to the Apostolic Church led by D. P. Williams. Daniel Powell Williams (1882–1947), a member of the Congregational denomination, was deeply affected by a visit to Loughor to hear Evan Roberts preach on Christmas day 1904. Williams was ordained in Hutchinson's Apostolic Faith Church in 1911, but after some disagreements over practice and accountability he resigned. Consequently, D. P. Williams and his brother William founded The Apostolic Church in 1916, with its centre at Pen-y-groes, West Wales.[86] The denominational distinctive of the Apostolic Church focuses on the permanent offices of Apostle and Prophet within the local church setting and, in particular, their roles for the guidance and leadership of the church. The Apostolic Church is currently the smallest of the major Pentecostal denominations in Britain.

The Elim Pentecostal Church emerged under the leadership of George Jeffreys (1889–1962). Jeffreys was converted during the Welsh Revival in November 1904 and Kay records that he was 'baptised in the Holy Spirit with speaking in tongues, probably in 1911.'[87] Jeffreys, a native of Nantyffylon, Maesteg, in South Wales, initially formed the Elim Evangelistic Band during a ministry

---

Essential reading on the history of Spirit baptism is found in Kilian McDonnell and George T. Montague, *Christian Initiation and Baptism in the Holy Spirit: Evidence from the First Eight Centuries* (Collegeville, MI: The Liturgical Press, 1991) also, Ronald Kydd, *Charismatic Gifts in the Early Church* (Peabody, MA: Hendrickson, 1984).

[85] W. K. Kay, 'Apostolic Church' in *NIDPCM*, 322–3; Kay, *Pentecostals in Britain*, 15–16 and Malcolm R. Hathaway, 'The Role of William Oliver Hutchinson and the Apostolic Faith Church in the formation of British Pentecostal Churches', *JEPTA* 16 (1996), 40–57. It is important to note that 'tongues' were not new to British Christianity and were a particular aspect of the ministry of Edward Irving see Arnold Dallimore, *The Life Of Edward Irving: Fore-Runner Of The Charismatic Movement* (Edinburgh: Banner of Truth, 1983).

[86] Kay, *Pentecostals in Britain*, 18–20. See also Hollenweger, *Pentecostals*, 191–3.

[87] Kay, *Pentecostal in Britain*, 20. See also Cartwright, *The Great Evangelists* and D. W. Cartwright, 'Jeffreys, George' in *NIDPCM*, 807–8 and D. W. Cartwright, 'Elim Pentecostal Church' in *NIDPCM*, 598–9.

visit to Ireland in 1915. After several years of evangelistic campaigns, the Elim Four Square Gospel Alliance of the British Isles was formed in 1926. The distinctive feature of the Elim denomination is its central structural development. The AoG's church polity, by contrast, insisted on the autonomy of local assemblies governed by a pastor and/or elders.[88] The importance of Wales in the development of Pentecostal teaching and experience cannot be overlooked. The Apostolic and Elim Churches owe their existence directly via their leaders and other members to the Revival of 1904–05 in Wales and it is necessary to evaluate to what extent AoG leaders within Wales were influenced by that revival.[89]

America: A Fountainhead of Pentecostalism

Tracing the possible links between Welsh Pentecostals—especially the AoG adherents of the early twentieth-century—and America introduces us to several significant individuals from both sides of the Atlantic such as: Pastor Joseph Smale, Frank Bartleman, William J. Seymour, T. B. Barratt, Cecil Polhill and A. A. Boddy. Each of these men had contact with, or was influenced by, the events both in Wales 1904–05 and, subsequently, at Azusa Street 1906–09. They were men from different backgrounds and continents but united by the Pentecostal doctrine of the initial evidence of speaking in other tongues.[90]

Joseph Smale (1867–1926) was born in England, the son of John and Anne Smale. After training at Spurgeon's College, London, in 1895 he emigrated to America and entered the Baptist ministry in Los Angeles, where he was pastor of First Baptist Church, 725 South Flower, Los Angeles. Smale received news of the Welsh Revival and being eager to witness it, he travelled to Wales in 1905. During this visit he met Evan Roberts, and on returning to Los Angeles

---

[88] Allen, 'Signs and Wonders', 91–130.

[89] James Robinson, *Pentecostal Origins: Early Pentecostalism in Ireland in the Context of the British Isles*, (Milton Keynes: Paternoster, 2005).

[90] Gibbard *On the Wings*, 55–77, 177–222, mentions the prominence of Smale, Bartleman, Barratt and Boddy. See also Tim Welch, *Joseph Smale: God's Moses for Pentecostalism* (Milton Keynes: Paternoster, 2013) who gives a fuller description of Smale's involvement and importance.

Smale began revival prayer meetings in order to seek God for a similar experience as that in Wales.[91] Bartleman records:

> June 17 (1905), I went to Los Angeles to attend a meeting at the First Baptist Church. They were waiting on God for an outpouring of the Spirit there. Their pastor, Joseph Smale, had just returned from Wales. He had been in touch with Evan Roberts, and was on fire to have the same visitation and blessing come to his own church in Los Angeles.[92]

Smale continued his prayer meetings but was confronted with internal opposition and subsequently left his Baptist pastorate. Accompanied by some 200 members Smale established The First New Testament Church early in 1906 and on Easter Sunday the first manifestation of tongues occurred amongst them.[93] Smale never experienced tongues himself but was an early supporter of the Pentecostal manifestation and was highly influenced by events in Wales.

Frank Bartleman (1871–1936) was an evangelist for forty three years who served with the Salvation Army, Wesleyan Methodists, Pillar of Fire and Peniel Missions but is best known as the Chronicler of the development of early Pentecostalism in Los Angeles. The Pillar of Fire was a holiness church founded by Alma White and based in Denver, Colorado. Bartleman left the Methodist denomination in search of more 'spiritual vitality'. The Peniel Mission was a rescue mission based in Sacramento, California. Bartleman worked there for a short time but internal problems caused him to leave and seek work/ministry in Los Angeles.

Bartleman wrote 550 articles, 100 tracts, and six books, many focusing on Pentecostalism. His eyewitness account of the Azusa Street revival is a key source of information, although as one reads it one gets the impression of Bartleman as an individual who was unsettled, wandering, opinionated and open to experience the latest 'new thing' in religious circles. He never settled in

---

[91] Bartleman: *Azusa Street*, 15–47 devotes a whole chapter to the return of Smale from Wales and his impact upon the church in Los Angeles.

[92] Bartleman, *Azusa Street*, 15.

[93] Robeck Jr., *Azusa Street*, 59.

one church or locality for any significant length of time, and also appears to seek the recognition for the beginnings of revival in Los Angeles. Bartleman was involved with both Smale and Seymour but eventually established another church on Eighth and Maple Streets a short distance from Azusa before continuing an itinerant ministry. Bartleman also demonstrates links with the events in Wales and records a series of correspondence between himself and Evan Roberts.[94] One of the replies by Roberts contained the following advice:

> My dear brother in the faith: Many thanks for your kind letter. I am impressed of your sincerity and honesty of purpose. Congregate the people together who are willing to make a total surrender. Pray and wait. Believe God's promises. Hold daily meetings. May God bless you, is my earnest prayer. Yours in Christ, Evan Roberts.[95]

Bartleman, as with Smale, was convinced of the necessity of a spiritual awakening in America and the background to the outbreak of revival at Azusa Street was an attitude of prayerful expectation that God was able to repeat the Welsh experience in Los Angeles. This leads to the most significant figure within the context of the spread of early Pentecostalism, namely, William Joseph Seymour.

The roots of the Azusa Street revival of 1906 stretch back to 2 May 1870 when William Joseph Seymour was born in Centerville, Louisiana the son of black African slaves.[96] As a young man Seymour was struck by a bout of smallpox, which left him blind in one eye; whilst recovering from this illness, he received a call to preach the gospel. Baptised as a Catholic, raised a Baptist and later coming under the influence of the Holiness Movement, Seymour—with no formal education—set out to preach the gospel.[97] In 1905, Seymour accepted

---

[94] Bartleman, *Azusa Street*, 18, 25, 28, 34, 37.

[95] Bartleman, *Azusa Street*, 18.

[96] Robeck, Jr. *Azusa Street*, in this publication Robeck provides an excellent outline of the various movements of Seymour until his arrival at Azusa Street, Los Angeles. He also gives interesting information regarding the racial conditions that were prevalent during the period. See also Bartleman: *Azusa Street*, Frodsham: *With Signs*, Liardon: *Azusa Street*, Wilmington Group: *The Great Azusa Street* and Cecil M. Robeck, Jr. 'William Joseph Seymour' in *NIDPCM*, 1053–58.

[97] The theological roots of Pentecostalism are vital in tracing its true identification the Holiness teachings and theology which originated with John Wesley are seen to weave itself into the development of Pentecostalism—for an excellent in-depth analysis of this issue see Dayton, *Theological Roots* see also David Allen, *The Unfailing Stream* (Tonbridge: Sovereign World, 1994), 65–124.

the pastorate of a Holiness church in Houston, Texas and it was here he would come into contact with Charles Fox Parham (1873–1929). Parham is credited with formulating the classical Pentecostal doctrine of 'initial evidence of speaking in other tongues' as the physical evidence of a baptism in or of the Holy Spirit. Parham whose background was in both Congregational and Methodist traditions became impressed by holiness doctrines.[98] In 1898 Parham established Bethel Healing Home in Topeka, Kansas which developed into a Bible and Missionary Training Centre it was here that the formulation of Pentecostal tongues theology occurred around 1900–1. Agnes Ozman had been the first of Parham's students to experience glossolalia, her utterance on the 1 January 1901. In 1905 Parham travelled to Houston, Texas where he came into contact with William J. Seymour.

Parham, the 'father' of Pentecostal doctrine, lost influence after being arrested on a charge of sodomy in 1907. Although the details are vague and the case was eventually dismissed, the events had a very negative effect upon Parham's influence. As a result it was Seymour who carried the torch for Pentecostalism into the new century.[99] Eager to learn more about his faith, Seymour enrolled in Parham's Bible Training School but the segregation laws dictated that Seymour had to sit in the corridor and listen through an open window or door. During this time, Seymour heard the new doctrine of speaking in tongues as constituting the initial evidence of being baptised in the Holy Spirit. Seymour immediately accepted this teaching on the basis of Acts 1 and 2; he now believed this to be the biblical model for all succeeding generations.

After spending a short time under the tutelage of Parham, Seymour accepted an invitation—through a friend Neely Terry—to preach in Los Angeles. On Seymour's arrival at the Nazarene church on Santa Fe Street, Los Angeles, he met with the pastor, Mrs Julia Hutchins, who invited him to the pulpit. One of his first sermons was based on Acts 2:4: 'And they were all filled with the Holy

---

[98] An important influence on Parham was Frank Sandford (1862–1948) see C.M. Robeck Jnr, 'Sandford, Frank' in *NIDPCM*, 1037–38.

[99] See J. R. Goff, 'Charles Fox Parham' in *NIDPCM*, 955–7. Vinson Synan, *The Holiness Pentecostal Movement* (Grand Rapids, MI: Zondervan, 1977), 99–105. Hollenweger, *Pentecostalism*, 18–24, Blumhofer, *Assemblies vol.1*, 97–110 and Robeck Jr., *Azusa Street*, 53–86.

Spirit and began to speak with other tongues as the Spirit was giving them utterance.'[100] Seymour wasted no time in beginning to propagate his newly embraced doctrine of initial evidence. At this point Seymour had not yet experienced personally this 'infilling' or 'baptism', but it did not hinder him from fervently preaching the necessity of the experience for all believers. Hutchins rejected Seymour's message, insisting that his teaching was out of line with the traditional holiness view on the role of the Holy Spirit so the church doors were closed to Seymour and he was not allowed over the threshold for the evening service. Harvey Cox comments that, 'Faced with a bolted door, Seymour did what thousands of Pentecostal preachers have done in similar circumstances. He carried on. With no money to rent a storefront, he began organizing prayer meetings in the humble homes of black friends and sympathizers.'[101]

Seymour felt the burden of his new Pentecostal message so greatly that nothing was going to hinder him in his search for, and propagation of, this 'power from on high'. Whatever the cost—wherever the location—he would carry on. Sympathetic supporters gathered around Seymour to listen to his teaching and pray with him. A small house at 312 Bonnie Brae Avenue, the home of Richard Asberry, became the centre of his operations. Members from Hutchins' holiness church, Smale's First New Testament Church, and others gathered to hear Seymour's Bible studies and the prayer meetings were attracting Christians hungry for a deeper experience of God. It is this general spiritual hunger which is so vital to the success of Seymour at Azusa.[102] The prayer meetings continued at Bonnie Brae Avenue for several days, then on 9 April 1906, the breakthrough came when a number of seekers spoke in other tongues. Questions remain as to whether or not Seymour experienced

---

[100] NASB.

[101] Harvey Cox, *Fire from Heaven* (London: Cassell, 1996), 54–5.

[102] Cox, *Fire from Heaven*, emphasises the socio-economic conditions in Los Angeles at this time as being a major contributory factor to the onset of revival at Azusa Street. He compares Los Angeles to the Jerusalem of New Testament times, a cosmopolitan centre ripe for new ideas. The study of the causes of revivals is an intriguing subject, and it is necessary to discover a balance between the social and cultural settings which may allow a revival to spread and the power of God at work within a people group or area at the inception of the revival. Robeck, *Azusa Street*, 52–86, also refers to the cosmopolitan situation in Los Angeles and provides interesting statistics on the church situation. Cf. Wesley Duewel, *Revival Fire* (Grand Rapids, MI: Zondervan, 1995), Andrew Walker and Kristin Aune, eds., *On Revival: A Critical Examination* (Carlisle: Paternoster, 2003).

glossolalia at this time, but news of the events spread with people from all over the city gathering to witness the extraordinary events. Seymour's personal Pentecostal experience with the initial evidence of speaking in other tongues was not received during his time with Parham, or during the initial stages of the Los Angeles revival, but occurred later in his spiritual quest yet he faithfully preached the necessity of the experience. Seymour is believed to have received this experience on 12 April 1906.[103]

The success of the Bonnie Brae meetings led Seymour and his congregation to look for larger premises, as the Asberry's front porch was no longer large enough to contain the eager disciples. The wandering Seymour at last found somewhere to put down his roots—312 Azusa Street, Los Angeles. The first service was held there on 14 April 1906. Some accounts of the revival leave a bitter taste regarding the racial attitudes of observers and participants. This segregationist culture has to be taken very seriously in the study of Azusa Street in 1906. Another vital aspect to consider is that of gender, Seymour had an inclusive outlook on the work of the Spirit, seeing a real Pentecostal experience as the key to wiping out the racial segregation and gender barriers and entering into a period of church history that would see black, white, Hispanic and Asian all worshipping under one roof. This former livery stable was to become the centre of attention in the religious world of 1906, the shock waves of which are still apparent through the modern day Pentecostal and Charismatic movements. As Seymour and his supporters moved into the Azusa Street building, they experienced what they described as a Pentecostal, spiritual visitation. Commentators generally agree with Vinson Synan who writes that, at Azusa Street, 'people not only spoke in other tongues, but sang hymns and prophesied in foreign languages. Reports of supernatural, interpretations of tongues, divine healing of diseases, visions of tongues of fire, and spectacular scenes of religious ecstasy.'[104]

As stated by Synan, the emphasis was on the supernatural, with men and women claiming to be operating under the influence of the Holy Spirit, as in

---

[103] Robeck, Jr., *Azusa Street*, 69.
[104] Synan, *Holiness-Pentecostal*, 117.

apostolic days. The person and work of the Holy Spirit was paramount to the inception and success of the Azusa Street phenomenon but Seymour was a man with his faith fixed on the centrality of Christ in the believers' experience. His focus was on the giver of the gifts of the Holy Spirit, not on the gifts. Seymour preached what he saw as a 'full gospel', calling men and women to repentance, salvation, sanctification and a baptism in the Holy Spirit, leading them on into the fullness of the Spirit's work. This evangelistic emphasis is encapsulated in Seymour's encouragement to the congregation at Azusa: 'Now, do not go from this meeting and talk about tongues, but try and get people saved.'[105] Seymour continued to pastor the Apostolic Faith Mission, Azusa Street, until his death on 28 September 1922, and this one man's vision can be regarded as the catalyst for a worldwide movement. His burden to unite race and gender under the umbrella of a Pentecostal theology was a dream which did not happen in his life-time but the sentiments of Harvey Cox regarding Seymour holds true; that despite his circumstances he 'carried on'.[106] The American influence spread from Azusa Street with a particular emphasis on evangelism and missionary work.[107]

America, in the early twentieth century, was viewed as a great source of wealth and in particular financial help for Christian ministry. Into this atmosphere arrived Thomas Ball Barratt, a native of Cornwall in England but a resident in Oslo, Norway. Barratt travelled to New York in 1906 seeking funds for his Oslo City Mission. His desired funding was not forthcoming, but he did encounter the news of Azusa Street and experienced his personal Pentecostal Spirit baptism. Barratt's teaching made its link with Wales through the influential ministry of A. A. Boddy who began to formulate a Pentecostal doctrine within

---

[105] Frodsham, *With Signs*, 38 this evangelistic emphasis is at the heart of Pentecostal theology, Spirit Baptism is an empowerment for service and in particular witness as based on Acts 1:8.

[106] In line with Seymour's vision at Azusa Street there are some interesting and helpful articles such as: Dale T. Irvin, 'Drawing All Together in One Bond of Love: The Ecumenical Vision of William J. Seymour and The Azusa Street Revival', *Journal of Pentecostal Theology*, 6 (1995), 25–53. Ted Olsen, 'American Pentecost', *Christian History* 17/2 (1998), 10–17. Grant Wacker, 'Hell Hatched Free Lovism', *Christian History* 17/2 (1998), 28–31.

[107] McClung,, ed., *Azusa Street*, this compilation provides an excellent overview of the missionary emphasis of the early Azusa Street members. See also Murray W. Dempster, Byron D. Klaus and Douglas Petersen, eds., *Called & Empowered: Global Mission in Pentecostal Perspective* (Peabody, MA: Hendrickson, 1991). Murray W. Dempster, Byron D. Klaus and Douglas Petersen, eds., *The Globalization of Pentecostalism: A Religion Made To Travel* (Oxford: Regnum Books International, 1999).

Britain.[108] His Pentecostal teaching, supported by the ministry of Rev. T. M. Jeffreys in Waunlwyd, attracted eager 'seekers' from South Wales. Some of the early leaders such as Mr and Mrs T. L. Hicks of Crosskeys visited the Sunderland conventions and returned to SE Wales to promote the experience of Pentecostal Spirit baptism.[109] Returning to Wales with great enthusiasm, they set about establishing house groups and Pentecostal ministry centres, some of which became AoG churches. The links with America continued and a group of Welsh Pentecostals, as mentioned above, contacted the American AG in 1921 regarding joining that denomination.

The impact of the American situation, especially the Azusa Street revival and in particular William J. Seymour cannot be overlooked in any history of the Welsh AoG churches. Seymour can rightly be viewed as the catalyst of Pentecost in America, and this in turn can be regarded as a fountainhead of Pentecostalism worldwide.

Having provided the main aims of this book and by way of introduction highlighted the major developments of Pentecostalism; the next chapter will examine the general social, political, economic and religious situation within SE Wales during this period.

---

[108] Wakefield, *Alexander Boddy*, 119–44, records Boddy's connections with Azusa Street via some prominent Americans who visited Sunderland, Stanley Frodsham (by then resident in Los Angeles), Levi Lupton, Pastor and Mrs. Kellaway, A. H. Post and Pastor J. H. King. Boddy also visited America on three occasions between 1909–12 when he travelled to the Azusa Street Mission where on one occasion he preached; see Robeck Jr., *Azusa Street*, 115.

[109] Wakefield, *Alexander Boddy*, 119–22, refers to visitors to Sunderland who eventually became prominent within British AoG circles, Smith Wigglesworth, H. Mogridge, Thomas Myerscough, Stephen Jeffreys along with Howard and John Carter.

Chapter 2 SE Wales: Background

This chapter aims to provide an overview of the economic, political and social conditions within Wales at the end of the nineteenth and the beginning of the twentieth centuries.[110] In addition it will consider the religious situation, especially in SE Wales, in order to identify, the possible roots of Welsh Pentecostalism.

Nineteenth Century Overview

The position of Wales in the industrialisation of Britain and the world cannot be over emphasised, David Ross comments:

> Wales was to be a key area in the rapid expansion of industrial growth that happened between 1780 and 1840. It has been variously described as a crucible and a cradle of the new industrial world. But if it was a cradle, then the baby was a foundling, put in from outside. Large-scale industry was thrust on Wales.[111]

If industry was 'thrust on Wales' the country reacted with vigour to the opportunities created by this new industrialisation. This vigour manifested itself in movements of population from various parts of Wales to the south east corner in order to seek employment, housing, higher wages and greater opportunities. These emerging industrial areas of SE Wales were faced, however, with the challenges of poor sanitary conditions, urban disease, overcrowding, poor food quality, inadequate medical support, and a high death rate.[112] The emergence of the Friendly Societies in the early part of the 1800s was the only means of assistance for individuals affected by economic difficulties due to illness, injury or bereavement.[113] These contributory factors led to the voice of social reformers being heard not simply in Wales but around Britain; and in Wales itself much attention was paid to the poor working and living conditions. Society needed reforming and this slow process of reform

---

[110] There is a plethora of excellent historical works on Wales for further in depth study, a cross section of which is contained within the bibliography.

[111] David Ross, *Wales: History of a Nation* (New Lanark: Geddes & Grosset, 2008), 169.

[112] Cholera outbreaks are recorded in 1832, 1849, 1854 and 1866.

[113] The Friendly Societies were established in order to assist people in economic difficulty, in the main societies were formed within different working/trade groups and following a period of regular payment of contributions individuals were then entitled to a small amount of financial assistance during difficult periods.

commenced in the mid-1800s with the emergence of groups such as the Chartists, under the leadership in SE Wales of John Frost; they were especially remembered for their march on Newport in 1839.[114] Although Chartism faded in its direct influence, nevertheless the Chartists had blazed a trail for social, economic and political reform and many of their aims were eventually achieved within society. This is illustrated by Alan Victor Jones within the area of SE Wales when he writes:

The abuse of child labour coupled with atrocious working conditions became a matter of such concern that between 1840 and 1842 the Government commissioned inspectors to go into these industrial areas to observe and report at first hand. As a direct result of this inquiry, women and children were excluded from underground work, as were boys under the age of 10 from March 1843.[115]

The changes were gradual and did not immediately address the poor working conditions faced by miners and iron workers who still risked their lives in order to feed their families. Rayner Rosser confirms this problem within the SE Wales coalfield:

> The average life of a collier was forty years. If he lived long enough, avoiding the terrible accidents that occurred on a daily basis in the mines, he would die of disease due to the conditions in which he lived and worked.[116]

There had been a shift in the economic landscape of Wales by the end of the nineteenth century from agriculture to the heavy industries of coal, iron and steel. By the 1850s iron was 'king' in South Wales, but coal was the pretender to the throne and soon emerged as the dominant force in Welsh industry. Within SE Wales the iron and steel industry was prominent in the northern region around Ebbw Vale; the first ironworks opening in Nantyglo in 1778,

---

[114] John Frost 1784–1877, a native of Newport Monmouthshire and eventual mayor of the town turned to radical politics and led the Newport Rising in 1839. See <www.chartists.net/John-Frost.htm>. Of interest here is the position of the village of Crosskeys which served as a meeting point for the groups of Chartists marching from the north and north-west of Newport.

[115] Alan Victor Jones, *Risca – Its Industrial and Social Development,* (Bognor Regis: New Horizon, 1980), 21.

[116] Rayner Rosser, *The Collieries of the Sirhowy Valley* (Abertillery: Old Bakehouse, 1996), 21

Beaufort in 1780 and Ebbw Vale 1790.[117] The south of the region was dominated by the growth of Newport which grew mainly due to the improved communications offered by the Monmouthshire Canal opening in 1796. Coupled with this was the building of the Sirhowy to Newport tram road in 1812 and the arrival of the railways from 1846 so the docks at Newport continued to expand until the demise of the coal trade around 1930. The central areas of the Sirhowy, Ebbw and Afon Llwyd valleys were major coal producing areas.[118] Eventually coal would dominate for almost a century; 'King Coal' was pushing Wales to the forefront of world industrialisation; A. H. Dodd commenting on this change states:

> It was in South Wales that the most spectacular developments were seen. Coal, instead of playing second fiddle to iron, came to dominate the economy: when Thomas Powell, who had pioneered the trade to France, died in 1863, he was the greatest coal exporter in the world.[119]

The world wanted Welsh coal, and Powell of Newport helped to fulfil the demand while steamships, railways, factories, and households were burning the high quality natural resource.[120] Sons followed their fathers to work at the coalface and the expanding coalfields dominated society. Coal masters and owners held their employees in a vice like grip, owning the tommy shop, houses and often being the local magistrates.[121] An example of the coal-owners hold over the workforce was payment in beer vouchers only redeemable at their privately owned and generally unlicensed beer houses. Gwyn A. Williams relates the fact that 'mass drunkenness' was considered a 'crippling social

[117] Arthur Gray-Jones, *A History of Ebbw Vale* second edition (Rogerstone: Gwent County Council, 1970, 1992), 45–64. Ebbw Vale iron/steel works continued to produce strip steel until 2002 <http://www.blaenau-gwent.gov.uk/theworks/archive/History%20of%20Ebbw%20Vale%20Steelworks.pdf>

[118] For detail see: Gray-Jones, *History of Ebbw Vale*, Peter Morgan Jones, *Hills of Fire and Iron* (Abertillery: Old Bakehouse, 1992) and John Cornwell, *Collieries of Western Gwent* (Cowbridge: D. Brown, 1983). See also Newport Borough Council, *A History of Newport* (Newport: Newport Council, 1986).

[119] A. H. Dodd, *A Short History of Wales* (London: B.T. Batsford, 1977), 147. Thomas Powell of Newport was a timber merchant, coal owner then exporter he died at the age of 83 in 1863.

[120] Rosser, *Collieries*, 113, records the export records of coal and coke from Newport docks in 1885, 1895, 1905 and 1914 each record shows significant increases with the 1914 total being 5,465,713 tons.

[121] The tommy shop was the local village store owned and supplied by the coal master who was then the recipient of the profits made from his own workforce.

disease' within the emerging industrial communities.[122] The social scene in SE Wales during this period was directly affected by the economic situation. Employment, health, and education were the major issues that needed to be addressed in the late nineteenth and early twentieth centuries, but Wales eventually benefitted from improvements in these social areas.[123] Within SE Wales the dominant social institutions were the chapel, public house, cinema and sports club.[124] The prevailing social conditions were maintained by the inherent class system which could be divided into three main strata i) the landed gentry, iron masters and coal owners, ii) the managers and iii) the labourers or workforce. The Anglicisation of the gentry was also an issue that slowly eroded the Welsh culture and society, with this landed class ruling Wales virtually unopposed; although this position changed gradually with the rise of Labour politics and unions within the workforce.[125] According to Dodd it was:

> During the 1870s trade unions began to acquire a firm footing in the principal industries, and were now throwing up their own leaders, instead of depending on outside initiatives.[126]

Many of these new local figures were proud Welshmen, Liberals in their political stance and Nonconformists in their religion, so these combined forces were highly influential during the next period of Welsh history.[127] This close link between politics and religion is illustrated by the presence of Lloyd George

---

[122] Gwyn A. Williams, 'The Emergence Of A Working-Class Movement', in A. J. Roderick, ed., *Wales Through The Ages/ Volume 2 Modern Wales* (Llandybie: Christopher Davies, 1960), 141.

[123] Educational changes are documented in D. Gareth Evans, *A History of Wales 1815–1906*, (Cardiff: University of Wales, 1989), 245–70. Jones, *Risca*, 78–94. Particularly significant are the Blue Books of 1847 the published reports of government inquiry in to the state of education in Wales.

[124] Welsh rugby's 1905 victory over the New Zealand All Blacks was the highlight of the sporting calendar amidst a generally mundane and harsh life style.

[125] For a general overview of the situation before 1912 see, Kenneth O. Morgan, *Rebirth of a Nation: Wales 1880–1980* (Oxford: O.U.P. 1981), 3–122, and John Davies, *A History of Wales* (London: Penguin Books, 2007), 387–493. See also D. Tanner, C. Williams and D. Hopkins, eds., *The Labour Party in Wales 1900-2000* (Cardiff: University of Wales Press, 2000).

[126] Dodd, *A Short History of Wales,* 149. For specifics on emergent Trade Unions see Evans, *History of Wales 1815–1906*, 285–94.

[127] The most well-known leader for the South Wales miners at this time was William Abraham also known as Mabon. The growing desire to regain the Welsh national consciousness is perhaps best illustrated in the composing and acceptance in 1856 of "Hen Wlad fy Nhadau" by Evan James of Pontypridd as a national anthem.

MP at the Quarterly Meetings of the Monmouthshire Baptist Association 1894 held at Hope Baptist Church Crosskeys.[128] The unexpected but welcomed and highly respected speaker used the opportunity to promote the Welsh Disestablishment Bill; Lloyd George was elected as president of the Welsh Baptist Union in 1909. Evans summarises this period of change within Wales; working-class organizations, both industrial and political, evolved; and there was the establishment of Welsh Nonconformity as a formidable ecclesiastical, social, and political force.[129]

The Liberal influence in Wales was transferred to Westminster when in the watershed election of 1868 twenty one Liberal MPs were returned from Wales.[130] David Williams describes the increasing friction and pressures between masters and workers:

> The English-speaking landowner and the iron-master were Anglicans; the Welsh-speaking tenant-farmer and industrial worker became increasingly Nonconformists; in fact, Nonconformity proved to be the most important link between rural and industrial Wales. Therefore it is seldom possible in the nineteenth century to disentangle social and economic considerations from religious motives.[131]

Coupled with the rising Liberal politicians, the evangelical thrust of Nonconformity was proving a major player in Welsh society. The three tangled threads of social, economic, and religious motives are indeed difficult to separate. David Ross emphasises this difference when examining the army of people who took up residence in South Wales stating:

> Their language was Welsh (90 per cent of the population of Merthyr spoke Welsh in the 1840s), their religion was based on the chapel. The Church of England, comfortable in its long-established parochial structure, was very slow to adapt to the fact that new communities were springing up in areas far from a parish church, where only before

---

[128] Graham O. Osborne, *A History of Hope Baptist Church Crosskeys* (Abertillery: Old Bakehouse, 2006).

[129] Evans, *A History of Wales 1815–1906*, 280.

[130] This trend continued at the 1892 election when Wales returned thirty-one Liberal members. The eventual rise of David Lloyd George to lead the country was possibly the apex of Welsh Liberalism.

[131] David Williams, *A History of Modern Wales* (London: John Murray, 1980), 246.

shepherds and foresters had wandered. Unitarians, Baptists and Congregationalists were far quicker to respond.[132]

The growth of industry coupled with the in-migration of a workforce with non-conformist leanings was to shape the political, economic, and religious conditions of Wales. Whatever the manoeuvrings in politics, chapel, and society the man in the street was still faced with terrible living and working conditions, as emphasised by Evans:

> The unavoidable risks to life and limb by violent accidents at work and a consciousness that they were prey to killing diseases and epidemics were the universal experiences of the working classes in this period.[133]

Despite this, the desire for improved remuneration caused people to leave their rural lives and seek employment in industry, especially in the coalfields of Glamorgan and Monmouthshire. The general situation in Wales toward the end of the nineteenth century was one characterised by employment in the heavy industries of steel and coal, improvements in education and the growth of Nonconformist denominations. An issue of major importance in this period of development is the prominence of a more militant working-class.[134] The social structure appearing towards the end of the nineteenth century paved the way for a boom in Welsh society at the beginning of the twentieth century; a boom built upon the shoulders of the working class.

Early Twentieth Century Developments: 1900–1918

In the early 1900s SE Wales was a heartland of heavy industry, and the men involved in these industries knew how to work and play hard. Collieries scarred the landscape, iron and steel works belched their toxic waste into the

---

[132] Ross, *Wales History,* 176.

[133] Evans, *A History of Wales 1815–1906,* 52. Within SE Wales three major collieries experienced disasters during the period under examination: Prince of Wales Colliery, Abercarn saw 259 fatalities on 11th September 1878, Universal Colliery, Senghenydd, Caerphilly saw 439 deaths in 1913 and Black Vein, Crosskeys was eventually closed in 1920 following three separate disasters during its history. See www.crosskeys.me.uk/history/pits.htm. See also Rosser, *Collieries,* 102, here Rosser lists the many mining disasters throughout Wales from 1837–1927 totalling 3508 deaths.

[134] Ross, *Wales History,* 202.

atmosphere and the docks at Newport connected it all to the outside world. Jones gives a précis of the situation as illustrated in the region around Risca:

> The predominant factor was that of coal, for Risca even though straddling the South Wales Coalfield had beneath its lands one of the most sought after varieties—steam coal—and it was this that attracted early pioneers to the area. Other industries also played their part, albeit more demurely, in the development role. [135]

The increasing demand for coal from SE Wales can be appreciated if one considers the number of mines that were sunk in the early twentieth century as, one of which was the Celynen North at Newbridge in 1913. This mine, sister to the already productive Celynen South established in the early 1870s, commenced its output with some 203 men employed in 1913. [136] Despite the new employment, families were touched by tragedy from the earliest years; Spencer refers to the men killed whilst working at the Newbridge mines and the first in 1914 being William Tedstone aged 32 years. [137] Amidst the hardship there were changing values in society and Evans highlights this shift:

> by 1906, a new industrial ethos prevailed in South Wales. Socialism and unionism gradually became the new religion of the working classes, and the language of the new creed was English. [138]

This 'new religion' of industrialisation and socialism was strengthened by the rise of the Independent Labour Party in South Wales, and in particular Kier Hardie breaking the stranglehold on Liberal politics when he was elected as Labour member for Merthyr Tydfil in 1906. [139] Pope provides an excellent

---

[135] Jones, *Risca*, 120–1, the other industries referred to by Jones are brick making and tin/steel works he also makes an important connection to the growth of better communications within the valley due to the arrival of an improved rail network linking the coal and other industries to Newport.

[136] Colin Spencer, *The Lamps Have Gone Out at the Celynen North & Graig Fawr Collieries* (Newbridge: Spencer, no date), contains scant bibliographical details and no page numbers. 1937 was the zenith of the North Celynen with some 1884 men employed. See also Cornwell, *Collieries*, Rosser, *Collieries*, 109, lists other mines opened 1900–1912.

[137] Spencer, *Lamps*, gives details of fatalities until 1976 referring to some as young as 16 years losing their lives at the coalface, some of the family names were those related to the early Pentecostals in the village e.g. Carpenter, Tyrrell and Lewis.

[138] Evans, *A History of Wales 1815–1906*, 313.

[139] Independent Labour Party was established in 1893 and after a period of affiliation to the Labour Party was eventually disbanded in 1973. Kier Hardie 1856–1915 was a native of Scotland who had been employed in the

summary of the difficulties faced by the Nonconformists during this period; Labour gradually drew Chapel members from the Liberal heritage and the New Theology infiltrated the pulpits.[140] Labour's rise to prominence was aided by the increasing militancy of the miners and in 1908 the Miners Federation of Great Britain affiliated itself to the Labour Party.[141] In SE Wales three individuals rose to prominence within the Labour/mining Federations: Tom Richards, William Brace and Alfred Onions. These men worked in the mining industry of SE Wales particularly in the area of Risca. Another influential figure was James Winstone, who became Vice president of the South Wales Federation (Miners) whilst Brace became president in 1911.[142] The growing unrest within society manifested itself through various demonstration, riots, and strikes. For example in SE Wales riots were recorded at Tredegar and Ebbw Vale in 1911, with their main cause being economic hardship and a desire for fairer levels of pay. K. O. Morgan suggests some possible reasons for this change in Welsh religion:

> A number of factors—the decline of the Welsh language, the change in patterns of population, the impact of Darwinism and biblical criticism— all helped to undermine the traditional influence of the chapel. Above all the silence of the churches in the face of the problems of industrialism cost them more and more working-class adherents. As the minister lost his authority, the miners' agent often took his place.[143]

Morgan suggests some important religious and theological issues that will need to be reviewed later, especially the rise of biblical criticism and liberal

---

coal industry and eventually moved into politics and finding political support in South Wales was elected to Parliament in 1906. For details of the numbers of MP within Wales see: <http://www.historylearningsite.co.uk/British_Electoral_History_1832.htm>

[140] Pope, *Building Jerusalem* and Pope, *Seeking God's Kingdom,* 11–16, for a further description of the 'New Theology' supported by Rev. R. J. Campbell and relating to the issue of interpreting Christianity in light of modern ethical thinking.

[141] Ross, *Wales,* 220–2, Ross here mentions the 1913 promise of a minimum wage for miners was to be introduced. See also T. I. Jeffrey-Jones, 'The Rise of Labour' in Roderick, *Wales Through the Ages,* 201–8.

[142] J. H. A. Roberts, *A View From The Hill* (Risca: Moriah Baptist Church, 1986).

[143] K. O. Morgan, 'Radicalism and Nationalism' in Roderick, *Wales Through the Ages,* 198.

theology, but his thoughts are to be contrasted to those of Brinley Thomas who comments:

> Instead of bemoaning the rural exodus, the Welsh patriot should sing the praises of industrial development which gave the Welsh language a new lease of life and Welsh Nonconformity a glorious high noon. [144]

If Morgan is correct in his assumption, did the vibrancy and social aspect of Pentecostalism bring new hope and faith to a people in such poor, often hopeless, conditions? Or from Thomas's perspective did the emergent Pentecostals simply benefit from the 'glorious high noon'? Pentecostals withstood the rise of liberal theology some of their new adherents left traditional denominations partly in opposition to the rising tide of such influences. Returning to the socio-economic conditions within SE Wales, Morgan writes:

> The overwhelming conclusion to be drawn about most of Welsh economic and social life in the years up to 1914 was that it was exceptionally thriving. The surging economic success of the industry and commerce of the South Wales coalfield meant opportunities of employment and a diffusion of wealth throughout the whole of the principality to some degree. By 1913 the south Wales coal industry was at its zenith. [145]

D. Gareth Evans concurs with Morgan's interpretation of the economic situation within Wales emphasising how Wales was brought from also-ran to major player in world economics. [146] Both Morgan and Evans portray a busy economic situation within Wales prior to 1914 emphasising the fact that although South Wales was the major producer of this new wealth yet all of Wales benefitted. A significant factor in the economic life of the valleys was population increase; by 1911 Monmouthshire and Glamorgan contained almost

---

[144] Brinley Thomas, 'The Growth of Industrial Towns', in Roderick, *Wales Through the Ages,* 192. See also Pope, *Building Jerusalem.*

[145] Morgan, *Rebirth of a Nation,* 125, see also Davies, *History of Wales* and Evans, *A History of Wales 1815–1906,* 15–74.

[146] Evans, *A History of Wales 1906–2000,* 9.

63% of the population.[147] The alteration in population distribution and the influx of immigrant workers gave South Wales an international outlook.[148] Not only did the in-migrants and immigrants bring an interesting blend of culture to the valleys but they also presented a new field of evangelism for Christians which was something the Pentecostals engaged in with zeal and commitment.

Within the changing political situation, two major issues can be identified as influencing conditions during this period. Firstly, the First World War proved a major disruption to the normal pattern of life. The second issue relates to both local and national government and the manoeuvrings between the Liberal Party and the rising Labour movement. The whole of Britain suffered as a result of the war, from issues such as food shortages due to panic buying and eventual rationing. A more dramatic impact is recorded by Andrew Marr:

> The way most people witnessed the war, however, was in the bodies of wounded men returning and the faces of those who had received a letter or telegram informing them of a bereavement. Above all, these were the years of visible death. A little more than 6 million men were mobilized to fight in the war, and more than 722,000 died.[149]

Of the six million mobilized at least 280,000 were Welsh and in 1914 a new Welsh division, the Welsh Guards was established. This figure is tempered by the fact that in 1914, 242,000 men were employed in the Welsh coal industry hence also supporting the war effort. At the centre of most major towns and villages in SE Wales is a cenotaph dedicated to those who gave their lives in the Great War of 1914–18. Wales was a nation that responded to the war effort with fervour encouraged by the presence of David Lloyd George, referred to by Marr as 'another Nonconformist shaker-upper', at Westminster.[150] Lloyd George served as minister of munitions, 1915, secretary of state for war, 1916

---

[147] Evans, *A History of Wales 1906–2000*, 10–13, quotes coal production in South Wales as 56.8 million tons in 1913 with employment peaking at 271,516 by 1920.

[148] Evans, *A History of Wales 1906–2000*, 1–13, gives population figures in 1801, 1851, 1901 & 1911 he records the population of Wales as 2,013,000 in 1901 and increasing by 400,000 to 1911.

[149] Andrew Marr, *The Making of Modern Britain* (London: Macmillan, 2009), 124. As well as the tragic death toll, 1.5 million were wounded which led to further difficulties within society.

[150] Marr, *Making of Modern Britain*, 20.

and prime minister, 1916–22. A. J. P. Taylor summarises the seismic shift in the British political arena when he comments:

> Lloyd George's accession to power in December 1916 was more than a change of government. It was a revolution, British-style. The party magnates and whips had been defied. The backbenchers and the newspapers combined in a sort of unconscious plebiscite and made Lloyd George dictator for the duration of the war. Lloyd George was the nearest thing England has known to a Napoleon, a supreme ruler maintaining himself by individual achievement. [151]

Lloyd George was a Welshman who advocated Welsh home rule, the temperance campaign and the disestablishment of the Church of England in Wales. [152] Although initially a pacifist, it was during his term at Westminster that conscription was introduced with many Welshmen, encouraged by some Welsh clergy, enlisting for military service. [153] It is worth noting here how both chapels and colleges donated funds to the war effort. The position of the some chapels in respect to war is highlighted by this popular view: 'Nonconformists ministers appeared to be preaching the creed "praise the Lord and kill the Germans."' [154] While this is an exaggeration, at least a number of ministers were actively encouraging recruitment to the armed services.

The industrial demands of the war effort also brought a heightened prosperity to South Wales. The requirements for coal to power the British naval fleet and for the production of steel saw the output from the valleys rise to new heights. The war effort was not supported by all and in particular some of the early Pentecostals took the stance of conscientious objectors. British pioneer AoG leader, A. Howard Carter, was imprisoned at Wormwood Scrubs and Dartmoor prisons between 1916 and 1918, and Donald Gee worked as a farm hand rather

---

[151] A. J. Taylor, *English History 1914–1945* (London: Book Club, 1977), 73.

[152] The Disestablishment campaign was the move towards making the Church in Wales separate from the Anglican Church, The Welsh Church Act of 1914 proved the watershed in this campaign it was 1920 before this Act came to fruition due to outbreak of World War I.

[153] Morgan, *Rebirth of a Nation,* 160.

[154] Morgan, *Rebirth of a Nation,* 162, see also D. Densil Morgan, *The Span of the Cross: Christian Religion and Society in Wales 1914–2000* (Cardiff: University of Wales Press, 2000), 41–77.

than be directly involved in the conflict.[155] Conscientious objection was not as widespread in SE Wales as many men were employed in the coal/steel industries which were supporting the war effort—this no doubt made the influence of early Welsh Pentecostals easier to accept by their co-workers.[156] The strength of its heavy industry promoted Wales to the forefront of world industry and with the rising industrialisation Wales was now catapulted to international significance. Riding the wave of success, despite the sometimes harsh life styles and impact of the Great War, the people of SE Wales enjoyed the bounty of their hard work. K. O. Morgan highlights the major achievements in Welsh society during this period:

> The Welsh Church had been disestablished; the University, Library and Museum came into being; there were Welsh laws, Welsh bishops, and Welsh regiments. The Welsh language was again officially taught in schools.... Wales, it seemed, was more than just a "geographical expression".[157]

As one assesses the early years of the twentieth century there is much positivity within Wales, however, the next period of Welsh history, post-World War I, is a time of change and decay yet also the most important period in the development of AoG in SE Wales.

Post-World War I: 1918–1924

One and three quarter million British men were killed or wounded by the time the armistice terms were presented to parliament by Lloyd George on 11 November 1918. With the end of hostilities came peace and a period of boom and prosperity but within a short time poverty returned, and the impact upon communities was crippling. Andrew Marr summarises the British situation:

---

[155] John Carter, *Howard Carter – Man of the Spirit* (Nottingham: AoG, 1971), 39–49. Richard Massey, *Another Springtime: The Life of Donald Gee Pentecostal Leader and Teacher* (Guildford: Highland, 1992), 23–33.

[156] An ex-miner who attended my home assembly in Newbridge always testified to the fact that his work gang where happier underground when he, 'their pentie' was with them as they believed his God would watch over him and hence they would be protected.

[157] Morgan, 'Radicalism and Nationalism', in Roderick, *Wales through the Ages,* 199. The University of Wales received its charter in 1893 and the National Library in Aberystwyth and the Museum in Cardiff were authorised in 1905.

In the immediate aftermath of the war, Lloyd George's triumph and Britain's seemed intermingled. The Royal Navy was bigger than any navy had ever been, or has ever been since. Soon, surely, the pound would again dominate the world's trading system, and London once more hum as the capital of capital. For the rest Lloyd George promised a new Jerusalem; and a short boom followed the mirth.[158]

Despite the victorious Lloyd George and the scenes of emotion and liberation in Britain, the gaiety was short lived as income tax remained high, government spending lowered, exports struggled to regain their foothold in the world economy and there were political problems at home and abroad.[159] Lloyd George's position became more tenuous and eventually the euphoria of victory in Europe gave way to the stark reality of slump and depression.

The change in Welsh politics did not help Lloyd George as his support base in Wales was slowly eroded; the Liberal Party lost its historic grip in South Wales while the Labour Party rose to prominence. Politics in SE Wales in 1918 was dominated by the Labour Party with the newly created constituencies in Monmouthshire being Monmouth, Newport, Abertillery, Ebbw Vale, Pontypool and Bedwellty. Charles Edwards was the elected member for Bedwellty and William Brace for Pontypool, and the SE Wales coalfield was to remain predominantly Labour from then on. Parallel to Labour's rise was the emergence of a more militant workforce that gave the Trade Unions added impetus. As the Labour Party gained dominance so the Nonconformists influence—so apparent in the Liberal Party—began to wane. Many Labour supporters were members in the Nonconformist chapels but they did endeavour to distance themselves from the anti-religious thinking of Lenin and Marx.[160] These political manoeuvrings influenced the life of the population of South Wales, yet all this is overshadowed by the effects of the Great War. Evans refers to Wales as 'a storm centre of industrial militancy and unrest;'[161] unrest which manifested itself in industrial action with its political and social

---

[158] Marr, *Making of Modern*, 218–9, see also Taylor, *English History*, 120–226.

[159] Major challenges at this time were in Ireland with the Republicans and Unionists, in Russia with the rising Communist state of Lenin and Trotsky and in India with the emergence of Gandhi and his peaceful campaigns that eventually brought an end to Britain's Indian Empire.

[160] Pope, *Building Jerusalem*.

[161] Evans, *History of Wales 1906–2000*, 73.

impact. Wages would again be the issue in the mining industry and Lloyd George suffered as a result of the lockout that commenced on 1 April 1921.[162] Unable to deliver on his promise of a 'new Jerusalem' and despite his successes in Downing Street, Lloyd George resigned from office in October 1922 throwing British politics into a period of turmoil. The subsequent general elections in 1922, 1923 and 1924 saw a 'new political battle' between Conservatives and socialists emerging.[163] Writing of the 1922 general election, Davies records:

> The Labour party polled 41 per cent of the Welsh vote compared with 31 per cent in 1918. It won every one of the fifteen seats in the mining valleys of the south – the beginning of complete electoral supremacy over these seats which would continue unbroken until the present day, at least at the Westminster level.[164]

Labour and socialism took a strong grip in south Wales but by 1925 the Welsh Nationalist Party emerged and although weak in its beginnings the efforts of Saunders Lewis (1893–1985) eventually brought it into the political circle.[165]

The post-war years proved difficult for many ordinary Welsh valley people. A generation of men had been taken from their families, employment, and chapels and buried in the fields of Europe. However harsh the effects upon the population were, the economic impact in SE Wales was wide-ranging.[166] Unemployment was to hit huge proportions within the valleys which were cast into economic depression and not only were the demands from the military reduced but foreign competition, especially coal from America, began to affect world trade.[167] Yet not all was doom and gloom, for the Celynen North and Graig Fawr collieries in Newbridge were expanding and sinking new shafts and employing more colliers. By 1923 the Celynen North employed some 921

---

[162] Taylor, *English History*, 146.

[163] Marr, *Making of Modern*, 213–38.

[164] Davies, *History of Wales*, 529.

[165] D. Hywel Davies, *The Welsh National Party 1925–45* (Cardiff: University of Wales Press, 1983).

[166] Taylor, *English History*, 1–261, who details the overall scene in Britain during this period. Wales features prominently if only because of David Lloyd George in British politics.

[167] Davies, *History of Wales*, 511 agrees with this view of the situation.

workers under the management of H. N. Forbes.[168] Spencer records some interesting personal details of colliers that help portray the essence of the period; for example Ivor Harris:

> I started in 1926. There was over a hundred horses when I started. Horses were thought more of than men. You only got paid for lump coal, you were never paid for small. For your lump you were paid two shillings and threepence a ton.

The grim story is continued by another miner, George Workman:

> I started in the Prince of Wales Colliery, Abercarn, in 1924. Fourteen on the Friday, started on the Monday. Wages in the Prince of Wales were 18 shillings a week. 3 shillings a day for six days. Boys in the Celynen North and South were paid 14 shillings.[169]

The prevailing attitude towards the workforce is summed up by Harris's views regarding horses, the meagre amounts paid for hard physical labour and the employment of boys as young as fourteen. The miners in Crosskeys Blackvein Colliery would begin their shift at 6am, and it would last until 2pm. Food was basic, generally consisting of bread and cheese, with cold tea or water drawn from a spout or tap at the top of Tredegar Street; a site preserved by the local council in the car park of Crosskeys Pentecostal Church. This site was also used as a convenient location for public rallies and meetings of the workforce. Other shifts during the day would be 2pm–10pm and a night shift from 10pm–6am. Coal was dug by hand and transported to the surface by trams drawn by horses.[170] These times and conditions were common in SE Wales during this period of industrial history, following a long hard shift cutting coal men would then be expected to return home to wash as pithead baths were not a common feature of the early mining industry. The overall impact of the coal industry on SE Wales is a major issue, affecting families, economy, social pastimes and leading to the growth of the town of Newport. Rayner Rosser sums up the impact:

---

[168] Spencer, *Lamps.*

[169] Spencer, *Lamps.*

[170] As late as the 1950s horses were still in use in the mines at Newbridge. The author's grandfather worked as the hostler, caring for the horses underground, and his father (who started work at the age of 15 in 1956) worked in the South Celynen with the blacksmith.

It took 300 million years to form coal, and a little more than 200 years to rip it out. Against that terrible scale of unimaginable time, 200 years is just a moment. Some would say it was a terrible moment, wasteful of lives and precious, unrenewable resources. Others, looking from a different perspective would see a glorious, heroic moment. Whatever our view, it cannot be ignored or forgotten.[171]

Many of the AoG adherents were miners by trade, and their impact in the mines is recorded in the example of George Pullen, a founder member of the Pentecostal Church in Newbridge.[172] The testimony of his influence was a lack of fear whilst underground and he would work anywhere, whatever the conditions, because he was not afraid to die. The hope of a heavenly reward was something which spurred men like George Pullen to work and testify of their faith and hope to some of the hardest men in the community: miners. These conditions were not solely experienced by miners, iron and steel workers also suffered horrendous working conditions. Peter Morgan Jones records an eyewitness testimony of furnace workers in Cwmbran:

> The puddler is exposed to scorching heat and light of the most dazzling brilliancy which no ordinary person could look at, the occupation is one of great personal exertion while exposed to an intense fire that no one not accustomed to it could even approach.[173]

Colliers and iron and steel workers alike endured some of the most difficult working conditions imaginable, but they were endured in order to provide a meagre living. An interesting observation, in respect to the social aspect of the mining and steel communities, is the effect material poverty may have had upon the spiritual outlook of ordinary people. Demonstrating one's faith by good deeds and kindness may have helped the emerging denomination to flourish in a low economic state; of which more later. Wales was very much a

---

[171] Rosser, *Collieries*, 109.

[172] Chris Palmer, *80 Years At Golden Grove 1923–2003: celebrating 80 Years of Pentecostal Testimony at Golden Grove*. I had researched the origins on Newbridge AoG in 2002 in order to produce this commemorative booklet. See also <www.aognewbridge.co.uk>

[173] Peter Morgan Jones, *Hills of Fire and Iron* (Abertillery: Old Bakehouse, 1992), 36.

nation in flux, and changes were apparent. D. Densil Morgan summarises the post-war situation in Wales:

> Yet it was apparent even then that post-war Wales would be a new, strange Wales, where the old values would be put aside and Christianity be increasingly regarded as an anachronism.[174]

This 'new, strange Wales,' which was experiencing major alterations in both economic and political circles, and at the outset of a rising nationalism, was the arena from which AoG emerged. Traditional churches were normally experiencing decline, but the Pentecostal teaching and experience offered hope.[175]

Having provided an overview of the socio-economic developments, I will now turn my attention to the tangled web of Nonconformity within Wales during the early period of the twentieth century.

The Christian Heritage of Wales

Evangelical Roots

British religious history from the mid-eighteenth century, including the development of evangelicalism with its strong missionary activity, can be viewed as one of the most significant periods in Protestant history.[176] D. W. Bebbington summarises this period within Britain as a whole to 1914:

> The hundred years or so before the First World War nevertheless deserve to be called the Evangelical century. In that period the activism of the movement enabled it to permeate British society. But, at least for a while, Evangelicals had remoulded British society in their own image.[177]

---

[174] Morgan, *Span*, 76.

[175] The eschatological focus of Pentecostalism was particularly strong in SE Wales where many early groups and especially those of the "mother church" at Crosskeys focussed on the Second Coming of Christ. This motivated people to witness and to look beyond the present suffering to a "glorious heavenly reward".

[176] Bebbington, *Evangelicalism in Modern Britain*, 20–74. It is important to note the development of overseas mission activity during this period, for example, William Carey travelled to India in 1793, see C. Silvester Horne, *A Popular History of the Free Churches* (London: Congregational Union of England and Wales, 1926), 312–38. Horton Davies, *The English Free Churches* (London: O.U.P., 1963).

[177] Bebbington, *Evangelicalism in Modern Britain*, 149–50.

Bebbington's claim is possibly somewhat exaggerated, but it reflects to a large degree the situation within SE Wales where the impact of evangelicalism had been wide-ranging: from the many local, regional and national revivals occurring in the eighteenth and nineteenth centuries until the outbreak, and aftermath, of the Welsh Revival of 1904–05.[178] Nonconformity had been growing in this period, chapels were expanding and society benefitted in various ways from its influence. Wales possessed a rich religious heritage and Christianity had played a crucial role in the formation of Welsh society. Wales has experienced various revivals of religion for example 1735, 1762, 1780, 1791, 1817, 1832, 1859 and 1904–05. These revivals were particularly significant among the Welsh Calvinistic Methodists but the Baptists and Congregationalists, and later the Wesleyan Methodists, also benefitted from these local and regional revivals.[179]

The first recognised Nonconformist chapel in SE Wales was established in the village of Llanvaches, Monmouthshire, in 1639; its beginnings attributed to William Wroth (1576–1642) and Walter Craddock (c. 1606–1659).[180] R. Tudur Jones provides an excellent and helpful summary of the antecedents of Congregationalism that emerged at Llanvaches; suggesting that an openness to change was an underlying principle of that new revolutionary movement.[181] Another pioneering Nonconformist chapel in the area was at Mynyddislwyn established in 1640 which later became New Bethel. The first pastor was Henry Walter who had been ejected from his position as curate of Mynyddislwyn due to a dispute over the Book of Sports.[182] The Penmaen Independent chapel near

---

[178] D. Geraint Jones, *Favoured With Frequent Revivals: Revivals in Wales 1762–1862* (Cardiff: Heath Christian Trust, 2001). See also Eryl Davies, *The Beddgelert Revival* (Bridgend: Bryntirion Press, 2004), 11–29 for a helpful overview of revivals and the social, political, religious and economic situation in Wales during the nineteenth century.

[179] Jones, *Favoured with Frequent Revivals.*

[180] Noel Gibbard, *Walter Craddock: A New Testament Saint* (Bridgend: Evangelical Library of Wales, 1977), Horne, *Popular History,* 299–311.

[181] R. Tudur Jones, *Congregationalism in Wales* (Bangor: University of Wales, 2004), 1–47.

[182] Len Burland, *A Historical Tour around Mynyddislwyn Mountain* (Abertillery: Old Bakehouse, 2002), 281–90. The Book of Sports was a document that allowed Sunday afternoon entertainment through sporting activities to any who had attended church on the Sunday morning, both William Wroth and Henry Walter refused to advocate such activity and hence were removed from their livings within the Anglican Church and proceeded in forming these early dissenting congregations.

Blackwood was also formed in 1640 by Henry Walter and gave added impetus to the rising Nonconformist cause in SE Wales.[183] From these early events in Llanvaches, Mynyddislwyn and Penmaen, Nonconformity spread throughout Monmouthshire and the influential denominations that emerged in this part of Wales were the Presbyterians, Independents (Congregationalists) and Baptists. D. Densil Morgan provides a helpful overview of the Christian nature of Wales, and with others, emphasises the importance of the Evangelical Revival, which began in Wales with the conversions of Daniel Rowland, curate of Llangeitho, (1713–90) and Howell Harris, Trefecca, (1714–73) in 1735.[184] There was also the particular influence of the hymns and writings of William Williams of Pantycelyn (1717–91). These developments in Wales were separate from, yet parallel with, those in England where John Wesley (1703–91) and George Whitefield (1714–70) had a wide impact.[185] In SE Wales the Independent Edmund Jones (1702–93) of Pontypool, known as the Old Prophet ('Yr Hen Brophwyd'), was a leading figure during this period.[186] The son of devout parents who attended the Independents meeting at Penmaen, Jones attended Howell Prosser's school in the Ebbw Fawr Valley near Penycae in the parish of Aberystruth (Ebbw Vale); he preached his first sermon at Penmaen in 1739. Jones was not offered the pastorate of the Penmaen chapel but became pastor at the Independent chapel in Tyllwyn, Ebbw Vale from September 1739 and served the congregation until 1779. Jones also founded another Independent chapel at the Tranch, Pontypool. A close friend of Howell Harris and George

---

[183] The Penmaen independent chapel is no longer a worshipping community though the building is now utilised as the home of the Mynyddislwyn Male Voice Choir. Ralph Thomas, *Oakdale – The Model Village* (Blackwood: 2004), 32–5.

[184] D. Densil Morgan, 'Continuity, Novelty and Evangelicalism in Wales, C. 1640–1850' in Michael A. G. Haykin and Kenneth J. Stewart, eds., *The Emergence of Evangelicalism: Exploring Historical Continuities* (Nottingham: Apollos - I.V.P., 2008), 84–102. See also E.D. Jones, 'The Methodist Revival' in Roderick, *Wales through the Ages*, 101–9, and Bebbington, *Evangelicalism in Modern Britain,* 1–19.

[185] John Pollock, *John Wesley* (Oxford: Lion, 1989), John Pollock, *Whitefield: The Evangelist* (Fearn: Christian Focus, 2009), John Morgan Jones and William Morgan, translated by John Aaron, *The Calvinistic Methodist Fathers of Wales* Vols. 1 and 2 (Edinburgh: Banner of Truth, 2008).

[186] Gwyn Davies, *A Light in the Land: Christianity in Wales 200–2000* (Bridgend: Bryntirion, 2002), 69–100. See also Lionel Madden, ed., *Methodism in Wales: A Short History Of The Wesley Tradition* (Llanrwst: Methodist Conference, 2003); William Williams, *Welsh Calvinistic Methodism*, (Bridgend: Bryntirion, 1998); E. D. Jones, 'The Methodist Revival' in Roderick, *Wales Through the Ages,* 101–9; Horne, *Popular History,* Knox; R. Buick, *Voices From The Past: History of the English Conference of the Presbyterian Church of Wales, 1889–1938* (Llandyssul: Gomerian Press, 1969); Brynmor Pierce Jones, *Sowing Beside All Waters* (Cwmbran: Gwent Baptist Association, 1985); Gray-Jones, *History of Ebbw Vale,* 27–9.

Whitefield, Jones read widely on theological issues and he was also deeply interested in superstitions, horoscopes and prophecies. Calvinistic in his theology, preaching a message of salvation by faith, adhering to infant baptism and known for the publication of a history of the Aberystruth parish in 1779, Jones was a prominent figure in SE Wales Nonconformist circles.

Following on from these initial activities, society in SE Wales began to change due to the growth of industry and subsequent surge in population the Nonconformists responded positively and rapidly commenced the expansion of chapels in the valleys. The following sample of churches within SE Wales offers a cross-section of the major denominations within Wales at this time and represents the main industrial centres that were the cause of much of the population shift and which later developed Pentecostal/AoG groups.

Examples of the Rise of Nonconformity in SE Wales

The development of Nonconformity in SE Wales can be illustrated at various locations throughout Monmouthshire, with the appearance of many chapels within this period of expansion.[187] The town of Risca was a prominent centre within the Ebbw Valley due to the opening of the Darren colliery in the 1730s, later industrial developments were the Pontymister Iron Works in 1835, and the brickworks established in 1835–39. The Nonconformist denominations took root within the area, offering spiritual guidance to the incoming workforce; the Welsh Baptists arrived in the mid-1700s, followed by both the Wesleyan (1798) and Calvinistic Methodists (1810), the Independents (1841) and, finally, the English Baptists (1855). Moriah Baptist, Risca, became a vibrant centre for Nonconformist activity, and sixty-five members transferred from Bethesda, Rogerstone (which had originally opened in 1746), to officially open Moriah on Christmas Day 1835.[188] Towards the end of the nineteenth

---

[187] <http://www.genuki.org.uk/big/wal/Dissent.html> Hywel D. Emanuel 'Dissent in the Counties of Glamorgan and Monmouth', *National Library of Wales Journal* Vol 8/4 (1954); 9/1 (1955); 9/2 (1955). In this three part series there is relevant information regarding the early Dissenting individuals within Monmouthshire.

[188] Abdiel Llewelyn and Dorothy R. Bailey, *Bethesda, Tydu: A Bicentenary Survey of the History of Bethesda Baptist Church Tydu* (Rogerstone: Bethesda Baptist, 1942, third edition 1984).

century Moriah recorded 283 members, with 620 attending the Sunday school in the care of 40 teachers.[189]

Building on the earlier ministry of Edmund Jones, the Ebbw Vale district was a beacon of Christian witness, and the first Wesleyan Methodist place of worship was established in 1808 by a Mr Evans, a furnace manager at the Harford iron works. By 1817 there was a meeting of Baptists and another Independent chapel in the district and within eight years (1825) there were also Calvinistic Methodist and Welsh Baptists chapels; by 1837 the Welsh Congregationalists had a permanent place of worship. The Ebbw Vale district was home to twenty one Nonconformist chapels by 1870, in contrast to two Anglican churches and a Roman Catholic school that was used for public services.[190]

The growth of Nonconformity is also reflected in the history of Tabernacle English Baptist Chapel, Newbridge, founded in 1859 as a mission from Beulah Welsh Baptist, Newbridge, which had opened much earlier in 1810.[191] Tabernacle was intended to provide for the spiritual needs of English speaking labourers who arrived in the Ebbw Valley to work in the collieries.[192] This new venture was well supported from the surrounding communities with visiting preachers travelling from other Nonconformist chapels in Pontypool, Blaenavon, Rhymney, Risca and Trinant. Subsequently Tabernacle Newbridge founded daughter churches at Chapel-of-Ease, Abercarn (1871) and Jerusalem/Bethel Crumlin (1905). Jerusalem Baptist church, Crumlin, opened as a result of the evangelistic fervour of people affected by the 1904–05 Revival; but this church merged with Noddfa, Crumlin in 1920, and became known as Bethel Baptist church.[193] Crumlin was also home to the Wesleyan Methodist chapel built in 1900 after a period of meetings held in a room in the Navigation Hotel. The progress of Nonconformity in Crumlin is further illustrated by the opening of the Presbyterian Church in 1915 through the ministry of the

---

[189] Jones, *Risca,* 103–114 and Roberts, *A View From The Hill.*

[190] Gray-Jones, *History of Ebbw Vale,* 64–76, 104, 139–50. More details are found in Brynmor Pierce Jones, *How Lovely Are Thy Dwellings* (Newport: Wellspring, 1999), 116–62 and Brian Collins, *Crumlin to Pontymister Places of Worship: A Sketchbook History* (Abertillery: Old Bakehouse, 2005).

[191] John Hopkin Butts, *A History of Beulah Baptist Newbridge* (Abertillery: Old Bakehouse, 2010).

[192] *Tabernacle English Baptist Chapel, Newbridge 150th Anniversary Souvenir Brochure,* 2009, <www.tabernacle-newbridge.org.uk> the first pastor was Mr. William Prosser of Pontypool College, ordained in 1864.

[193] The Noddfa chapel was sold and became the Crumlin Rugby Club. Bethel Baptist still functions as a place of worship.

Forward Movement; the first minister of the chapel on Whitethorn Street was Rev. D. D. Jones.

The Temple Church in High Street, Newbridge was opened in 1891 and was affiliated to the Presbyterian denomination; following the 1904 Revival and to accommodate the influx of a larger labour force, a new chapel was built in 1912. Temple, Newbridge, through the work of the Forward Movement, established chapels at Pentwynmawr (1900), Crumlin (1915), Abercarn (1915), and Oakdale (1916). The necessity of providing both Welsh and English language services, due to the changing labour force, is also illustrated in Newbridge at Zion Congregational Church. Zion, built in High Street in 1898, accommodated both resident Welsh and incoming English speakers; in the early part of the twentieth century, the Welsh speakers built another chapel, Zoar, off Victoria Terrace. [194]

Towards the south of the region, the expansion of Nonconformity was represented by the establishment of Tabernacle Congregational Chapel, Rhiwderin. [195] This chapel provided opportunities for Christian worship for the families of in-migrants who moved to the village seeking employment in the newly opened tin works. From 1865 Rev. Jones of Machen, Rev. Edwards of Newport and Rev. Hughes of Maesycwmmer commenced regular services in Rhiwderin, so that by 1872 a church was formed that met in the canteen of the tin works. In 1884 a newly constructed chapel was opened with Rev. Mon Evans of New Inn, Pontypool being installed as the first pastor.

In the Eastern (Afon Lywyd) Valley, events at Pontymoile, Pontypool, serve as a good example of the expanding ministry of Nonconformist chapels. The Pontymoile Mission Hall was established in 1878 by Thomas Wintle, who preached first in a cottage before building the mission hall, a ragged school for neglected children, and a rescue home for abandoned and abused girls of the

[194] The site at Golden Grove, Newbridge, was home to the Methodists then Congregationalists and now the AoG. The decline of Nonconformity in the late twentieth century is seen at Newbridge in the fact that Zion is now residential housing; Zoar is a car park and Temple a new police station and car park.
[195] Raymond Saunders, *1881: Memories of Tab* (Rhiwderin: self-published, 2006).

district.[196] Wintle's evangelistic efforts continued with the establishing of other missions in Pontnewydd, Cwmffrwdoer and Pontypool.

The largest town in southern Monmouthshire—Newport—was home to numerous chapels during this period; for example Duckpool Road Baptist was established in 1875. Initial services were commenced by three ladies and one man in a private house and by 1875 a group of twelve were meeting who then invited the nineteen year old A. T. Jones (1856–1935), of Raglan to be their minister; a role he fulfilled for forty two years.[197] Another Baptist church in Newport was founded at Lliswerry in 1889 where a group of believers who worshipped at nearby Nash Baptist Church (opened 1821) proposed opening a new church. The original nine members led by Mr Thomas Delahaye, Pastor at Nash, grew to thirty-six by the end of the first year.[198] The membership continued to grow under the continued guidance of Mr Delahaye with a Sunday school consisting of eighty individuals led by a Mr Wills and six teachers. This grew to one hundred and eighty attendees and eleven teachers by 1917.

Hope Baptist Church, Crosskeys, was opened in February 1882 as a result of open air preaching and prayer meetings conducted by a group of Baptists from Bethany Baptist Risca (1855). Hope opened with thirty-three members and seventy children connected to the Sunday school. Bethany and Hope's influence may also be seen in the establishing of Baptist churches; one was at Zion, Cwmcarn that emerged from a Sunday school in 1892 to become a recognised church by 1914. Then also Abercarn Baptist was also officially formed in 1847 but the village had seen Baptist witness since 1747, however, due to the need of Welsh language services a group of miners joined Chapel-of-Ease Baptist a mile from Abercarn. The Welsh speakers eventually established their own church at Caegorlan (1883) on the opposite side of the valley and the English speakers held their services at Chapel-of-Ease.

---

[196] At the time of writing Pontymoile Mission still maintains an evangelical witness.

[197] *Duckpool Road Baptist Church 1875–2000, 125th Anniversary Booklet* (Duckpool Road Baptist, official Church history, produced by the pastor and members of Duckpool Road). See also Jones, *Sowing Beside,* and Jones, *How Lovely,* 158–162.

[198] Lliswerry Baptist Church, *Lliswerry Baptist Church 1889–1939: Momento of Jubilee* (Lliswerry, 1939).

In some places, the disused Nonconformist chapels became home to new Pentecostal groups; this was the case in Newbridge where the old Methodist chapel at Golden Grove became home to the Pentecostals. After several years of renting the premises it was finally purchased in 1928 for the sum of £750.[199] A similar story is seen in Abercarn where the Primitive Methodist chapel became home to the Pentecostal Full Gospel Mission which commenced public worship there in the mid-1940s. These situations are a sample illustrating the steady expansion of Nonconformist chapels in the area of SE Wales both pre- and post- 1904–05; it was from within these chapels that many of the pioneer Pentecostals would emerge. The major issue that arises from this sampling of local churches is the fact that evangelical Christianity, within SE Wales, was vigorous and in certain places expanding while maintaining an influence within society on both a religious and social level. The growing discontent within some of the local denominational chapels was, however, to affect the rise of Pentecostalism as some dissatisfied with liberal theology gradually began to be attracted to the biblical emphasis and experiential vitality of the new charismatic groups.

Struggles and Success

The growth of Nonconformist chapels in SE Wales was encouraged by the ministry of organisations such as the Forward Movement, established in 1891, by the evangelistic fervour and tireless service of its gifted leader, Dr John Pugh (1846–1907).[200] Seth Joshua (1858–1925) and his brother Frank (1861–1920) of Upper Trosnant, Pontypool were converted after their family moved to Treforest, Pontypridd in 1882; the brothers eventually joined with Dr John Pugh in the work of the Forward Movement of the Presbyterian Church of Wales. The main purpose of this organisation was to take the gospel message to the people by means of evangelistic campaigns. Their particular aim was to evangelise the lower working classes in the industrial communities of South

---

[199] *80 Years at Golden Grove, 1923-2003*, the AoG chapel still operates from the same site. The Wesleyans moved location but still function within the village of Newbridge, at Wesley Hall situated on Bridge Street.

[200] Geraint Fielder, *Grace, Grit and Gumption* (Fearn: Christian Focus, 2000); T. Mardy Rees, *Seth and Frank Joshua The Renowned Evangelists The Story Of Their Wonderful Work* (Wrexham: Principality Press, 1929); Cauchi, *Welsh Revival CD ROM* and Howell Williams, *The Romance Of The Forward Movement Of The Presbyterian Church Of Wales* (Denbigh: Gee & Son, 1948).

Wales and especially the English speaking immigrants. The evangelistic efforts of the Forward Movement had a profound effect upon local society in ministering to the poor and also the morally lax individuals; at every opportunity, they presented the gospel message. As mentioned above, Howell Williams records that within three to five years of the founding of the Forward Movement centres had opened at Crosskeys, Abercarn, Abertillery, Elliotstown, Ebbw Vale, Blaina, Llanhilleth, Pontypool, and Six Bells.[201] Coupled to this expansion into the eastern valleys the work in Newport continued to grow and became a key centre of ministry for the Forward Movement.[202]

Another yet distinctly different evangelical para-church ministry of the period was the Keswick Movement (commenced 1875), and particularly the Keswick-in-Wales, 'daughter conventions', held in Llandrindod Wells (commenced 1903).[203] The emphasis upon the Holy Spirit's activity in the life of the believer was paramount at Keswick. This teaching was one possible precursor to Welsh Pentecostalism and, as mentioned in chapter 1, Sidney Mercy of Pontywaun had been a visitor to Llandrindod Wells. It was here that he would have been introduced to the teaching of men such as Evan Hopkins and Dr G. Campbell Morgan who presented the necessity of experiencing the fullness and power of the Spirit.[204]

Cyril G. Williams provides an insight into this link by providing five issues found within Keswick teaching that Pentecostalism inherited or more correctly developed:

> 1) That there is a blessing to be sought and to be received subsequent to and distinct from conversion

---

[201] Fielder, *Grace, Grit and Gumption*, Collins, *Crumlin to Pontymister*, Jones, *How Lovely*, Rees, 'Seth and Frank Joshua the Renowned Evangelists', Williams, *Romance of the Forward Movement*, 98–108.

[202] Williams, *Romance of the Forward Movement*, 109–23.

[203] Steven Barabas, *So Great a Salvation* (Eugene, OR: Wipf & Stock, 2005) and John Charles Pollock, *The Keswick Story: The Authorized History of the Keswick Convention* (Fort Washington, PA: CLC, 2006). See also Dayton, *Theological Roots*, 104–6.

[204] Stevenson, ed., *Keswick's Authentic*, 461–77, within both of these sermons no Pentecostal experiences are advocated.

2) That one must seek to be led by the Spirit in all the affairs of life.

3) That revivals and camp meetings ought to be utilized for the purpose of winning converts and rejuvenating the spiritual lives of the faithful.

4) That believers should maintain a vibrant hope in the imminent return of Christ, and

5) That one ought to forsake the world and shun all manifestations of 'worldliness' – amusements, jewellery (sic), use of cosmetics, luxury.[205]

Although some of these theological positions were found within the teaching of the traditional denominations, neither they nor the Keswick 'second blessing' teaching were by any means Pentecostal. Instead, both the more traditional theological positions and Keswick teaching centred on sanctification and the path to holiness. Evidence of the Spirit's presence in the believer would be recognised within areas such as a greater love of Jesus, prayer, Bible study, evangelism and a desire for purity of life.

Another important figure at this time was Reader Harris K. C. (1847–1909) who established the Pentecostal League in 1891.[206] The focus of this group was to promote holiness, seek revival in the churches and pray for the baptism in the Holy Spirit. Although Harris used the term 'Pentecostal' in his movement's signature it was not to be defined in the way later Pentecostals would understand; they did not see this as related to speaking in tongues. The use of terminology adopted by the Pentecostals and in particular the 'baptism in the Holy Spirit' should not cause one to see an automatic link between Keswick, the Pentecostal League, and the AoG. The doctrinal differences are easily recognised, especially with the AoG's development of an emphasis upon

[205] J.T. Nichol cited in Cyril G. Williams, *Tongues of The Spirit: A Study Of Pentecostal Glossolalia And Related Phenomena* (Cardiff: University of Wales Press, 1981), 49.

[206] Reader Harris was also a supporter of British Israelism the theory that suggests the Anglo-Saxons are descended from the Children of Israel. In 1908 he published his book *The Lost Tribes of Israel*. His teaching was accepted by Charles Fox Parham the American 'Father of Pentecostalism'.

tongues and spiritual gifts. The Pentecostals did, though, adopt the
terminology of 'the baptism in the Holy Spirit', endeavouring to give it a more
succinct definition and purpose i.e. evidential tongues and power for service
based upon Acts 1:8. [207]

At the beginning of the twentieth century individuals such as Joseph Jenkins
(1859–1929), W.W Lewis (1856–1938), E. Keri Evans (1860–1941), W. Nantlais
Williams (1874–1959), J. Cynddylan Jones (1841–1930) and R. B. Jones (1869–
1933), rose to prominence. [208] These men, and others like them, stood for the
divine inspiration and inerrancy of the Bible and recognised its content as the
divine rule for life and conduct; they made valuable contributions to Welsh
Nonconformity. [209] Along with their ministry was the social and gospel
ministry of the Salvation Army established in 1865 by William Booth (1829–
1912), which responded particularly to the social injustice and economic
hardship of the labourers of SE Wales. [210]

Despite such developments, the growth of evangelicalism in SE Wales faced
significant opposition [211] from the appearance of liberal theology which
revolved around two major issues: i) liberalism in biblical study—challenging
the authority, historicity and divine inspiration of the Bible which subsequently
lead to, ii) liberalism in doctrine—undermining and denial of the traditional
doctrines of the faith. [212] In SE Wales, some individuals within the established

---

[207] This use of evangelical theology is apparent in the Statement of Faith of AoG which covers all the major
theological tenets but adds the belief in initial evidence and spiritual gifts.

[208] B. Jones, *The King's Champions 1863–1933* (Surrey: B. Jones, 1968). See also Fielder, *Grace, Grit and
Gumption*, and Brynmor Pierce Jones, *The Spiritual History of Keswick in Wales 1903–1983* (Cwmbran: C.L.P.,
1989) and Stevenson,, ed., *Keswick's Authentic*. Robert Ellis, 'Living Echoes of the Welsh Revival 1904–05', in
Cauchi, *Welsh Revival on CD ROM*.

[209] R. B. Jones was particularly influential through his work at the Bible Training School in Porth, Rhondda. See
Noel Gibbard, *R. B. Jones: Gospel Ministry in Turbulent Times* (Bridgend: Bryntirion Press, 2009), 118–36. See
also Jones, *King's Champions*.

[210]   <http://www.salvationarmy.org/ihq/www_sa.nsf/vw-local/United-Kingdom-with-the-Republic-of-Ireland>
Roger Joseph Green, *The Life and Ministry of William Booth: Founder of the Salvation Army* (Nashville, TN.:
Abingdon Press, 2005). Salvation Army, *The Salvation Army: its Origin and Development* (London: Salvationist
Publishing and Supplies Limited, 1927, Revised 1945).

[211] Jones, *Faith and the Crisis*.

[212] The development of liberal Protestantism in the nineteenth century is widely accepted as originating with the
German theologian Friedrich D. E. Schleiermacher (1768–1834). For an overview of liberal theology and
suggested further reading see Alistair Mason, 'Liberal Protestantism' in Adrian Hastings, ed., *The Oxford
Companion To Christian Thought* (Oxford: O.U.P., 2000), 385–7 and B.A. Gerrish, 'Schleiermacher, Friedrich
Daniel Ernst', in Hastings, ed., *Oxford Companion,* 644–6. Mark Hopkins, *Nonconformity's Romantic*

denominations may have become disillusioned with the rise of liberal theology, and they began to look outside their chapels for spiritual input. However there is no written evidence that those who were attracted to Pentecostalism were so due to the impact of liberal theology. The emerging Pentecostals had little influence upon the evangelical world, a fact which could be due to the lack of serious theological training received by their early leaders. These people emphasised the Spirit's role in the Christian experience and did not become overly concerned with theological differences in the denominations. The publication of Charles Darwin's *On the Origins of Species* in 1859 also helped in the slow erosion of biblical truth by which Wales had been governed; these issues would have cut to the heart of Welsh Nonconformity.[213] These external doubts, coupled to the burgeoning desires of materialism and leisure pursuits, ushered in the age of decadence; this caused many to lose sight of God or the need for religion and faith. Eifion Evans provides an excellent summary of the declining situation within Welsh evangelicalism:

> By 1904 those very doctrines which had formed the backbone of the historic denominations were relegated to a place of secondary importance. If they were not strenuously opposed at least they were regarded with scornful indifference. Consequently the 1904 revival came to a church which was doctrinally off balance.[214]

This became a major cause of concern for the leading Nonconformists within Wales; men such as Nantlais Williams, R. B. Jones, and the Joshua brothers. Despite the instances of chapel growth as mentioned above and the impact of the Forward Movement, the early years of the twentieth century saw a steady decline in organised religion in Wales, changes in the social structure, the economic effects of the Great War and the slow desertion of traditional biblical

---

Generation: Evangelical and Liberal Theologies in Victorian England (Milton Keynes: Paternoster, 2004). J. Gresham Machen, *Christianity and Liberalism;* (Grand Rapids, ML: Eerdmans, 2001). Davies, *Light in the Land*, 85–109; Eifion Evans, *The Welsh Revival* (Bridgend: Bryntirion Press, 1969), 35–48 and Gibbard, *R. B. Jones*, 157–68.

[213] http://darwin-online.org.uk Darwin's theory was placed in total opposition to the biblical doctrine of creation see also Davies, *Light in the Land*, 94–109.

[214] Evans, *Welsh Revival*, 34.

theology affected this slow demise.[215] The period should not be considered as the death-knell of Welsh Nonconformity because of the fact that both before and after 1904–05, mission halls and chapels, as illustrated above, were appearing in order to fulfil the spiritual needs of the community. Noel Gibbard encapsulates this state of flux in the title of his book *R. B. Jones: Gospel Ministry in Turbulent Times.* This turbulent period continued before, as well as after, the hiatus that was the 1904–05 Revival.[216] Commenting on the religious scene in Wales before, during and after the Revival of 1904–05, Gibbard writes:

> The religious life of Wales was characterised by a stubborn denominationalism. During the Revival of 1904–05 the denominations were brought closer together, only to divide afterwards. This pattern was repeated in many countries. The Pentecostals believed that the Revival in Wales had prepared the way for the real Pentecost.[217]

This is a generalisation that lacks sufficient supporting evidence, although Gibbard (in line with Gee, Kay and Massey), refers to the conversions of such significant individuals as D. P. Williams and George and Stephen Jeffreys. Hence the hypothesis that the Welsh Revival 1904–05 may well have prepared the way for the emergence of Pentecostalism, in the fact that significant individuals were converted during those years and not in the contribution of distinctly Pentecostal theology, is highly probable.[218] Some were drawn to the new Pentecostal groups that preached the necessity of a 'new birth' and a baptism in the Holy Spirit with the evidence of speaking in tongues coupled to a vibrant hope in the imminent return of Christ. This theological emphasis led to a vibrant missiology and aggressive evangelism within the local communities that saw Pentecostals reach out to others with the gospel. To a lesser degree there may also have been the effect of liberal theology which may have caused some to seek a different emphasis within the emerging Pentecostal groups. However within SE Wales the major factor that led to the rise of

---

[215] Jones, *Faith and the Crisis,* 87, in his publication Jones provides an excellent and in-depth review of Welsh religion at this time. See also Davies, *History of Wales,* 493.

[216] Gibbard, *R. B. Jones.*

[217] Gibbard, *On The Wings,* 222.

[218] Gibbard, *On The Wings,* 184–90, 220–2, Gibbard *Fire on the Altar,* 181–4.

Pentecostalism was the arrival of Pentecostal interpretation from America. The purpose of outlining the religious situation in Wales at this period is to examine some of the factors leading to the emergence of AoG.

During the late nineteenth and early twentieth centuries, South Wales was a society in turmoil; the industrial boom and accompanying social unrest coupled with the challenge from increasingly liberal views and the impact of the Great War left traditional orthodox Christianity in a precarious position. There were those who endeavoured to stand against the tide of decline and controversy by proclaiming the necessity of the 'new birth' and the authority of the Bible. One such group to emerge was the Pentecostals, with their emphasis on biblical truth and the experiential; with an added emphasis on eschatology and pneumatology, accompanied by an urgent missiology, this group became increasingly set apart from traditional Welsh Christianity.

The next chapter will examine the general theological influences that were present within SE Wales that may have influenced the emerging Pentecostals.

Chapter 3 Possible Antecedents of Pentecostalism in SE Wales – 1901–07

This chapter will explore whether or not there were streams of influence within Wales which may have contributed to the experience and thinking of those involved in the emergent AoG in SE Wales. The period 1901–07 is crucial within the development of global Pentecostalism and within SE Wales as well. These dates are important as 1901 saw the emergence of Pentecostal theology through the teaching of Charles Fox Parham in America, and 1907 witnessed the commencement of events at Sunderland and the ministry of A. A. Boddy.[219] Both of these wider ministries eventually fed into the local situation in SE Wales.

The focus of the Pentecostal denominations is, the 'baptism in the Holy Spirit'; a variety of thinking on this subject emerged immediately prior to, during and following the Revival in Wales 1904–05.[220] It is outside the scope of this dissertation to examine the 1904–05 revival in detail; it is a subject which has attracted considerable attention from historians.[221] But were there influences from that period which may have affected, or teachings which were later adopted by, the emerging AoG followers in SE Wales?

Wales benefited considerably from the revival as chapels grew and many areas of society experienced a significant decrease in alcohol abuse, gambling, domestic cruelty, and immorality; and the influence of the revival was felt even in other nations.[222] However the effects of the revival in Wales soon began to ebb and most people were left to contemplate a return to the old

---

[219] See chapter 1

[220] E. H. Andrews, *The Promise of the Spirit,* (Welwyn: Evangelical Press, 1982) provides a helpful critique of Reformed, Pentecostal, and Charismatic views of the ministry of the Holy Spirit.

[221] See, Eifion Evans, *The Welsh Revival of 1904* (Bridgend: Bryntirion Press, 1969); Noel Gibbard, *Fire on the Altar* (Bridgend: Bryntirion Press, 2005); R. B. Jones, *Rent Heavens The Revival of 1904* (London: Stanley Martin, 1930); Jessie Penn-Lewis, *The Awakening in Wales* (Fort Washington, PA.: CLC, 2002).

[222] Jones, *Rent,* 63–97; Wesley Duewel, *Revival Fire* (Grand Rapids, MI: Zondervan, 1995), 178–286. See also Colin Whittaker, *Great Revivals* (Basingstoke: Marshalls, 1984), 89–156; Helen S. Dyer, *Revival in India 1905–1906* (Maharashtra, India: Alliance, 1907/1987) and Noel Gibbard, *On The Wings of the Dove* (Bridgend: Bryntirion Press, 2002) who deals with the specific international influences of the Welsh Revival.

denominational issues and styles of worship.[223] Despite the influence of liberal theology in many local chapels and the spread of conventional religiosity, coupled with the emergence of political, social, and cultural activities, at least two factors are important at this point.[224]

First, significant numbers of Revival converts remained in the chapels and churches of Wales with a good proportion of them continuing to adhere to their new faith. It is important to note that the traditional denominations were not all losing ground and the spiritual health of Wales at this time was relatively strong. The rising Pentecostals were simply another option for those enthused by the Revival of 1904–05 and who may have become disheartened with the slow decline in some churches.[225] As Morgan indicates, there were a growing number of alternatives to the traditional denominations emerging the main ones being: Brethren and independent mission halls as well as the Pentecostal halls and denominations.[226] Secondly, there was a group of Welsh ministers who endeavoured through preaching conventions to deepen the spiritual experience of people and urge the necessity of remaining in the blessing of revival.[227] B. P. Jones outlines the attempts of these evangelical leaders who fought for their version of biblical truth, encouraging others to follow their lead.[228] Jones and Gibbard suggest that the emerging Pentecostals were sympathetic to this group of preachers.[229] Their teaching highlighted the

---

[223] William Kay, 'Why Did the Welsh Revival stop?' *Revival, Renewal and the Holy Spirit Conference,* (University of Bangor, June 2004). D. Densil Morgan, *The Span of the Cross Christian Religion and Society in Wales 1914–2000* (Cardiff: University of Wales Press, 1999); R. Tudur Jones, *Faith and the Crisis of a Nation Wales 1890–1914* (Cardiff: University of Wales Press, 2004) and Dyfed W. Roberts, ed., *Revival, Renewal and the Holy Spirit* (Milton Keynes: Paternoster, 2009).

[224] Robert Pope, *Building Jerusalem Nonconformity, Labour and the Social Question in Wales, 1906–1939,* (Cardiff: University of Wales Press, 1998), 14–30

[225] Morgan, *Span,* 5–40 for a more detailed account of the state of religion in 1914, the effects of the Great War as mentioned in chapter two had a dramatic effect upon the religious conscience of the Welsh.

[226] Morgan, *Span,* 13–15.

[227] This group represented by men such as R. B. Jones and Keri Evans was also responsible for the publication of *Yr Efenglydd* a journal promoting evangelical theology. See Noel Gibbard, *R. B. Jones Gospel Ministry in Turbulent Times* (Bridgend: Bryntirion Press, 2009), 85–9 and B. Jones, *The King's Champions* (Cwmbran: CLP, 1986), who refers to this publication throughout his work.

[228] Jones, *King's Champions,* special attention is paid by Jones to R. B. Jones who was a leading figure within this group of Welsh Evangelical leaders, see also Gibbard, *R. B. Jones.*

[229] Jones, *King's Champions.*

importance of the Second Coming and the work of the Holy Spirit; both themes which were to appeal greatly to early Pentecostals. This is further illustrated by the fact that Pentecostal evangelist Stephen Jeffreys believed R. B. Jones to be one of the greatest preachers of his generation.[230] 'R. B.' was an influential figure during this period that had been influenced by men such as F. B. Meyer, Gypsy Smith, Alexander Dowey and R. A. Torrey, all of whom impressed Jones with the content and style of their ministry.

The question to be addressed is how AoG teaching emerged and flourished in SE Wales. Consequently an attempt will be made to identify and assess any streams which may have affected those involved with the emerging Pentecostal movement.

General Streams

Welsh Evangelicalism in 1901 was not Pentecostal in theology or practice and the revival events in Wales 1904–05 predated the 'Pentecostal outpouring' at Azusa Street by two years.[231] It has already been suggested that the detailed Pentecostal pneumatology was imported from America, albeit via Sunderland.[232]

Teaching by the churches on the ministry of the Holy Spirit had been common in Wales since the time of the Methodist Revival under Harris and Rowland. The historic denominations, whether Calvinistic or Arminian, had believed in and preached the necessity of the Holy Spirit's ministry in the lives of believers and in the corporate life of the church and its witness.[233] This interest is illustrated in the sermon of the great Welsh preacher John Elias (1774–1841) entitled *Praying for the Spirit;* in his concluding remarks he calls on his hearers

---

[230] Edward Jeffreys, *Stephen Jeffreys the Beloved Evangelist,* (London: Elim, 1946), 17; Iain H. Murray, *D. Martyn Lloyd-Jones: The First Forty Years 1899–1939* (Edinburgh: Banner of Truth, 1982), 192–3 for a differing view of R. B. Jones.

[231] There were other Revivals during this period that also predated Azusa Street for example in India see Duewel, *Revival Fire,* 204–277.

[232] Chapter 1

[233] Charles H. Spurgeon, *Twelve Sermons on the Holy Spirit* (Grand Rapids, MI: Baker, 1973).

to be aware of and open to receiving the Spirit and on God to send the Spirit.[234] As E. H. Andrews states:

> One thing is plain; habitual fullness of the Spirit is a Christian privilege and duty.... To be filled with the Spirit is the norm to which the child of God should conform.[235]

Davies retraces the importance of the ministry of the Holy Spirit to some of the 'giants' of Welsh preaching from across the denominational divide.[236] The use of such terminology as 'pouring', 'awakening', 'revival' or 'baptism of fire' were commonly used to describe the coming of the Spirit upon preachers and congregations. R. B. Jones illustrates this point in a communication with O. M. Owens dated 15 April 1903:

> O, is there not a need for us to be *filled with the Spirit*? [my emphasis] I believe that there is a tide in God's wise providence, and if we are caught in its flood we will be carried on to great success in our work.[237]

The desire to be filled with the Spirit was close to the heart of Welsh evangelical preachers such as R. B. Jones who were simply following in the traditions of their forefathers. R. B. Jones developed a greater desire to experience the Holy Spirit following his introduction to the Keswick teaching.[238] The later Pentecostals were therefore no pioneers in their

---

[234] John Elias, 'Praying for the Spirit', in Joel Beeke, ed., *The Experimental Knowledge of Christ and Additional Sermons of John Elias (1774–1841),* (Grand Rapids, MI: Reformation Heritage Books, 2006), 43–54.

[235] Andrews, *Promise of the Spirit,* 156.

[236] Gwyn Davies, *A Light in the Land Christianity in Wales 200–2000* (Bridgend: Bryntirion Press, 2002), 86; Lionel Madden, ed., *Methodism in Wales A Short History of the Wesley Tradition,* (Llandudno: Methodist Conference, 2003), 87–103 and Herbert F. Stevenson, ed., *Keswick's Authentic Voice* (London: Marshall, Morgan & Scott, 1959), 461–5. Emotionalism and Welsh religious activity were not previously unknown; see Peter Howell Williams, 'Jumpers – Blessed Enthusiasts or Bizarre Episodes?' *Historical Journal of the Presbyterian Church of Wales,* 29–30 (2005–06), 43–72.

[237] Gibbard, *R. B. Jones,* 29. See also John MacNeil, *The Spirit Filled Life* (Sven Pederson, 2006, first published in Australia 1895, 2011) and Andrew Murray, *The Full Blessing of Pentecost,* (Plainfield, NJ: Logos, 1974) both MacNeil and Murray's teaching exerted a wide influence. See J. I. Packer, *Keep In Step With The Spirit: Finding Fullness In Our Walk With God, New Expanded Edition,* (Leicester: I.V.P., 2005) for a helpful overview of the major issues regarding the work of the Spirit with particular reference to the terminology "baptism in the Spirit", sanctification and holiness.

[238] Jones, *King's Champions,* 45–51, these events predate the 1904–05 Revival. See also Gibbard, *R. B. Jones,* 137–51.

insistence upon the necessity of engaging with the Spirit. However, where the Pentecostals differed was in their definition of Spirit baptism; the AoG later accepting the distinctive teaching of Spirit baptism as post-conversion experience evidenced in tongues speaking as well as the operation of other charismata.[239]

The emphasis upon holiness in late nineteenth and early twentieth century Wales was promoted prominently through the Keswick in Wales Conventions.[240] Emerging from the American Holiness Movement, the Keswick teaching on sanctification, 'Higher Life' or fullness of the Spirit was one expression found in Britain.[241] The main emphasis of Keswick teaching was the Lordship of Christ and the essential ministry of the Holy Spirit with emphasis upon what McQuilkin describes as 'experiential sanctification'.[242] This area of the doctrine of sanctification, as McQuilkin suggests, is that which centres on how the Christian may enjoy freedom from sinful thoughts and actions: this also is a controversial area. The receiving of the 'fullness of the Spirit' was a subsequent act of faith that gave power for living a 'victorious Christian life'.[243] This 'victory' was over the power of known sin but the realisation of this power is a gradual development throughout the individual's life. In its teaching Keswick holiness moved away from the eradicationist views of the American holiness teaching and the use of terminology such as 'sinless perfection'. In contrast Keswick moved towards a suppressionist view of dealing with a person's sinful nature. Keswick sanctification or 'baptism in the Holy Spirit' was a definite distinct act that could be repeated as times of special blessing at times of particular spiritual need. There is within the Keswick

---

[239]Carl Brumbeck, *What Meaneth This?* (London: Elim, 1946), David Petts, *The Holy Spirit An Introduction* (Mattersey: Mattersey Hall, 1998), 63–102.

[240] John C. Pollock, *The Keswick Story* (Fort Washington, PA: CLC, 2006), 159–70 who briefly highlights the emergence of the Keswick in Wales conventions and the interplay between Keswick leaders and those of the Welsh Revival 1904–05. See also Steven Barabas, *So Great Salvation* (Eugene, OR.: Wipf & Stock, 1952).

[241] D. D. Bundy, 'Keswick Higher Life Movement', in Stanley Burgess, ed., *NIDPCM* (Grand Rapids, MI: Zondervan, 2002), 820–21; Chad Owen Brand, *Perspectives on Spirit Baptism*. (Nashville, TN: B&H Publishing, 2004), 11; Donald Dayton, *Theological Roots of Pentecostalism* (Metuchen, NJ: Hendrickson, 1887), 104–6; Vinson Synan, *The Holiness-Pentecostal Tradition* (Grand Rapids, MI: Eerdmans, 1997), 143–66; J. Robertson McQuilkin, 'The Keswick Perspective' in Stanley N. Gundry (ed,) *Five Views on Sanctification* (Grand Rapids, MI: Zondervan, 1987), 151–95; Ian M. Randall, *Evangelical Experiences: A Study in the Spirituality of English Evangelicalism 1918–1939* (Milton Keynes: Paternoster, 1999).

[242] McQuilkin, 'Keswick Perspective', in Gundry, ed., *Five Views,* 159.

[243] Barabas, *So Great.*

thinking a possibility of two strata of Christian experience. Firstly all are indwelt by the Spirit at conversion and secondly those who are later 'filled' with the Spirit. These subsequent infillings produce within the believer a greater earnestness in pursuit of the abundant life promoted at Keswick which was intended subsequently to reinvigorate the church. Many early Pentecostals would have been in agreement with this position, with only some accepting the more radical interpretation that unless a person had been baptized in the Spirit they were not a true Christian. Most, however, saw a difference between mature and immature Christians (Heb 5:11–6:3) which was the same position promoted by Andrew Murray (1828 1917) who spoke of those with and without the indwelling Spirit. [244] Andrew Murray was a South African Christian leader who travelled extensively in Africa, Europe and America, influenced by the holiness movement and was a speaker at Keswick. [245] Murray particularly through his writings and teaching on individual Christian experience helped in shaping modern day Pentecostalism. [246]

Another pivotal figure in Britain was John MacNeil (1854–96) a Scotsman resident in Australia who was widely used in the promotion of holiness teaching. His book *The Spirit Filled Life* was particularly influential during this period and set out the necessity of the fullness of the Spirit for every believer; MacNeil's work was translated into Welsh and was popular. With Murray, MacNeil believed that the fullness of the Spirit was the birthright of every born again believer and promoted the necessity of victory and soul satisfaction in the battle against sin. [247] He regarded it as a divine command to be; 'filled with the Spirit' (Eph 5:18) and any Christian who was not enjoying this spiritual experience was disobeying God's command. [248] A failure to experience this fullness was a sin for it was something to be obtained with diligence; so

---

[244] Murray, *Full Blessing,* 2 who promotes the position of the twofold Christian life. See I. Hexham, 'Murray, Andrew' in Sinclair B. Ferguson and David F. Wright, eds., *New Dictionary of Theology* (Leicester: IVP, 1988), 447.

[245] Stevenson, ed., *Keswick's Authentic,* 292–300, 425–35.

[246] Andrew Murray, *The Spirit of Christ* (London: Marshall, Morgan & Scott, 1893) and Murray, *Full Blessing,* were/are read widely amongst Pentecostals.

[247] Murray, *Full Blessing.*

[248] MacNeil, *Spirit Filled,* 1–14, see also Gibbard, *Fire,* 167–78.

MacNeil's position would have been popular with Pentecostals. Modern Pentecostals would likewise encourage all believers to seek and experience a Spirit baptism. Gibbard notes that the terminology 'filled' is not synonymous with 'baptism' and hence it is unwise to impose a Pentecostal interpretation on the writings of MacNeil.[249] However, Pentecostals would develop his teaching further to incorporate a definite experience of evidential tongues connected to the baptism of the Spirit. MacNeil was popular with the holiness movement and influenced Keswick teaching, although due to his untimely death at the age of forty-two he never preached at the Llandrindod Convention. American Presbyterian Dr Arthur Tappan Pierson (1837–1911) was an influential speaker at the Keswick Conventions and had an impact in Wales.[250] He preached in eight Keswick conferences and also preached in Wales with the Welsh taking Pierson to their hearts and supporting his ministry during his visits to Britain. F. B. Meyer (1847–1929) was also a prominent figure during this period and was a regular visitor and speaker at Keswick in Wales.[251] Another influential speaker was R. A. Torrey (1856–1928) who preached at Keswick in Wales and also throughout Wales; for example in Cardiff in 1904.[252] The Keswick teaching with its variety of preachers and teachers was influential throughout South Wales, as Jones records:

> Even so, the converts who had such glorious experiences during the 1905 convention (held at Llandrindod) went home and learned by hard experience what it meant to take up the cross and follow. Scores of chapels failed to provide for their needs. Many saved up all the year round in order to go up to Llandrindod in August and hear the great Bible teachers.[253]

Jones here offers a glimpse of the nominalism affecting some churches in failing to provide for the spiritual needs of individuals. The annual visit to Llandrindod provided them with the opportunity of hearing challenging

---

[249] Gibbard, *Fire on the Altar*, 170–72.

[250] Pollock, *Keswick Story*, 154–70 and Brynmor Pierce Jones, *The Spiritual History of Keswick* (Cwmbran: CLP, 1989), 7–16.

[251] Bob Holman, *F.B. Meyer* (Fearn: Christian Focus, 2007) and Stevenson, *Keswick's*, 66–70, 204–8.

[252] R. A. Torrey, *What the Bible Teaches* (Springdale, PA: Whittaker House, 1998); Gibbard, *Fire on the Altar*, 169 and 195; Jones, *Spiritual History* and Stevenson, ed., *Keswick's Authentic*, 443–52.

[253] Jones, *Spiritual History*, 17 see also Jones, *King's Champions*.

preaching which was applied to their lives. The influence of Keswick's holiness teaching was felt throughout Wales through the ministry of such individuals as R. B. Jones, Keri Evans and Mrs Jessie Penn-Lewis. Sydney Mercy (AoG) of Wattsville was one of those who saved money from his shoe selling business and visited the Llandrindod Conventions and was deeply affected by the teaching he received.[254] Returning to his home chapel, Trinity Congregational Pontywaun, he continued his search for a deeper experience of God. Mercy was instrumental in establishing Crosskeys Pentecostal Church in 1912 following a difference of opinion with the Congregationalists regarding the imminence of the return of Christ. D. P. Williams (Apostolic) and George Jeffreys (Elim) also visited the Keswick in Wales conventions.[255]

Jessie Penn-Lewis (1861–1927) influenced the theological scene during this period in Wales.[256] A native of Neath and brought up in the 'lap of Calvinistic Methodism,' Jessie Jones married William Penn-Lewis at the age of nineteen and they moved to Surrey in search of employment.[257] Converted on New Year's Day 1882 she came under the influential ministry of Rev. Evan H. Hopkins (1837–1918) in Surrey. It was whilst under the influence of Hopkins that Penn-Lewis became aware of the theology associated with the Keswick Movement.[258] Hopkins was known as the theologian of the Keswick movement and along with Penn-Lewis was instrumental in establishing the Keswick in Wales conventions.[259] Following her conversion and contact with Hopkins, Penn-Lewis embarked on Christian ministry and service and became more desirous of experiencing the fullness of the Spirit and God's power. The kernel of her thinking is to be found in a seven point summary of her personal

---

[254] Penn-Lewis, *Awakening in Wales*, 81, who refers to two unnamed Keswick preachers visiting various parts of Wales and in regard to this research mentions visits to Monmouthshire.

[255] Gibbard, *Fire on the Altar*, 146, Jones, *King's Champions*, 49–50, Desmond Cartwright, *The Great Evangelists* (Basingstoke: Marshall Pickering, 1986), 30–5 and E. Jeffreys, *Stephen Jeffreys*, 17.

[256] Brynmor Pierce Jones, *The Trials and Triumphs of Mrs. Jessie Penn-Lewis*, (North Brunswick, NJ: Bridge-Logos, 1997); J.C. Metcalfe, *Molded by the Cross* (Fort Washington, PA: CLC, 1997), Penn-Lewis, *Awakening in Wales*.

[257] Metcalfe, *Molded by the Cross*, 13.

[258] Pollock, *Keswick Story* and Stephenson, *Keswick's Authentic*, 157–67, 301–7, 332–7, 436–42, 461–5.

[259] Pollock, *Keswick Story*, 17–19, Jones, *Spiritual History*, 7–16, Metcalfe, *Molded by the Cross*, 20.

enduement with the Holy Spirit recorded by J. C. Metcalfe.[260] This subsequent spiritual experience or 'enduement' was, for her, a distinct and joyous experience but she did not accept evidential tongues speaking; a position she held throughout her life. However, further study of Jessie Penn-Lewis's writings, especially *The Work of the Holy Spirit* provides much that could be said to have been adopted by Pentecostals.[261] As with traditional teaching the Spirit is portrayed as a gift, the guide into truth, the Comforter, the means of victory over sin but, unlike later Pentecostalism, the work contains no direct teaching on tongues as initial evidence of conversion or Spirit baptism. Penn-Lewis was an individual who was totally opposed to the emerging Pentecostal teaching in Wales and further afield.[262]

The Keswick position with its mix of denominational leaders led to ambiguities that have made it difficult to standardise the teaching; nevertheless the work of Steven Barabas is invaluable in endeavouring to ascertain the central message of Keswick.[263] The Keswick view of Spirit baptism focuses more on sanctification with an element of empowerment for service, which differs significantly from the Pentecostal view of power for service and the operation of spiritual gifts. Embryonic Pentecostalism had common roots within the holiness traditions of America and this was mirrored to some extent by the influence of the Keswick teaching in Britain.[264] The combination of the traditional denominational positions, Keswick and the teaching of prominent individuals such as MacNeil, Penn-Lewis, and Murray, led to a cross-fertilization of thinking, teaching and practice in the realm of pneumatology.[265] The promotion of holiness 'second blessing' teaching in the late nineteenth and early twentieth centuries could be viewed as another stream which fed into Pentecostalism.

---

[260] Metcalfe, *Molded by the Cross*, 40–1.

[261] Jessie Penn-Lewis, *The Work of the Holy Spirit*, (Fort Washington, PA: CLC, 1992).

[262] Jones, *Trials and Triumphs*, 169–207.

[263] Barabas, *So Great*. See also Blumhofer, *Assemblies of God, vol.1*, 59–60, who records A. T. Pierson's attempt at summarising Keswick teaching.

[264] Dayton, *Theological Roots*, Synan, *Holiness-Pentecostal* and Allan Anderson, *An Introduction to Pentecostalism* (Cambridge: C.U.P., 2004).

[265] MacNeil, *Spirit Filled;* Murray, *Full Blessing;* Penn-Lewis, *Work of the Holy Spirit;* Torrey, *What the Bible*.

Stanley M. Horton states that the Wesleyan Holiness teaching on a distinct second work of grace following conversion was the most important contributory factor in the nascent Pentecostal movement.[266] The American Holiness Movement developed from Wesleyan Methodist teaching, significant early supporters who helped to develop the position being Charles G. Finney (1792–1875) and Phoebe Palmer (1807–74). As the holiness teaching developed so the traditional Methodists rejected the details of the teaching and hence the holiness movement came into existence c. 1895 through the ministry of men such as Phineas Bresee (1838–1915). One of the most significant denominations to develop in the Holiness Movement was the 'Church of God' (Cleveland, Tennessee).[267] Significant early Pentecostal leaders such as Charles Fox Parham and William J. Seymour had holiness roots.[268] However there are significant differences between the nature and purpose of the experience pursued, namely, Wesleyan entire sanctification or the Pentecostal baptism of power for service and evidential tongues.

Charles Fox Parham, the 'father' of modern Pentecostalism, commenced his ministry as a Methodist preacher from which he received the 'second work' of grace teaching on sanctification.[269] This teaching was developed by Parham during his time at Topeka, Kansas, and introduced to the religious world in 1901 with the new emphasis of Spirit baptism as being essentially power for service which is evidenced by tongues-speaking. This position was further supported by the work of William Seymour at Azusa Street.[270] Dayton

---

[266] Melvin E. Dieter, 'The Wesleyan Perspective' in Gundry,, ed., *Five Views,* 11–57 and Stanley M. Horton 'Spirit Baptism: A Pentecostal Perspective' in Brand,, ed., *Perspectives,* 47–104. See also Packer, *Keep in Step,* 120–33 for an interesting critique of the Keswick teaching where Packer offers his views on both the strengths and weaknesses of Keswick theology; Keswick practitioners see Packer's assessment as an attack on their position. See also McQuilkin, 'Keswick Perspective', in Gundry, ed., *Five Views,* 183; Synan, *Holiness-Pentecostal,* 1–83; Dayton, *Theological Roots;* C. E. Jones, 'Holiness Movement', in *NIDPCM,* 726–29.

[267] C. W. Conn, 'Church of God (Cleveland, TN)' in *NIDPCM,* 530–34.

[268] See Dayton, *Theological Roots,* for an in depth evaluation of this position see also Synan, *Holiness-Pentecostal.*

[269] Sarah E. Parham, Mrs, *The Life of Charles F. Parham: Founder of the Apostolic Faith Movement,* (Joplin, MO: Tri-State Publishing, 1930) available from <www.revival-library.org> Melvin E. Dieter, 'The Wesleyan Perspective' in Gundry,, ed., *Five Views,* 11–46.

[270] Cecil Robeck Jr., *The Azusa Street Mission and Revival* (Nashville, TN: Thomas Nelson, 2006); Frank Bartleman, *Azusa Street An Eyewitness Account* (Gainesville, FL: Bridge-Logos, 1980).

emphasises the Methodist roots in America where Wesleyan thinking was more apparent in the development of Pentecostalism than it was in Britain, where it was less widespread.[271] British Pentecostals did not embrace the Wesleyan doctrine of entire sanctification, and one must note other influences in Britain including SE Wales.[272] Within the formation of British AoG there were some who joined from Methodist churches and who became influential within the denomination. Colin Whittaker mentions in particular Harold Horton (1880–1969) who served as a Methodist lay preacher and who became very influential through his teaching on spiritual gifts when he joined the staff at Hampstead Bible School in 1926/7.[273] Whittaker also mentions the Wesleyan heritage of healing evangelist Smith Wigglesworth (1859–1947), who also had Brethren links.

The development of Pentecostalism in America eventually led to a division in the understanding of sanctification and Spirit baptism. This division manifested itself in the 'Finished Work Controversy'.[274] One group emerged advocating the Wesleyan Holiness tradition, accepting that sanctification could be a crisis experience or second work of the Spirit following salvation which they sometimes referred to as a baptism in the Spirit; this was followed by another experience evidenced by glossolalia. Another group emphasised that sanctification was a process following from salvation; the AoG adopted this latter view of progressive sanctification which was more aligned to Keswick and also traditional teaching. The latter position allowed some flexibility for a different emphasis upon Spirit baptism as an empowering for service. Their position is illustrated in the original Statement of Fundamental Truths of the AoG published in 1924 which contains two separate clauses, numbers 6 and 7, which read: we believe in:

---

[271] Randall, *Evangelical Experiences*, 209.

[272] Dayton, *Theological Roots*, 35–84.

[273] Colin Whittaker, *Seven Pentecostal Pioneers* (Basingstoke: Marshalls, 1983), 21,131–45, see also Donald Gee, *Wind and Flame* (Croydon: AOG, 1967), 150–2, Keith Malcomson, *Pentecostal Pioneers Remembered* (Xulon Press, 2008), 359–66 and Harold Horton, *The Gifts of The Spirit,* (Nottingham: AoG, 1934).

[274] Stanley M. Horton, 'The Pentecostal Perspective' in Gundry, ed., *Five Views*, 105–48; Timothy Jenney, 'The Holy Spirit and Sanctification' in Stanley M Horton, ed., *Systematic Theology.* (Springfield, MO: G.P.H., 1994), 397–421; D. Powell, 'The Doctrine of Holiness' in S. Brewster,, ed., *Pentecostal Doctrine* (Cheltenham: Elim, 1976), 357–70; Keith Warrington, *Pentecostal Theology A Theology of Encounter.* (London: T&T Clark, 2008), 206–45 and R.M. Riss, 'Finished Work Controversy', in *NIDPCM*, 638–9.

6. The baptism in the Holy Spirit, the initial evidence of which is the speaking with other tongues...

7. Holiness of life and conduct in obedience to the command of God, "Be ye holy for I am holy"...[275]

Here one discerns the distinctiveness of the AoG position in contrast to the Holiness teaching; particularly the evidence of tongues but also that holiness is a process lived out daily in the strength of the Holy Spirit rather than crisis experience linked to Spirit fullness or baptism. However, Keswick, Wesleyan, and Pentecostal teaching agree that the power of the Holy Spirit is essential in the personal battle against sin. Tongues-speaking, too, was not a new phenomenon; it had been experienced in Britain through the ministry of the controversial Church of Scotland minister Edward Irving (1792–1834).[276] Vinson Synan also records how D. L. Moody experienced an instance of 'tongues' during a meeting in London, 1875.[277]

Another rising stream contributing to the distinctive Pentecostal teaching was that of premillennial theology; this was particularly the case at Crosskeys. John Nelson Darby (1800–82) a founding father of the Brethren movement and a developer of premillennialism was particularly influential.[278] Darby's position was popularised by the publication of the Scofield Reference Bible in 1909. Cyrus Ingerson Scofield (1843–1921) first a Congregational then Presbyterian minister, was a great defender of dispensational premillennialism.[279] C. I.

---

[275] AoG Minutes, 1st February 1924, 2.

[276] Arnold Dallimore, *The Life of Edward Irving: Fore-Runner of the Charismatic Movement* (Edinburgh: Banner of Truth, 1983). See also David Allen, *The Unfailing Stream* (Tonbridge: Sovereign World, 1994), 80–92, for an AoG view of Irving and D. D. Bundy, "Irving, Edward" in *NIDPCM*, 803–4 where Irving is categorised as a Scottish-Presbyterian.

[277] Synan, *Holiness-Pentecostal*, 87–8 and Stanley N. Gundry, *Love Them In The Life and Theology of D.L. Moody* (Chicago: Moody Press, 1976), 157–62.

[278] Marion Field, *John Nelson Darby: Prophetic Pioneer* (Godalming: Highland Books, 2008); Floyd Elmore, 'Darby, John Nelson' in Mal Couch,, ed., *Dictionary of Premillennial Theology* (Grand Rapids, MI: Kregel, 1996), 82–5; Malcomson, *Pentecostal Pioneers*, 27–39; Crawford Gibben, 'Evangelical Eschatology And 'The Puritan Hope', in Michael A. G. Haykin and Kenneth J. Stewart, eds., *The Emergence of Evangelicalism* (Nottingham: Apollos, 2008), 375–93, for an overview of the developments in Evangelical eschatology. See also Randall, *Evangelical Experiences,* 142–66.

[279] Charles Gallaudet Trumbull, *The Life Story of C. I. Scofield* (New York: O.U.P., 1920, digitized version), <www.WholesomeWords.org>

Scofield was an American converted in 1879 who was highly influenced by the writings of Darby. The premillennialist theory holds that Christ will return to earth before a millennial age commences and a kingdom will emerge over which Christ will rule. During this period Israel's covenants will be fulfilled and a time of peace will be inaugurated which will last for one thousand years. At the end of this millennium, God will deal with Satan, the Antichrist and the false prophet (Revelation 20) and the eternal state will begin for all believers.[280] The contribution of Scofield to twentieth century evangelicalism, and in particular Pentecostalism, was significant through his Reference Bible.[281] Bebbington suggests that premillennial theology and Keswick Holiness teaching became intertwined and that this was apparent in some aspects of Welsh evangelicalism.[282] This may be realised in the increase of interest in the Parousia although the doctrine of the Second Coming of Christ was not new to Welsh churches. According to Gibbard, the concept of a millennial reign of Christ was present in the 1859 Revival, particularly through the preaching of Humphrey Jones (1832–95).[283] This teaching remained unpopular within Welsh evangelicalism following 1859 and Gibbard, commenting on the ministry of R. B. Jones, states that he 'was aware that he was dealing with an unpopular doctrine, and one that was unacceptable to most theologians of his day.'[284]

Not only was this an unpopular doctrine but according to R. B. Jones premillennialism was almost unheard of in Wales pre 1904–05.[285] According to Gibbard, R. B. Jones referred to the influential work of Scofield within his teaching on the Second Coming.[286] Jessie Penn-Lewis was also interested in

---

[280] Modern day Pentecostals are slowly moving away from the certainty of a Millennium period but in their earliest thinking this was a major teaching. Stanley N. Gundry, ed., *Three Views of the Millennium and Beyond* (Grand Rapids, MI: Zondervan, 1999); J Rodman Williams, *Renewal Theology*, vol. 3 (Grand Rapids, MI: Zondervan, 1996), 289–508; D. J. Wilson, 'Eschatology, Pentecostal Perspectives', in *NIDPCM*, 601–5. See also Bob Hyde, *Do Pentecostals need to be Premillennial? A Discussion Paper submitted to the General Council of the Assemblies of God.* (October 2002, available through AoG HQ) and David J. Garrard, *The importance of keeping the Premillennial rider in any statement of Faith regarding the Second Coming of Christ.* (2002, available from AoG HQ).

[281] C. I. Scofield, *The New Scofield Reference Bible* (New York: O.U.P. 1967).

[282] D. W. Bebbington, *Evangelicalism in Modern Britain* (London: Routledge, 1993), 191–4

[283] Gibbard, *Fire on the Altar*, 178–81.

[284] Gibbard, *R. B. Jones,* 151–6.

[285] Gibbard, *R. B. Jones,* 151 and Gibbard, *Fire on the Altar,* 178–81.

[286] Gibbard, *R. B. Jones,* 153.

this teaching and accepted the dispensational position and the millennial reign of Christ. She developed an interest in the final battle against the kingdom of Satan, emphasising the necessity of spiritual preparation for this spiritual warfare.

Emerging Pentecostalism was vociferous in its proclamation of the second advent of Christ, their double edged message centred on spiritual preparation and warning of impending judgement. The Pentecostals were not innovative or revolutionary in their teaching on the subject but were insistent upon it and its effect upon personal holiness and evangelism.[287] The combination of these theological positions led to a powerful eschatological pneumatology that expressed itself in a militant missiology. Premillennial theology is a central tenet of Pentecostal groups and in particular the AoG. They then expanded or enhanced it with a strong eschatological pneumatology based on their interpretation of Acts 1:8 and Acts 2. Many early Pentecostals adopted Scofield's eschatology although differing with him over his position relating to Spirit baptism and gifts, his understanding being more in line with his Presbyterian roots.[288] For many in SE Wales, the hardships endured due to the difficulties of heavy industry, World War 1 and economic recession were tempered by the joy and hope of a heavenly redemption vigorously promoted by the early Pentecostals. This drew people to their house meetings and eventually led to some accepting their doctrine and experience. This theological emphasis within Pentecostal groups led some within the established churches to become wary and even uncomfortable and for many years both in Crosskeys and the surrounding district the label Second Comers was attached to the new group.[289] Eschatology must be viewed as the central tenet that caused the growth of the Pentecostal assembly at Crosskeys, for it

---

[287] Brewster, *Pentecostal Doctrine,* 149–58, 259–91, Walter J. Hollenweger, *The Pentecostals* (London: SCM, 1972), 413–23; Stanley M. Horton, 'The Last Things' in Horton, ed., *Systematic Theology,* 597–638 and Warrington, *Pentecostal Theology,* 309–23.

[288] Couch, ed., *Dictionary of Premillennial,* 389–93 and H. Alexander 'Scofield Reference Bible' in *NIDPCM,* 1044–5. A summary of Scofield's teaching regarding spiritual gifts is found in his reference Bible in the notes relating to Acts 2 and 1 Corinthians 12–14.

[289] The opposition to the Second Comers/Pentecostals continued for many years in the valley towns of SE Wales I have myself recently been confronted with such opposition in local Baptist and Congregational Churches.

was some two years after its formation that the congregation was introduced to Pentecostal pneumatology.

Ian Randall suggests that the Brethren tradition exerted a more significant influence on the development of British Pentecostalism towards premillennial teaching[290] (although the Brethren tradition was in no way Pentecostal and rejected any suggestion of a 'second blessing'). Both Randall and Allen suggest that the link with the Brethren tradition is particularly seen in their emphasis on a weekly observance of the Lord's Supper.[291] The importance of the commemoration of the Lord's Supper is indicated by its inclusion in the Fundamental Truths of the AoG in 1924.[292] Malcomson further suggests the Brethren influence is seen in the simplicity of their traditions, a move away from the formalism of other denominations and in particular their emphasis upon biblical teaching. Some early Pentecostal leaders such as W. F. P. (Willie) Burton (1886–1971), John Carter (1893–1981), and Thomas Myerscough (1858–1932) were influenced by the regular Bible exposition of Brethren teachers.[293]

The experience of pioneer AoG leader John Nelson Parr (1886–1976) illustrates this combining of influences. Parr was raised in a Holiness church in Manchester, visited the Keswick Conventions, and then joined a Plymouth Brethren group in Stanley Hall, Manchester, who were praying for a Pentecostal Spirit baptism.[294] Parr became the pastor of this group and then a significant figure in the establishing of the AoG denomination in Britain through his ministry at Bethshan Tabernacle, Manchester.[295] The wider influence of the Brethren movement on the English leaders was not reflected within the valleys of SE Wales, with Jones highlighting how although there

---

[290] Randall, *Evangelical Experiences*, see also Ian M. Randall, 'Old Time Power: Relationships between Pentecostalism and Evangelical Spirituality in England', *PNEUMA* 19/1 Spring (1997), 53–80.

[291] David Allen, *Neglected Feast: Rescuing the Breaking of Bread* (Nottingham: New Life Publishing, 2007), 48 and Randall, *Evangelical Experiences*, 215–16. Many AoG groups still endeavour to keep the weekly Lord's Supper although this central ordinance is becoming of less importance. See also Robert Letham, *The Lord's Supper: Eternal Word in Broken Bread* (Phillipsburg, NJ: P&R Publishing, 2001).

[292] Minutes, 1924, 3, statement 9.

[293] John Carter, *A Full Life* (London: Evangel Press, 1979), 38 and Malcomson, *Pentecostal Pioneers*, 167–77, 229–42.

[294] William K. Kay, *Inside Story* (Mattersey: Mattersey Hall, 1990), 53–4; John Nelson Parr, *Incredible*, (Fleetwood: John Nelson Parr, 1972) and Desmond Cartwright, 'Parr, John Nelson' in *NIDPCM*, 957.

[295] Kay, *Inside Story*, 67, who records the early Pentecostal leaders and their variety of non-Conformist heritages.

were five Brethren Gospel Halls in Newport, there were none in the surrounding valleys.[296] R. B. Jones concurs that the presence of the Brethren movement in South Wales was insignificant and their theological influence was almost non-existent.[297] It must be noted that the basic theological tenets of the Brethren Movement would have been in line with mainstream evangelical thinking. Hence its influence would not have been in any way detrimental to the ongoing work of gospel presentation. The Brethren Halls grew in the more middle class areas of the larger towns and cities and made little impact in the working class valleys of SE Wales.[298] This position is supported by Morgan who agrees that development of the Brethren movement was seen mainly in the urban areas: however Morgan surmises that there was a proliferation of Brethren, Independent Halls, and Mission Halls that could have been the spiritual homes for up to 3000 worshippers.[299]

Randall, Allen, and Malcomson regard the impact of Brethrenism to have been more widespread amongst the English Pentecostal leaders such as Burton, Parr, Carter, and Myerscough yet the influence within Wales was less noticeable. And it must be remembered that it was the English AoG figures that took the lead in later theological thinking, development and training. However the wider Brethren influence was recognised in weekly Bible teaching, premillennialism, regular remembrance of the Lord's Supper and simplicity in public worship. These issues were also gaining popularity in SE Wales, yet there were other more significant influences in the area as people were drawn from the established or traditional denominations.

Another stream was the apparent decline of biblical ministry in the chapels which led to some becoming disillusioned with what Iain Murray refers to as 'cold worship'.[300] As a result of the fervency of the Welsh Revival, some searched for a more satisfying expression of church life that was biblical but also experimental. Some who emphasised the new birth and the authority of

---

[296] Brynmor Pierce Jones, *How Lovely Are Thy Dwellings* (Newport: Wellspring, 1999), 158–61.

[297] Jones, *Rent Heavens*, 90–3.

[298] This appears to be so at the time of writing as there are few if any Brethren Halls in the valleys of SE Wales and those in the Newport area are in decline.

[299] Morgan, *Span*, 13.

[300] Murray, *D. Martyn Lloyd Jones: The First Forty Years*, 192.

the Scriptures left their denominations and established Mission Halls that promoted the new birth and the infallible authority of scripture. Kay indicates that these Halls served as a 'safety net' for those new converts who were not sufficiently welcomed or helped in the established denominations.[301] In SE Wales some turned to the growing number of Mission Halls which stood against liberal theology and the danger of nominalism.[302] Mission Halls appeared in such places as Cwmsyfiog (New Tredegar), Hengoed, Ystrad Mynach, Llanbradach, Pontymoile, Rogerstone, Crosskeys and Oakdale. Some, such as at Crosskeys Full Gospel Mission eventually accepted the Pentecostal teaching and experience, others such as Pontymoile continued to promote the gospel without becoming Pentecostal. As mentioned in chapter 2 some such as the Mission Hall at Pontymoile, served the community especially through compassionate ministries and gospel preaching. Political lectures, fund raising events and church teas were replacing the prayer meeting and Bible study in a number of churches. Some took exception to these developments and found a more biblical centred preaching at the Mission Halls or the embryonic Pentecostal groups. This was the case in Crosskeys where families left the local Baptist, Methodist, and mainly the Congregational churches and attended the Pentecostal Mission Hall because there they heard what they regarded as gospel preaching.[303]

Graham Osborne records some interesting comments from the church minutes regarding the spiritual condition of Hope Baptist Church, Crosskeys, which illustrates the conditions which prevailed at the time:

> Financial difficulties were at their worst in 1899. The strain must then have been beginning to tell for there are complaints that "*the financial conditions are due to the lack of spiritual life in the church and to the inactivity of the officers*" and that "*the same members are contributing all of the time*".[304]

---

[301] Kay, 'Why Did the Welsh Revival Stop', 7.

[302] Davies, *Light in the Land*, 106–7, Jones, *How Lovely*, 116–42.

[303] Phyllis Lewis 84 years old (2010) related to me in conversation during a pastoral visit the story of how her parents left the Methodists in the early 1920s to join the Gladstone Street 'Second Comers'.

[304] Graham Osborne, *A History of Hope Baptist Church* (Abertillery: Old Bakehouse, 2006), 13

It appears that following the resignation of Rev. Evans (1914) the church began to decline so that by 1919 the church minutes were once again recording the 'poor spiritual life at Hope'. Osborne also notes that this demise in church life was not confined to Hope Baptist Church, Crosskeys, but that churches in the region were losing members on a regular basis. Hence in Crosskeys some moved from the local chapels due to the dissatisfaction with the content of the preaching, others because of the increasing prevalence of nominalism, and others left due to objections to their emphasis on the Parousia. Some of those disillusioned believers found solace in the Pentecostal mission where there was a premium on basic biblical preaching and fervency in worship. These general streams contributed to the religious world of SE Wales and in particular upon those involved with emergent Pentecostalism. However there was also the major catalyst of this time, namely the Welsh Revival of 1904–05.

Revival Begins

Evan Roberts is a name synonymous with Welsh religious history due in the main to his involvement in the Revival of 1904–05 in which he was one of several leading figures. Roberts was born in Bwlchymynydd, Loughor, West Wales on 8 June 1878 to Henry and Hannah Roberts.[305] Loughor was home to an Anglican Church, a Baptist, and Congregational chapel while Sunday worship for the Roberts family would take place a mile from their home at Moriah Calvinistic Methodist chapel, Loughor. From the age of twelve employment for Roberts came at both the colliery and a blacksmith's forge but neither were to keep his attention for long and by 1903 he responded to a sense of call to the Christian ministry. He commenced his training at Newcastle Emlyn Grammar School with the intention of continuing his theological studies at Trefecca College. His plans were thwarted by the

---

[305] Henry Roberts experienced a mining accident and was left with a damaged leg which prevented him from carrying out all his duties underground. At the age of 12 years Evan joined his father underground serving as a door boy, opening and closing the doors underground in order to allow the horse drawn trams of coal to pass. See Jones, *Instrument,* for a detailed account of the life of Evan Roberts.

outbreak of the Revival in the locality and Roberts broke off his training and became engaged in an itinerant ministry.[306]

Revival was present in Wales before Evan Roberts' involvement in the autumn of 1904 and to ignore this fact is an injustice to other faithful ministers who were seeking God for a fresh awakening.[307] The return of W. S. Jones (c. 1860–1930) from ministry in America was a pivotal element in establishing the desire for revival within Wales by emphasising the work of the Holy Spirit.[308] His influence over some prominent evangelical leaders was significant; he had been affected by the ministry of students of D. L. Moody in America. Moody had been propagating a message that the baptism in the Holy Spirit was an empowering experience that would assist the individual in evangelising.[309] W. S. Jones experienced what he described as receiving 'power from on high' in 1893 which in turn gave him a greater desire for spiritual awakening. Upon his return to Wales (1893) he began to propagate a new 'abundant life' teaching.[310] Following another similar 'baptism' in 1900, he encouraged people to yield their whole lives to God in the pursuit of holiness, such teaching assisted the promotion of revival desires within Welsh evangelicalism. W. S. Jones was a regular and respected speaker at conventions throughout Wales; he spent time preaching in Monmouthshire where he continued to propagate this 'new' teaching.[311] The renewed emphasis on the ministry of the Holy Spirit is a key issue in tracing the rise of AoG.

Christopher Turner suggests that the events of the Wales Revival of 1904–05 could more correctly be seen as a 'movement of the laity' and as being directed by the Spirit of God, not by men.[312] His position may find some support in the

---

[306] Trefeca College was established in 1768 by The Countess of Huntingdon and still operates as a Lay Training centre under the ownership of the Presbyterian Church of Wales. <www.trefeca.org.uk>

[307] William Kay, 'Revival: Empirical Aspects' in Andrew Walker and Kristin Aune, eds., *On Revival: A Critical Examination*, (Carlisle: Paternoster, 2003), 187–91.

[308] Jones, *Rent Heavens*, 23–38.

[309] Stanley N. Gundry, *Love Them In*, Jones, *King's Champions*, 35–52 and Brand, *Perspectives on Spirit Baptism*, 49–50.

[310] Jones, *King's Champions*, 37

[311] Jones, *King's Champions*, 84, 262.

[312] Christopher Turner, 'A Movement of the Laity': The Welsh Religious Revival of 1904–05.' *Historical Journal of the Presbyterian Church of Wales*, 34 (2010), 130–60. Turner also makes some interesting comments regarding the rise of Pentecostalism, 131. See also Robert Pope, 'Demythologizing the Evan Roberts Revival,' *Journal of Ecclesiastical History*, 57/3 (2006), 515–34.

fact there was not one central figure responsible for the Revival but there were a number of ordained ministers who were prominent within the movement. Partly due to the influence of Evan Roberts, there was a move away from the dominance of deacons or elders who 'controlled worship', for those in the pew were now encouraged to be more active in corporate worship. This move towards a greater voice for the laity was often a characteristic of the 1904–05 Revival in Wales. The revival preachers encouraged all believers to participate in corporate worship and receive blessing from God. Despite the move towards a greater emphasis upon the laity, there were some key ministers active within the revival years. One was Rev. Joseph Jenkins of Tabernacle Calvinistic Methodist Chapel, New Quay, West Wales and his introduction of a series of conventions entitled: 'For the Deepening of the Spiritual Life'. The first was held on 31 December 1903 and 1 January 1904 with subsequent conventions organised for Aberaeron 30 June–1 July and for Blaenannerch in September 1904. Events at New Quay saw a deepening of people's appreciation of God and the need for evangelism leading to conversions. Correspondence from Jenkins to Evan Philips (1829–1912) on 28 March 1904 contains the kernel of the events at Tabernacle Church, New Quay:[313]

> The Spirit of God has fallen on our young people. I am unable to do anything I am in the middle of the sound of the wind. God himself is here. I have never seen anything like it before. It is spring and I don't know what to say – only weep and yet I cannot weep. Twenty-year-old girls are prophesying. It is the early hours of the morning and I am unable to go to bed. I must try to pray ... the tide now is truly powerful.[314]

It is interesting to note that such terminology as 'prophecy' is recorded as occurring within the Revival and could possibly be linked with future Pentecostal teaching.[315] Nevertheless apart from the complex matter of the

---

[313] Evan Phillips minister of Bethel Calvinistic Methodist Church Newcastle Emlyn had been influenced by the Revival of 1859.

[314] Kevin Adams, *A Diary of Revival* (Farnham: CWR, 2004), 46.

[315] For an AoG view of prophecy see David Petts, *Body Builders* (Mattersey: Mattersey Hall, 2002), 39–56, 136–48; William K. Kay, *Prophecy!* (Mattersey: Mattersey Hall, 1991) and C.M. Robeck Jr., 'Prophecy, Gift of,' in *NIDPCM*, 999–1012.

interpretation, the incidents of Pentecostal like manifestations recorded are spasmodic and produce no pattern that could be seen as clearly Pentecostal in doctrine. The spiritual fervour recorded in New Quay preceded Evan Roberts' involvement in the Revival by some months and helped to pave the way for a wider awakening within the land. Revival had begun and a prominent theme as intimated by Jenkins was the essential ministry of the Spirit of God.[316]

The village of Blaenannerch, Cardigan, West Wales was the site of the conference at which Seth Joshua was the invited speaker, the meetings commenced on 25 September 1904. At this time Evan Roberts visited these meetings—an experience which is recorded at length by the journalist 'Awstin'.[317] To experience the fire of God had been Roberts's desire since his conversion some thirteen years previously. A need of spiritual preparation related in Old Testament sacrificial language is applied by Roberts to his personal situation so all that remained was for God to visit and ignite the offering of his life. His desires were fulfilled at Blaenannerch on 29 September 1904 when he underwent a highly emotional experience; Awstin records the description of the events.[318] The now famous prayer of Roberts: 'Bend me! Bend me! Bend us!' was first uttered during his experience at Blaenannerch. The effect of God's dealings with Evan Roberts set the tone for the emotionally charged ministry he commenced. His desire for evangelistic endeavour born in these early days of revival activity affected Wales on a wide scale over the following months. In the months up to December 1905 Roberts embarked upon a demanding series of revival meetings with visits to many of the towns and villages of South Wales. His desires and expectations are summarised in the following extract from a personal letter written to his friend Elsie Phillips in November 1904 which records the centrality of the Spirit's work:

> Then I told them of the work the Spirit was and is doing at New Quay and Newcastle-Emlyn, and urged them to prepare for the baptism of the

[316] Adams, *Diary of Revival*, 35–47, Evans, *Welsh Revival*, 49–75 and Jones, *Rent Heavens*, 23–38.
[317] Awstin, 'The Religious Revival In Wales', vol.3, Western Mail (Jan. 1905); Cauchi, *Welsh Revival on* CD ROM. Awstin was the pen name for the Western Mail journalist T. Davies a close follower of revival events in Wales 1904–05. Gibbard, *Fire on the Altar*, 173–4; Geraint Fielder, *Grace, Grit and Gumption* (Fearn: Christian Focus, 2004), 139–51; Brynmor Pierce Jones, *An Instrument of Revival* (South Plainfield, NJ: Bridge, 1995).
[318] Awstin, 'The Religious Revival in Wales'; Cauchi, *Welsh Revival on CD ROM*.

Holy Spirit. Now, this is the plan I have taken under the guidance of the Holy Spirit—there are four things to be right:

If there is some sin or sins in the past not confessed, we cannot have the Spirit. Therefore, we must search, and ask the Spirit to search us.

(2) If there is something doubtful in our life, it must be removed—something we say of it we do not know whether it is wrong or right. This thing must be removed.

(3) Total surrender to the Spirit. We must do and say all He asks us.

(4) Public confession of Christ.

These are the four things leading us to the grand blessing. [319]

Through this statement Roberts showed a close allegiance to the Keswick position of dealing with 'known sin' which displayed the influence of the Holiness teaching upon his thinking. The urging of his hearers to prepare for the 'baptism of the Holy Spirit' is a common call throughout his ministry although what exactly he defined as 'grand blessing' is not developed; his letter further explains some of the events which unfolded at Loughor. [320] He records definite conditions which lead to the experience of individuals being 'baptised in the Spirit' and of it being a recognisable event. By promoting this position Roberts moved away from the traditional Calvinistic Methodist teaching he would have been taught. [321] An earnest desire expressed in the words 'send the Holy Spirit for Jesus Christ's sake' epitomises the deep longing for a greater experience of God. This earnestness was characterised by fervent prayers for a

---

[319] D. M. Phillips, *Evan Roberts, The Great Welsh Revivalist and His Works* (London: Marshall Brothers, 1923), 225–6, Cauchi, *Welsh Revival* on CD ROM.

[320] Phillips, *Evan Roberts, The Great Welsh Revivalist and His Works*, 232. See also Gresham Jr., *Charles G. Finney's Doctrine*, 58–63 where similar conditions to receiving the baptism in the Holy Spirit are suggested and 70–5 for a comparison of Finney and Keswick.

[321] Calvinistic Methodists, *The History, Constitution and Confession of Faith of the Calvinistic Methodists in Wales, drawn up by their own Associated Ministers* (Memphis: General Book Club, 1827/2010), 40–1, 43. See also Walter C. Kaiser Jr. 'The Baptism in the Holy Spirit as the Promise of the Father: A Reformed Perspective', in Brand, *Perspectives on Spirit Baptism,* 15–46 and Anthony A. Hoekema, 'The Reformed Perspective' in Gundry,, ed., *Five Views,* 61–101. See also A. A. Hoekema *What About Tongue Speaking?* (Exeter: Paternoster, 1966) and B. B. Warfield, *Counterfeit Miracles* (Edinburgh: Banner of Truth, 1972).

baptism of the Holy Spirit with fire, emotional outbursts, weeping, and public confession of sin, praise and spontaneous congregational singing throughout Wales.[322] The methods employed by Evan Robert were unorthodox in the context of Welsh evangelicalism:

> I have been asked concerning my methods. I have none. I never prepare the words I shall speak. I leave all that to Him. I am not the source of this revival. I am only one agent in what is a growing multitude.[323]

This pronouncement by Roberts appears to contradict the earlier letter written to Elsie Phillips in which he sets out four definite conditions or 'methods' for receiving the Spirit.[324] This could be further challenged by the emotive contents of Roberts' campaigns and his continual practice of 'testing the meeting' could be understood as a definite emotional method of gaining converts.[325] Coupled to this was his method of preaching which although usually brief, was at times lengthy, and regularly saw Roberts walking up and down the aisles waving his Bible and encouraging people to respond to God's presence. His suggested lack of preparation could be viewed as presumption; yet he would have seen this attitude as illustrating his total dependence upon the Spirit of God. One of the drawbacks of Roberts's approach was that although the emotionally charged atmosphere allowed for spontaneity in worship, adequate provision was not made for a period of deeper biblical ministry. This lack of biblical preaching and teaching would have thwarted spiritual understanding and growth in his converts and led in fact to nominalism.[326] Despite this, Roberts believed that he was under the complete control of the power of the Holy Spirit and acting and speaking solely in accordance with the will of God. This would have been something to which early Pentecostals could have been attracted. Their belief in the moving or leading of the Spirit and of extempore ministry or exhortation was an

---

[322] Jones, *Rent Heavens*, 49–60 and Brynmor Jones, *Voices From the Welsh Revival* (Bridgend: Evangelical Press, 1995), 65–86.

[323] Evan Roberts, 'A Message to the World by Evan Roberts', in *The Story of the Welsh Revival by Eyewitnesses*, www.dustandashes.com

[324] Pope, 'Demythologising the Evan Roberts Revival', 520.

[325] Evans, *Welsh Revival*, 163–68, Pope, 'Demythologising the Evan Roberts Revival', 519; Jones, *Rent Heavens*, 49–60.

[326] Evans, *Welsh Revival*, 163.

important feature of their early preaching. Robert Pope makes some poignant comments on the position of Evan Roberts and the relation to pneumatology, reinforcing his links with Keswick:

> Yet during the early meetings his (Evan Roberts) message was not so much Christocentric as pneuma-centric, a result of the influence of the Holiness movement, especially the teaching of Keswick. He emphasised the need for Christians to be empowered through the baptism of the Holy Spirit. Confession then was not enough, and neither was faith. Each believer needed to be filled with the Spirit. [327]

This call for people to be filled with the Spirit is a constant theme in the ministry of Roberts, but his theological tendencies were towards the Keswick model rather than that of an emerging Pentecostalism. Pope also deals with some of the popular 'myths' that surround Evan Roberts and his 'leadership' of the Revival. He suggests that Roberts was not the sole architect of the movement while as noted above there were numerous others involved in the Revival ministry. Pope also credits the emerging Pentecostals with continuing the emphasis upon Spirit baptism as a second blessing and an empowerment for service. Yet one must still differentiate between a continuance of terminology and a continuance of experience. The emergent Pentecostals accepted the terminology of the Revival but enlarged it, or even, imposed upon it the experience of initial evidence.

Gibbard makes some crucial observations regarding the terminology associated with a baptism of the Holy Spirit but states categorically that Roberts did not speak in tongues and even discouraged their use. [328] He does relate the Revival of 1904–05 to events of Acts 2, but without suggesting any connection with later Pentecostal belief in 'initial evidence'. [329] Gibbard's position is similar to Edith Blumhofer; namely, that the Revival could be described as 'Pentecostal in character'. This understanding relates to such areas as emphasising the leading of the Spirit, giving much time to singing and public participation in meetings,

---

[327] Pope, 'Demythologising the Evan Roberts Revival,' 521.
[328] Gibbard, *Fire on the Altar,* 164.
[329] Gibbard, *Fire on the Altar,* 38, 81, 169–78.

but not in doctrine or subsequent expected experience.[330] As Pentecostal theology at the time was only in embryo in America, it is difficult to connect the specifics of that theology to any theological interpretation of Revival terminology.[331] Gibbard also provides interesting insights regarding the relationship of the Revival and Pentecostalism recording both the expansion of, and opposition to, the new teaching. Allen concurs with Gibbard, correctly stating that it was not the conventional churches alone that criticised Pentecostalism but that some leading evangelicals such as F. B. Meyer, Graham Scroggie and Campbell Morgan joined the condemnation.[332]

By 1905 Britain was still to experience the new wave of teaching which commenced with the ministry of A. A. Boddy in Sunderland.[333] Many people travelled to Wales in order to experience the remarkable revival events – one such visitor was Boddy and another Joseph Smale of Los Angeles—both of whom were impressed by the Revival, and in particular Evan Roberts.[334] They also had some influence upon emergent Pentecostalism.[335] Charismata or the gift of tongues were not expected within early twentieth century Welsh chapel life, and references to 'new tongues' within the Revival period referred to a change in people's speech in refraining from swearing and blasphemy, rather than speaking in unlearned or unknown languages. This interpretation of 'new tongues' as a result of the Spirit's presence is more closely related to the holiness or Keswick inspired model of sanctification rather than the Pentecostal view of initial evidence.[336]

---

[330] Gibbard, *On The Wings*, 184–90 and Edith W. Blumhofer, *The Assemblies of God: A Popular History* (Springfield, MO.: Radiant Books, 1985), 20–2.

[331] Anderson, *Introduction to Pentecostalism*; Bartleman, *Azusa Street*; Robeck, *Azusa Street*.

[332] Allen, *Unfailing Stream*, 120.

[333] Gavin Wakefield, *Alexander Boddy Pentecostal Anglican Pioneer* (London: Paternoster, 2007), Neil Hudson, 'The Earliest Days of British Pentecostalism,' *JEPTA* 21 (2001), 49–67; William K. Kay, 'Sunderland's Legacy in New Denominations,' *JEPTA* 28/2 (2008), 183–99.

[334] Tim Welch, *Joseph Smale: God's 'Moses' for Pentecostalism* (Milton Keynes: Paternoster, 2013) Welch adds a great deal to Pentecostal historiography with a re-evaluation of Smale and his impact on rising Pentecostalism; especially in relation to the standard position espoused by Bartleman.

[335] Wakefield, *Alexander Boddy*, 75–7. Bartleman, *Azusa Street*, 15–47 and Synan, *Holiness-Pentecostal*, 84–7 records how Smale led the First New Testament Church Los Angeles and maintained a congregation of one thousand members, see also Welch, *Joseph Smale*.

[336] Stevenson, *Keswick's Authentic*, 403–528 who provides a summary of the various sermons given on the subject by Keswick Conference speakers.

Historians and commentators differ over their understanding of any Pentecostal phenomena being present during the Revival. B. P. Jones records how W. S. Jones was especially prominent in visiting churches and chapels that had experienced outbursts of 'tongues'. He visited in order to assist the resident minister in dealing with these emotional outbursts and other 'foreign' phenomena by emphasising the necessity to teach biblical principles to counter such emotions. [337] J. Edwin Orr states that speaking in Pentecostal type tongues was not experienced in the Welsh Revival 1904–05. Orr suggests that the return of Pastor Joseph Smale from Wales to Azusa Street, Los Angeles provided the opportunity for Pentecostal teaching to be linked to revival terminology. [338] This was no doubt enhanced by the correspondence between Evan Roberts and American based Frank Bartleman who had contact with Smale in Los Angeles. [339] That the issue of Pentecostal tongues occurring during the Welsh Revival is debatable: Vinson Synan disagrees with Orr on the subject, reporting that people who did not know the Welsh language yet who spoke in 'Old Welsh', and that a Dutch Pastor—without any ability in English—preached an entire sermon in English. [340] Whether this experience was rightly described by Synan, is questionable but also whether it would be classed as glossolalia or xenolalia would be debated among the various Pentecostal groups. However, Synan's position (that tongues occurred during the 1904–05 Revival) is supported by the *Christian Herald* reporter who recorded the following experience:

> The Gift of Tongues Repeated. – A remarkable statement is made regarding the Welsh revival which recalls the "gift of tongues" mentioned in the New Testament. Young Welshmen and Welshwomen who know little or no Welsh, it is reported, take part in these services in a language which they were supposed hitherto not to be able to

---

[337] Jones, *King's Champions*, 62.

[338] J. Edwin Orr, 'The Welsh Revival Goes Worldwide', *Western Mail*, 9 December 1974.

[339] Bartleman, *Azusa Street*, 18, 25, 28.

[340] Synan, *Holiness-Pentecostal*, 86–8.

understand, yet which trips off their tongue with an ease which might be supposed to indicate long and familiar usage. [341]

Furthermore, Edith Blumhofer records that the *Times* newspaper accounts of the use of 'classical Welsh' in some revival meetings and also stated that this 'old Welsh' was far beyond the normal linguistic abilities of those who used it in these services. [342] Neither Blumhofer nor the *Christian Herald* reporter made any reference to these 'new tongues' as being initial evidence of a baptism in the Holy Spirit. One could suggest that these occurrences were due to the Holy Spirit producing this Pentecost like phenomenon but, as Williams notes, there is no substantial evidence of the practice of glossolalia during the Welsh Revival. [343] If, as these records may suggest—and as Jones and Synan claim— tongues were experienced at this time, these occurrences were not considered as the initial evidence of baptism in the Holy Spirit.

Evan Roberts claims that he experienced two powerful, personal experiences of God that could be labelled as 'baptisms in the Holy Spirit'. The first was a prolonged experience at Loughor during the spring of 1904. The second was his more public experience at Blaenannerch in September 1904. [344] His experience is recorded as follows:

> His Spirit came to me one night, when I was upon my knees I asked Him for guidance, and five months later I was baptized with the Spirit. He has led me as He will lead all those who, conscious of their human weakness, lean upon Him as children upon a father. [345]

Roberts records a definite experience of the Spirit's presence, one which he interpreted as a baptism in the Holy Spirit. However, there is no reference to any glossolalia as evidence of this experience being present or expected. Eifion Evans provides a 'definition' of the term, 'baptism in the Holy Spirit' as promoted and experienced by Evan Roberts:

---

[341] *Christian Herald Welsh Revival Issue*, (CPO: 2007), 9, this publications gives further insights into the work of the Revival in Monmouthshire.

[342] Edith Blumhofer, 'The Welsh Revival 1904–1905'; *Paraclete* 20/3 (1986), 1–5.

[343] Cyril G. Williams, *Tongues Of The Spirit* (Cardiff: University of Wales Press, 1981), 51–6.

[344] Evans, *Welsh Revival*, 190 and Jones, *Instrument of Revival*, 9–41.

[345] Roberts, 'Message to the World'.

The baptism of the Holy Spirit may be described as an influx, sudden or gradual, of the Spirit of God into man's spirit, which liberates it from the vessel of the soul, and raises it into a place of dominance over soul and body. The freed spirit then becomes an open channel for the Spirit of God to pour through it an outflow of divine power. The mind receives, at the same time, a clarifying quickening, and the "eye of the understanding" is filled with light (Ephesians 1:18). The body becomes entirely under the man's complete control, as the result of the dominance of the spirit, and often receives a quickening in strength for endurance in the warfare service he finds he has emerged into. [346]

This definition, supported by the influential Jessie Penn-Lewis, promotes a baptism that relates much to the individual's victory over sin and strength for service, but there is no reference to Pentecostal evidential tongues. [347] This account also assumes that Roberts embraced a tri-partite doctrine of man in terms of body, soul and spirit based largely on Hebrews 4:12. [348] It is the 'spirit' which is directly in touch with God the Holy Spirit, is capable of victory over sin, and allows intimate fellowship with God. [349] This would not have been the teaching he received under the Calvinistic Methodists which was a more traditional body/soul distinction. Roberts clearly had come under the influence of Holiness teaching similarly as Watchman Nee (1903–72) had done so in this period through Penn-Lewis. [350] For Roberts, the encounter with the Spirit of God allows a person to be liberated from the carnal attitudes and enter into a deeper Christian experience of holiness and service. It must be noted that

---

[346] Evans, *Welsh Revival*, 191.

[347] Gibbard, *Fire on the Altar*, 168–9.

[348] F. F. Bruce, *The Epistle to the Hebrews: Revised Edition* (Grand Rapids, MI: Eerdmans, 1990, NICNT), 111–14.

[349] Wayne Grudem, *Systematic Theology* (Leicester: IVP, 1994), 472–89 and Williams, *Renewal Theology, vol. 1*, 197–219.

[350] Through her writings Penn-Lewis's influence reached beyond Wales as is seen in Watchman Nee, *The Spiritual Man* (New York: Christian Fellowship Publishers, 1968) which shows particular similarities to Jessie Penn-Lewis with Evan Roberts, *War On The Saints* (Burgess Hill: Meadow Books, 2005). See also Watchman Nee, *A Living Sacrifice* (New York: Christian Fellowship Publishers, 1972) and Watchman Nee, *Spiritual Knowledge* (New York: Christian Fellowship Publishers, 1973). Nee supported the tri-partite view of man: body, soul and spirit, he was also influenced by the writings of Andrew Murray and J. N. Darby. See <www.watchmannee.org>

neither Roberts nor Penn-Lewis believed that sin was eradicated in the believer due to the baptism in the Spirit and that sanctification was a progressive experience. A careful reading of their volume *War on the Saints* reveals a confusing concentration on negative and demonic influences. At times Penn-Lewis emphasised these matters to an extent that detracted from the true work of conversion that occurred in the Revival 1904–05.[351]

Kay makes some interesting comments regarding the overall situation that led to the slow demise of the Revival fervency paying particular reference to the role played by Jessie Penn-Lewis. Kay refers to her over-bearing influence on Evan Roberts which may have been detrimental to both Roberts' personal ministry and the progress of the Revival. This adverse influence could have been due to a lack of true Pentecostal teaching on charismata and the insistence by Penn-Lewis upon Calvinistic teaching. There is also evidence that the anti-Pentecostal attitude of Penn-Lewis was a significant factor that prevented the development of the Revival in any truly Pentecostal direction. This attitude was revealed in her hostile correspondence with A. A. Boddy.[352] Kay may well be right in his general thesis, although since (as he correctly highlights) Pentecostal theology was still in embryo in America, teaching on such matters was still unknown in Britain. However it does appear that Penn-Lewis endeavoured to extricate Roberts from Wales at every possible opportunity and bring him to her home in Leicester.[353] His eventual retreat to Leicester did provide a cessation of his public ministry. The influence of Penn-Lewis was important within South Wales particularly through the Keswick in Wales conferences; however she was an over-bearing individual who endeavoured to control Evan Roberts. Her theology as expressed particularly in *War on the Saints* is at times confusing and difficult to follow; I therefore submit that she was no great theological thinker but an individual who was prominent through her letters and apparent 'control' of Evan Roberts. Although speculation it would be interesting to think of the possible further extent of the Welsh Revival if Roberts had not been diverted from his public ministry by Penn-Lewis.

---

[351] Gibbard, *Fire on the Altar*, 156–9.

[352] Jones, *Trials and Triumphs*, 183–94.

[353] Kay, 'Why did the Welsh Revival stop,' 9–12.

Eifion Evans relates how 'Pentecostal manifestations' were prominent within the revival and that Evan Roberts was the chief promoter of them. Nevertheless he does not elaborate on the nature of these manifestations apart from reference to them being termed 'baptism in the Holy Spirit'.[354] Penn-Lewis and Roberts reveal a deeper understanding of the position on this crucial Pentecostal doctrine. The co-authors state:

> The Baptism of the Spirit is THE ESSENCE OF REVIVAL.... The hour of Revival is the hour of crisis and possible catastrophe. A crisis in the history of every individual, as well as in the history of a country, a church or a district. A crisis for the unregenerate man, wherein he settles his eternal destiny, as he accepts, or rejects conversion to God; a crisis to those who receive the fullness of the Holy Spirit, and to those who reject Him; for to the believer who bends and receives the Holy Spirit, it is the day of the visitation of the Most High, but to others it means the decision whether they will become spiritual men or remain carnal (1 Cor 3:1); whether they will elect to remain in defeat in the personal life, or determine to press on as overcomers.[355]

This explanation by Penn-Lewis and Roberts with its 'crisis' emphasis reflects the Keswick emphasis on the victorious life and overcoming in the battle of personal holiness, which normally involves a crisis stage but here they relate it especially to revival. However, they are using the term 'revival' in a restricted sense to refer to personal awakening which may lead to wider and more public blessing.[356] Pentecostals can be excused for being excited by later mention of an influx of divine power resulting in empowerment for service, the distribution of spiritual gifts and the Spirit supplying true knowledge of Christ. However the authors are cautious, even dismissive, over the question of

---

[354] Evans, *Welsh Revival*, 190. See also G. Campbell Morgan, 'The Lessons of the Revival' in Arthur Goodrich, 'The Story of the Welsh Revival', in Cauchi *Welsh Revival* on CD ROM, 34–48; Jones, *Faith and the Crisis*, 283–311 where Jones highlights some of the thinking concerning baptism in Holy Spirit but also recognises some of the inconsistencies in Roberts' thinking. Adams, *Diary of Revival*, 35–119. See also Gibbard, *On The Wings*, 186–90. An interesting chapter on baptism in the Holy Spirit is found in Penn-Lewis, *War*, 195–222.

[355] Penn-Lewis, *War on the Saints*, 195.

[356] Penn-Lewis, *War on the Saints*, 198–201.

tongues and denied its necessity.[357] The words of Jessie Penn-Lewis are highlighted in the Pentecostal journal *Flames of Fire*. She states that the Pentecostal character of the Welsh Revival was 'unmistakably clear'.[358] The events in Wales are related to the Joel prophecy and she suggests that such supernatural occurrences had not been seen since the time of the early church in Acts. The use of Penn-Lewis's words here by the editor of *Flames of Fire* highlights the possibility of pro-pentecostal writers adopting the words of prominent individuals and the use of significant terminology in order to connect their thinking and experience with the Revival events. Throughout her account of the Revival Penn-Lewis employs the terms 'Pentecostal' and 'Pentecost' to refer to Wales in 1904–05 and states that it was 'the Acts of the Apostles up to date'.[359] However she had already distanced herself from the rising Pentecostalism before this extract was reprinted in *Flames of Fire*.[360] This is best summarised by the account of Penn-Lewis' dealings with Mr and Mrs Garr—Azusa Street missionaries to India. They had commenced a Pentecostal based ministry encouraging people to seek Spirit baptism with the sign of tongues. The position of Penn-Lewis is made clear in the following words:

> Speaking of the Garrs, she asked why they lacked meekness and love and why did they make this *unscriptural claim* (my emphasis) that the gift of tongues is "the invariable evidence of being baptized". She asked why they made such a fuss about gifts and signs that could merely excite the flesh or even lead us into the sin of pride.[361]

Penn-Lewis leaves us in no doubt that she opposed the developing Pentecostal view. The early Pentecostals would have had similar concerns about 'exciting' the flesh or pride even if they accepted that in some instances their teaching

---

[357] Penn-Lewis, *War on the Saints,* 205.

[358] *Flames of Fire*, March (1912), 3–4, contains an extract from Jessie Penn-Lewis, 'Pentecost and the Gift of Tongues', *Life of Faith*, Nov.10 (1909); cf. Penn-Lewis, *Awakening in Wales;* Gibbard, *On The Wings*, 187–90; Rees, *Seth and Frank Joshua,* 44; Cauchi, *Welsh Revival* on CD ROM.

[359] Penn-Lewis, *Awakening in Wales,* 51.

[360] Jones, *Trials and Triumphs,* 131–43.

[361] Jones, *Trials and Triumphs,* 141. See also, Gary B. McGee, 'Early Pentecostal Hermeneutics: Tongues As Evidence In The Book Of Acts', in Gary B. McGee, *Initial Evidence Historical and Biblical Perspectives on the Pentecostal Doctrine of Spirit Baptism* (Eugene, OR: Wipf & Stock, 2007), 102–3 for a discussion of how the Garrs had to alter their position on xenolalia due to a fruitless excursion into missionary work in India.

was abused and misused.[362] Pentecostals would agree that being aware of counterfeit demonstrations of power is essential in the life of the believer, however it appears that Penn-Lewis and Roberts over-emphasised this thus detracting from the possibility that God may work in this way.[363] Jones assesses how Penn-Lewis reacted to the tongues movement revealing that her correspondence with A. A. Boddy shows a rejection of its teaching. Penn-Lewis was particularly concerned about the teaching of T. B. Barratt, the 'apostle' of European Pentecostalism. The correspondence between Penn-Lewis and Boddy was hostile and placed the two opposing views beyond any reconciliation.[364] This division between Penn-Lewis, Roberts, and Boddy highlights the difficulties in openly accepting any firm theological links between the Welsh Revival and emerging Pentecostalism.

Eifion Evans helps clarify the relationship between the 1904–05 Revival in Wales and Pentecostalism when he states:

> The movement's exponents in Wales drew their inspiration from the revival, their distinctly Pentecostal emphases were traceable to its rarer occurrences and incidental features. The mainstream revival continued to run in the channels of the historic denominations without losing its impetus or character.[365]

For Evans these possible 'pentecostal' occurrences were 'rarer' and 'incidental' yet the 'inspiration' gained may have attracted some to emerging Pentecostal groups. The tone of Evans's words here suggests that 'Pentecostal' type activity was very much on the periphery of the Revival. There does appear a contradiction in Evans' description of Pentecostal phenomena, in the first instance he says they were prominent yet his next reference is to their being 'rarer' or 'incidental'.[366] At best it could be held that Pentecostal type phenomena were peripheral during the Revival. Geraint Fielder deals briefly

---

[362] Jones, *Trials and Triumphs*, 169–94 for an interesting view of Penn-Lewis and the "Tongues Movement" in Britain.

[363] Kay, 'Why did the Welsh Revival stop,' 9.

[364] Jones, *Trials and Triumphs*, 183–94.

[365] Evans, *Welsh Revival*, 192.

[366] Note Evans' description regarding Pentecostal phenomena in Evans, *Welsh Revival*, 191–2.

with this subject in relation to John Pugh and the Joshua brothers; Pugh called for people to seek a baptism of the Holy Spirit for power in Christian service. It was his belief that the Forward Movement evangelists had experienced such power for service and thereby had been able to reach the apparently unreachable with the gospel. As well as his work with the Forward Movement, Seth Joshua was also involved in the Keswick in Wales Conventions. He accepted the general theological stance of that movement although he held reservations regarding the interpretation of the baptism in the Spirit and how to obtain it. Spirit baptism for Seth Joshua led to the personal assurance of salvation and did not have a particular crisis event on the path to holiness, as Keswick taught. Unlike later Pentecostal teaching, Joshua's interpretation did not include a desire for, or belief in, tongues as initial evidence.[367] He believed that a 'dose' of Calvinistic theology would have corrected the emphasis emerging from Keswick. As Gibbard rightly notes, even though Joshua held a high regard for Calvinistic doctrine he was not afraid to employ Arminian evangelistic techniques during his ministry.[368] To Pentecostals, the baptism of the Spirit would 'energise' or empower an individual's ministry, but 'tongues' were a paramount, introductory, and initial experience. The Keswick model and the more traditional denominational positions were to the forefront of much of the teaching on this subject. Whether the Joshua brothers were embracing Pentecostalism or not, Frank had openness to what the Spirit was doing. This is illustrated by his hosting a Pentecostal meeting at his chapel in

---

[367] Fielder, *Grace, Grit and Gumption*, 153–4. See also D. Martyn Lloyd-Jones, *Joy Unspeakable* (Eastbourne: Kingsway, 1984), who believed in the baptism of the Spirit but did not relate its occurrence to receiving any particular gift as proof. According to Gibbard, Lloyd-Jones regarded the baptism of the Spirit as 'revival', Gibbard, *On The Wings*, 190. See also Iain H. Murray, *Lloyd-Jones Messenger of Grace* (Edinburgh: Banner of Truth, 2008), 127–63, Murray sheds some interesting light on the views of Lloyd-Jones regarding the subject of baptism in the Spirit. From a Pentecostal stand point Lloyd-Jones is to be supported in his insistence upon the necessity of the power of the Holy Spirit within the preacher and his preaching, Murray, *Lloyd-Jones*, 29–54.

[368] Gibbard, *Fire on the Altar,* 174, see also Charles G. Finney, *Principles of Revival* (Minneapolis, MN: Bethany House, 1987); Charles Grandison Finney, *Revivals of Religion* (London: Morgan and Scott, 1910) and John L. Gresham, *Charles G. Finney's Doctrine of the Baptism of the Holy Spirit* (Peabody, MA: Hendrickson, 1987). Finney's teaching was developed during his time at Oberlin College 1835–1866. His influence upon later Pentecostalism is significant as he emphasised a second experience or baptism of the Spirit as the means by which individuals are more aware of the spiritual realities and is also very similar to the Keswick position. See also David Prothroe, 'An Analysis and Theological Evaluation of Revival and Revivalism in America from 1730–1860' (PhD Dissertation, University of North West South Africa – Potchefstroom – 2004).

Neath. His personal involvement in a meeting with Dutch Pentecostal pioneer Gerrit Polman (1868–1932) is recorded in *Confidence*.[369]

> Neath was the next place that God wanted us to testify. Dear Bro. Frank Joshua had invited us to come and hold a meeting in his chapel, which seats about 2,000. For this meeting on Monday evening Bro. Joshua had only invited some Christians, and about 250 had come together, and we had the privilege of testifying for the glory of God of what He had done in and for us. We felt that God blessed the words, and we pray that God may bless dear Bro. Joshua, and that the Lord may give him very soon the desire of his heart—the Pentecostal Baptism.[370]

According to Boddy and Polman, and as recorded in *Confidence,* Frank Joshua was seeking the 'Pentecostal Baptism' but whether this was ever experienced by Joshua is not recorded in *Confidence*. Frank Joshua clearly was open to God working in his life through the Holy Spirit and also happy to hear of, and learn from, Pentecostals.

The Revival years in Wales should not focus solely on Evan Roberts for there were others who were used during 1904–05 and who held personal or denominational theological positions regarding the baptism of the Spirit.[371] These various understandings of the baptism in the Holy Spirit are not to be directly compared to later Pentecostal practice. However, the convergence of teachings and practices in the Revival period prepared some individuals for the arrival of the specific Pentecostal teaching on glossolalia. The latter was imported from America via Sunderland when Spirit baptism was defined differently as being evidenced in tongues and providing power for service as modelled on Acts 1:8 and Acts 2:4. There was a particular emphasis on Acts 2:39 where early Pentecostals understood Peter's words as a literal fulfilment in

---

[369] Gerrit Roelof Polman was the founder of Dutch Pentecostalism. He had been influenced by the Welsh and Azusa Street revivals and began a Pentecostal assembly in 1907.

[370] *Confidence*, April, 1910, 94.

[371] Evan Roberts was not the only individual who believed in the baptism of the Spirit see, Gibbard, *R. B. Jones*, 137–56; Williams, *Tongues of the Spirit*, 51–6; Jones, *Spiritual History*, 40–5 and Stevenson, ed., *Keswick's Authentic*, 403–525. See also various articles in *Life of Faith 1905*.

their experience for they were a part of the 'as many as the Lord our God will call.'

The major Pentecostal groups that attracted later attention were led by either D. P. Williams (Apostolic) or George Jeffreys (Elim) and still later the emergent AoG congregations. It is important to note that D. P. Williams did not come into contact with Pentecostalism until c. 1909 and George Jeffreys until 1910. Whether a Pentecostal interpretation of spiritual manifestations was present in the Welsh Revival of 1904–05 remains a question which is still difficult to answer. Scholars differ over the issue but Pentecostal theology, with its distinctive view of the gifts and Spirit baptism was still not present in any obvious way within Wales.

The Revival Influences SE Wales

Between 1904 and 1905 throughout SE Wales, hardened labourers were brought in to the local chapels on a wave of religious fervour. Conversions soared, so that in 1906 there were 549,000 chapel members in South Wales compared with 369,494 as recorded in the 1851 religious census.[372] The dramatic occurrences of 1904–05 had alarming effects upon the mining communities of the south-eastern valleys and there was a wide ranging influence from Roberts and other revivalist preachers.

The first visit of Evan Roberts to SE Wales was to Caerphilly on 5 and 6 December 1904 but others, apart from Roberts, took the gospel message to the region.[373] Men such as Sidney Evans, Seth Joshua, W. S. Jones and Dan Roberts made preaching tours of the valleys and meetings were conducted at such places as Abercarn, Abertillery, Ebbw Vale, Newbridge, Abergavenny, and Newport.[374] H. Elvet Lewis records the significant ministry of Sydney Evans in Monmouthshire:

> The young leader was not present: he had started on his first missionary journey. His place was taken by Mr Sydney Evans, his comrade from the

---

[372] Kenneth O. Morgan, *Rebirth of a Nation Wales 1880–1980* (London: Oxford University Press, 1981), 134. See also Jones, *Faith and the Crisis*, 10–40; Gibbard, *Fire on the Altar*, 132–6 and Evans, *Welsh Revival*, 146.

[373] Jones, *Voices from the Welsh*, 46–7.

[374] Gibbard, *Fire on the Altar*, 42–63 see also Rick Joyner, *The Power To Change The World* (Fort Mill, SC, Morning Star, 2006), 84–94 and Jones, *Voices from the Welsh*, 81–2.

first and co-worker in the mission, though not together in the same meetings. The latter, after the inauguration of the movement in the western parts of Glamorgan, became more distinctly connected with the mission in the mining valleys of Monmouthshire, both Welsh and English. His singing companion was Mr Sam Jenkins, and together they did a work second in public importance only to that of the leader and his immediate helpers.[375]

Sydney Evans, a close friend and ministry associate of 'the young leader' Evan Roberts, recognised the spiritual needs within the industrial communities of SE Wales. Accordingly he and Sam Jenkins complimented the ministry of the Forward Movement, which had already had an impact there. Evans commenced his ministry in Newport and following an inauspicious start he eventually attracted crowds to hear his gospel preaching. From Newport he and Jenkins travelled north to Cwmbran, Beaufort and Ebbw Vale and they saw encouraging results. The ministry of Evans and Jenkins in the east of Wales ran parallel to that of Evan Roberts and others in West Wales. Another who worked in the valleys of SE Wales was Dan Roberts, Evan's brother; who commenced a five week ministry campaign in the early months of 1905. The influence of the revival activity in the area is summarised by various eye-witnesses such as Rev. Thomas Theophilus of Tredegar:

> I remember the Revival which thrilled the people about forty-five years ago. Its eccentricities, as showing its human side, were greater then than in connection with the present one. There appears to be, on the whole, greater sobriety and inward intensity about the one now prevailing. It was much needed. We could not help feeling the coldness and formality which pervaded professors of religion and the especial outpouring of the Holy Spirit on humble means has come with healing. We have had Prayer Meetings in our large vestry.[376]

---

[375] H. Elvet Lewis, *With Christ Among The Miners*, 36; Cauchi, *Welsh Revival* on CD ROM. Jones, *Voices from the Welsh*, 52–61 emphasises the important role played by gospel singers during the Revival months; Sam Jenkins of Llanelli became known as the "Sankey of Wales".

[376] 'Church and People', 16/11 February (1905), 20; Cauchi, *Welsh Revival*, on CD ROM. Thomas Theophilus was a native of Llandovery, Carmarthenshire. He was married to Emily Elizabeth with one daughter Maria

These words of Anglican vicar Theophilus and similar sentiments of Pastor Luther Davies (1872–1909) of St. Marys Street Baptist Church, Newport, illustrate how the Revival crossed denominational barriers.[377] This cross denominational influence is seen in the attitude of Dr Handley Moule, Bishop of Durham, who was supportive of the events in Wales and was also of A. A. Boddy who was a vicar within Moule's diocese. Of interest is the fact that Moule was involved with the Keswick Convention illustrating how he was keen to see the Christian influenced by the power of the Holy Spirit.[378] However his desires would not have been Pentecostal in interpretation.

Following various visits by the missioners the Revival spread and the south east area was greatly affected. D. M. Phillips records the Western Mail Revival Pamphlets that collated some of the various reports of conversions in eastern valleys during the Revival.[379] The villages, towns, and surrounding districts that eventually saw AoG chapels established were deeply affected by the Revival of 1904–05. It is impossible to accurately record the number of lasting conversions but newspaper reports list the numbers affected: Pontnewynydd, Talywain, Garndiffaith and Varteg 180, Abertillery 1000, Abertridwr 166, Aberbeeg 206, Abercarn 330, Abersychan and district 455, Abertillery and district 3,487, Beaufort 100, Bedwas 39, Blackwood 365, Blaenavon 1,200, Blaina 1,069, Brynmawr 466, Caerphilly 459, Crosskeys 600, Crumlin 16, Llanhilleth 251, Machen 815, Newbridge 500, Risca 654, Rogerstone 450.[380] According to the Western Mail reporter these figures are only an estimate and a guide as many conversions were not reported at other centres of revival activity; suffice to say the numbers brought into the churches and chapels were considerable. With regard to the emergence of AoG in SE Wales, one

---

Dingal still living at home in 1911, <www.1911census.co.uk>. There is no evidence that Theophilus had any future involvement with the Pentecostals and no apparent links with Boddy save their common Anglicanism. See also Jones, *Voices of the Welsh*, 200, who records the thoughts of Luther Davies, Newport.

[377] Evans, *Welsh Revival*, 98–119 and Gibbard, *Fire on the Altar*, 59–63 who records some of the influence of the revival upon the Anglican churches, see also *Christian Herald Welsh Revival Issue*, 4, Pollock, *Keswick Story*, 90–6. Memoirs of Ministers available from the Baptist Union of Great Britain for information on Luther Davies.

[378] Stevenson, *Keswick's Authentic*, 51–6, 521–4.

[379] Phillips, 'Evan Roberts the Great Welsh Revivalist and His Works,' 425; Cauchi, *Welsh Revival Library*, on CD ROM.

[380] Kevin Adams and Emyr Jones, *A Pictorial History of Revival: The Outbreak of the 1904 Welsh Awakening* (Farnham: CWR, 2004), 110–11. *Western Mail*, Religious Revival in Wales No. 2, December 1904 and No. 3 January 1905.

significant individual converted at this time was Tom Mercy, Crosskeys. Mercy later became very influential within Welsh and British AoG, serving as pastor at Crosskeys and also as an executive board member with a particular interest in foreign missions.

It was not the chapels alone that saw the effects of the Revival, for the wider communities were deeply affected. For a period, prayer meetings were held in the workplace and especially in the coal mines of Monmouthshire.[381] Events in the valley towns were also distinctly different due to the Revival. James A. Stewart records:

> Blaenavon. On Saturday evening, a band of young lads between the ages of fourteen and sixteen held prayer meetings in the different places in the principal streets.
>
> NEWBRIDGE. An official of the Colynen (sic) colliery, when asked how the religious fervour had expressed itself underground, said: "This is a blessed time. When I go around on my inspection now I rarely ever hear a blasphemous word of oath. There is a glorious change for the better".[382]

Teenagers were praying in the streets, miners praying underground, nightly services (some prayer meetings continuing until midnight), individuals responding to the gospel message, and book shops running out of Bibles. All this illustrates how deeply SE Wales was affected by the revival. William Kay highlights some of the sociological and psychological effects of the Welsh Revival 1904–05 and compares them to effects of the Azusa Street Revival in Los Angeles.[383] Kay's conclusion on this issue is interesting, in that he states it is difficult to 'rigorously' apply his findings to every revival as they are all 'undisciplined' events.

---

[381] T. Davies ('Awstin'), 'The Welsh Evangelist: A Monthly Pictorial Record and Review', 12 in Cauchi, *Welsh Revival Library* CD ROM. See also: 'The Quarterly Mail', No.72, April 1905, 21–2 in Cauchi, *Welsh Revival Library* on CD ROM.

[382] James A. Stewart, *Invasion of Wales By The Spirit Through Evan Roberts,* (Fort Washington, PA: CLC, 1963), 44–53, see also Joyner, *Power*, 84. See also, *Gibbard*, Fire on the Altar, 50–2, 91–2.

[383] Kay, 'Revival: Empirical Aspects', in Walker, ed., *On Revival,* 196–202.

Revival Themes

Certain key themes current in the Revival contributed to the emergent Pentecostalism. Firstly, there was the Revival's emphasis on the ministry of the Holy Spirit, which was later developed distinctively under other influences from England and America. As Larry Hart suggests, the development which focused on the issue of subsequence and the baptism of the Holy Spirit was pivotal in Pentecostalism from its beginning.[384] This development caused distrust and scepticism towards the emergent Pentecostals on the part of historic denominations.[385] While the ministry of the Holy Spirit had played a prominent part in traditional Welsh denominational theology, and had been a vital element of their preaching, the Pentecostal interpretation of the doctrine was neither apparent nor desired. The linking of the experience of tongues to the doctrine of the baptism of the Spirit was widely promoted only following events at Azusa Street in 1906. There had already been a variety of terms used to express Spirit baptism, but it was the Pentecostals who developed the narrower definition of tongues and empowerment for service. The crisis element of the Keswick teaching and the Holiness doctrines were adopted by some within Welsh theology (including Jessie Penn-Lewis) and can be considered a forerunner of Pentecostal teaching.[386] Such engaging with the Spirit is a crucial element in understanding the ministry of Evan Roberts; for however his experiences are expressed or interpreted, they set the tone for his 'Spirit awareness' in his public ministry.

Secondly, the evangelistic zeal which characterized the Revival was heightened by the Pentecostal sense of eschatological urgency due to the presumed imminence of the Parousia.[387] The statement of Jesus as recorded in Acts 1:8

---

[384] Larry Hart, 'A Charismatic Perspective' in Brand, *Perspectives on Spirit Baptism*, 145; William Kay, 'Assemblies of God: Distinctive Continuity and Distinctive Change', in Keith Warrington, ed., *Pentecostal Perspectives* (Carlisle: Paternoster, 1998), 51–63.

[385] Gibbard, *Fire*, 167–78 provides a helpful summary of the theological differences held by the leading figures of 1904–05, especially in relation to the work of the Holy Spirit. For Pentecostal/AoG views see Horton, *Gifts of the Spirit;* Petts, *Holy Spirit;* and Donald Gee, *Concerning Spiritual Gifts* (Springfield MO: GPH, 1972).

[386] Metcalfe, *Molded by the Cross* and Penn-Lewis, *Work of the Holy Spirit.*

[387] Blumhofer, *Assemblies Vol. 1,* 17–36, for an overview of the major theological influences upon late nineteenth and early twentieth century American theology that led to Pentecostalism. It must also be noted that it wasn't the Pentecostals alone who embarked upon evangelism, others such as Gypsy Smith (1860–1947) were prominent at this period. See David Lazell, *Gypsy from the Forest* (Bridgend: Bryntirion Press, 1997).

drew together the emphasis of Spirit baptism with evangelism; something Pentecostals emphasised in their search for the experience.[388] The evangelistic zeal of the Pentecostals was prevalent in the simplicity of their preaching and their recourse to personal testimony of God's deliverance from their sin and their 'hope of heavenly glory'. Although Densil Morgan pays scant attention to the rising Pentecostals, he states that Pentecostalism could be labelled as 'unsophisticated'.[389] Morgan does not elaborate on this description other than to emphasise that Pentecostalism was a popular movement among the working classes; a view supported by Pastor Paul of Germany who saw the tongues movement particularly prominent among people of immature belief.[390] Morgan and Paul are correct in that the majority of early adherents were drawn from the poorly educated working-class; however, not all converts to Pentecostalism came from the coal seams and blast furnaces of SE Wales. The label 'unsophisticated' relates most probably to the general lack of education, and especially theological education, evidenced in preaching; this was often direct and simple, with an emphasis laid on 'the leading of the Spirit.' Such extemporary exhortation often took the place of biblical exegesis, and they also placed a greater emphasis upon personal testimony and pneumatology; especially the engagement with the gifts recorded in 1 Corinthians 12.[391] Morgan does, however, credit the Pentecostals with offering adherents a taste of the 'vitality and excitement' of the New Testament.

---

[388] Christopher Palmer, 'Mission: The True Pentecostal Heritage as Illustrated in Early British AoG Thinking', *JEPTA* 30/2 (2010), 39–50. This article assesses the necessity of returning to an evangelism based paradigm for Spirit baptism which should be at the heart of AoG teaching. It may be appropriate to classify AoG as a missionary organisation rather than a denomination, since the focus of their distinctive Spirit baptism is evangelism/mission. See also Allan Anderson, *Spreading Fires The Missionary Nature of Early Pentecostalism* (London: SCM, 2007).

[389] Morgan, *Span,* 13–14.

[390] Jones, *Trials and Triumphs,* 171–2. See also Carl Simpson, 'Jonathan Paul and The German Pentecostal Movement – The First Seven Years, 1907–1914' *JEPTA* 28/2 (2008), 169–82.

[391] This issue of 'Spirit leading' is a major criticism of some early Pentecostals. The lack of emphasis on theological training and biblical studies is an issue that I find unhelpful and something that has hindered the development of an appropriate Pentecostal theology. This issue has been addressed with a widening of Pentecostal theological institutions and scholarly debate as illustrated by organisations such as The European Pentecostal Theological Association: www.eptaonline.com this website provides links to various Pentecostal theological groups and educational facilities. There is also an increasing library of Pentecostal based theological books available, for example Warrington, *Pentecostal Theology.*

The third major theme which the early Pentecostals carried over from the Revival was that the movement was experiential rather than doctrinal—a fact which partly manifested itself in their style of corporate worship. The meetings during the Revival years were characterised both by liberty in singing and by greater congregational participation. Pentecostals embraced this new-found liberty in worship and encouraged freedom of expression within their assemblies. Some of the Revival meetings, in particular those presided over by Evan Roberts, were characterised by spontaneity in singing and prayer, which at times lasted for several hours, as well as an emphasis on the leading of the Holy Spirit. Roberts allowed some of his meetings to proceed in what may be termed an 'unordered manner' with a desire to see the Holy Spirit lead; often he did not preach at all.[392] But other revival figures held up the necessity of preaching the gospel in order to see the 'sinner converted' through the Holy Spirit working upon the preached Word of God.[393]

As Kay suggests, the links between the Revival of 1904–05 and Pentecostalism in SE Wales must be recognised more in terms of individuals affected by the fervour of the gospel rather than the presence of Pentecostal theology and teaching in that revival. The convergence of the results of the Revival and the importation of Pentecostal theology allowed for certain individuals to continue their spiritual experience following the decline of the fervour of 1904–05.[394] Following the Revival there is a gap of two years until the emergence of Rev. T. M. Jeffreys at Waunlwyd, Ebbw Vale and A. A. Boddy at Sunderland, then another five years to the commencement of events at Crosskeys. However, the vigour of the Welsh Revival lived on in the experiences of those attracted to the new Pentecostal teaching. Bridging the time span between late 1905 revival and the emergence of AoG will be important in tracing the development of the pioneer Pentecostals and their theology and experience. Some of those converted in 1904–05 the so called 'Children of the Revival' were of particular significance within nascent AoG circles.

---

[392] Gibbard, *R. B. Jones,* 148–51, where he relates Jones's dismay over those who did not preach within the Revival meetings. See also Jones, *Rent Heavens*, 49–60.

[393] Gibbard, *R. B. Jones*, 45–68. See also Fielder, *Grace, Grit and Gumption*, who emphasises the biblical ministry of the Joshua brothers.

[394] Gibbard, *Fire on the Altar*, 183–4.

'Children of The Revival'

It is widely accepted by Pentecostal historians such as Gee, Kay, and Massey that the major influence of the Wales Revival 1904–05 upon Pentecostalism was the conversion of significant individuals who were instrumental in establishing the main Pentecostal denominations in Britain.[395] Although this is largely correct, there were other significant streams feeding into the rising Pentecostal and AoG movement. However, in respect of this historically accepted hypothesis, it is necessary to mention some of those principal figures and their rise to prominence. This will require a summary of the lives of two important national figures, namely, Stephen Jeffreys and Donald Gee, as well as one local figure, Tom Mercy of Crosskeys, before turning in the next chapter to other local figures within SE Wales.[396]

Stephen Jeffreys (1876–1943) a native of Nantyffylon, Maesteg, was converted on 20 November 1904 at his home church, Siloh Independent Chapel, Maesteg, through the ministry of Rev. Glasnant Jones.[397] The significance of the Jeffreys family for Pentecostal history centres on the conversions of both Stephen and his brother George. Edward Jeffreys comments:

> If the Jeffreys Brothers only had been converted through the Welsh Revival, it had been worthwhile. Probably only Eternity will reveal the magnitude of their evangelistic efforts.[398]

This significant event in the life of Stephen Jeffreys eventually led him to an evangelistic ministry within the Pentecostal movement that had worldwide repercussions. The influence of the Sunderland outpouring is also seen in Jeffreys' experience, his son Edward recording:

---

[395] Allen, *Unfailing Stream*, 109–12; Kay, *Inside Story,* 11; Richard Massey, *Another Springtime* (Guildford: Highland Books, 1992), 8.

[396] I have dealt with the important contributions of D. Williams (Apostolic) and George Jeffreys (Elim) and do not intend to expand any further on their respective ministries see chapter 1.

[397] E. Jeffreys, *Stephen Jeffreys.* See also Cartwright, *Great Evangelists;* Donald Gee, *These Men I Knew* (Nottingham: AoG, 1980), 52–4; Alfred E. Missen, *The Sound of a Going* (Nottingham: AoG, 1973), 19–23; Gee, *Wind and Flame,* 77–8 , 91–2 and Whittaker, *Seven Pentecostal,* 47–78. There are numerous references to the ministry of Stephen Jeffreys in both *Life of Faith* and *Confidence.*

[398] E. Jeffreys, *Stephen Jeffreys*, 4.

It was spread abroad that the Lord was pouring out His Holy Spirit in Sunderland, and that great things were happening under the ministry of Church of England vicar, A. A. Boddy. Special meetings were arranged in Maesteg, and my father received a mighty experience which he declared was a 'Baptism in the Holy Ghost', accompanied with the speaking of tongues. In that service God was preparing for the "Pentecostal Movement" one of the most powerful evangelists ever known.[399]

Again the influence of A. A. Boddy at Sunderland is significant in the life of emergent Welsh Pentecostalism. Stephen Jeffreys initially accompanied his brother George in the work of Elim, but it was as an independent itinerant evangelist that he is best remembered. Jeffreys continued work as a miner before responding to the call to Christian ministry following his preaching at an evangelistic service held at Cwmtwrch, Swansea in October 1912.[400] He returned to Cwmtwrch in December 1912 and conducted a seven week evangelistic campaign and saw numerous conversions. News of these events reached a wider audience and some significant visitors included Cecil Polhill, Mrs Crisp and Frank Bartleman, all of whom enhanced the relationship between Cwmtwrch and the Pentecostals. Mrs Eleanor Crisp (1856–1923), a native of Devon but residing in London following her marriage to William Crisp, was a well-known Pentecostal in the early years of the movement in Britain. She was the principal of the women's training Home of the PMU in Hackney and was a popular speaker at Pentecostal conventions.[401]

Following these events, Jeffreys received many invitations to preach including at Boddy's Sunderland Convention in 1913.[402] He combined itinerant evangelism with pastoral duties at Island Place Mission, Llanelli. In 1920 Jeffreys conducted a mission at Dowlais and established a church there, becoming the pastor though he still continued to travel widely on evangelistic itineraries. Jeffreys' campaigns were noted for his simple but powerful

---

[399] E. Jeffreys, *Stephen Jeffreys*, 5.

[400] George Griffiths, *What God hath Wrought: A Brief Account Of The History Of The Tro'r Glien Mission Hall, Cwmtwrch On The Occasion Of Its Half-Century Celebrations* (Cwmtwrch: George Griffiths, 1962, 1984).

[401] See Gee, *These Men*, 34–36 and Malcomson, *Pentecostal Pioneers,* 179–86.

[402] *Confidence*, April 1913,p. 74.

preaching and the occurrence of divine healing. The whole issue of divine healing was promoted by the early Pentecostals and is still a major aspect of AoG doctrine and ministry.[403] His reputation as an evangelist grew until in 1921 he was invited to hold a campaign at Horbury Congregational Chapel London by Cecil Polhill, in which many were converted and healed. During these meetings Jeffreys met Donald Gee, who was acting as pianist for the services and commenced a long association with the AoG leader. When AoG was formed in 1924, Stephen Jeffreys was invited to hold campaigns on its behalf and for approximately three years he travelled extensively for that denomination.[404] Following this he embarked upon a worldwide ministry visiting America, South Africa, Australia, and New Zealand. On returning to Britain and with failing health he retired to the seaside town of Porthcawl, where he died on 17 November 1943. Stephen Jeffreys left a lasting legacy especially through his work alongside the AoG, establishing many new assemblies, encouraging growth in others and seeing some of his converts and friends enter full time Christian ministry both at home and abroad. Stephen Jeffreys can certainly be regarded as a significant link between the Welsh Revival of 1904–05 and the emergent Pentecostalism and in particular AoG.

Another vital link between the Welsh Revival of 1904–05 and British AoG was Donald Henry Frere Gee (1891–1966).[405] The son of a London based sign writer, he was converted at Finsbury Park Congregational Church, London, during a visit by the Welsh Revival preacher Seth Joshua in 1905.[406] John Carter records how Joshua's methods were not widely appreciated by the Church and only three people, Gee being one, were converted. R. Tudur Jones

---

[403] David Petts, *Just a Taste of Heaven: A Biblical and Balanced Approach to God's Healing Power* (Mattersey: Mattersey Hall, 2006). See also Donald Gee, *Trophimus I left Sick* (London: Elim, 1952.); F. Martin, 'Healing, Gift of', in *NIDPCM*, 694–98 and R. A. N. Kydd, 'Healing in the Christian Church', in *NIDPCM*, 698–711. John Alexander Dowie (1847–1907) was influential in the area of divine healing through his ministry in Australia, America, and Britain: see Allen, *Unfailing Stream*, 99–101; E. L. Blumhofer, 'Dowie, John Alexander' in *NIDPC*M, 586–7 and Donald Dean Smeeton, 'John Alexander Dowie: An Evaluation', *Paraclete* Spring (1981), 27–31.

[404] E. Jeffreys, *Stephen Jeffreys*, 69–84.

[405] John Carter, *Donald Gee – Pentecostal Statesman*. (Nottingham: AoG, 1975) and Massey, *Another Springtime*, Whittaker, *Seven Pentecostal*, 79–99.

[406] Jones, *Faith and the Crisis*, 348; Gee, *Wind and Flame*, 34 and Massey, *Another Springtime*, 7–8.

records that Gee was 'a Welshman' but in fact he was born and raised in London and his only connection with Wales was through the ministry of Joshua. Following his conversion, Gee joined his mother in attending a Baptist church and it was during this time that Gee's mother was introduced to Pentecostals.[407] Carter further relates how Gee's first contact with the Pentecostal teaching came whilst on holiday on the Isle of Wight in 1912; it was here he first heard the ministry of E. W. Moser of Southsea, an influential figure in early Pentecostalism. Mrs Gee finally convinced a reluctant son to attend the Pentecostal meetings held at the home of American widow Mrs Margaret Cantel, 'Maranatha', in Highbury New Park, London. This served as a Missionary Rest Home, and drew many eager new Pentecostals from London and beyond.[408] Mrs Cantel's home became a centre for the emergent Pentecostal movement in Britain, especially as she received many American Pentecostal missionaries who were passing through London on their journeys to foreign fields. These meetings were often led by Cecil Polhill and it was as a result of these services that in 1913 Gee received his personal baptism in the Spirit, an experience he states revolutionised his Christian life.

> I was in a condition of spiritual ecstasy and taken up wholly with the Lord. For the first time I personally tasted the experience referred to by Paul: 'He that speaketh in an unknown tongue speaketh not unto men but unto God. In the spirit he speaketh mysteries'. (1 Cor 14:2). Increasing glory flooded my soul until I began to speak in new tongues in public. Also I would sing very much in the Spirit in new tongues when the little assembly would be moved in this way by the Holy Spirit during our times of prayer and worship. My whole Christian experience was revolutionised.[409]

This spiritual revolution set Gee on a course of wide service within the Pentecostal movement, though his involvement was initially curtailed by the outbreak of World War 1. Gee, a conscientious objector, was ordered to seek employment of national importance. So he found work on a farm near High Wycombe but continued to propagate the Pentecostal teaching. Following the

---

[407] Carter, *Donald Gee,* 11–15.
[408] Gee, *These Men,* 31–3
[409] Whittaker, *Seven Pentecostal,* 84.

Great War, Gee returned to his occupation of sign writing and during these years continued to preach at various Pentecostal gatherings, eventually entering the Pentecostal ministry at Bonnington Toll Chapel, Leith, Edinburgh in 1920. A gifted musician, Gee served the AoG and wider Pentecostal movement as a pastor, teacher, author, and editor of the magazine *Pentecost* until his death in 1966.[410] He was regarded as a 'statesman' of the AoG denomination on both a national and international level, and due to his balanced biblical approach he received the title, the 'Apostle of Balance'. Walter Hollenweger gives a summary of Gee's involvement in the Pentecostal movement and paid him the compliment of calling him a 'Pentecostal Gentleman'.[411] Donald Gee's ongoing contribution to the AoG and the wider Pentecostal movement came about as a result of a Welsh preacher, deeply involved in the 1904–05 Revival in Wales, preaching in London. Michael Harper wrote a fitting tribute to Donald Gee:

> The Pentecostals should always feel indebted to this great man's major contribution to their movement. He became a world figure, and helped to build the young movement on firm scriptural foundations, a bulwark against the fanaticism which was to ruin some other branches of the Pentecostal movement.[412]

Both Stephen Jeffreys and Donald Gee had significant involvement in the emergent AoG GB&I both as a direct result of contact with the Welsh Revival of 1904–05; their influence is still apparent respectively in the assemblies they helped to establish and in their writings. Although they were converted through the Revival, their Pentecostal theology was not received through the Welsh Revivalist preachers but from subsequent encounters with later Pentecostalism.

Tom Mercy (1883–1935) is a significant local link between the Revival of 1904–05 and AoG in SE Wales.[413] He was born in 1883, his parents being devout

---

[410] Donald Gee,, ed., *Pentecost Magazine 1947–1966,* on CD ROM, (Tony Cauchi, Revival Library: Bishop's Waltham, 2008).

[411] Hollenweger, *Pentecostals*, 208–13.

[412] Michael Harper, 'Donald Gee – A Tribute' in Massey, *Another Springtime.*

[413] Malcomson, *Pentecostal Pioneers,* 345–52.

members of Trinity Congregational Church, Pontywaun; his father Sidney—
who served as a deacon—being involved with the work of the daughter church
(Zion) in Wattsville. Sidney Mercy had been influenced by visits to the
Keswick in Wales Llandrindod Conventions which gave him a greater desire
for more of God. Working in the local coal mine, a job he never resigned even
whilst a pastor, Mercy was converted in the days of the Welsh Revival 1904–05.
Following the revival, he joined with a group who were seeking a deeper
experience of God and meeting in a private house in Wattsville. This situation
had arisen due to the request for them to leave the Congregational church at
Pontywaun, because of their insistence on the doctrine of the Second Coming
of Christ. Eventually this group founded Crosskeys Full Gospel Mission which
later became Crosskeys AoG with Tom Mercy as its first pastor.[414] Mercy's
initial contact with Pentecostalism came during a visit to London in 1914
where he attended a meeting at the Pentecostal home of Mrs Cantel. Upon
returning to Crosskeys, Mercy informed others in the group of Pentecostal
theology and of the 'outpouring' at Sunderland. As a result Mr and Mrs Tom
Hicks of Wattsville travelled to Sunderland and having accepted Spirit baptism
returned and began to propagate this new teaching within the area. Tom
Mercy's contribution to the expanding witness of AoG will be treated in the
next chapter.

Summary

The essential question that remains for the Pentecostal historian is: were there
tendencies, attitudes or influences within the revival movement which were
conducive to the emergence of Pentecostalism in SE Wales? As Gee, Kay and
Blumhofer have shown this was primarily in the conversion of individuals who
became significant leaders in Welsh and British Pentecostalism. However there
were other vital elements that contributed to the growth of the movement and
may have influenced these leaders namely: Keswick teaching, Wesleyan
Holiness, Brethrenism (in particular premillennialism), spontaneity in worship,
and the experiential aspect of the Welsh Revival with a greater emphasis on the
ministry of the Holy Spirit and evangelism.[415]

---

[414] Jones, *How Lovely*, 127–31.
[415] Blumhofer, 'The Welsh Revival 1904–05', 1.

Along with these specific theological emphases there was also the fear that formalism was affecting the mainstream evangelical churches. Although possibly unsophisticated in their theology, Pentecostals endeavoured to preach a simple gospel reflecting clear biblical truths. This may well have attracted some who were dissatisfied with the current trends in Welsh Chapel life. Nigel Wright makes some insightful comments regarding the methods of Evan Roberts and the overall influence of the Welsh Revival on the Principality, stating that one of the major impacts of the revival was the emergence of Pentecostalism.[416] The fact that, although emphasising the ministry of the Holy Spirit, and believing that the initial evidence of Spirit baptism was the receiving of the spiritual gift of tongues, the Pentecostals held to widely accepted evangelical truth, is testimony to their emergence from the existing churches.[417] Hence it seems that the confluence of theological and social streams following on from the Welsh Revival of 1904–05 may well have influenced those involved in Pentecostalism; yet in their own view their movement was simply the result of a divine visitation that enabled people to return to the fervour of the Book of Acts.

R. Tudur Jones correctly summarises this period in Welsh Christianity as complex and turbulent; for despite the hiatus that was the Revival 1904–05, the church struggled with the ravages of war, social, economic challenges and liberal theology.[418] The religious scene in Wales after 1905 became increasingly affected by secularism and soon returned to its previous denominational norm.[419] However the experience of the Pentecostal groups was different as they concentrated on promoting their teaching and experience around the valleys. The early AoG adherents were particularly influential in the mines of SE Wales; their evangelistic zeal manifested itself in personal witness and many were converted even whilst underground. As a result of the ministry among the working classes the theological debates proceeding in the chapels

---

[416] Nigel Wright, 'Does Revival Quicken or Deaden the Church? A Comparison of the 1904 Welsh Revival and John Wimber in the 1980s and 1990s', in Walker, ed., *On Revival*, 121–35.

[417] A review of the Statement of Fundamental Truths of AoG 1924 shows remarkable similarities with the major evangelical denominations in Britain at that time.

[418] Jones, *Faith and the Crisis*, 412–19.

[419] Jones, *Faith and the Crisis*, 368–69.

and colleges of Wales had little impact upon them. Pentecostalism and in particular AoG took root within SE Wales and promoted a particular doctrine of Spirit baptism with the initial evidence of speaking in tongues.

Chapter 4 The Emergence of Pentecostalism in SE Wales

The previous chapter suggested the existence of a combination of streams that were present within Wales influencing those involved in rising Pentecostalism. This chapter will trace the specific Pentecostal influences within Britain that affected SE Wales and led to the establishing of the 'Assemblies of God in Wales and Monmouthshire' (abbreviated to AoG W&Mon). It was this group of churches that was instrumental in initiating the process that led to the formation of AoG in Great Britain and Ireland in 1924.

Tracing the roots of Pentecostalism in SE Wales is a difficult task as the early activity was confined to house groups or cottage meetings with few or no records maintained or preserved.[420] The problem of a lack of primary source material is further compounded by the fact that those involved in the early years have died; much of the information available is, at best, of a secondary nature. Within the local context, two documents written by Price Davies and W. G. Attwood are particularly important.[421] Despite the scarcity of material, some important details relating to the beginnings of Pentecostalism and in particular AoG can be gleaned from local chapel records and some older members who still remember the pioneer leaders.

Commenting on the relationship between the 1904–05 Revival in Wales and Pentecostalism Donald Gee wrote, 'Then came the great Welsh Revival of 1904. It is impossible, and would be historically incorrect, to disassociate the Pentecostal Movement from that remarkable visitation of God.'[422]

Although Gee relates the events of the Welsh Revival 1904–05 to emergent Pentecostalism, he does not provide any supporting evidence for this claim.

---

[420]The Donald Gee Centre contains no reference material of the pre-AoG years regarding the development of the cottage meetings around SE Wales; I have now supplied them with a copy of W. G. Attwood, *How Pentecost Came to Crosskeys* (c. 1940).

[421] Attwood, *How Pentecost* and Price Davies, *A Testimony and a Brief Record of the Beginnings of the Pentecostal Movement in the Merthyr Borough, Bedlinog and the Aberdare Valley*, (c. 1961), <www.dustandashes.com/624.htm>

[422] Gee, *Wind and Flame*, 5. See also Kay, *Inside Story*, 11; Massey, *Another Springtime*, 8; Williams, *Tongues of the Spirit*, 46–71.

His assumption is that the Welsh Revival brought a spirit of expectancy to evangelicals that God could yet do greater things among them: and in his interpretation, that was realised in Pentecostalism.[423] Gee further suggests another important reason that can be added to the streams mentioned in chapter three; namely, that the Pentecostal movement resulted from a direct visitation of God. Although shaped by the various theological influences present during this period, Pentecostals believed that their movement emerged as a direct result of divine intervention within a failing evangelical church. This view would be linked to, and heightened by, events of the 1904–05 Revival which was seen as a judgement on the parlous state of conventional religion at the time. This intervention by a sovereign God provided an escape for those weary of the spiritual decline in their chapels, unhappy with the onset of liberal theology, and dismayed by a social gospel which seemed inimical to true spiritual life. Alfred Missen concurs with Gee's analysis but relates it specifically to Pentecostalism in Wales:

> Undoubtedly the great Welsh revival of 1904 was a stepping stone to the formation of the Pentecostal work in that country.[424]

Missen's support for this claim focuses on those he labels as the 'Sons of Wales,' whose desire to keep the revival fires burning eventually led them into Pentecostalism. T. M. Jeffreys also agrees that the 'Children of the Revival' were a key link between the phenomena of 1904–05 and Pentecostalism. He relates that although some converted in the Revival were seeking an even greater experience of God, the churches had been slowly returning to their pre-Revival condition. Due to this some people began meeting in homes for prayer and Bible study and it was in some of these groups that the teaching on Spirit baptism and tongues was promoted.[425] William Kay and Richard Massey continue this connecting theme by mentioning individuals such as Seth Joshua and 'Children of the Revival' like D. P. Williams, George and Stephen Jeffreys, and Donald Gee.[426] Gee, Massey, Kay, and Missen point to this personal

---

[423] Gee, *Wind and Flame*, 6.

[424] Missen, *Sound of a Going*, 46.

[425] *Confidence,* April, 1909, 'Special Supplement', vol. II, No.4 Report of the Cardiff Easter Convention 1909.

[426] In respect of this dissertation the conversion of Donald Gee is a significant event as he proceeded to be a prominent figure in the AoG denomination until the 1960s. Gee, *Wind and Flame* and Massey, *Another Springtime.*

influence of these 'Children of the Revival' rather than specific theological views as the significant link between the Revival of 1904–05 and Pentecostalism. However as mentioned in the previous chapter, it is impossible to separate the 'Children of the Revival' from theology as it was a specific doctrinal stance that helped shape the religious world that nurtured embryonic Pentecostalism.

Embryonic Pentecostalism in Britain

Thomas Ball Barratt (1862–1940), an Englishman resident in Norway, is regarded as the 'Apostle' of European Pentecostalism and was largely responsible for its promotion in the early twentieth century.[427] Barratt had visited America where he received what he regarded as a post-conversion experience of the baptism in the Holy Spirit in 1906, and returning to Scandinavia he began to promote the new teaching. Consequently, Boddy visited Norway in order to hear Barratt and his teaching; he then invited him to Sunderland with the result being Boddy's acceptance of the Pentecostal theology and experience. Boddy's influence was particularly significant between 1907 and 1914, especially through the annual Whitsun Conventions in Sunderland and the publication of the journal, *Confidence.*

Barratt, Polhill, Boddy and Sunderland

T. B. Barratt was born in Albaston, Cornwall, England; his mining family emigrated to Norway in 1867. Barratt began preaching at the age of 17 within the Methodist Episcopal Church of Norway; in 1902 he founded the Oslo City Mission. Barratt eventually established the Filadelphia Church in Oslo which he pastored until his death in 1940. In 1905–06 Barratt travelled to New York in search of funding for the new City Mission; whilst there he heard of events at Azusa Street and, although he never visited the revival centre, he received his personal Pentecostal Spirit baptism. Enlivened by this experience, he

---

[427] David Bundy, 'Thomas Ball Barratt: From Methodist to Pentecostal', *JEPTA* 13 (1994), 19–49. D. D. Bundy, 'Barratt, Thomas Ball' in *NIDPCM,* 365–6, T. B. Barratt, 'The Gift Of Tongues: What Is It? Being a Reply to Dr. A. C. Dixon' (Kristiana, Norway, June 20th 1914), available from <www.revival-library.org> David Bundy, 'Spiritual Advice to a Seeker: Letters to T. B. Barratt from Azusa Street 1906', *Pneuma* 14:2 (1992), and T. B. Barratt, 'How Pentecost Came to Great Britain in 1907', *Redemption Tidings* (Oct. 1933), 3.

returned to Norway—with no money, but having experienced a deep sense of spiritual renewal—and commenced a Pentecostal ministry. David Bundy supplies interesting information on T. B. Barratt suggesting his Methodist roots, contact with the 'Higher Life' teaching, and with Evan Roberts, allowed him to accept more readily the Pentecostal influence discovered in America in 1906.[428] Barratt spread the Pentecostal message to England through his contact with A. A. Boddy at Sunderland. Wakefield sums up this connection when he writes:

> News of the events in Azusa Street in 1906 and then in Oslo in early 1907 reached Boddy and in March 1907, he visited Barratt's meetings in Oslo for four days.[429]

Barratt's eventual visit to All Saints, Monkwearmouth in 1907, coupled with Boddy's experiences in Wales in 1904 and the outworking of Azusa Street ushered in the Pentecostal movement to Britain. The relationship between Barratt and Boddy is the vital link to the importation of Pentecostal doctrine to Britain. Upon his arrival in Sunderland Barratt commenced a seven week preaching and teaching ministry at All Saints Parish Church; it was during this period that much of the Pentecostal thinking was formed in the mind of Boddy. Boddy's theology of tongues will be discussed later.[430]

Amongst the significant individuals who formed part of the chain of events linking Britain and America, was Cecil H. Polhill (1860–1938), one of the 'Cambridge Seven', who became the first major promoter of Pentecostal missions in Britain.[431] The Cambridge Seven emerged from Cambridge University under the leadership of C. T. Studd and joined with the China Inland Mission in 1885. Due to health reasons Polhill returned to his native England from missionary work in China in 1908; en-route he visited Azusa

---

[428] Bundy, 'Thomas Ball Barratt: From Methodist to Pentecostal'.

[429] Gavin Wakefield, *Alexander Boddy Pentecostal Anglican Pioneer* (London: Paternoster, 2007), 81.

[430] Alexander Boddy, 'A Vicar's Testimony,' 11; Tony Cauchi, *The Works of Alexander Boddy* on CD ROM (Bishop's Waltham: Revival Library, 2010).

[431] John Pollock, *The Cambridge Seven* (Fearn: Christian Focus, 2006); Cecil Robeck, Jr. *The Azusa Street Mission and Revival* (Nashville, TN: Nelson, 2006), 288–9. See also John Usher, 'The Significance of Cecil H. Polhill for the Development of Early Pentecostalism', *JEPTA* 29/2 (2009), 36–60 and Leigh Goodwin, 'The Pneumatological Motivation and Influences of the Cambridge Seven' *JEPTA* 30/2 (2010), 21–38. D. Hocken, 'Polhill, Cecil, H.' in *NIDPCM*, 991–2.

Street where he received his personal Pentecostal Spirit baptism. Polhill's involvement at the Azusa Street Mission is witnessed by his particularly generous financial donation to the sum of £1500 that helped clear the debt on the building.[432] Arriving back in England, Polhill linked up with Boddy at Sunderland and with his inherited wealth established the Pentecostal Missionary Union (PMU). Polhill was the main benefactor of early British Pentecostal mission; the PMU eventually merged with the AoG in 1925.[433] Boddy and Polhill, encouraged by Barratt, were the driving force behind Pentecostalism in Britain. There were other very influential future leaders who visited Sunderland such as T. H. Mundell (d. 1934), Henry Mogridge (1854–1931), Ernest W. Moser (1865–1950), Norwegian sailor Eilif Beruldsen, and Arthur Booth-Clibborn (1855–1939) along with his son William (1893–1969). Two figures who would become prominent in AoG may also be added to this list—Howard Carter (1891–1971) and John Carter (1893–1981). There can be no doubt of the wide-ranging influence which Boddy had on the early Pentecostal movement.[434]

However, not all the emerging Pentecostals were impressed with Boddy; W. F. P. Burton was scathing in his attack on Boddy for his unwillingness to leave the Anglican Church. Garrard makes this assessment of Burton's view of the links with Boddy and the PMU, recording Burton's words: 'I unhesitatingly deny that Pastor Boddy is an Elder in the Church of God'.[435] Burton insisted that, for him, a truly Pentecostal Spirit filled believer would have to leave the established Church of England since it was not (he said) a true model of what the Church should be. This would perhaps be a difficult issue to approach

---

[432] Robeck, *Azusa Street*, 289.

[433] Peter Kay, 'The Pentecostal Missionary Union and the Fourfold Gospel with Baptism in the Holy Spirit and Speaking in Tongues: A New Power for Missions?' *JEPTA* 19 (1999), 89–104; D. Hocken, 'Pentecostal Missionary Union', in *NIDPCM*, 970–1.

[434] See Neil Hudson, 'The Earliest Days of British Pentecostalism', *JEPTA* 21 (2001), 49–67; Donald Gee, *These Men I Knew* (Nottingham: AOG, 1980), 17–19, 64–66; Keith Malcomson *Pentecostal Pioneers Remembered* (Xulon Press, 2008), 139–49, 151–65; and William Booth Clibborn, *The Baptism in the Holy Spirit: A Personal Testimony,* (Portland, OR: Ryder, 1936). A testimony from Mrs. Beruldsen is recorded regarding Boddy's visit to Edinburgh in January 1908, *Confidence,* April, 1908, 5.

[435] David J. Garrard, 'Burton's Early Years of Ministry and Doctrine under the auspices of the PMU', *JEPTA* 32/1 (2012), 3–14.

today, especially since the 'Charismatic Renewal' from the 1970s which has invaded both Anglican and Catholic churches.[436]

The Apostolic Faith magazine published by Seymour at Azusa Street contains much information as to the spread of the Pentecostal experience of tongues around the world. A letter received in March 1907 illustrates how the movement was growing in London:

23 Gairloch Road, Camberwell, SE London, Jan. 20: A little band of Christians have been waiting here about nine months for their Pentecost and am glad to say that one sister has received her Pentecost with tongues. Praise Him! Will you continue to pray that all may receive, the writer included. I feel very hungry. Yours in Jesus Christ, C. H. Hook.[437]

Rev. A. A. Boddy traces early Pentecostalism in Britain to some five or six personal acquaintances scattered throughout the country that had experienced the gift of tongues but sadly he does not provide the biographical details.[438] *Confidence* records the first alleged instance of Pentecostal Spirit baptism and links it to the experiences of the Welsh Revival:

TUESDAY AUGUST 8TH, 11 A.M. Rev. T. Hackett (Church of Ireland) said that very day, August 8th, was the anniversary of his first visit to Heathfield, at the August Convention of 1907, he was first brought into direct contact with this wonderful work of God, and met the one (Mrs Price, of Brixton) first thus visited by our God in England. He gave a most interesting account of her experience, when in January, 1907, heart being deeply stirred by the Welsh Revival and the manifestation of the Spirit in speaking in tongues in Los Angeles, U.S.A, April, 1906. She, her husband, and a friend had been seeking the Lord in united prayer each evening for a full outpouring of the blessed Spirit. An address in Holborn Hall by a Welsh speaker upon 1 Thess v., 23–24, brought the

---

[436] Andrew Walker and Kristin Aune, eds., *On Revival A Critical Examination* (Carlisle: Paternoster, 2003), 171–251 for interesting insights into modern revival phenomena.

[437] *Apostolic Faith*, March 1907, 5.

[438] Cauchi, *Works of Alexander Boddy* on CD ROM. See also Hudson, 'The Earliest Days of British Pentecostalism', and Gavin Wakefield, 'The Human Face of Pentecostalism: Why the British Pentecostal Movement began in the Sunderland Parish of the Church of England Vicar Alexander Boddy,' *JEPTA* 28/2 (2008), 158–68; William Kay, 'Sunderland's Legacy in the New Denominations,' *JEPTA* 28/2 (2008), 183–99.

matter to a crisis. At the close she said, sadly enough to the speaker, 'I do not see I am much further on', though for years she had experienced heart-cleansing and holiness. 'Sister', was the reply, 'Faithful is He that calleth YOU, Who also will do it'. It was a living word from God to her soul. That night in her home the Spirit fell, and she was speaking and singing in tongues; and again the following forenoon, and in the evening in a large meeting at the Lewisham Hall, under the power of the Spirit she found herself speaking in tongues, while on every side men and women were on their faces seeking their God.[439]

This apparent first record of a Pentecostal type Spirit baptism was encouraged due to the experiences of the Welsh Revival and news from Azusa Street. The reported instances of such occurrences steadily grew, leading eventually to the denominational distinctive associated with AoG. Rev. Thomas Hackett (1850–1939) was a graduate of Trinity College Dublin and served as a curate in the Church of Ireland.[440] By 1903 Hackett was disappointed with his life's ministry and sought a deeper experience of God; his search led him to Switzerland. It was here that Hackett was deeply affected by the holiness ministry of Rev. Labilliere who later became a propagator of the Pentecostal teaching.[441] Following his experience in Switzerland, by 1907 Hackett had heard of, and initially rejected the Pentecostal message, but soon changed and embraced the message of initial evidence. Following visits to Boddy at Sunderland, Hackett took the Pentecostal message to Ireland and became a regular preacher at Pentecostal conventions.

By April 1908, Boddy records that the number of people experiencing tongues had risen to approximately five hundred.[442] Unfortunately, Boddy does not

---

[439] *Confidence,* August 1910, 20–25; and *Confidence*, Oct. 1916, 11. See also Desmond Cartwright, 'From the Backstreets of Brixton to the Royal Albert Hall: British Pentecostalism 1907–1928', *European Pentecostal Theological Association,* (Leuven, Belgium, December 1981), 1 <www.smithwigglesworth.com/pensketches/brixton.htm>

[440] Malcomson, *Pentecostal Pioneers,* 160–2 and James Robinson, *Pentecostal Origins Early Pentecostalism in Ireland in the Context of the British Isles* (Milton Keynes: Paternoster, 2005), 108–19.

[441] Rev. Labilliere of Switzerland remained involved with the Pentecostal Movement as is seen by his entry in *Confidence*, August 1909, 16.

[442] *Confidence,* April 1908, 3.

supply either the names or locations of any of these people. However, the April 1908 edition of *Confidence* records Pentecostal activity in South Wales at Waunlwyd (T. M. Jeffreys), Bridgend (Pastor W. G. H.) and Port Talbot (F. Williams), though no further biographical information is made available.[443] The initial growth of British Pentecostalism was slow but Boddy credits the Welsh Revival as having an influence on the birth of the Pentecostal movement. *Confidence* records Boddy's assessment of 1904–05:

> Indeed he [Boddy] cannot tell the story of the beginning of this Pentecostal outpouring without many personal references, or without telling how the Welsh Revival prepared the way in Sunderland, and made hearts more hungry for the Living God.[444]

As with Gee and Missen, Boddy suggests that the events in Wales 1904–05 were the preparation for the arrival of Pentecostalism and the baptism in the Holy Spirit. Boddy later relates the importance of the Welsh Revival as the time of widespread conversion prior to the arrival of the Spirit, linking it to the account in Acts 10 – a pivotal account for Pentecostals.[445] Hence Boddy supports the Pentecostal paradigm of subsequence i.e. conversion and separate Spirit baptism.[446] The wave of conversions that took place in 1904–05 produced an intense sense of expectancy; this period of spiritual preparation was viewed as the first blessing within a two blessing paradigm of conversion and Spirit baptism. Boddy returned to Sunderland in 1904 with a greater zeal to see people converted and, once converted, seeking after a greater experience of God through the essential ministry of the Holy Spirit.

Any possible links between the Welsh Revival and the rise of Pentecostalism is summarised by Pastor T. M. Jeffreys: 'It was like the days of the Welsh Revival. All the fervour, but more of the Spirit than in those marvellous gatherings.

---

[443] *Confidence,* April 1908, 13–15.

[444] *Confidence*, August 1910, 20–1.

[445] See also Acts 1:4–8, 2:1–13, 19:1–6, which Pentecostals rely on to support their doctrinal stance. For an AoG perspective on this issue see: Harold Horton, *The Gifts of the Spirit*, (Nottingham: AoG, 1934), David Petts, *Body Builders: Gifts to Make God's People Grow*,(Mattersey: Mattersey Hall, 2002) and David Petts, *The Holy Spirit: An Introduction* (Mattersey: Mattersey Hall, 1998).

[446] A. A. Boddy, *Pentecost for England, (and other lands) With Signs following.* (Sunderland: Boddy, 1907) available from <www.revival-library.org> see also A. A. Boddy, 'A Vicar's Testimony'.

Again and again we sang, with right hand uplifted, and then with Bibles held high.'[447]

Jeffreys further suggests that the Pentecostal outpourings placed a greater emphasis upon the ministry of the Spirit, which he later develops in line with Boddy's teaching on tongues and gifts. It is difficult to assess whether this statement is a fair comparison, as the two events had very different emphases. The 1904–05 Revival was a period of evangelistic fervour when many were converted, whereas the Pentecostal outpourings around SE Wales were occurring within already established congregations: churches, chapels, and cottage meetings. The fervour may well have been dramatic, and some of the worship similar, but the overall purpose was distinctly different; the former being evangelistic and the latter representing a change of theological and experiential emphasis. In respect to the freedom in worship experienced in Pentecostal meetings, Jeffreys offers some words of caution, especially in regard to the people of Wales. His concern is that as an 'emotional race' the Welsh could easily take the freedom of the Pentecostals and allow it to become licence. Jeffreys further states that definite teaching on the order, as well as the liberty, of the Spirit was essential.[448] This attitude is also supported by another *Confidence* correspondent, a Mr Andrews of Swansea. He asks people to pray for a greater work of the Spirit than in the Revival, and indicates that the sign of tongues was becoming the major issue drawing disparate groups together around S. Wales.[449] Jeffreys certainly saw a connection between the Welsh Revival and emergent Pentecostalism in SE Wales. As with Boddy, he interpreted the Revival in terms of the spiritual preparation of individuals who were seeking a greater experience of God.

It has been noted that it was 1907 before Britain experienced this new theology via A. A. Boddy and his contact with T. B. Barratt. It was indicated in chapter 1 that Charles Fox Parham (1901), the events at Azusa Street (1906), and complimented by the ministry of Boddy in Sunderland (1907–1926), were the

---

[447] *Confidence,* June 1908, 20.
[448] *Confidence,* April, 1909, 'Special Supplement', Vol. II, No.4 report from the Easter Convention Cardiff 1909.
[449] *Confidence*, April 1910, 22.

main sources of Pentecostal teaching. Boddy adopted this new teaching and his purpose in disseminating it is summarised as follows:

> We are learning to put the Gifts in their right place. To look to the Giver far more than to His gifts. To honour Jesus, to keep closer and closer to His Word. To detect the flesh in some extravagances, in some messages, in some manifestations, but to go forward fearlessly and to exalt Jesus far above all. [450]

Boddy desired to interpret the Bible in that contemporary situation for the benefit of people and believed a return to New Testament gifts was a reality for all who would seek them. Here Boddy states an important principle which is often overlooked in the critique of historical Pentecostalism. Boddy's desire was clearly for the movement's teaching to be centred on Christ, the giver of the gifts, and not solely on the spectacular. He saw this as important to avoid the abuse of spiritual freedoms.

As well as illustrating the growth of Pentecostalism in Britain, *Confidence* also contains an early indication of further links between Boddy and America. This link is in the form of a 'Pentecostal Manifesto' drawn up by pastors, teachers, and evangelists in Ohio, USA, in June 1908 and records the basis for future Pentecostal Missions practice. [451] This five point manifesto is interesting in that it does not encourage the formation of separate Pentecostal denominations, yet accepts the necessity of an 'affiliation of Pentecostal Missions', this being similar to the emergence of the PMU from Sunderland.

Other important issues to arise from the manifesto were: a necessity to prepare for overseas ministry through Bible study and practical work. This would allow for those who had previously accepted xenolalia as a gift of 'missionary tongues' (only to become disillusioned by their experiences in foreign lands) to properly prepare for service. An essential reference is also made to the accountability of all Pentecostal missionaries to their home or sending church, hence discouraging 'rogue' false apostles or teachers. All Pentecostal missionaries were to be well grounded in the faith and not to be novices, so that they might discern false teaching where it arose. The manifesto is one of

---

[450] *Confidence,* June 1908, 4.

[451] *Confidence,* August 1908, 9, see Appendix 3.

sensible, biblical application which sought to avert the embryonic Pentecostal movement from possible spiritual disaster. Boddy was impressed by this manifesto and utilized it within his own ministry as reference to the formation of the PMU in 1909 will substantiate.[452] The American influence is also briefly highlighted in the case of Annie Griffiths of Merthyr Tydfil who was healed of 'Tuberculosis Hop'.[453] As a result of this divine healing, she became interested in all things Pentecostal and from c. 1908 was receiving Pentecostal publications from Spokane USA, illustrating and recording the 'large numbers' who were receiving the Pentecostal baptism.[454]

Further American influence is highlighted by Boddy who was particularly thankful for the support of Mr and Mrs Emery of Akron, Ohio, and Rev. and Mrs J. Mead of 'America' for their input in establishing the Pentecostal testimony in Sunderland.[455] Again, one is conscious of the importation of Pentecostal teaching from America being disseminated throughout Britain by Boddy via *Confidence*, the annual Sunderland conventions and his many publications.[456]

Boddy was a prolific writer and published many small pamphlets and leaflets which were freely available to the public via his office in Sunderland. An example of this was a pamphlet entitled *Pentecost for England (and other lands) With Signs Following*.[457] It was through publications like this that Boddy and his associates promoted and explained the teaching on such subjects as the baptism of the Holy Spirit, speaking in tongues, and charismata. Boddy was not hesitant in distributing the Pentecostal testimony around Britain and, with time, his magazines and pamphlets received a worldwide readership. The development of Pentecostal theology and practice was largely due to Boddy's unceasing labours in Sunderland. According to

---

[452] *Confidence*, January 1909, 13–16 contains the initial statement on the formation of the PMU see also Wakefield, *Alexander Boddy*, 135–55.

[453] An illness that restricted her ability to walk.

[454] Davies, *Testimony*, chapter 5.

[455] Boddy, 'A Vicar's Testimony', 8–9.

[456] Mark Cartledge, 'The Early Pentecostal Theology of *Confidence* Magazine (1908–1926): A Version of the Five-Fold Gospel'? *JEPTA* 28/2 (2008), 117–30.

[457] Boddy, *Pentecost for England*.

Wakefield, Boddy was not an 'exceptional theologian' but endeavoured to formulate a framework for Pentecostal theology and practice.[458] Any reading of Boddy's literature reveals a more pastoral and experiential application of truth rather than deep theological debate and exegesis.[459] In his booklet entitled *Pentecost for England (and other lands) With Signs Following*, Boddy states that the experience of tongues is biblical and that it is to be viewed as 'peculiarly and exclusively a Pentecostal sign'. As a result of experiencing the baptism of the Spirit, a believer was encouraged to expect physical manifestations based upon texts such as Acts 5:36 (*sic* – Acts 4:31) and that the baptism is but one of the manifestations of the Spirit.[460] Boddy's call to his readers is that:

> Pentecost is to be sought: diligently, fervently, trustfully, as the heart may be free to it. 'In the day thou seekest me with all they heart I will be found of thee'. 'And the Lord whom you seek shall suddenly come to his Temple'.[461]

Boddy further emphasises that Pentecost is a vital enduement to assist in the service of God; power to witness and work was a paramount reason for Boddy's encouragement to seek Spirit baptism. Boddy was also careful to teach the necessity of holiness of life and the growth of spiritual fruit as well as the essential nature of Spirit baptism. For him, the gifts and fruit of the Spirit were complimentary manifestations. However, his framework was based upon the centrality of Christ and allowed for a development of spiritual experience through tongues, charismata, and healing. Boddy also supported the essential Pentecostal aspect of the imminent return of Christ which motivated him to exercise a wide influence upon Pentecostal world mission. Despite his wide influence upon the development of Pentecostal theology and practice, Boddy himself never joined any of the new Pentecostal denominations but remained

---

[458] Wakefield, *Alexander Boddy*, 156–90 and Cauchi, *Works of Alexander Boddy*.

[459] Boddy, *Pentecost for England*.

[460] Boddy, *Pentecost for England*, 6, the reference to Acts 5:36 appears to be a misprint in the text; I suggest it should read Acts 4:31.

[461] Boddy, *Pentecost for England*, 12.

an Anglican until his death in 1930.[462] It was his desire for all Christians to receive, and enjoy, the fuller Pentecostal-type baptism of the Holy Spirit.

SE Wales, T. M. Jeffreys and Waunlwyd

The presence of Pentecostal activity in SE Wales can be traced to the influential ministry of Rev. Thomas Madoc Jeffreys (c. 1878–1950) at Tabernacle Congregational Church, Waunlwyd, Ebbw Vale. Jeffreys—no relation to George and Stephen Jeffreys—was married to Ann Margretta and they had one daughter, Lilian Margretta, born in 1904. Jeffreys became aware of the events in Sunderland and visited Boddy in 1907, returning to Wales with 'Pentecost'. The slow spread of the Pentecostal message is highlighted by the recipients of *Confidence* with the first record of copies being sent to T. M. Jeffreys in Ebbw Vale in April 1908. Jeffreys welcomed the arrival of *Confidence,* stating in a letter to Boddy:

> I am very glad to learn that you have been led to issue The "Confidence." Its pages will provide a meeting place where many of us who are separated by wide distances, but truly joined in one Spirit, can unite in mutually distributing our experiences, and thus greatly encourage each other in this blessed struggle to regain the lost gifts of the Church.[463]

Jeffreys relates how the availability of *Confidence* would allow people drawn to Pentecostalism to be united by its regular updates and teaching. In the first issue, Jeffreys states how his church in Waunlwyd had been deeply affected by the Welsh Revival and had endeavoured to carry on the fervour of that visitation of God through evangelism, prayer, and practical ministry in the community. The Pentecostal teaching and experience was embraced by this congregation as they saw in it a return to that religious expectancy they had tasted in 1904–05. It was also their desire that through this new teaching, the

---

[462] Kay, 'Sunderland's legacy in new denominations', see also Cornelius van der Laan, 'Alexander Boddy: Anglican Father of Dutch Pentecostalism', *JEPTA* 31/1 (2011), 93–110 and Robinson, *Pentecostal Origins* who traces the wider impact of Boddy in Europe and particularly in Ireland.

[463] *Confidence,* April, 1908, 13.

'lost gifts' of the church could be regained in their quest for a return to New Testament Christianity.

Endeavouring to establish an initial link between SE Wales and emergent Pentecostalism, J. Edwin Orr agrees with Jeffreys and correctly points to the visit of American Ansel Howard Post (1850–1931) to Waunlwyd in 1907.[464] Post preached in Waunlwyd at the invitation of Jeffreys, and this was a major factor that led to Pentecostalism taking root in SE Wales.[465] These early experiences are recorded by T. M. Jeffreys in a report in the first edition of *Confidence* magazine:

> The definite seeking for Baptismal Fullness began as a result of a Mission conducted by Pastor Niblock, of Aston, in November last. He very faithfully and boldly taught the Pentecostal Blessing, though he himself had not, at that time, received the definite Baptism, but subsequently he went to Sunderland (God ever bless Sunderland!) and returned with the gift of the Holy Ghost, accompanied by the Sign of Tongues ... Bro. Niblock, together with Bro. A. H. Post, of Los Angeles (now at Colombo, Ceylon), were greatly used in guiding and counselling us, and ever since December 1st we have pressed on, holding tarrying meetings nightly.[466]

H. Post, a former Baptist minister, came into contact with Pentecostalism at Azusa Street where he received his personal baptism in the Holy Spirit in 1906. Along with his wife, Henrietta, Post became an independent Pentecostal pioneer missionary to India and Sri Lanka (1907–14). In 1914 they joined the Assemblies of God USA and travelled to Egypt in 1916. It was during his early journey, en route to India, that Post visited Britain and made an initial short visit to Waunlwyd on 22 December 1907. He was accompanied by Mr Alexander Moncur Niblock (1876–1951) of London and they promoted the Pentecostal teaching. Niblock was the principal of the first PMU Bible School

---

[464] E. J. Gitre, 'Post, Ansel, Howard' in *NIDPCM*, 994 and Robeck, *Azusa Street*, 95, 205–10, 243 for a further examination of early Pentecostal missionary activity. See also Allan Anderson, *Spreading Fires* (London: SCM, 2007).

[465] Orr, 'The Welsh Revival Goes Worldwide', *Western Mail*, Dec. 9th 1974. See also Gee, *Wind and Flame*, 34–7 and *Confidence*.

[466] *Confidence*, April 1908, 13, this early article also contains reports of Pentecostal occurrences in Port Talbot and Bridgend.

in London which opened in July 1909. After serving within British Pentecostal circles fulfilling a largely itinerant ministry, Niblock eventually settled in New Zealand entering the Anglican ministry. He died at his home in New Plymouth, Taranaki, New Zealand in March 1951.[467] The official PMU training school was soon moved to Preston under the guidance of Thomas Myerscough (1858–1932) and produced a number of Pentecostal pioneer missionaries, most notable among them being W. F. P. Burton, Jimmy Salter and Teddy Hodgson.[468] A further Bible school was opened by Cecil Polhill in London, in October 1913.[469]

A result of Post's visit to Waunlwyd was the instigation of nightly 'tarrying' or 'waiting' meetings which were a regular feature of Pentecostal assemblies; it was during these meetings that individuals would wait or tarry for the baptism in the Spirit. This practice was seen as a continuation of the command of Jesus to his disciples as recorded in Acts 1:4 to wait in Jerusalem for the promised Spirit. At this time, Pastor T. M. Jeffreys received his personal Spirit baptism and launched into a Pentecostal ministry that saw him work closely with Boddy, Polhill, and the PMU.[470] *Confidence* records the experience of Jeffreys and others in Waunlwyd hence emphasising the pivotal role of Waunlwyd in the spread of Pentecostalism:

> The Lord, very graciously, did not keep us waiting long. I had a prophecy given me concerning the time when heaven's blessing would descend (Dan ix., 23: x., 13), and surely, on December 22nd, at a wonderful praise meeting held in my study, the Holy Ghost fell upon Bro. John Jones (now one of my deacons), and the temple was filled. I do praise God for thus greatly honouring our dwelling place. I think we can say that, here, Pentecost first broke out in Wales. Since then, glorious experiences, too many to attempt to describe, have been ours,

---

[467] Gee, *Wind and Flame*, 61; William K. Kay, *Pentecostals in Britain* (Carlisle: Paternoster, 2000), 17; *Confidence*, April 1908, 13–14; and Colin Whittaker, *Seven Pentecostal Pioneers* (Basingstoke: Marshalls, 1983), 49 <www.anglicanhistory.org/nz/blain_directory>

[468] David Womersley and David Garrard, eds., *Into Africa* (Preston: Central Africa Mission, 2005), 25–32.

[469] Gee, *Wind and Flame*, 62–3; *Flames of Fire*, October 1913; Malcomson, *Pentecostal Pioneers*, 167–77. The AoG training centre is now located at Mattersey Hall, Mattersey, Doncaster, England.

[470] Robeck Jr., *Azusa Street*, 204–8, 243.

and now, seven in all (including myself, Hallelujah!) have definitely received the Pentecostal Baptism with the sign of Tongues.[471]

Jeffreys believed that Waunlwyd was the location of the first Pentecostal activity in Wales and there is no evidence to counter his claims. Following this, events at Waunlwyd continued to give impetus to the emergence and consolidation of Pentecostalism in SE Wales. The prominence of Barratt, Boddy, Niblock, and Post suggests greater evidence of the importation of Pentecostal theology from the USA and England. However, Waunlwyd served as the catalyst for the proclamation of the Pentecostal testimony in Wales. Jeffreys records how people had visited his Congregational church from Maesycwmmer, Dowlais, Abertillery, and Merthyr in order to experience a personal baptism in the Spirit; one such visitor was Mr Fry of the Salvation Army Corps at Cwm, and another being Rev. David Price of Maesteg.[472]

Another significant visitor to Waunlwyd, and a man who became very influential in the spread of Pentecostalism, was Price Davies (1881–1966).[473] Price Davies was born and raised in Dowlais and attended Calvaria Welsh Presbyterian Church, Caeharris, Dowlais. He had worked at various local coal mines by 1904, eventually finding employment at Nixon's Navigation Colliery, Mountain Ash. During this period he was affected by the Welsh Revival, and was converted on 21 November 1904 at Bethlehem Chapel, Mountain Ash through the ministry of Evan Roberts. Following his conversion, Davies had a deep desire for a greater experience of God and this eventually led him to Waunlwyd and the Pentecostal ministry of Jeffreys. Upon his return to Dowlais, he began a Pentecostal work and entered on a ministry within the Pentecostal movement, serving in: Dowlais, Aberaman, Six Bells, Abertillery, Aberbeeg, Builth Wells, Penrhiwceiber, and, for a short time, in Talke, Stoke on Trent, before his retirement after a period as pastor of Ystrad Rhondda AoG in 1952.[474] The recollections of Price Davies emphasises the role played by Post and Niblock, coupled to dramatic healings in the growth of Pentecostalism in

---

[471] *Confidence,* April 1908, 14

[472] *Confidence,* May 1908, 10; *Confidence,* August 1910, 24 and Malcomson, *Pentecostal Pioneers,* 159.

[473] Davies, *A Testimony,* ch. 5.

[474] Davies, *A Testimony,* ch. 5.

south Wales.[475] Davies also had an influence in the Tonypandy area as a result of interaction with George Vale (b. 1876) who became the first pastor of that Mission Hall; Tonypandy could be considered amongst the first future AoG assemblies established in Wales c. 1910. The influence of Davies also reached to Gorseinon, when Vale moved to pastor the new work there c. 1911–12. Davies further relates how the Vale's home, as well as the churches, became a centre for Pentecostal testimony.[476] It is of interest that Tonypandy is not listed in the 1924 AoG Constitution, neither is the assembly at Gorseinon. This is despite the fact that Gee states these assemblies were in embryo by 1908 due to the influence of Jeffreys at Waunlwyd and the afterglow of the Revival of 1904–05. Further growth came at Bedlinog, Sirhowy, Beaufort, and Brynmawr as a result of the influence of Price Davies. Whilst ministering at Six Bells and Aberbeeg, Davies had contact with Tom Mercy of Crosskeys and Leonard Jenkins (b. 1890) of Crosskeys and Newbridge. He also utilised the ministry of Crosskeys based evangelist Billy Lewis c. 1923.

The assemblies at Aberbeeg, Aberaman, Bedlinog, Penrhiwceiber, and Ystrad Rhondda were all initial signatories to the first AoG Constitution in 1924, Price Davies being listed as pastor of the Aberbeeg group. George Vale of Gorseinon was present at the initial 1922 meeting of prospective AoG churches. Although he is not listed on the 1924 document, along with his son Garfield (b. 1900), a missionary to India and Congo, Vale had a significant influence upon later AoG in South Wales. However important the influence of Price Davies may have been, his initial encounter with Pentecostalism came at Waunlwyd on Easter Monday 1908 through the ministry of Jeffreys, Post, and Niblock.[477] Following Gee's position, Hudson refers to the important role of both Waunlwyd and Gorseinon in the early days of Welsh Pentecostalism. However, unlike Gee, he does not comment on the central role played by the emergent congregation at Crosskeys.[478]

---

[475] A. A. Boddy also held to the teaching of divine healing following the experience of his wife who was healed from chronic asthma; see Boddy, 'A Vicar's Testimony' 6–7.

[476] Davies, A Testimony and Gee, Wind and Flame, 34–6, 66–7 Gee indicates that Tonypandy became a centre for Pentecostal power in Wales. The assembly is still functioning at Tonypandy <www.livingwaychurch.org>

[477] Davies, Testimony, Chapter 5.

[478] Hudson, 'The Earliest Days of British Pentecostalism', 65.

The Spreading Fire: Pentecostalism Spreads

In order to understand how the Pentecostal message spread across Wales, it is interesting to study the locations of subscribers to *Confidence*. Its circulation in Wales gradually increased and it became more influential throughout the Principality. The early influence of *Confidence* in Wales is seen from the December issue of 1908 which contains an entry regarding copies posted to Nelson and by October 1909 recipients were located in Cwmfelin, Abertillery, and Abergavenny. By 1910 there were eighteen recognised Pentecostal centres around South Wales; these centres were Waunlwyd, Tonypandy, Pen-y-groes, Pontarddulais, Pen-y-graig, Clydach Vale, Aberkenfig, Maesteg, Cross Hands, Llandeilo, Mountain Ash, Grovesend, Ammanford, Cwmtwrch, Dowlais, Llwynhendy, Port Talbot, and Aberaeron. In respect to this research, only one—Waunlwyd—was recognised as being in SE Wales, the other locations being further west.[479] According to Desmond Cartwright, by 1912 this group of eighteen Pentecostal centres no longer contained Waunlwyd, although T. M. Jeffreys still had contact with the PMU and Boddy after 1912.[480] Cartwright may not be correct in his assumption as there are numerous references to *Confidence* being supplied to Waunlwyd after 1912. However, this may not have been Waunlwyd Congregational chapel but other Pentecostal supporters in the village.[481] This supposed lack of further references to Waunlwyd may well be due to the fact that Jeffreys became actively involved with the PMU, travelling to Armenia and Greece. Following a service at Peniel, London on 28 June 1910, Jeffreys made a missionary visit to Armenia where he endeavoured to preach the gospel and expound Pentecostal doctrine.[482]

The propagation of the new Pentecostal message was very much a driving force of the PMU and this is substantiated by articles in the first two editions of its journal, *Flames of Fire*. Within these articles, the basis for the belief in a baptism of the Holy Spirit and fire is established, this is the message that

---

[479] *Confidence*, August 1910, 24. See also Davies, *A Testimony*.

[480] Cited in Noel Gibbard, *On the Wings of the Dove* (Bridgend: Bryntirion, 2002), compare, 259 n. 16 and 260 n. 20.

[481] References to *Confidence* being supplied to individuals in Waunlwyd are present in numerous editions of the Journal, see May 1914, Dec. 1914, July 1915, Nov. 1916, and Jan.1923.

[482] *Confidence,* July & September 1910 contain separate reports of this trip.

Jeffreys would have preached both home and abroad.[483] Upon his return to Wales, Jeffreys continued to minister in Waunlwyd until 1914 when he assumed the pastorate of the Congregational Church in Aberdare, and then in 1920 moved to Cardiff.[484] He was also a regular speaker at the various Pentecostal conventions held in Britain, and assisted at the PMU training school before returning to pastoral ministry. *Confidence* contains letters, articles and reports from the influential T. M. Jeffreys relating to his missionary travels as a PMU representative. Jeffreys also spent some time as editor of *Omega* and *Overcoming Life* for a short time from 1910.[485]

The growth of the Pentecostal movement in South Wales is highlighted by two interesting entries in *Confidence*: firstly an advertisement for 'cheap excursions' to Sunderland for the Whitsun Convention 6–17 June 1908.[486] The second being the introduction of a Welsh Conference first held in the Park Hotel, Cardiff during Easter week, April 1909 at which A. A. Boddy, Cecil Polhill, A. Moncur Niblock, T. M. Jeffreys and Smith Wigglesworth were present. Smith Wigglesworth (1859–1947) became a leading evangelist within early Pentecostalism. A Bradford plumber, Wigglesworth—who undoubtedly fitted Morgan's designation of being 'unsophisticated'—received his personal Spirit baptism at Sunderland in 1907 after which he embarked upon a unique worldwide evangelistic and healing ministry.[487] During this first Welsh Conference, people gathered in Cardiff from various parts of Wales including Tonypandy, Llanelli, Bridgend, Aberkenfig, Tondu, Aberaeron, Abertillery, and Waunlwyd. T. M. Jeffreys concluded that the conference was a success in that it provided for those 'Children of the Revival' who were endeavouring to continue their spiritual journey to discover a further move of God in their land:

---

[483] *Flames of Fire,* October 1911, 1 and *Flames of Fire*, November 1911, 1.

[484] Dr. Williams Library Congregational Church Records, <www.dwlib.co.uk/dwlib/family/index.html>

[485] <www.1911census.co.uk> and Malcomson, *Pentecostal Pioneers*, 158–60. Thanks are due to Desmond Cartwright for assisting with information of Jeffreys' further ministry.

[486] *Confidence*, May 1908, 9–10.

[487] *Confidence*, April 1909, 12. See also *Confidence*, April 1909, 'Special Supplement' 2/4, 2–4 for the account given by T. M. Jeffreys of this first conference. See also Jack Hywel-Davies, *Baptised by Fire: the Life of Smith Wigglesworth* (London: Hodder and Stoughton, 1987), Roberts Liardon, compiler, *Smith Wigglesworth: The Complete Collection of His Life Teachings* (Tulsa, OK: Albury Publishing, 1996).

this was realised for some in the Pentecostal movement.[488] As Jeffreys made Pentecostal teaching and practice available in SE Wales, some of his fellow Welsh pioneers such as Tom Hicks (b. 1885) of Wattsville and Crosskeys visited Boddy's Whitsun conventions at Sunderland. They were encouraged in their search for a greater experience of God through the Holy Spirit and aided by the teaching in *Confidence* and Boddy's other numerous publications.[489]

Following on from the initial scenes in Waunlwyd it is possible to trace a progression of interest in Pentecostalism within South Wales via the subscriptions and donations lists contained in *Confidence.* The first records of financial contributions towards the printing of *Confidence* received from South Wales were: Waunlwyd, 5 shillings and Pentre, Rhondda, 2 shillings. According to *Confidence,* the Pentecostal Convention at Dowlais, Christmas 1910, saw visitors from Abertillery, Llanhilleth, and Waunlwyd and this appears to have been an important convention in terms of the spread of the Pentecostal message in SE Wales.[490] Following this series of meetings and in the period to 1924, *Confidence* was posted to new destinations; Newport, Oakdale, Blackwood, Monmouth, Wattsville, Aberbeeg, Crosskeys, Machen, Bedwas, Argoed, and Earlswood. In respect to this research, the arrival of *Confidence* in Wattsville, July 1915, and Crosskeys, April 1916, could be very significant but sadly the recipients of *Confidence* are not listed. A careful examination of these magazines reveals a number of Pentecostals who were unnamed individuals scattered throughout the eastern valleys who also contributed to the ongoing needs of Pentecostal missions. Jeffreys promoted the circulation of *Confidence* from Waunlwyd beginning in 1908 and its influence gradually spread throughout the region, reaching a peak in distribution between 1916 and 1918.

A desire by those of Wales to be involved with the Pentecostals is also recognised in their attraction to the London Missionary Conferences held by the PMU.[491] The continued interest in Pentecostal missionary activity is seen

---

[488] *Confidence*, April 1909, 'Special Supplement', 2/4, 2–4.

[489] Wakefield, *Alexander Boddy*, 236–8 for a list of Boddy's publications and Cauchi, *Works of Alexander Boddy* on CD ROM.

[490] *Confidence*, January 1908, 5.

[491] *Flames of Fire*, July 1915, 9.

in the donations given via Boddy and the PMU and which are recorded in each issue of *Confidence*. These lists serve as an example of the interest in mission from the earliest days. Every issue of *Confidence* from 1908 contained some update or list of financial contributions towards mission.

A. A. Boddy had a particular interest in mission and was a man who travelled widely supporting the work. The first PMU missionaries to leave Britain were Kathleen Miller of Exeter and Lucy James of Bedford, both of whom travelled to India. Financial contributions to missions are recorded as being received from readers in Scotland and 10 shillings from an anonymous donor.[492] The January–March 1919 edition of *Confidence* records the financial contributions which illustrate the continued interest: Machen £2–16s, Earlswood £3, Crosskeys £7–10s (for China), £14–10s 6d (for India) and Machen £2 (to support Miss Knell). Considering that Britain was emerging from the ravages of the First World War, this generosity of believers for overseas missions highlights the intense interest for evangelism within these embryonic Pentecostal groups. By 1919, PMU had twenty-six missionaries in India and China.[493] Donald Gee speaks highly of the generosity of the economically challenged Welsh in their support of 'the Lord's work' during the difficult times after World War I and beyond.[494]

Pentecostalism in SE Wales was emerging from a religious milieu whose theology was by no means Pentecostal. B.P. Jones concurs with Jeffreys that the emergent Pentecostals were viewed by some within the evangelical community as wolves, serpents, tares, deluded and deceptive; some even labelled the new sect as demonic.[495] As the Pentecostal groups grew, this opposition increased and Jeffreys records how those involved faced prejudice and antagonism due to their testimony to the 'Scriptural Baptism in the Holy Spirit'.[496] Nevertheless, Pentecostalism took root in SE Wales against a background of doubt, cynicism, and open opposition; and in time, the Pentecostals began to establish their

---

[492] *Confidence*, March, 1909, 23.

[493] *Confidence,* Jan–Mar 1919, 11.

[494] Gee, *Wind and Flame*, 78.

[495] Brynmor Pierce Jones, *How Lovely are Thy Dwellings* (Newport: Wellspring, 2009), 12; *Confidence*, May 1908, 10.

[496] *Confidence*, May 1908, 10.

own house groups and mission halls. Jones pays particular attention to the emergence of the Apostolic Church, the first official Pentecostal denomination to be established in Wales.[497] The position of Jones relating to the latter is also relevant to the other Pentecostal groups that were emerging and which joined either Elim or AoG. Life within the established denominations for the 'tongues people' was gradually proving more difficult, and eventual separation became their necessary or preferred course of action. After 1904–05 the established denominations reverted to their traditional forms of worship; yet some who had been deeply affected by the Revival searched for a return to the informal and spontaneous forms of worship experienced in the Revival period. The Pentecostals gave some the opportunity to experience spontaneity and liberty in corporate worship; and it was here people were presented with the teaching concerning an experience labelled as a 'baptism in the Holy Spirit with the initial evidence of speaking in tongues'. This definite crisis event identified a further spiritual experience which provided people with a definite understanding of the baptism in the Holy Spirit. This experience now had a focus and a purpose: tongues and evangelism.

The various pressures that were apparent within society caused some to be drawn to the prospect of eternal release from suffering through the hope of heaven. The Pentecostals promoted a message of salvation and offered people the hope of eternal liberty and it was this evangelistic fervour that brought people to the cottage meetings and into contact with the doctrine of Spirit baptism. As they presented a 'four-square gospel' message of Christ as Saviour, Baptiser in Holy Spirit, Healer and Coming King so individuals came into contact with this new teaching on tongues and spiritual gifts for the advancement of the Kingdom of God and personal edification.[498] The Pentecostals were one religious group that grew in the post-war years.[499] After the initial economic prosperity of the immediate post-war years, by 1920 there

---

[497] Jones, *How Lovely*, 17. See also James E. Worsfold, *The Origins of the Apostolic Church in Great Britain* (Wellington, NZ: Julian Literature Trust, 1991).

[498] John Christopher Thomas, *Toward a Pentecostal Ecclesiology: The Church and the Fivefold Gospel* (Cleveland, TN: CPT Press, 2010).

[499] Others that functioned were the Independent Mission Halls and from the late 1920s Dr M. Lloyd Jones at Sandfields. See Iain H. Murray, *D. Martyn Lloyd-Jones The First Forty Years 1899–1939* (Edinburgh: Banner of Truth, 1982). See also D. Martyn Lloyd-Jones, *Joy Unspeakable* (Eastbourne: Kingsway, 1984).

was further economic depression and a loss of the religious fervour of 1904–05. Despite this, there were some groups that emerged that became associated with the Pentecostal movement and, in particular, with the later established AoG.

Within three years of the end of the Great War, the AoG W&Mon was formed. This unofficial denomination was in existence by Saturday 22 October 1921 as letters from SE Wales representatives to AG America indicate.[500] The first available letter of 5 December 1921, written by Mr Hubert Crook (b. 1888) of Pontnewydd, speaks of earlier communication. This correspondence is a key issue in discovering the vital role played by a group of Welsh assemblies in the eventual establishing of AoG GB&I. The specific content of these letters to America will be assessed below.

Apostolic, Elim or AoG?

It would be historically inaccurate to suggest, or even imply, that there was a quantum leap between the Revival of 1904–05, the formation of AoG W&Mon in 1921, and the official recognition of the AoG denomination in 1924. As well as the ministry of the traditional denominations, which is highlighted by Pope, there was also the rising Pentecostal movement which has its British roots in Sunderland and its denominational structure formed in Wales.[501] The life and ministries of D. P. Williams (Apostolic) and George Jeffreys (Elim) providing the impetus for the widening phenomenon.[502]

It is recognised that the Apostolic Faith Church, Bournemouth, was the first official British Pentecostal denomination; however, it fell into decline following

---

[500] Letter Number 3, Appendix 1

[501] Robert Pope, *Building Jerusalem* (Cardiff: University of Wales Press, 1998), 115 for statistics on the membership of Nonconformists denominations 1904–39.

[502] <www.apostolic-church.org> and <www.elim.org.uk> for an outline of their respective histories and theological position. See also: H. B. Llewellyn, *A Study of the History and Thought of the Apostolic Church in Wales in the Context of Pentecostalism* (MPhil. Diss. University of Cardiff, 1998); W. K. Kay, 'Apostolic Church' in *NIDPCM*, 322–3 and D. W. Cartwright, 'Elim Pentecostal Church', in *NIDPCM*, 598–9; Tony Cauchi, *The Elim Evangel: 1919–1934 on CD ROM* (Bishop's Waltham: Revival Library, 2004) and Robinson, *Pentecostal Origins*, 90–232 and 233–95.

the impropriety of its leader William Hutchinson (1864–1928).[503]
Consequently it was the emergence of the Apostolic Church in Wales under
the leadership of D. P. Williams and Elim under George Jeffreys which set the
foundation for the denominational structure in British Pentecostalism. There
were, however, some groups or small Pentecostal mission halls that were not
attracted to the teaching of these emerging Pentecostal denominations.[504] In
time, these other disparate groups, led by men based largely in Crosskeys,
united to form the AoG W&Mon eventually joining with their English
counterparts to form AoG GB&I. These Welsh groups were not theologically
sophisticated as their leaders were drawn from the working class: miners, steel
workers, and factory workers who had not had the opportunity to study
theology formally, many not even finishing their schooling due to the
desperate needs of their families for an additional source of income. It was
these people who approached the AG in America for suitable support in
doctrinal and organisational matters. However, within Britain as a whole the
development of an AoG theology and the struggles with both Apostolic and
Elim Churches are best summarised in the writings of Donald Gee. It was he
who was at the forefront of the defence of what was to become the AoG
position on three crucial areas: firstly, the authority of the apostle and prophet
in the local assembly; secondly, a rejection of the so called doctrine of
'Ultimate Reconciliation'; and, thirdly, an acceptance of initial evidence.
However, these two later issues were combated by Gee within the context of
the wider British AoG post-1924. The major issue or perceived threat faced by
the Welsh proto-AoG groups was that of Apostolic Church Government.

Apostolic Authority

William Hutchinson of Bournemouth had been influenced by the events of the
Welsh Revival of 1904–05 and the ministry of Boddy in Sunderland. On his
return to Bournemouth, people began to receive the Pentecostal Spirit baptism

---

[503] Malcolm R. Hathaway, 'The Role of William Oliver Hutchinson and the Apostolic Faith Church in the
formation of British Pentecostal Churches', *JEPTA* 16 (1996) 40–57.

[504] Hollenweger, *Pentecostals*, 191–6; Kay, *Inside Story*, 76–80; Kay, *Pentecostals in Britain*, 1–36; Gee, *Wind and
Flame*, 124–30 and Massey, *Another Springtime*, 57–77 who discuss the problems that emerged in relation to
theological differences.

and the first official Pentecostal Assembly in Britain was opened in 1908.[505] Daniel Powell Williams came into contact with the Pentecostal teaching and experience whilst on holiday in Aberaeron in 1909; it was here that he received his personal Pentecostal type Spirit baptism. Upon returning to his home village of Pen-y-groes he established a house meeting in February 1910; it was known as 'Yr Eglwys Efengylaidd' (The Evangelical Church) and became a centre for Pentecostal activity. D. P. Williams visited the Bournemouth assembly and invited Hutchinson to travel to Wales, the result being the opening of an Apostolic Faith Church at Pen-y-groes in May 1914 in which Williams was installed as the apostle and pastor. Following a variety of concerns over Hutchinson's leadership and financial accountability, Williams resigned from the denomination and established 'his own' denomination: 'The Apostolic Church in Wales' at Pen-y-groes in 1916. The new denomination slowly spread and has been an influential Pentecostal force worldwide.[506] It is interesting to note that there were Pentecostal groups in the far western extremities of Wales that were receiving *Confidence* from Boddy, hence emphasising the widespread influence of the Anglican Pentecostal.[507] It would not be unreasonable to associate some of those listed in *Confidence* with the groups that became strongly associated with the Apostolic Church in Wales. The first official Apostolic assemblies are noted by Worsfold as: Pen-y-groes, Cross Hands, and Aberaeron.[508] However, not all of these initial Pentecostal centres joined the Apostolic Church—it being based mainly in West Wales; and although Williams was a major player in the early years of Pentecostalism in Wales, it remains T. M. Jeffreys at Waunlwyd to whom Welsh Pentecostals owe their primary debt of gratitude.

---

[505] Kay, 'Apostolic Church' and Hathaway, 'The Role of William Oliver Hutchinson and the Apostolic Faith Church in the formation of British Pentecostal Churches'. See also J. A. Hewett, 'Apostle, Office of', in *NIDPCM*, 318–21 and William Henry Lewis, *And He Gave Some Apostles,* (Yorkshire: Puritan Press, 1954).

[506] Worsfold, *Origins* and Apostolic Church, *Introducing the Apostolic Church: A Manual of Belief, Practice and History* (Apostolic Church: Penygroes, 1988), 93–102 and <www.apostolic-church.org>

[507] *Confidence*, August, 1910, 24.

[508] Compare *Confidence,* August, 1910, 24 and Worsfold, *Origins,* 169–70 there are a further 16 Apostolic assemblies listed by Worsfold, they being Llwynhendy, Llanelli, Dafen, Tumble, Morriston, Pontardawe, Birchgrove, Skewen, Trecynon, Dowlais, Llanon, Pontypridd, Ystrad, Glannamman, Tyr-y-dail, and Tycross. Joining these Welsh centres were Apostolic churches in Birmingham, Hereford, Glasgow, and Belfast.

The defining theological tenet of the Apostolic Church is their insistence (on the basis of Ephesians 4:11) on the authority of apostles and prophets within the local assembly. While the other Pentecostals agreed with their theological stance, the perceived over-emphasis on the primary roles of apostle and prophet disturbed the other groups. In commenting on the tenets of faith produced by the Apostolic Church in Britain, Gordon Weeks states:

> Our unique Tenets is No. 9 believing as we do that it was never the purpose of God that the recognised (and obeyed) ministry of the Apostles and Prophets should cease at any time in the "Church Age". We believe that these united ministries are the Biblical channels for Theocracy today as is further explained later in this data.[509]

Ian Macpherson and William Rowe provide an Apostolic consideration of the theological stance on apostles and prophets thus supporting their ministry within the local church and of their necessity in carrying on the work of the original New Testament Apostles. The apostle would be viewed as the senior figure and leader of the denomination with ultimate control. The prophet fulfils a more active role within local assemblies and works in unison with the apostle to bring his direction to the church body. Whilst the AoG would not promote this as a central tenet, they would recognise people with 'apostolic' ministry and be open to the use of prophecy within the local assembly.[510] This concern was highlighted by Gee who stated a strong disagreement over bestowing titles upon people and expecting them to fulfil the role; he stated that such insistence upon titles was no more than; 'children playing at church'.[511] This apparently harsh and derogatory statement reflected tensions resulting from the tendency among the Apostolics to proselytize other Pentecostal bodies. Congo missionary W. F. P. Burton also supported Gee in

---

[509] <www.apostolic-church.org/history.phtml> See also Apostolic Church, *Introducing The Apostolic*, 177–85; William, A. C. Rowe, *One Lord One Faith* (Apostolic Publications: Penygroes, 1988), 237–310 and Ian Macpherson, *The Faith Once Delivered* (Milton Keynes: Word, 1988), 299–313. See also Appendix 2 for full statement of faith.

[510] Petts, *Body Builders*, 21–56.

[511] Gee, *Wind and Flame*, 74, 104–6. See also Donald Gee, *The Ministry Gifts of Christ* (Springfield, Mo: G.P.H. 1930) and Massey, *Another Springtime*, 73–7.

his insistence upon care within the arena of seeking instruction from 'prophets'.[512]

The role of Burton in the establishing of the AoG GB&I cannot be overstated; his homeland furlough in 1921–22 gave him ample opportunity to endeavour to unite the disparate Pentecostal groups around Britain due in the main to his observation of the possible pitfalls in theology emerging from such groups as the Apostolic Church. This scepticism of Apostolic teaching is further illustrated by a letter sent to American Pentecostals by E. C. W. Boulton warning them of the imminent invasion by the 'distinctly unscriptural' teaching of the Apostolics.[513] Gee formulated the AoG position in an attempt to preserve their stance and protect from 'false' teaching the culmination of his thinking is summarised as follows. Apostles are present today although they are different from the original twelve of the New Testament; however these men will have:

> Outstanding spiritual gifts, and a deep personal experience, resulting in power to establish churches and provide adequate spiritual leadership for the people of God is to be legitimately demanded.[514]

On reflection one may be more inclined to suggest that there are those in Gee's estimation who hold an 'apostolic-like' ministry that is they have certain qualities of the New Testament apostles but lack that vital element of having seen the Lord. W. F. P. Burton is widely regarded in AoG circles as a man with such apostolic-like ministry. The main areas of identity of an apostle would be: preaching accompanied by signs, church planting, foundation laying, authority over churches, and training others. The argument against modern day apostles would suggest that these are roles carried out by the offices of evangelist, pastor, and teacher.

Gee also entered the debate over the office of a prophet by concluding that prophets were:

---

[512] Massey, *Another Springtime*, 75–6. See also W. F. Burton, *Teachings from the Word of God*, (Upington, S. Africa, n.d. translated by Arie and Alice Blomerus), 41–4.

[513] Robinson, *Pentecostal Origins*, 282, *Pentecostal Evangel*, August 5 1922, 9; Gee, *These Men*, 23–5.

[514] Gee, *Ministry Gifts*, 36.

> Not to add anything to the perfect revelation of the Scriptures, but for the building up of the body of Christ through an inspired and an inspiring ministry-gift that interprets and applies those Scriptures with new light and life and power to every generation and circumstance by a fresh and immediate operation of the Holy Spirit.[515]

AoG proponents Gee and Petts remain steadfast in their belief that Scripture is the infallible word of God from which every Christian should seek their guidance.[516] Whilst they advocate those 'prophets' who through their spiritual gift can encourage and confirm to people God's desires, they insist that such prophets should never bring specific direction either to the individual or the corporate body of Christ, for this is supplied through the perfect revelation of the Scriptures. Gee laid great emphasis upon the preaching of the Word of God indicating that within such preaching ministry the gifts of prophecy, words of wisdom and knowledge could operate. Again, it could be suggested that such ministry could be fulfilled by a suitably equipped Spirit-led pastor or teacher as they expound the word of God to their congregations.

Ultimate Reconciliation

As well as the perceived threat from the rising Apostolic Church, the Welsh proto-AoG groups were also troubled by the growing influence of A. E. Saxby (1873–1960) and his support of the doctrine of Ultimate Reconciliation.[517] A Baptist minister, Saxby was introduced to Pentecostalism in London around 1912 by his wife, in the home of Mrs Cantel. As a result of his acceptance of the message, Saxby left his Baptist congregation to commence a Pentecostal mission known as Derby Hall, in 1915. Saxby was a widely respected preacher and a prominent figure in early British Pentecostalism and a popular speaker in Wales. However by 1921 he had adopted the liberal doctrine of 'Ultimate Reconciliation' or universalism. This view holds that as the love of God cannot

---

[515] Gee, *Ministry Gifts*, 44; Petts, *Body Builders*, 21–56; Aaron Linford, *A Course Study on Spiritual Gifts* (London: AoG, 1969); Wayne Grudem *Systematic Theology* (Leicester: IVP, 1994), 904–49

[516] Gee, Ministry Gifts, 44–45 and Petts, *Body Builders,* 55.

[517] Gee, *These Men,* 80–3; Massey, *Another Springtime,* 69–73. Saxby was Gee's pastor in London in his early years of Pentecostalism: Malcomson, *Pentecostals Pioneers,* 415–21 and Robinson, *Pentecostal Origins,* 189–94. See also Daniel B. Pecota, 'The Saving Work of Christ' in Stanley M. Horton, *Systematic Theology* (Springfield MO: GPH, 1994), 325–73; Keith Warrington, *Pentecostal Theology* (London: T&T Clark, 2008), 34–8 and Grudem, *Systematic Theology,* 1140–57.

ultimately be thwarted, and so everyone in the end will be saved. Not surprisingly he was accused of heresy and forced to sever his Pentecostal links. Massey provides a summary of Gee's opinion and records his appraisal of Saxby—his former pastor and a man whom he held in high regard:

> It seems fair now to suggest that Mr Saxby did not possess the theological training and ability to see through all the implications of his doctrine. Some have felt that had he been led more sympathetically he could have been won to a more balanced position.[518]

As Gee's former pastor, Saxby had a great influence on his formative Christian experience. However, Gee could not agree with any undermining of the doctrine of eternal reward and punishment. According to the AoG Statement of Faith, the denomination holds to:

> The everlasting punishment of all who are not written in the Book of Life. Rev 20:10–15.

The AoG position has never altered in respect to eternal rewards and punishment believing in a God of love—as did Saxby—but also one of justice.[519]

Elim and Initial Evidence

The later development of the Elim churches concerned the AoG due to their insistence upon central government and the rejection of the 'initial evidence' doctrine. George Jeffreys had established Elim in 1916 and had worked exclusively in Ireland until 1920, it was only then that he was urged to bring his ministry to the mainland.[520] Jeffreys was the sole leader of Elim and this caused some problems within the denomination, though they have continued to be governed by a general secretary until the present day.[521] An interesting

---

[518] Massey, *Another Springtime*, 72. See also John Carter, *Donald Gee Pentecostal Statesman* (Nottingham: AoG, 1975), 17, who gives a summary of Gee's defence against Saxby's teaching.

[519] See Bruce R. Marino, 'The Origin, Nature, and Consequences of Sin', in Horton, *Systematic Theology*, 255–90 and Stanley M. Horton, 'The Last Things', in Horton, *Systematic Theology*, 597–638. See also Warrington, *Pentecostal*, 317–20.

[520] See Robinson, *Pentecostal Origins*, for an in depth analysis of the work of Elim in Ireland.

[521] <www.elim.org.uk>

question regarding Jeffreys is why a Welshman, converted in the Revival 1904–05, decided to minister in Ireland rather than the land of his birth. Robinson suggests that the pull of the American dollar was strong on British evangelicals but Jeffreys never made it further west than Belfast.[522] This may be a very simplified view of Jeffreys and his Irish work; however Elim did not directly affect the proto-AoG groups in Wales until the later formation of AoG GB&I after 1924. The possibility of a merger between the two denominations was discussed in 1963 but never materialised.[523] The AoG position on denominational governance holds to the fact that each assembly is autonomous with both the executive and the denominational structure in place to foster inter-congregational fellowship and to arbitrate in matters of dispute. Although this was the essence of the original constitution of 1924, in recent years this sense of fellowship has waned and the denomination has become more centralised.[524] Kay states the major stumbling block to unity between AoG and Elim was over the insistence by AoG adherents of the word 'initial' in regards to Spirit baptism and evidential tongues. Under the heading 'Holy Spirit' the Elim Tenets of Faith states:

> We believe in the deity of the Holy Spirit who proceeds from the Father and the Son and the necessity of His work in conviction of sin, repentance, regeneration and sanctification, and that the believer is also promised an enduement of power as the gift of Christ through the baptism in the Holy Spirit with signs following. Through this enduement the believer is empowered for fuller participation in the ministry of the Church, its worship, evangelism and service.[525]

Hence Elim believed in a Spirit baptism and the use of all the charismata but, unlike AoG, does not insist upon 'initial evidential tongues'.

---

[522] Robinson, *Pentecostal Origins*, 120.

[523] Kay, *Pentecostals in Britain*, 58–60. It is also noteworthy that Gee considered joining Elim in 1923: see Richard D. Massey, 'A Flirtation with Elim – Donald Gee's Negotiations to join the Elim Pentecostal Alliance in 1923,' article extract from Richard Massey, 'A Sound and Scriptural Union' (PhD Diss, Birmingham, 1987).

[524] A number of Welsh AoG churches, Crosskeys included, have resigned their affiliation due in the main to issues with the national leaders and in particular their perceived move towards a more centralised form of government.

[525] <http://www.elim.org.uk/Groups/112249/What_we_believe.aspx> See Appendix 2 for full statement of faith.

There was then a perceived theological threat to the independent Pentecostal missions in Wales particularly from the Apostolic Church. As the Pentecostal message spread throughout the valleys of SE Wales, some of the leaders recognised the necessity of uniting in order to defend their theological position.

AoG in Wales and Monmouthshire

As a result of concerns over theological differences with the Apostolic Church, the non-affiliated Pentecostal mission halls in SE Wales moved towards forming a loose fellowship of like minded believers. This desire for unity and security led to the formation of AoG W&Mon c. 1920 which was ratified on Saturday 22 October 1921 at a meeting held most probably at Crosskeys. It was this group that commenced correspondence with the AG in America seeking affiliation to that denomination in 1921.

The correspondence between Wales and America has not been given adequate consideration by Pentecostal historians such as Allen, Gee, Kay, Massey, and Missen; all of whom make only fleeting reference to its existence. As Gee states it was these letters that 'stung the English brethren into action'.[526] Allen follows Gee in referring to the Welsh as a 'small group' but the fact is that they were far more significant than has been realized in the past.[527] Massey simply suggest that about twelve Welsh assemblies were in correspondence with American AG and Kay follows Gee in suggesting that these letters were first dated 1923.[528] Missen mentions contact between Wales and America and rightly emphasises that there were some thirty four Welsh Assemblies active by 1923–24.[529] None of these authorities give sufficient credence to the letters that were in existence before 1923. A careful examination of these will show that the AoG GB&I had its roots in South Wales, and not in England, even if the English leaders were the driving force in establishing the denomination in

---

[526] Gee, *Wind and Flame*, 126–30.

[527] David Allen, 'Signs and Wonders The Origins, Growth, Development and Significance of Assemblies of God in Great Britain and Ireland 1900–1980' (PhD Diss. University of London: unpublished, 1990), 110–11.

[528] Massey, *Another Springtime*, 50 and Kay, *Inside Story*, 78.

[529] Missen, *Sound of a Going*, 11–12.

1924. The significance of the four letters written before 1923 will now be assessed. [530]

Letters to America

American AG was established in the spring of 1914 at Hot Springs, Arkansas, following a fellowship of Pentecostal ministers and pastors who determined that unity was expedient to the spread of the Pentecostal message. [531] A major figure in these discussions was Eudorus N. Bell (1866–1923), a former Baptist pastor who was influenced by the Pentecostal ministry of William Durham (1873–1912) in Chicago. [532] Bell became a prominent leader in the AG in America serving as chairman in 1914 and 1920–23. It was with Bell, in his capacity as chairman, that the Welsh proto-AoG were in correspondence from 1921. The AG denominational system established in America allowed for an executive presbytery of twelve who were 'safe, sane, and trained brethren', who would be the guiding lights to the new denomination offering theological and practical advice to the growing number of assemblies. [533] The second general council in November 1914 increased the presbytery representation to sixteen and decided to establish the AG headquarters at St. Louis. The growth of the new denomination allowed for these immediate changes and the office in St. Louis began publishing the *Christian Evangel* on a weekly basis. [534] Significant growth occurred between 1916 and 1926; in 1916 there were a registered 118 churches and by 1926 this had grown to 671 churches with 47,950 members. As this growth required organisational control, the offices in St. Louis became vital to the denomination as it oversaw the activities of the national district councils. The Americans were no strangers to doctrinal pressures, having navigated the troubled waters of such theological debates as the 'Finished Work' controversy, eventually accepted by AG, and the rise of the Oneness

---

[530] Appendix 1.

[531] Edith Blumhofer, *Assemblies of God, vol. 1* (Springfield, MO: GPH, 1989), 197–243; Blumhofer and C. R. Armstrong, 'Assemblies of God', in *NIDPCM*, 333–40 and Gee, *Wind and Flame*, 84–7.

[532] See W. E. Warner, 'Bell, Eudorus, N.' in *NIDPCM*, 369 and R. M. Riss, 'Durham, William H', in *NIDPCM*, 594–5.

[533] Blumhofer, *Assemblies, vol. 1*, 204.

[534] The *Christian Evangel* (later the *Pentecostal Evangel)* had been published previously by Joseph James Roswell Flower (1890–1970), who was another highly influential figure at this time. The American AG resource Flower Heritage Centre is named after J. R. Flower. Englishman Stanley Frodsham (1882–1969) edited this journal until 1949. AG America is now located in Springfield, Missouri <www.ag.org>

Pentecostals in 1918.[535] As the organisational structure was in place, and a system of doctrine accepted, those small and anxious groups in SE Wales turned their attention to the USA in hope of help, direction and security.

The AoG W&Mon was established c. 1920, with its existence being ratified in 1921—unfortunately there is no written reference to the exact date of its emergence other than general comments in the letters now under discussion. This group focused on the leaders at Crosskeys and was represented by: Tom Hicks of Crosskeys, Richard Anthony of Crosskeys, William Attwood of Crosskeys, Tom Mercy of Crosskeys, Price Davies of Aberbeeg, and Hubert Crook of Pontnewydd.[536] This group, in which the Crosskeys assembly was heavily represented, needed assistance to see how best to defend their movement against the perceived threat of Apostolic proselytising.

The first letter extant is dated 5 December 1921 and was sent by the secretary, Hubert Crook, on behalf of the Welsh grouping, in response to at least two earlier letters that had traversed the Atlantic between Crook and E. N. Bell. The desire of the AoG W&Mon was to form a 'Council' affiliated to the American denomination. Bell had agreed to this possibility in principle and the process began with the ordering of thirty-two copies of the combined minutes of the American AG. It could be suggested, therefore, that there were some thirty-two individuals or assemblies interested in this proposal throughout Wales and Monmouthshire. This is supported by the fact that the 1924 Constitution of AoG GB&I lists some thirty-eight assemblies in Wales and Monmouthshire. Crook also asked to receive a copy of the American 'Ordination Certificate' in order to ratify the pastoral roles given to the leaders of assemblies. The urgency of Crook's letter is summed up in his closing statement; 'this matter must be dealt with at once with us here'. Crook included the necessary financial outlay of £1 and 15 shillings to cover the cost of the minutes and copies of *Evangel*.

---

[535]J. L. Hall, 'A Oneness Pentecostal Looks At Initial Evidence' in McGee, ed., *Initial Evidence,* 168–88 and D. A. Reed, 'Oneness Pentecostalism', in *NIDPCM,* 936–44 and R. M. Riss, 'Finished Work Controversy', in *NIDPCM,* 638–9.

[536] Letter Number Three, 6 Feb. 1922.

The second letter is dated 13 December 1921 in which Crook is designated as 'Elder', thus suggesting his position in the local assembly at Pontnewydd. Pentecostal groups and later AoG churches operated under a system of church government of pastors, elders, and deacons; in the event that a church did not have a pastor, the elders would be designated with authority within the assembly. However, within AoG circles the pastor is often, but not always, viewed as a 'first among equals' within the leadership team of an assembly, holding the casting vote in any proposed church activity. Bell's response is very positive to the request from Wales stating that they would be 'glad to consider your application as soon as we get the customary information'. Bell seeks to obtain the minutes of the meeting held in Wales that led to the approach to America, plus the names and addresses of the participants. Bell assures Crook that upon receipt of these details the application process would be considered. As Bell enclosed copies of the Ordination Certificate and Fellowship Certificate one can assume that the American believers were keen to 'adopt' this Welsh district. Bell offers further advice upon the appointment of ministers to the new assemblies in Wales; he states that caution was required due to the changing of views by individuals within embryonic Pentecostal theology. The practice in America was for an annual review of credentials given to ministers as this allowed any with differing views to the Statement of Faith to be released to other organisations or denominations. The Welsh believers no doubt would have been heartened by the decision of Bell to send the necessary paperwork and to have offered 'any further service' they may require.

The third letter to traverse the Atlantic is dated 6 February 1922 and is from Crook to Bell. The opening greetings are followed by a note of thanks for the consideration being given to the application. Following this, Crook includes a copy of the minutes taken at the meeting held on 22 October 1921 and 'convened by one of the largest Assemblies in Wales and Mon.', presumably Crosskeys which had been located at its home on Gladstone Street since 1914 and was at that time drawing a congregation of up to 120 on a Sunday morning.[537] The minutes refer to the necessity of union between the assemblies while the content of these minutes dates the official recognition of

---

[537] Sidney Mercy, 'Pentecost in South Wales' *Pentecostal Evangel,* June (1928), 8. <www.ifphc.org/pdf/PentecostalEvangel/1920-1929/1928/1928_06_16pdf#page8>

AoG W&Mon from 22 October 1921, although fellowship and discussion had been in progress before this date.[538] It was at the October 1922 meeting that the definition of the title 'Assemblies of God' was stated and they also reveal how the disparate groups of various designations were drawn together:

> Resolved, that recognising ourselves as a GENERAL DISTIRCT COUNCIL of (Spirit Baptized) Saints from local Churches of God in Christ, Assemblies of God, various Apostolic Faith Missions, Full Gospel Pentecostal Missions and all Assemblies of like faith in Great Britain. Also That [sic] we recognize all the above said Assemblies of various names, and speak to them and refer to them by the general Scriptural name "Assemblies of God". And recommend that they all recognize themselves by the same name:- "Assembly of God" and adopt it as soon as practicable.[539]

This statement provides some evidence that the Welsh believers were not possessed of a narrow mentality but were open to the prospect of English, Scottish, and Irish groups joining their ranks. Crook then proceeds to list the central figures within AoG W&Mon: Tom Hicks (chairman), Hubert Crook (secretary), Richard Anthony (treasurer), William Attwood, Tom Mercy, and Price Davies. Following the supply of the necessary information, Crook requested a manual and sufficient credential, fellowship, and ordination certificates for '50 ministers'. On the official certificates they desired an addition of 'Assemblies of God Great Britain'. The Welsh proto-AoG was thus allowing for their local denomination to be accepted as a British denomination—paving the way for the AoG GB&I to be formed in 1924.

It is important to note the backgrounds of each of these men. Tom Hicks was born in Machen in 1885, the eldest son of Thomas and Elizabeth Hicks and brother to John, Owen, and Kinvyn. In 1921 Tom Hicks was resident at 63 Islwyn Road, Wattsville near Crosskeys; it was here that some of the initial Pentecostal meetings took place. Hicks worked as a collier at the coal face and

---

[538] See Davies, *A Testimony,* and Attwood, *How Pentecost,* who both relate the interaction between various Pentecostal Missions in South Wales and especially the strong links within the Ebbw Valley between Crosskeys and the surrounding areas such as Newbridge, Aberbeeg, Pontllanfraith, Machen, and Newport.

[539] Letter Number 3, paragraph 4.

was a member of Zion Congregational Church, Wattsville. Hubert Crook was born in 1888 the son of Zebina and Alice Ann Crook at Llanfrechfa, Monmouthshire. He was brother to Agnes, George, Jabez, and Miriam; his job description is that of a weigher at the local tinplate factory; and by 1921 he was resident at: 4 Tynewydd Road, Pontnewydd, Monmouthshire. The third member of the group was Richard Anthony of 3, Beechwood Avenue, Wattsville, Crosskeys, Monmouthshire. Born in 1890 he lodged for a few years at the home of Joseph and Elizabeth Probert at 26 Duffryn Terrace, Wattsville. Anthony's occupation was that of collier. Details as to the life of William Attwood are difficult to locate other than to state that he was a miner and that by 1921 he was resident at Risca Road, Crosskeys; eventually he served as pastor at the Risca Assembly. Price Davies of Hafod Arthem Farm, St. Illtyds, Aberbeeg, Monmouthshire was an influential figure throughout South Wales Pentecostalism.[540]

Tom Mercy is probably the most well-known and influential of these figures. Born in 1878 to Sidney and Elizabeth Mercy, he was one of sixteen children.[541] Tom Mercy was married to Elizabeth a native of Dinas, Glamorgan, and worked as a Checkweigher at Nine Mile Point Colliery Wattsville. They lived at 15 Islwyn Road, Wattsville, Crosskeys, Monmouthshire and it is interesting that Tom never resigned his secular work whilst continuing to lead the new mission at Crosskeys.[542] Donald Gee refers to Tom Mercy as 'an outstanding figure in the Welsh Assemblies', and notes his strong belief in divine healing. Yet, neglecting medical advice and trusting the Lord to heal him during a battle with illness, he died on 17 August 1935 from exhaustion leading to heart failure.[543] This group of Welsh miners, tin-workers, and farmers provide some support for Morgan's view of the 'unsophisticated' nature of early Welsh Pentecostalism. However, this group of manual labourers were open to God's working in their midst, studying the Bible and seeking a greater experience of God in their lives. To them, their initial fulfilment came through the

---

[540] Davies, A Testimony.

[541] Malcomson, Pentecostals Pioneers, 345–52. The dates supplied by Malcomson are incorrect; the 1911 Census gives 1878 as the birth year of Tom Mercy and Gee, These Men, 61–3. I have found no record of Sidney Mercy on the 1911 Census for Crosskeys or surrounding district.

[542] In 1911 Tom Mercy is recorded as living at 143 Islwyn Road Wattsville.

[543] Gee, These Men, 61–2.

Pentecostal movement in Britain and found its haven in the AoG denomination which they all supported until their deaths.

Letter number four is the crucial piece of correspondence which led to the involvement of the Welsh with the wider British scene. It is dated 29 March 1922 and was sent from Bell to Crook. Bell introduces the fact that the formation of a Welsh district was still plausible but that further information had come to light that may affect the way forward. This crucial matter was a similar approach from England:

> We have just received notice from another bunch of good ministers, namely in England, who are planning to come together in what they call a Leaders Conference, and are to hold their meeting during the Swanwick Convention in April. The call for this meeting is issued by W. Burton, E. C. Boulton, A. Carter, J. Douglas, Geo. Jeffreys, T. H. Jewitt, G. Kingston, Thos. Myerscough, E. W. Moser, J. Tetchner, J. & L. Walshaw, E. Blackburn. Correspondence is to be addressed to Pastor E. C. Boulton, 2 May St. Hull, Yorks. [544]

The English group had also applied to the American AG for copies of minutes and credentials in order to follow their example in the formation of a new British denomination. Bell suggested that the Welsh group make contact with their English counterparts and pool their resources into the formation of one significant British organisation. Bell indicates his intention to write to the English group and suggest a similar course of action offering a basis of 'mutual fellowship' between America and any new British denomination. Although the 1922 meeting at Swanwick was a failure, this list contains the names of some of the most significant British Pentecostal leaders—especially W. F. P. Burton, A. Howard Carter, and Thomas Myerscough who were very influential in the eventual establishing of the AoG GB&I in 1924. [545] Bell's suggestion allowed for a practical and wise outcome to be achieved during a difficult period within Welsh Pentecostalism. The Apostolic Church in Wales was not the preferred destination for these independent groups and Elim was still very much an

---

[544] Letter Number 4, paragraph 2.
[545] Gee, *Wind and Flame,* 98–101.

evangelistic organisation based in Ireland. A new denomination was about to be born with Bell, Crook, and the team in Wales instrumental in focusing their attention on a much needed British grouping.

The Appeal of Pentecost in Working Class Wales

Since Pentecostalism became popular among the poorer working class in Wales, a question of interest to this author is whether there is any correlation between Pentecostalism and poverty? Woven into the fabric of Pentecostalism is an appeal to the oppressed and rejected; this allows its principles to make headway with those who are economically dispossessed. This was so in Los Angeles in 1906, where racial segregation and the 'Jim Crow' laws hampered the work of Seymour; and it was so among the Welsh mining communities in the early twentieth century.[546] Harvey Cox makes much of this proposal when he reviews the birth of the movement at the Azusa Street Mission, stating that Pentecostalism is mainly an urban based religion, benefitting from the cosmopolitan mix within the industrial districts.[547]

Within Wales, the prevailing socio-economic conditions seemed to have been conducive to the new teaching, which brought the common people an opportunity to find peace, joy, and hope in their new faith. The mix of immigrant industrial workers and the indigenous South Wales population brought cultural differences; economic hardship was guaranteed by often ruthless mine owners and political upheaval with the rise of the Labour movement allowed Pentecostalism its voice.[548] It can be suggested that as the socio-political structures of society were being challenged by the rise of Labour and the unions, so too the traditional chapel values came under threat. Even so, during this upheaval, the Pentecostal testimony with its robust evangelism was allowed to flourish in the industrial heartland of Wales. Coupled to this, those who were attracted to the Pentecostal meetings were not stigmatised or

---

[546] There is also the phenomenal growth of Pentecostalism in Africa, Latin and South America largely in the urban sprawls and amongst the poorer section of society see D. B. Barratt and T. M. Johnson, 'Global Statistics' in *NIDPCM*, 284–302 and Anderson, *Introduction to Pentecostalism*, 63–143.

[547] Harvey Cox, *Fire from Heaven* (London: Cassell, 1996), 3–78.

[548] See Pope, *Building Jerusalem*, for a detailed examination of the socio-economic conditions in Wales at this time. Although Pope does not interact with Pentecostalism, he does highlight this important principle and possibly illustrates how the traditional denominations lost sight of their true ministry in the battle with rising Labour.

criticised for their lack of learning but simply encouraged to allow God to use them in his service. The unsophisticated preaching style of the early Pentecostal leaders was an added dimension in the growth of the movement within the valleys. The local embryonic AoG adherents appealed to the working-class as they were familiar with their thought forms and spoke the language of the 'man in the street'. An example of this was the influence of Tom Mercy in Crosskeys through his continued work in the coal mines and the N.U.M. whilst still leading the Pentecostal work in the village. Many of the miners and iron or steel workers were spared from the worry of conscientious objection as they were employed in industry of national importance; hence they faced no stigmatism and opposition such as that which was endured by Gee or Carter in England.

Many early Pentecostals drew great encouragement from the words of Acts 4:13, in which the Sanhedrin viewed the apostles as 'uneducated and untrained men'. It led them to believe that although education was not essential, the presence and enabling of the Spirit was paramount. As a result of this general position, many within SE Wales Pentecostalism frowned upon the establishing of Bible schools and training centres during the early years. They were initially concerned with the impact of liberal theology within the established Bible Colleges. Sadly, the concern over the traditional colleges led to a growing scepticism in some circles about the necessity of any formal biblical and theological training: the Spirit was the centre of their theology and he could inspire anyone to preach, lead, operate charismata, and evangelise: who needed a degree?[549]

However Bible schools were not unknown in Pentecostal circles. Thomas Myerscough opened a training school in Preston that was to have major influence through the ministry of George Jeffreys, W. F. P. Burton and many other Congo missionaries; Howard Carter served the denomination at the Hampstead Bible School in London, and later when it relocated to Kenley in London. The current AoG Bible College at Mattersey Hall Doncaster provides

---

[549] To illustrate this attitude, I have experienced opposition from some older Pentecostals in SE Wales to my attendance at Mattersey Hall to gain a Masters degree and to my pursuit of a further higher degree; one man accused me of it being 'nothing but pride!'

for ministry training and theological education to PhD level. Within these difficulties, the emerging Pentecostals were confronted with, and experienced, what to them could be labelled the 'raw power of God in action'. So what did Pentecostalism offer to these poor, unsophisticated working class folk?

Hope and Deliverance

There are four main areas I suggest that encouraged people to join these groups in SE Wales c. 1912:

Firstly, a hope of deliverance summarised as ultimate eternal release from the humdrum life faced by so many; Pentecostals often refer to Paul's words in Romans 8:18 in preaching this ultimate hope of deliverance. Within their eschatological framework, the words of Revelation 21:1–4 are often quoted by Pentecostal adherents, their desire being the ultimate hope of redemption in the heavenly Jerusalem.

Secondly, Pentecostalism offered people a joy and freedom in public worship which gave them relief from the harshness of existence in the mine, steel mill, or factory. There was a constant desire within Pentecostal circles to 'get to the meetings' and enjoy the presence of God and the exuberance of public worship. Meetings were known to proceed for hours, often long into the night, tarrying or waiting for a divine visitation; miners would often leave their shift after twelve hours of hard labour and walk directly to the local Mission Hall. [550]

The third principle that is offered by Pentecostalism is an expectation of divine blessing in one's life. In a society in which temporal blessings and comforts were few, and where there was no free medical help, the possibility of receiving spiritual blessings from God brought great comfort to the participants. [551] For the early Pentecostals, the thought that 'God is interested in us' was almost unbelievable; however, they sought his presence and blessing.

The fourth and final principle I suggest that was offered to men such as Tom Mercy was an assurance of God's presence in their lives. Matthew 28:20 reads, 'And, behold I am with you always, to the end of the age' and this assurance

---

[550] See Attwood, *How Pentecost.*

[551] The National Health Service (NHS) was officially formed in 1948, as Welshman Anuerin Bevin (1897–1960) spearheaded the move to national health provision.

allowed these labourers and workers to live with no fear of death (a very present reality in the mines), or of hostility towards their faith. It also allowed them to evangelise with no fear of reproach, as they believed their God was with them always. These four areas of Pentecostalism were present in the ministry of the group at Crosskeys; they held on to them securely and looked to God to take them forward in their work, ministry, and witness.

AoG Great Britain & Ireland

The result of the correspondence that passed between Bell, Crook, and Boulton was the invitation of the Welsh believers to join their English counterparts at the Hayes Conference Centre at Swanwick, Derbyshire, England, in April 1922.[552] It was there that the initial steps towards denominational formation were taken. By the spring of 1922 there was a call, driven by W. F. P. Burton, on furlough from the Congo, for a 'leaders' gathering in order to investigate any common ground which could lead to unity within the disparate Pentecostal groups.[553] Burton had travelled the British Isles and had become conscious of the diversity of thought and practice among the independent Pentecostal groups. In his estimation, the solution to the situation lay in the formation of a 'fellowship' of like-minded people or assemblies in order to regulate the Pentecostal testimony. A conference was arranged for Sheffield on 23–24 May 1922, when thirty-eight persons were present. A 'Provisional General Council' was elected consisting of Thomas Myerscough (president), E. C. Boulton, James Tetchner, A. Carter, E. W. Moser, Charles Flower, George Jeffreys, W. Henderson, Tom Mercy and George Vale. These men signed a draft Constitution on Pentecostal doctrines entitled:

CONSTITUTION OF THE GENERAL COUNCIL OF THE ASSEMBLIES OF GOD IN GREAT BRITAIN AND IRELAND.

This document provided a seven point outline of recommendations concerning the operation of the denomination, a ten point statement of fundamental

---

[552] Gee refers to Swanwick conferences in 1920 and 1921. It was during the 1921 meetings that the issue of Ultimate Reconciliation proclaimed by Saxby was dealt with and rejected; this suggests that there was already some interaction between English proto-AoG groups.

[553] Allen, 'Signs and Wonders', 100–18; Gee, *Wind and Flame,* 110–30; and Kay, *Inside Story,* 69–83.

truths, and two ordinances for observance in the church. It was mailed to
Mission halls, cottage meetings, and house groups of similar doctrinal
understanding; there was also attached a 'tear off slip' to be signed by the
pastor/elders of any fellowship seeking to adhere to the AoG then returned to
the secretary, E. C. Boulton. This meeting was not successful and as Gee
states, 'the time was not fully ripe'. Events at Swanwick and Sheffield were a
disappointment to the organisers and in particular to W. F. P. Burton who had
invested much energy in its formation.[554]

According to Gee, there was a further exchange of correspondence between
Wales and America following the abortive meeting of 1922; Allen states that
the Welsh were 'tired of the timidity of their English brethren'.[555] Coupled to
this frustration with the English and the increased pressure from the Apostolic
Church, the Welsh proto-AoG saw no hope of a British denomination; hence
America was again viewed as their 'promised land'. As mentioned above, Gee
believed this further correspondence 'stung the English brethren into action,'
thus paving the way for a reconvening of the '1922 committee' under the
leadership of Parr and Myerscough but minus the Elim contingent. Kay further
relates that a visit to Britain during the intervening years from South African
Archibald Cooper had once again given rise to the issue of organisational
structure in order to solidify the fluid Pentecostal situation.

In collusion with Myerscough and Parr, Cooper resurrected the discussions on
unity and following another letter of 23 November 1923 a Pentecostal leader's
conference was arranged at Aston, Birmingham on 1 February 1924. Twelve
leaders responded, namely: J. Nelson Parr (Manchester), R. C. Bell
(Hampstead), Charles Buckley (Chesterfield), A. Howard and John Carter
(London), Mrs Cantel (London – the only woman), J. Douglas (Stratford),
Donald Gee (Edinburgh), Tom Hicks (Crosskeys, representing the AoG
W&Mon), Arthur Inman (Mansfield Woodhouse), E. W. Moser (Southsea),
Fred Watson (Blackburn), and Arthur Watkinson (York). Apologies were
received from Thomas Myerscough who was detained due to illness. This
group elected Parr as its chairman and introduced a system of local assembly
autonomy within a fellowship of like-minded assemblies who adhered to the

---

[554] Gee, *Wind and Flame,* 126, Kay, *Inside Story,* 70–1.

[555] Allen, 'Signs and Wonders', 111, Gee, *Wind and Flame,* 126–30.

same fundamental truths. This group adopted the title 'Assemblies of God in Great Britain and Ireland' and those present ratified the new AoG GB&I constitution.[556] Wales, and in particular the small mining village of Crosskeys, played a major role in establishing the AoG in Britain. This is illustrated by the fact that the first executive presbytery in Britain consisted of: W. Davies (Caerau), T. Hicks (Crosskeys), A. H. Carter, T. Myerscough, J. N. Parr, F. Watson and H. Webster, hence two of the seven representatives were from Wales.[557] This gathering also decided to publish a quarterly magazine to be called *Redemption Tidings* with Parr as the editor. By March of 1924, some seventy assemblies had agreed to join the new denomination and approximately half were from Wales. When the full minutes of the new denomination were published later in 1924 there were thirty-eight assemblies listed in England and Ireland but also thirty-eight in Wales alone. Thus with fifty percent of the total AoG churches located in Wales, one must give greater credit to these pioneer Welsh Pentecostals who turned firstly to America and then to unity within Britain. Although the English Pentecostals drove the new denomination forward, the Welsh input through their initial contact with America and their heeding of Bell's helpful advice was not insignificant. The desire expressed by the Welsh for the creation of a specific denomination gave others within British Pentecostalism the motivation to construct the AoG GB&I.

The majority of the significant figures involved in AoG W&Mon were from Crosskeys, with Tom Mercy and Tom Hicks involved in the formative talks of the British AoG. The next chapter will assess the role of Crosskeys assembly which is held to be the first AoG assembly established in SE Wales. This assembly was to have a wide ranging influence upon AoG both at home and abroad. Its origins and growth between 1912 and 1934 when a new larger meeting hall was opened will be examined.

---

[556] Significant Elim figures not in attendance were George Jeffreys and E. C. W. Boulton.

[557] The structure of AoG has evolved over the period between 1924 and 2011; however Welsh representation on the Executive has been a constant concern, with Leonard Jenkins, Eric Dando and in more recent years Allan Hewitt all serving for long periods on the Committee.

Chapter 5 Crosskeys: The Mother Church of AoG in SE Wales

Following the fervour of the Revival in Wales 1904–05, a house group commenced in Wattsville, that later became the AoG assembly in Crosskeys. That assembly was set to have a major impact upon Welsh and British AoG, providing executive council delegates and a number of pastors and missionaries within that denomination.[558] The members of Crosskeys wholeheartedly supported world mission through generous financial commitments, and their annual Whitsun conventions, at which many of the leading AoG figures from home and abroad were the invited speakers, became important events in the early history of the movement.[559]

I am indebted to the work of the late Pastor W. G. Attwood, one of the original members at Crosskeys, and later pioneer pastor at Clyde Street AoG Risca, for the information on this fellowship.[560] There are also available some financial records dating from 1930 which record the annual missionary offerings dating from 1916–29. It is possible from these to glean the names of some influential Pentecostal/AoG preachers who were regular visitors to Crosskeys.[561] Another source is the recollections of Paul Mercy, an AoG pastor, who wrote a series of articles in *Redemption Tidings* between November 1985 and May 1987.[562] One major constraint on this research is that a number of years ago the Crosskeys Pentecostal Church was burgled, the safe was stolen and the contents destroyed, hence all the historical records were lost. This chapter will consider

---

[558] Some of the members who entered AoG ministry were: Tom Mercy, Leonard Jenkins, W. G. Attwood, Alf Mitchell, Wilfred Mercy, W. T. H. Richards, Paul Mercy, David Kidd, Peter Jenkins and Haydn Jeffreys.

[559] At the time of writing the annual Whitsun convention is still held at Crosskeys.

[560] W. G. Attwood, *How Pentecost came to Crosskeys* (c. 1940). This document was made available to me by the late Mr William Davage of the Crosskeys Assembly in 2011. See also Sidney Mercy, 'Pentecost in South Wales', *Pentecostal Evangel,* June 1928, 8; <www.ifphc.org/pdf/PentecostalEvangel/1920-1929/1928/1928_06_16pdf#page8>

[561] These records dated 1930 – 1951 were discovered in the estate of the late Mr William Davage who had served the Crosskeys assembly for many years as secretary and treasurer. There are also the Missionary accounts from 1945–1968 these have been made available to me by Mrs Lorna Smith a member at Crosskeys.

[562] I am grateful to Paul Mercy, grandson of Sidney Mercy for allowing me to copy these articles and use them in this research. One major drawback to these articles is their personal and narrative nature hence with no serious engagement or critical analysis of the theological implications. However Mercy does confirm some details contained within the work of Attwood.

the origins and growth of the Crosskeys Assembly from its inception in 1912 to the opening of the new larger hall in 1934. This date will allow for an evaluation of the impact made by Tom Mercy (d. 1935), the first officially recognised pastor and an influential figure in the AoG GB&I.

Crosskeys: Local Churches

Crosskeys is a small village situated at the confluence of the Ebbw and Sirhowy rivers, approximately seven mile north of Newport in SE Wales; it was built around the Blackvein coal mine.[563] At the time of the emergence of the proto-Pentecostal group, religious life in Crosskeys could be viewed as a microcosm of the wider Welsh situation.[564] According to Pope, the Baptist churches were numerically stronger in Monmouthshire during this period and this appears to have been the case in Crosskeys.[565] The village was served by St. Catherine's Anglican Church (established 1906), Hope Baptist Church (est. 1882) and led by Rev. William Evans (1894–1914), the Primitive Methodists (est. 1880) under the oversight of Rev. W. Wilcock and the Wesleyan Methodists located on High Street (meetings commenced c. 1850). Three other significant chapels in the vicinity were Trinity Congregational Pontywaun (est. 1870) under the guidance of Rev. Harold Davies, Zion Congregational Wattsville (commenced 1907 as a daughter church of Trinity), and Bethel Baptist in Wattsville (a daughter church of Hope Baptist which began holding services in 1905).

Despite the proto-AoG group that emerged from Trinity Pontywaun and Zion Wattsville, the health of the churches in the vicinity of Crosskeys between the 1890s and 1914 was prosperous. This was particularly true of Hope Baptist. During the ministry of Rev. William Evans, the congregation grew and planted Bethel, Wattsville and Zion (Cwmcarn), as daughter churches. Graham Osborne records that the congregation of Hope in 1903 stood at 350 people with 400–500 children in the Sunday school.[566] It was also proposed that the

---

[563] Rayner Rosser, *Collieries of the Sirhowy Valley* (Abertillery: Old Bakehouse, 1996), 99–103, who records some 120 deaths at the mine in 1880.

[564] D. Densil Morgan, *The Span of the Cross* (Cardiff: University of Wales Press, 1999), 5–40 and in particular 12–23, where the strength of the principal non-conformist denominations is highlighted.

[565] Robert Pope, *Building Jerusalem* (Cardiff: University of Wales Press, 1998), 115.

[566] Graham O. Osborne, *A History of Hope Baptist Church* (Abertillery: Old Bakehouse, 2006), 14.

church be extended following the influx of converts from the Revival of 1904–05. Alongside this outward 'success' there were, nonetheless internal issues that led to the slow decline of the church.

Osborne suggests that the major issues in Hope were financial, but there were also some problems that arose with certain strong personalities in the church that caused division. Osborne also hints at another possible problem: the promotion of politics. It appears that some church leaders were keen to have Lloyd George to speak in order to raise funds to pay the debt on the building. However there was opposition to this and the lecture was never given; within Wales there was tension between church and politics. Osborne suggests that some had a keen interest in the social and political issues of the day, perhaps neglecting the spiritual emphasis of the church, and surrendering it for a more nominal Christianity.[567] Coupled to these issues, the outward expansion of daughter churches at Cwmcarn and Wattsville saw members of the mother church 'relocate' to support these new congregations in their own villages. Despite these difficulties the witness of Hope has continued to the present day.[568]

Trinity Congregational Church, Trinity Hill, Pontywaun, played a vital role in the emergence of the Crosskeys Full Gospel Mission.[569] Trinity had commenced worship as a positive response to the influx of English speaking labourers and workers in the mid-late nineteenth century and worship was first held in the building in 1870. Rev. D. G. Davies, of the Glyn Congregational Church, Risca, responded to the need of the immigrant workers by planting a new church in Crosskeys. Initially they met in the Long Room of the Crosskeys Hotel until the site in Pontywaun became available; a building was erected for the cost of £680 with much of the finance being raised by a Samuel Morley of Bristol who helped many Congregational churches in Wales. From its inception in 1870 Trinity Congregational Church was a member of the Congregational Union and also on a local level the Monmouthshire English

---

[567] Morgan, *Span*, 5–40.

[568] R. Tudur Jones, *Faith and the Crisis of a Nation* (Cardiff: University of Wales Press, 2004), 368–9 and 412–19 for a summary of the other possible strains placed upon the Evangelical communities of Wales.

[569] Brian Collins, *Crumlin to Pontymister Places of Worship* (Abertillery: Old Bakehouse, 2005), 91–3. For a wider picture of the Congregational denomination in Wales see R. Tudur Jones, *Congregationalism in Wales* (Cardiff: University of Wales Press, 2004).

Union.[570] Although the early records of Trinity have been lost, it appears that the chapel grew numerically and in 1911 a Sunday school hall was added to the site.[571]

Sidney Mercy (1857–1934), later known affectionately as 'Father Mercy', is a central figure in the establishing of Crosskeys AoG. He was converted at the age of twenty-five from a life of gambling and violence; he described himself as someone 'that hated everything that was good'.[572] He records how on two occasions he had decided to kill a man; one a policeman for insulting him, and the other his step-father for abusing his mother. His conversion was the result of his entering a local Congregational chapel in Machen, his place of residence at that time, in order to find shelter from the cold weather. He prayed that God would reveal the awesome reality of hell in order to convince him of the necessity of following Christ. His conversion came one morning as he walked to the local coal mine to start his shift. Of this experience he wrote: 'One morning when about to go down to the mines to my work, the Lord saved me all through from my head to my toes; something went through me, and I was absolutely sure my sins were forgiven.'[573]

From this moment Mercy was so transformed as to cause people to think he had 'religious mania'. His desire was to spread the gospel message and see his workmates and family converted to Christ. Mercy's mother died at the age of forty-four from heart complaints, a problem that Sidney himself inherited. As a result his work in the mines had to cease, and he then turned his attention to his wife's occupation of shoe sales and repairs. The family then moved to live in Crosskeys. Sidney Mercy was married to Elizabeth (b. 1856) and they had nine children, Tom (b. 1878), Emma (b. 1880), Albert (b. 1888), Lill (b. 1889), May (b. 1891), John (b. 1893), Wilfred (b. 1895), Agnes (b. 1897), and Ada (b. 1898).[574] Whilst living in High Street, Crosskeys they attended Trinity

---

[570] Information available from the Congregational Library, London and is contained within the collection of Year Books, www.dwlib.co.uk my thanks to Mr David Powell of the Congregational Library for his assistance in this matter.

[571] According to Leon Jenkins (Church Secretary in 2005) see Collins, *Crumlin to Pontymister,* 91–3.

[572] Mercy, 'Pentecost in South Wales'.

[573] Mercy, 'Pentecost in South Wales'.

[574] <www.1901censusonline.com>

Congregational Church, Pontywaun where Sidney served faithfully as a deacon and became recognised as the 'senior deacon'.[575] He had been a faithful member at Trinity Congregational, Pontywaun, and was involved with the establishing of Zion, Wattsville. Mercy had been particularly impressed with and influenced by the deeper life teachings of the 'Keswick in Wales' movement. Under the influence of Keswick, he would have heard the ministry of such individuals as Jessie Penn-Lewis, R. B. Jones and A. T. Pierson to name but a few.[576] As a result of this strong influence Mercy believed that he could experience more of God following conversion; he admits that he struggled with the mastery of 'inbred sin'.[577] His family had also experienced the direct effects of the Welsh Revival 1904–05 during which time his son Tom was converted.

Zion Congregational, Wattsville, also had a particular significance in relation to the emergence of Crosskeys AoG, as some of its original members emerged from that congregation. The church was built as a daughter church of Trinity Congregational Church in Pontywaun when the residents of Wattsville, who had to travel three miles to worship in Pontywaun, decided it would be more practical to provide a church in their own village. The land was donated by the organisation which was later known as the National Coal Board and construction began. The initial building was intended to be a schoolroom attached to a larger chapel; but there were insufficient funds and the larger chapel was never built. The benches which were used as pews came from the deck of a liner which had been sent to C. H. Bailey's shipyard in Newport to be decommissioned. Mrs Bailey was an influential supporter of the Congregational churches in the Newport area and often provided items to furnish the church buildings in the surrounding valleys. The first service was held at Zion in November 1907. Zion was an active church for most of its life with a large Sunday school and sisterhood contributing to the worship. The church was also very proud of its choir which was trained by a series of highly respected local musicians. Public worship ceased there in 2002.[578]

---

[575] This was the title used by Paul Mercy to designate his grandfather's position of prominence with the Trinity congregation. Sidney Mercy gives the brief insight into his conversion in Mercy, 'Pentecost in South Wales'.

[576] Brynmor Pierce Jones, *The Spiritual History of Keswick in Wales 1903–1983* (Cwmbran: CLP, 1989).

[577] Sidney Mercy, 'Pentecost in South Wales'.

[578] Information from <www.urc-wales.org.uk>. A small, faithful group continued to worship at Zion until, in the autumn of 2001, the report from the buildings inspector confirmed that the chapel was structurally unsound and

One interesting issue that has arisen in this narrative is the prominence, in early Pentecostalism in SE Wales, of members of Congregational churches. Sidney Mercy joins the list of Congregationalists impressed with Pentecostalism, which consists of other notable figures such as: T. M. Jeffreys of Waunlwyd, George and Stephen Jeffreys of Maesteg, D. P. Williams and on a wider British scene Donald Gee of Finsbury Park London. The Congregationalists or Independents trace their origins to the time of Queen Elizabeth I (1558–1603); however Albert Peel traces their origins to the time of the New Testament. Peel argues that all New Testament churches were Congregational in polity, answering to Christ as the true head of the church, and not affiliated to any one denomination.[579] The Congregational Union of England and Wales emerged in 1831, setting down some general guidelines of belief and practice; though with no intention to interfere with the autonomy of local churches.[580]

Despite the union of 1831, some Congregational Churches did not employ a confession of faith, believing that the Bible alone was their basis for faith.[581] This lack of stringent doctrinal parameters was a reaction to the tight doctrinal controls of the other mainline evangelical denominations. As Davies states '[some] people began to regard the old Calvinistic teachings as narrow and restricting.'[582] This desire for openness was a factor in the spread of liberal theology in South Wales, an attitude which had both a positive and negative impact, for as, Kirby suggests, the Congregational Union was slowly 'imbibed by Liberal Theology.' This too could have proven a reason for Mercy and his

---

remedial work was prohibitively expensive. The members held a meeting on 2 June 2002 at which it was decided with great sadness that the last service would be held at Zion on 30 June 2002. The last service of thanksgiving for the life of the church at Wattsville, for its witness in the community and for the many blessings received by all those who had shared fellowship in the 'schoolroom' over the past 95 years. Zion Wattsville is no longer in existence and is now the location of residential housing.

[579] Albert Peel, *These Hundred Years 1831–1931* (London: Congregational Union, 1931), see also G.W. Kirby, 'Congregationalism' in Sinclair B. Ferguson, ed., *NDT* (Leicester: I.V.P. 1988), 159–61, see also Tudur Jones, *Congregationalism in Wales* and Tudur Jones, *Faith and the Crisis*.

[580] Peel, *These Hundred Years,* 69–74.

[581] This was also apparent in some early Baptist churches; however, other Congregational Churches were strong on doctrine and had strong leadership in the form of elders. The situation within the Congregational Church in Wales appears to have been as much of a melee as the general Welsh Religious scene.

[582] Gwyn Davies, *A Light in the Land* (Bridgend: Bryntirion Press, 2002), 97.

fellow dissenters to leave their respective churches.[583] However, these Congregationalists were sincere in their belief and their position allowed for more openness and freedom in responding to any new biblical teaching. It could be said that if this 'Congregational flexibility'—a theme in historical Congregationalism reaching back as far as the Puritans William Wroth and Walter Craddock—was in the ascendance in Pontywaun and Wattsville, then these people would have been more receptive to a new interpretation of pneumatology. According to Paul Mercy, Trinity Pontywaun did not hold a definite statement of faith, hence allowing Sidney Mercy to be more open to new teaching.[584] Another issue rising from this strong Congregational heritage in Wales is the eventual structure of the AoG W&Mon and later AoG GB&I. They too were initially formed along similar lines to the Congregational Union.

Insistence upon the independence of the local Christian community was never regarded as precluding a loose fellowship of independent local churches for purposes of mutual consultation and edification.[585]

The later embryonic AoG denomination also stated that their assemblies were a loose fellowship of 'Spirit filled' believers who were members of independent and autonomous local assemblies. However they did all accept a fundamental statement of faith and agree to close co-operation and fellowship.[586]

Wattsville, 'Second Comers' and Crosskeys

B. P. Jones continues the unfolding saga of the emergence of Pentecostalism in SE Wales when he records events in Wattsville that led directly to the establishing of Crosskeys AoG:

> A group of Revival converts continued to meet in Mrs Eatwell's house under the guidance of Josiah Purnell, but the first flush was over and God came down to stir them again. An attempt to set up their own Hall was stifled by the officers of Zion, Wattsville, who opposed the doctrine of the Second Coming. Later on, a crisis was reached when Mrs Watts

---

[583] Kirby, 'Congregationalism'.

[584] Paul Mercy made this statement to me during a private conversation in February 2012. As mentioned earlier the records of Trinity have been lost so it is impossible to ascertain if they did or did not have a Statement of Faith c. 1911.

[585] Kirby, 'Congregationalism'.

[586] AoG Minutes 1924 and *Redemption*, July 1924.

preached in her chapel on the Second Coming in the summer of 1912 and was asked to resign.[587]

The identity of Mrs Watts remains difficult to ascertain; however a Mrs Emily Eatwell (b. 1867) was resident at 24 Duffryn Terrace, Wattsville. She was a native of Wiltshire and married Thomas (b. 1858) who was employed as a colliery timberman, and they had two daughters Winnifred (b. 1898) and Evelyn (b. 1899).[588] There is no record of the Eatwell family being involved with the Crosskeys Full Gospel Mission following its establishment in 1912.

There is also some conjecture as to the identity of Josiah Purnell. Reference is made to two Josiah Purnells, they being a father and son. One was born in 1849 and resident in Risca and employed as a fireman in the local coal mine, and the other was born 1892 and who worked as a grocer's assistant in Crosskeys.[589] Either of these could have been the man mentioned by Jones. If it was the latter then he would have been a mere twelve years old at the time of the Welsh Revival and seems unlikely to have been the leader of a prayer meeting. However, the Revival in Wales had remarkable effects upon children so it is not impossible to link this young man with such a group.[590] If Josiah is considered too young, and the reference is not to his father (who had died by 1911), an alternative candidate could have been Jacob Purnell (b. 1882) who was converted in Zion Baptist Church, Brynmawr during the 1904–05 Revival.[591]

Purnell subsequently received his personal Pentecostal type baptism in the Holy Spirit independently of any outside teaching on the subject; he then embarked on an itinerant ministry. In 1920 Purnell came into contact with Pastor D. P. Williams (Apostolic Church) and established Apostolic missions in the area of Ebbw Vale, Beaufort, Cwm, and Brynmawr. By 1933 some twenty

---

[587] Brynmor Pierce Jones, *How Lovely are Thy Dwellings* (Newport: Wellspring, 1999), 128 and 'The Late Pastor Jacob Purnell's Testimony: The Monmouthshire Valleys', unpublished testimony obtained from Mr. Colin Evans of Abergavenny Apostolic Church.

[588] Census 1911.

[589] See <www.1901censusonline.com> and <www.census1911.co.uk>

[590] Kevin Adams, *A Diary of Revival* (Farnham: CWR, 2004), 106, who records girls as young as twelve receiving the Spirit during the Revival services.

[591] There is no reference to Josiah Purnell senior in the 1911 census.

Apostolic churches had been established within Monmouthshire, mainly through the ministry of Jacob Purnell. Before this time his itinerant ministry could possibly have taken him to Wattsville where he could have influenced the revival converts in their search for a greater outpouring of God's Spirit. However, there is no link between this post-Revival group and the Apostolic type Pentecostalism that Jacob Purnell is associated with throughout the rest of Monmouthshire. The identity of Josiah Purnell is open to debate; however, if one disregards Jacob Purnell, it is most interesting to note that the Crosskeys Pentecostal Church could have been formed as a result of a prayer meeting led initially by a teenage grocer's assistant. B. P. Jones makes a direct link to some converts of the 1904–05 Revival who gathered for further prayer and Bible study at the home of Mrs Eatwell and the emergence of Crosskeys AoG. It must be noted here that the group referred to by Jones may have pre-dated the 'second comers' by some six or seven years. This group was then joined by an influx of eager 'second comers' and they continued to meet and evolved into the embryonic AoG church in Crosskeys.

Gladstone Street, Crosskeys Full Gospel Mission

In 1914 a Pentecostal mission was opened in Gladstone Street, Crosskeys, in a derelict billiard hall that had begun life as a Presbyterian chapel.[592] But this Mission Hall was a result of the house group that met in Wattsville before 1912. Recording the history of the region, Gee writes:[593]

> About 1912 a Pentecostal work took root in the large village of Crosskeys, where two narrow valleys meet about nine miles north-west of Newport, Mon., that was destined to become a fruitful centre both of influence throughout Wales, and foreign missionary interest.[594]

Attwood agrees with Jones that the assembly began life as a result of the house group that emerged in Wattsville. However, Attwood supplies further details of an increase in the numbers gathering so that two homes were necessary to house the worshippers. These met officially from 1912 at the home of Tom

---

[592] This date, 1912, is the first official record I can find as to the commencement of the fellowship at Crosskeys and is contained within the financial records.

[593] Attwood, *How Pentecost*. The Crosskeys Pentecostal Church still worships at this same site.

[594] Donald Gee, *Wind and Flame* (Nottingham: AoG, 1967), 77.

Mills in Hafod Tudor Terrace, and Tom Hicks on Islwyn Road, Wattsville. Missen suggests that the meetings commenced on 6 October 1911 and he records the circumstances of their commencement as relating to the same doctrinal issue of the Second Coming of Christ. [595] However, it is best to accept Attwood's date of October 1912 for two reasons: one, he was himself involved with the initial meetings, then, secondly, this date also concurs with the financial records available which record 6 October 1912 as the commencement of the mission. However, it must be noted that the roots of the dissident group of Congregationalists reaches back to the effects of the Keswick teaching and to the fervour of the 1904–05 Revival. A further challenge to their theological understanding came around 1911, which may well be the date Missen records, when they were initially confronted by teaching on the Second Advent.

It is essential to recognise that not everyone was dissatisfied with liberal theology, conventional religiosity and the emphasis upon socio-political issues in some of the chapels joined the rising Pentecostal movement. Many remained in the independent mission halls or moved to biblically strong local chapels where they continued their Christian growth and development. [596] There was significant opposition to the growing Pentecostal movement within the established denominations, with many labelling it as heretical and emphasising overt emotionalism to the detriment of solid biblical teaching.

The events recorded at Wattsville, focusing more on eschatology than pneumatology, led to the formation of Crosskeys Full Gospel Mission. The content and urgency of the message preached in the summer of 1912 gripped some individuals, causing them to research the biblical teaching concerning the personal return of Christ. Sidney and Tom Mercy along with Tommy Davies, Tom Mills, W. G. Attwood, Tom Selathiel, and Tom Hicks gained the title 'Second Comers' as this theological emphasis shaped their ministry and preaching. Their insistence (some might say obsession) with the return of Christ became the driving force of this group. Members of the dissident group

---

[595] Alfred E. Missen, *A Sound of a Going* (Nottingham: AoG, 1973), 47.

[596] Jones, *King's Champions,* who highlights the growth of traditional evangelical churches at this time.

were regularly to be found walking the local mountains praying for the communities. Attwood records:

> We were miners and sometimes we worked on the afternoon shift (2pm–10pm). One week there were five or six of us working afternoons, so we agreed to meet one night at 11:30, after coming from the pit and take a walk together. We reached the top of Twym Barlwm mountain and then on to our knees in prayer. The dear Lord met us in a wonderful way and heaven came down, our souls to greet and Glory crowned the Mercy seat. So near we were to heaven that night, that we felt we could hear the song of the angels. Personally, the impression of that experience I have never forgotten. We came down from the mount that morning filled with joy and the Holy Ghost, enjoying a new experience with our Lord Jesus Christ and one we would never forget. [597]

Attwood records how they were full of the Holy Spirit—yet this experience came prior to their later Pentecostal understanding of being filled or baptised with the Spirit. These were already committed Christians, who would have been familiar with their denomination's pneumatology, and would have been aware of the terminology and experiences of the 1904–05 Revival. They had also been particularly influenced by the Keswick teaching, supported at Wattsville by Sidney Mercy. Hence they were not unfamiliar with the essential ministry of the Spirit in their lives but were committed to prayer and desired to experience the fullness of God. It was this 'new experience' which eventually led them to emergent Pentecostalism.

One wonders how the eventual theological position of this proto-pentecostal group might have developed differently had they been involved in chapels with a strong biblical ministry. This could possibly have made a significant difference in their understanding and experience; however they were left to discover their own way forward in regards to spirituality and in particular Pneumatology. As a result of their own biblical study the route to Pentecostalism became clear to this particular group. Faced with local opposition Mercy and his friends began to promote a new teaching which eventually combined with Pentecostalism and began to spread from Crosskeys

---

[597] Attwood, *How Pentecost*, 2.

to the surrounding villages and towns in SE Wales. This situation in Crosskeys mirrors, to some extent, the events at Azusa Street, Los Angeles, when William Seymour, the catalyst of Pentecostalism, was barred from local churches and so was forced to establish meetings first in local homes and then in the derelict livery stable on Azusa Street.[598]

Mercy and his associates began to promote the necessity of holiness of life and evangelism in light of the imminent return of Christ. It was this premillennial stance that concerned the leadership of Trinity and Zion. The weekly Bible class became dominated by conversation and debate over the Second Coming and the protagonists were told to stop emphasising the Parousia or leave; consequently the 'Second Comers' left the church.[599]

As mentioned in chapter three, the doctrine of the Second Coming was not new to Welsh evangelicalism, however the emphasis placed on the imminence of the Parousia and the urgency of mission was the significant theological issue that concerned the traditional Congregationalists. These proto-pentecostals expected the return of Christ 'today', this expectancy led to a greater emphasis on prayer and evangelism. The dissident Congregationalists continued their house meetings for approximately eighteen months until the houses became too small for the increasing numbers. After much prayer and searching they located a vacant property on Gladstone Street, Crosskeys, a former Presbyterian church which had been purchased by Mr Millership and utilised as a billiard hall. The hall had fallen into disrepair and Mr Hicks and Mr Attwood approached the owner regarding the possibility of purchasing it and restoring it to its original purpose as a church. Mr Millership agreed to sell the vacant hall for £400, so the 'Second Comers' believed it to be God's will to

---

[598] Cecil Robeck Jr., *The Azusa Street Mission and Revival* (Nashville, TN: Nelson, 2006); Frank Bartleman, *Azusa Street* (Gainesville, FL: Bridge, 2006).

[599] For a summary of the major views on eschatology see: Louis Berkhof, *Systematic Theology* (Edinburgh: Banner of Truth,1958 repr. 1998), 695–738; Wayne Grudem, *Systematic Theology* (Leicester: I.V.P. 1994), 1091– 167; and J. Rodman Williams, *Renewal Theology Three Volumes in One* (Grand Rapids, MI.: Zondervan, 1996) Volume Three, 289–515. For a Pentecostal perspective see: Allan Anderson, *An Introduction to Pentecostalism* (Cambridge: C.U.P., 2004), 206–24, D. J. Wilson 'Eschatology, Pentecostal Perspectives on' in Burgess, *NIDPCM*, 601–5; Stanley M. Horton, 'The Last Things' in Stanley M. Horton, ed., *Systematic Theology* (Springfield, MO: GPH, 2004), 597–63;8 and Keith Warrington, *Pentecostal Theology*, (London: T&T Clark, 2008), 309–23.

purchase and so commenced the process of renovating it into a suitable place of worship.

Pentecost in Crosskeys

Eschatology had shaped the early years at Wattsville/Crosskeys but it was not until 1914 that they were introduced to the Pentecostal teaching. During a visit to 'Maranatha', the missionary rest home of Mrs Cantel in Highbury, London, in 1914, Tom Mercy, the first recognised pastor at Crosskeys, encountered the new Pentecostal teaching.[600] Cantel's home held a significant role in connecting travelling American Pentecostals with the British constituency. Cecil Polhill was a regular visitor and often led the services at 'Maranatha'; another frequent attendee was Donald Gee.[601] Tom Mercy's visit would, therefore, have introduced him to some of the leading figures of the Pentecostal movement and to the ministry of Boddy in Sunderland. Upon his return to Crosskeys, Mercy spoke of the new teaching and experience, directing people's attention to the events in Sunderland. Later in 1914, Mr and Mrs Tom Hicks and Emma Mercy (Tom's sister) visited Sunderland where Mrs Hicks and Emma Mercy received their personal Spirit baptism;[602] hence Pentecost arrived in Crosskeys.

Others who became aware of the emerging Pentecostal testimony in 1914 were Leonard Jenkins, an elder at Crosskeys, and Billy Buggit. Both visited Belfast in order to listen to the preaching of George Jeffreys. During this visit, Leonard Jenkins, following an encounter with Congo missionary James Salter, received his personal Spirit baptism with the initial evidence of speaking in tongues; this spiritual experience occurred on 31 July 1914.[603] Upon their return to Crosskeys they promoted the Pentecostal experience with great vigour and added fervour. The meeting between Jenkins and Salter, who worked with W. F. P. Burton and the Congo Evangelistic Mission (CEM), led to a long

---

[600] Gee, *Wind and Flame*, 80–4 for an eyewitness account of events at Maranatha.

[601] Richard Massey, *Another Springtime* (Guildford: Highland, 1992), 9–13 and Donald Gee, *These Men I Knew* (Nottingham: AoG, 1980), 31–33.

[602] I am reliant on the word of Paul Mercy for this inclusion of Emma Mercy—I have been unable to substantiate her visit to Sunderland.

[603] Missen, *Sound of a Going*, 47.

association with many visits made to Crosskeys by CEM missionaries.[604] Although Mercy was the recognised leader of the Crosskeys Full Gospel Mission he had not yet received his personal Spirit baptism; therefore Leonard Jenkins took the primary role in dealing with all things pneumatological within the church. By 1923 Leonard Jenkins had left Crosskeys to assist in the establishing of the Pentecostal work in Newbridge, some five miles north of the village.[605]

Keswick in Wales was still having an influence amongst the churches of South Wales and in August 1914 twelve people from Wattsville/Crosskeys visited the Llandrindod convention. They attended in order to hear more of the Keswick teaching of entire surrender and the deeper life in the Spirit. The importance of the Keswick teaching cannot be overstated in the Crosskeys situation, for the holiness background of that teaching alerted the Crosskeys congregation to an awareness of a greater work of the Holy Spirit in the life of the believer. Their visit to the 1914 convention was cut short due to the outbreak of the Great War. Despite the curtailment, they did, however, meet a pastor Richard Howton (b. 1855) of Glossop Derbyshire, who had a widely recognised healing ministry.[606] Howton was married to Charlotte (b. 1860) and was the Pastor of the Gospel (?) Union in Glossop, by 1911 they lived in Spire Hollins Bethrapha, a 'Rest Home', in Glossop.[607] Howton had been approached by Sidney Mercy in his quest for healing from his heart condition. Upon Mercy's request for prayer Howton asked if he had been baptised by full immersion. Mercy, a strong Congregationalist, stated that infant baptism had been sufficient in his upbringing.[608] Howton explained that in his opinion, full

---

[604]David Womersley & David Garrard, eds., *Into Africa* (Preston: CAM, 2005); W. F. Burton, *God Working With Them* (London: Victory Press, 1933); E. Hodgson, *Fishing For Congo Fisher Folk* (London: AoG, 1934). This connection is still maintained between Crosskeys and the now named Central Africa Mission (CAM) missionaries.

[605]Missen, *Sound of a Going*, 47.

[606] Attwood, *How Pentecost*, and Mercy, 'Pentecost in South Wales', who both refer to the pivotal role played by their meeting with Howton.

[607] The census records are poorly reproduced and it is difficult to ascertain the name of the church or mission of which Howton was the pastor. See Richard Howton, *Divine Healing and Demon Possession* (London: Ward, Lock & Co., 1909), Mercy 'Pentecost in South Wales' and Attwood, *How Pentecost*.

[608] David Petts, *You'd Better Believe It* (Mattersey: Mattersey Hall, 1999), 69–78.

immersion was necessary and that Mercy was disobeying scripture by avoiding this rite. After some thought, a very physically weak Mercy agreed to water baptism. Following this event he was anointed with oil, prayed for and healed of his heart condition. This interaction over water baptism and healing led to them becoming foundational teachings at Crosskeys. Despite Howton's healing ministry he was very sceptical of the rising Pentecostal movement and during their conversation, Howton, a staunch Baptist, had warned Mercy of the counterfeit power of Pentecostalism. He was, according to Mercy, particularly concerned with the Pentecostal based ministry of an evangelist named James Tetchner (d. 1928), an associate of Boddy in Sunderland. A few of the Crosskeys members kept in communication with Howton and visited his Easter convention the following year. Following this encounter, Sidney Mercy decided to seek out Tetchner and hear him for himself, so an invitation was extended for Tetchner to visit Crosskeys.

A native of Sunderland, Tetchner attended the Salvation Army meetings in that city, eventually coming into contact with Boddy in 1907. This contact led to him receiving the Pentecostal baptism in the Holy Spirit and commencing an itinerant ministry propagating the Pentecostal testimony. Tetchner continued as a Pentecostal evangelist, joining the AoG at its formation in 1924, and remained a member until his death in 1928. J. Tetchner is listed as an initial signatory of the AoG Constitution in 1924; he represented the assembly at Horden, Durham.[609] Tetchner was very influential in the formation of the Pentecostal witness in Crosskeys.[610] Sidney Mercy was impressed by Tetchner and his teaching, believing God had something more for those with the desire for a deeper spiritual experience. This 'new' Pentecostal experience was the thing that Mercy was searching for. He along with others in Crosskeys received his personal Spirit baptism as a result of Tetchner's ministry. It is ironic how the warning of Howton to avoid Tetchner and Pentecostalism actually led to a strong relationship between Tetchner and Crosskeys. According to Gee, Tetchner would have appealed to the Welsh believers due to his fiery nature and striking appearance describing him as a modern day 'John the Baptist'.[611]

---

[609] AoG Constitution, 1924, also lists T. Tetchner as representative at Scarborough.

[610] Keith Malcomson, *Pentecostal Pioneers* (Xulon Press, 2008), 153–4; Mercy, 'Pentecost in South Wales'.

[611] Gee, *Wind and Flame,* 68.

The new Pentecostal experience led Mercy to hold 'receiving meetings' at Crosskeys; these were times when people would wait for the baptism of the Spirit and evidential tongues. Many of the congregation came into this experience. Mercy recounts events:

> I was as ignorant as a donkey as to how such a meeting should be conducted. Early in the proceedings, four or five present were prostrated. I saw that this manifestation corresponded with Acts, when some said on the Day of Pentecost, "These men are full of new wine." I danced for joy, since in our ignorance God had met us so wonderfully and a member of my own family spoke in tongues.[612]

This exuberance, reminiscent of occurrences in the Welsh Revival 1904–05, but with the added ingredient of initial evidence, set the foundation for the Pentecostal nature of the Crosskeys Full Gospel Mission. One issue which is clear from Mercy's comments is the simplicity of his faith in believing that God could reproduce the Acts 2 events in a modern context. This is a belief that has been paramount in AoG (and wider Pentecostalism) since its inception. The acceptance of the Pentecostal doctrine by Tom Mercy, Tom Hicks, Leonard Jenkins, and Billy Buggit enabled them to return to Crosskeys confident of the fact that the others of the congregation, who had been significantly influenced by Keswick, were open to a deeper work of God: for them this was found in the emergent Pentecostalism. Not all the Mercy family were in favour of Pentecost. Sidney's wife was initially sceptical of the move from Trinity, Pontywaun. A Welsh speaker and ardent chapelgoer, the thought of such a modern day Pentecost was abhorrent to her; however, a remarkable incident led to her conversion to Pentecost. During a meeting there was a message in tongues which Mrs Mercy recognised as being in the Welsh language. To her surprise, a non-Welsh speaker, Mr Tom Mills, gave a word for word interpretation of the tongues – hence Mrs Mercy's scepticism was dissolved and she accepted the Pentecostal teaching.[613] Although the title 'Second Comers' was linked to

---

[612] Mercy, 'Pentecost in South Wales'.
[613] Paul Mercy, *Redemption*, March 1986.

the Crosskeys assembly, from 1914 they became a Pentecostal congregation emphasising Spirit baptism with the initial evidence of speaking in tongues.

Belief and Practice

Writing in 1928, Sidney Mercy commented on the theological stance of the Crosskeys Full Gospel Mission by stating that the fellowship believed in the, 'verbal inspiration of the Bible, Divine healing, Holiness, the Gifts of the Spirit, the Lord's Second Coming and Pentecost with the sign of Tongues.'[614]

This later summary of the beliefs of the Crosskeys Assembly has broadly evangelical foundations but with the added dimension of their specific pneumatology. This theological position is in line with the AoG stance and the earliest constitutional minutes of Crosskeys Pentecostal Church state:[615]

> The Church is called "The CROSS KEYS PENTECOSTAL CHURCH", and is in fellowship with the Assemblies of God, Great Britain and Ireland.

As a result the fundamental beliefs are those as set down by the AoG in 1924 and these have remained the standard for the church until the time of writing. Within the context of local church policy, it was agreed that all elders and deacons were to be men who have been baptised in the Holy Spirit as suggested by Acts 2:4, and who also fulfilled the qualifications as set out in 1 Timothy 3:1–13 and Titus 1:5–9. Of interest here is that Spirit baptism is given as the first qualification for eldership rather than the biblical standard as set out in the Pastoral Epistles; this approach emphasises further the fact that this congregation was primarily Pentecostal in belief and practice.

As the congregation steadily grew, another important doctrinal issue became prominent in Crosskeys—water baptism by total immersion. This act followed conversion, and was regarded as the public confession of faith and the introduction to a new lifestyle. The original hall on Gladstone Street did not have a baptismal pool, and so those who desired to 'follow the Lord through the waters' were transported by horse drawn cart to the 'Lighthouse', a site at

---

[614] Mercy, 'Pentecost in South Wales'.

[615] Unfortunately there is no date supplied on these minutes however they must be post-1924 as this was the time of the formation of AoG GB&I.

the mouth of the river Usk, near Newport. The first baptismal service was held in the cold waters of the Bristol Channel on a Saturday afternoon early in 1914. This service attracted much attention, with some villagers even suggesting that 'Father' Mercy was going to attempt to 'walk on the water' in order to demonstrate the power of the Holy Spirit in his life. Baptismal services were held occasionally in the Sirhowy River, a short walk from the chapel, however, due to the amount of pollution from coal and iron works, this was not a popular site.

Miraculous Outcomes

During the early years of growth and development at Crosskeys, the church was helped in its ministry by the effecting of miracles within the community. The miraculous—with a particular emphasis on divine healing—made an impact on individuals which resulted in them experiencing a religious conversion and joining the Pentecostals. As a result of this the Crosskeys assembly also served as a magnet for the early Pentecostals in the locality.

Many of the interested parties were miners, who generally commenced their shift underground at 6am. It became their standard practice to spend an hour in prayer before leaving for work, and so for them to rise at 4am was not unusual. Paul Mercy relates how that even following such a long shift in the mines, men would walk from Machen in the next valley to be at the Crosskeys midweek services. Some testified to the fact that their return journey home was 'in the Spirit', so that having taken the first step from the chapel in Gladstone Street, it seemed to them that they arrived at their own front doors very quickly.[616]

As noted, a significant emphasis was placed on divine healing at Crosskeys, with many people claiming to have been healed from a variety of illnesses.[617] Sidney Mercy records a number of such instances of healing; one such incident was the healing of his daughter Ada (later Ada Dixon), who had suffered with a

---

[616] Paul Mercy, *Redemption,* Nov. 1985.

[617] Mercy, 'Pentecost in South Wales'. See also, Anna C. Reiff, 'Mining – From Coal to Men', *The Latter Rain Evangel*, October, (1922), 14–16 <www.ifphc.org/LatterRainEvangel/1920-1929>

serious speech impediment.[618] She was prayed for in the Crosskeys Mission hall. Her problem was cured and she went on to be a well-known and respected preacher in Pentecostal circles. Others were healed of cancers, consumption, and heart problems; with some of these healings leading to the Pentecostal message spreading throughout the valleys. Mercy states that the Pentecostal centres which grew in Llantwit, Rhydfelin, Pontyclun, Peterstone, Machen, Bedwas, Aberbargoed, Thomastown, Caerphilly, and Newport came into being as a direct result of healing miracles.[619] This claim is supported by Paul Mercy who records the healing of a Tom Jones, of Machen, from tuberculosis.[620] It is claimed that the miraculous manifestation of God's power was even witnessed through the 'healing' of a pig, owned by Arthur Kidd of Crosskeys, which was prayed for by Les Oliver of the Full Gospel Mission.[621] Paul Mercy further reports that one member prayed for his crop of broad beans in order that they may be protected from blight. This prayer was answered as he was the only man in the allotments that particular year to have a good crop of beans![622]

These events may appear trivial—or even far-fetched—but whatever these events are to be understood, the result of them was genuine conversion of families to Christ, with David Kidd (son of the pig owner) eventually entering the AoG ministry and serving as pastor at Crosskeys.[623]

Early Leaders at Crosskeys

As the Crosskeys Full Gospel Mission became established, there was a necessity to appoint an appropriate leadership. Sidney Mercy was the initial driving force of the group and was considered by many to be the first leader, but it was his son Tom who was recognised as the first pastor.

Tom Mercy was a man greatly respected in the community, not only because of his strong Christian standards but also because he served as the secretary and

---

[618] Missen, *Sound of a Going*, 48.

[619]David Petts, *Just a Taste of Heaven* (Mattersey: Mattersey Hall, 2006). See also Donald Gee, *Trophimus I have Left Sick* (London: Elim, 1952).

[620] Paul Mercy, *Redemption*, Nov. 1985.

[621] Paul Mercy, *Redemption,* June 1986.

[622] Paul Mercy, *Redemption Tidings,* July 1986.

[623] David Kidd, my maternal uncle, served at Rogerstone, Crosskeys, Newport, and Risca AoG churches before his death in 2012.

chairman of the Welsh National Union of Mine Workers. As mentioned in chapter four, the issue of conscientious objection did not trouble the emerging Welsh Pentecostals; hence the house groups and mission halls did not lose a generation of leaders to the war. The initial elders who supported Tom Mercy were: Tom Hicks, Tommy Davies, Tom Mills, and Leonard Jenkins—all of whom were employed in manual labour of 'national importance' and so were exempt from conscription. The unsophisticated style of the local leaders in Crosskeys helped to draw people who could relate to the vibrant and robust Pentecostalism of their working class colleagues. This gospel presentation offered in everyday language—and aimed at the hearts, not the intellects of people, with sincerity and simplicity—was an effective tool of evangelism in the mining community.

In order to assist the ongoing evangelistic zeal of the mission, W. G. Attwood was appointed as evangelist with the responsibility of helping any new assemblies that opened. He was responsible to the board of elders at Crosskeys, a fact which supports Missen's designation of Crosskeys as the mother church in the area. Jack Matthews often accompanied Attwood in his evangelistic work and they were also joined in their efforts by William (Billy) Lewis, a former member of Trinity Congregational, Pontywaun. This approach to the ministry of the church at Crosskeys was well ahead of its time with the introduction of team ministry in order to support the ongoing work of the gospel.[624] This approach was necessary as there were initially insufficient funds to employ a full time pastor. The use of lay-leaders became a common aspect of many AoG/Pentecostal assemblies. It is apparent that the church depended much on the use of visiting preachers. Tom Mercy was not a great preacher and he was aware of the necessity to bring in outside speakers in order to supplement his ministry.[625] Nevertheless he was a caring pastor and leader of

---

[624] Team Ministry has become a widely used term in recent church structure and leadership models.

[625] This view of Tom Mercy was suggested to me by some of the older members of Crosskeys who recollected some of his later ministry before his death in 1935. The same view is held regarding his brother Wilfred, his successor. See also Gee, *Wind,* 78 and Missen, *Sound of a Going,* 48–9.

his congregation, who witnessed substantial growth so that by 1928 the average Sunday attendance was one hundred and twenty people. [626]

Evangelism and Foreign Mission

Another aspect of the work in Crosskeys that attracted much attention was the dramatic conversions of some inhabitants of the village. Many of these were looked upon as the worst of citizens, miners who spent much money and time in the drinking taverns, involved in gambling and often violent towards their families. These received the gospel and Pentecost via the simple testimony of fellow miners such as Tom Mercy and were radically converted, as was the local GP, Dr Smith, who was converted just ten days before his untimely death on board ship to Australia. [627]

A recurring theme throughout the valleys of SE Wales is the impact of Pentecostals within the mining communities. Due to their eschatological urgency and hope, they did not fear death and were always ready to witness to their faith in Jesus Christ. Many other miners were brought to faith in these early years due to the example and lifestyles of these pioneers. The desire for evangelism instigated by a focus on the return of Christ caused these pioneers to hold open-air services within the communities of Wattsville and Crosskeys. A regular meeting place was near the Workman's Institute in Wattsville, which was known as 'penniless corner' for it was the place where the local unemployed gathered to seek employment or financial assistance from the passing locals. [628] The Pentecostals would offer these penniless people hope through the gospel but also food and limited financial assistance. This practical approach drew some to the meetings and eventually their conversion. Despite some turning to God the participants in these services were often verbally or physically abused yet this did not deter them and they carried on the practice for many years. The threat of abuse or even violence seemed to them insignificant in light of the urgency of their message of salvation.

---

[626] Mercy, 'Pentecost in South Wales'.

[627] *Redemption,* Jan. 1986.

[628] See <www.crosskeys.me.uk> for photographs of 'penniless corner' and other historical images of the village from the 1920s

The congregation developed a love for all aspects of mission and evangelism, both at home and overseas. The significance of the open air ministry was wide-ranging and the faithful members would take their message to neighbouring villages where they held open air services. It was this ministry that led to the formation of Pentecostal assemblies in Abercarn, Cwmcarn, Aberbeeg, Newbridge, Risca, and Rogerstone. Indeed all of these areas (except Cwmcarn) were home to AoG churches, as listed in the 1924 constitution. Sidney Mercy records that by 1928 there were thirty-six assemblies who owed their existence to the ministry of Crosskeys as the mother assembly.[629]

As a result of the increase in the congregation at Crosskeys the decision was made to build a larger meeting place. The site on Gladstone Street was considered the best suitable location and work commenced in July 1933. The church was built largely by volunteer labour, consisting mainly of miners from the Nine Mile Point and Black Vein Collieries, which at this time were on strike; these men gave of their time and money in order to dig away the side of the hill, install deep foundations and build the chapel. It was eventually opened at a cost of £1600 and furnished with the modern amenities of electric lighting and central heating, with seating for six hundred people. The opening service was held on Saturday 3rd March with both Tom Mercy and his father Sidney taking part in the service; they were joined by some twenty-four pastors and evangelists and a large congregation.[630] The officers of the Crosskeys Pentecostal Church at this time were: Tom Mercy (pastor), Gwilym Farmer (secretary), Rd. Williams (missionary secretary), and Ben Davies (Sunday school secretary).

As well as promoting the Pentecostal testimony and evangelising the local community, there was also a keen interest in foreign mission at Crosskeys. Tom Mercy served as the missionary secretary for the South Wales region within the developing AoG and fostered a particular link with the CEM and in particularly W. F. P. Burton, James Salter, Teddy Hodgson, and later with the

---

[629] Mercy, 'Pentecost in South Wales'.

[630] 'New Crosskeys Church', *The Ocean and National Magazine*, March/April (1934), 121.

Womersley family.[631] The keen interest in mission was reflected in the extent of their giving. Mercy wrote, 'We preach tithes and freewill offerings and in eleven years the sum of approximately $16,236 has been contributed to foreign missions alone, which does not include considerable amounts contributed for home needs.'[632]

The financial contributions to missions during this period which included the Great War and depression were considerable. The financial records reveal the extent of the generosity and are recorded in pounds, shillings and pence:

> 1916 - £68.2.9, 1917 - £119.15.10, 1918 – £303.15.6, 1919 - £433.18.7, 1920 - £454.7.10, 1921 - £403.2.7, 1922 - £316.19.6, 1923 - £380.7.11, 1924 - £408.15.8, 1925 - £250, 1926 - £198, 1927 - £200.0.11, 1928 - £176.3.4, 1929 - £170 and £14.4.4 making a grand total £3987.14.11.[633]

Some of the missionaries who regularly visited Crosskeys are listed in the financial records; they were: Miss B. Terrell (a Crosskeys member who travelled to India in 1924), Mr & Mrs Newington, Mr Fisher, Mr Burton, Mr Salter, Mr Hodgson, Mr Womersley (all C.E.M). Also, monthly donations were made to AoG Missions, British and Foreign Bible Society, SW Mission (possibly that which became The Welsh District Council Missionary Fund, namely, those missionaries supported specifically by the group of South Wales AoG churches). Regular contributions were also made to a Pentecostal Jewish Mission and the Home Missions department of AoG. The link with the Congo Mission was particularly strong in Crosskeys. According to Paul Mercy, who recollects his father Wilf's testimony, this link is illustrated by the fact that the assembly was the first to send a financial contribution to Burton and Salter in South Africa.[634] The sum of approximately £8 was sent to the pioneer missionaries as they contemplated their next move. Their options were to remain in South Africa with the little funds they had or, if enough finance was

---

[631] Elizabeth Donald, 'The Rushing Wind' in *Sunday Companion*, 8.4.1961, 15.4.1961, 22.4.1961 and 29.4.1961 is a fitting tribute to Teddy Hodgson. See also, Burton, *God Working* and Womersley & Garrard, eds., *Into Africa*.

[632] Mercy, 'Pentecost In South Wales'.

[633] Financial Records Full Gospel Mission, Crosskeys, Mon. I have been informed by the late Mr. William Davage of Crosskeys that the 'bulk' of this finance went to Burton's CEM. The missionary financial records post-1945 reveal a monthly contribution made to CEM.

[634] This fact was also given to me by the late Mr. William Davage of Crosskeys; however I find no reference of it in Burton, *God Working*.

made available in the next week then, they would follow their initial calling to Congo. Within a week the first money arrived from Crosskeys which allowed them to make the first tentative steps in to Equatorial Africa. By 2012 there were approximately one million believers connected with the denomination established in the Congo by Burton and Salter.

The financial records also provide insight about the early Pentecostal/AoG leaders who visited Crosskeys to preach at various meetings and the annual Whitsun Convention. Howard Carter, Donald Gee, Harold Horton, and Smith Wigglesworth were all guest preachers at the Crosskeys Convention. Many people over a wide area were attracted to the Whitsun meetings in order to hear the prominent Pentecostal teachers and preachers, but due to the limited size of the Mission Hall, the annual Convention was held at the Primitive Methodist Hall further along Gladstone Street.[635] From 1934, the Crosskeys assembly had sufficient seating to cater for congregations in excess of three hundred; one publication reported some six hundred seats.[636] Men such as Harold Horton and C. L. Parker (former Fellow and Tutor of University College, Oxford) helped to counter-balance the 'unsophisticated' Pentecostal preachers when they joined the staff at Hampstead Bible School under the leadership of A. Howard Carter.[637] These too visited Crosskeys to preach at the Whitsun Conventions.

The Crosskeys assembly grew steadily under the leadership offered by Tom Mercy and, following his premature death in 1935, the pastorate passed to his brother Wilfred. Tom Mercy had a significant influence not only in Crosskeys but also within AoG GB&I. He was a welcomed participant in national executive meetings and was frequently a source of godly counsel to the other executive members. Tom Mercy collapsed and died in the arms of David James Williams (1893–1957) pastor of 'The Power House' Treorchy, whilst officiating

---

[635]It is reported that one could see up to twenty coaches parked along Gladstone Street bringing people to the Convention meetings.

[636] *The Ocean and National Magazine,* March/April, (1934), 121.

[637] Colin Whittaker, *Seven Pentecostal Pioneers* (Basingstoke: Marshalls, 1983), 112, 131–45. See also, Gee, *Wind and Flame,* 150–2; William K. Kay, *Inside Story* (Mattersey: Mattersey Hall, 1990), 121–31 and Missen, *Sound of a Going,* photographs printed between pages 58–9 where C. L. Parker is listed as General Secretary of AoG 1932–1936.

190

at the opening ceremony of a new assembly at Trealaw, Rhondda on 17 August 1935.[638] As Mercy turned the key in the door, he collapsed, and as Gee poetically records: 'he fell back dead and entered—not the chapel but the presence of the Lord'.[639] The news came as a shock to the congregation at Crosskeys, but also the wider community and the Pentecostal Movement in general. It is reported that some two thousand people attended Mercy's funeral. Gee speaks highly of Mercy's influence:

> [He was] their beloved pastor (at Crosskeys) throughout the years, and his genial personality, administrative ability, and high qualities of Christian character endeared him to multitudes outside the Pentecostal Movement, and far beyond the borders of South Wales.[640]

Following the death of Tom Mercy, a prophetic vision received by Hubert (Bert) Hone (b. 1892), a member at Crosskeys, was shared with the church. In this vision, Wilfred Mercy was seen to be head and shoulders above the other leaders, so as a direct result he was installed as the pastor and he served the community for thirty years.[641] In addition, Missen relates a conversation between Donald Gee and Wilfred Mercy in which Gee appears to favour this appointment. Whilst attending the funeral of Tom Mercy, Gee is reported to have said: 'Well, Wilf, the mantle has fallen on you'.[642] Wilfred Mercy was inducted to the pastorate of Crosskeys Pentecostal Church on 17 September 1935.

The influence of the Mercy family has been considerable in Crosskeys, both within the local church and the wider community. The current membership owes a debt of gratitude to this family for the step of faith taken initially by Sidney in planting the church and seeing it through the initial years of difficulty and opposition. The significance of Tom Mercy cannot be overstated in the development of both Crosskeys and AoG W&Mon. A tribute to Tom

---

[638] This information was supplied to me by during a phone conversation with Mrs. Moira Jones of Cwmcarn, D. J. Williams' daughter, on 4.4.2012 and is the result of conversations she had with her parents as a child.

[639] Gee, *Wind and Flame*, 78.

[640] Gee, *Wind and Flame*, 78.

[641] Gee, *Wind and Flame*, 78 and Missen, *Sound of a Going*, 48–9. There are references to a Bro. Hone receiving 10 shillings from the Crosskeys assembly—most probably payment for ministry for example May 1932, Dec. 1932 and May 1933.

[642] Missen, *Sound of a Going*, 48–9.

Mercy was given by his nephew Paul in *Redemption Tidings* where he recalled Tom's 'gifting' with words of knowledge was much appreciated by the AoG Executive Council. He often provided the answer to difficult situations faced by the young body.[643] Coupled to this he was a man with a pastoral heart, caring for the congregation at Crosskeys often to the detriment of his own health.[644]

The Influence Spreads

The majority of the information in this next section has been taken from W. G. Attwood's personal recollections as recorded in his *How Pentecost Came to Crosskeys*.[645] The influence of Crosskeys continued to expand in SE Wales. Sydney Mercy was instrumental in sending out preachers to other local groups interested in Pentecostal teaching; such groups were emerging in Newbridge, Cwmfelinfach, Risca, and Pontllanfraith. The results of their prayers and preaching were soon felt in other parts of the valleys; the first people from outside the Wattsville and Crosskeys area to respond to their message were from Machen. Members of Machen Baptist church would walk over the mountain from the neighbouring valley in order to listen to their teaching on the Second Coming. They returned to their village and began meetings in the house of Mr Charlie Cox (b. 1875). From Machen, the message spread to Bedwas and the leaders at Crosskeys took responsibility for these emerging 'Second Comer' congregations, regularly sending preachers to support them in their ongoing search. Initially men from Crosskeys, such as Billy Lewis, Leonard Jenkins, and Tom Hicks, would travel to Machen, Bedwas, Earlswood, Risca, Newbridge, Pontllanfraith, Newport, and Abercarn in order to promote the doctrine of the Second Coming as well as (later) the Pentecostal testimony.

The Machen Pentecostal Assembly was officially recognised in 1924 under the leadership of Mr T. Early. Bedwas AoG church was led by Mr H. Richards and both were original signatories of the first AoG Constitution in 1924.

---

[643] Paul Mercy, *Redemption*, October 1986.

[644] See Appendix 5 for a list of the pastors of Crosskeys Pentecostal Church since its inception in 1912. The dates of this list are incomplete due to the loss of the chapel records.

[645] Attwood's account is not an academic piece of writing and lacks any substantiating footnoted evidence; however as an eyewitness of events in Crosskeys his thoughts are extremely helpful. I have had particular difficulty in tracing the backgrounds of some of those mentioned in his writing.

The next village to receive the message of the Second Coming was Pontllanfraith where three individuals were greatly impressed by the teaching. These three men were William Treasure (b. 1860 or 1887),[646] William Moore (b. 1895) and Harry John. William Moore was installed as the first pastor of Pontllanfraith AoG church and was another signatory of the first AoG constitution in 1924. The village of Earlswood, near Chepstow, was another recipient of the Pentecostal teaching via Crosskeys. A Mrs Davies of The Farm in Crosskeys began to attend the services at Gladstone Street. Mrs Davies introduced her sister, Mrs Phelps of Earlswood, to Pentecost and meetings commenced in Cherry Orchard Farm, Earlswood. According to Attwood, the leading figures in Earlswood were Mr Bovet, Tom and Horace Lewis, and Trefor Knight. Mr Bovet was an initial signatory of the 1924 AoG Constitution. Every weekend someone would travel from Crosskeys to Earlswood—a distance of approximately twenty miles—to preach and lead the seekers into the Pentecostal experience. When the gospel was preached at Earlswood, a number of people were converted; one significant convert being John (?) North (b. 1880), who quickly commenced meetings in the nearby village of Crick. A J. (or possibly T.) North is listed as the pastor of Crick Assembly and was an initial signatory of the 1924 AoG Constitution.[647]

Another outpost for Pentecostals was Newport, with meetings commencing there in 1916. A leading figure at Newport was Richard Anthony who saw his sister, Mrs Williams of Green Court Farm, Malpas, converted. Meetings were then commenced at the farm. From there the message spread to a Mrs Gibbs who opened her home at 91 Alma Street to the Pentecostals, with Richard Anthony and W. G. Attwood being responsible for the services. In order to unite these groups, a hall was found in Dock Street, with Richard Anthony leading the group. Anthony was the recognised pastor who signed the 1924 AoG Constitution.

According to Missen, by 1934 Crosskeys was 'directly or indirectly' responsible for the formation of some forty Pentecostal assemblies with the ministry of

---

[646] I have found reference to two men named William Treasure, both resident in Pontllanfraith. Either of them would have been the possible first pastor at Pontllanfraith.

[647] I would suggest that there is a typing error in the 1924 constitution and that T. North should read J. North.

both Tom Mercy and Tom Hicks being particularly influential.[648] Missen does not give any indication as to the identity of these forty assemblies but this would be consistent with Mercy's statement in 1928 that the figure stood at thirty-six.[649] The sentiment of Missen illustrates the wide ranging influence of Crosskeys during the early years of development in SE Wales.

Newbridge

Situated five miles north of Crosskeys and built around the success of the South and North Celynen collieries, the village of Newbridge has been home to a Pentecostal witness since 1918.[650] Until 1910, the town was well served by a variety of other evangelical denominations such as Beulah Welsh Baptist (1809), Tabernacle English Baptist, (1859), Wesley Hall Methodist, Temple Presbyterian (1891), Zoar Welsh Congregational (c. 1900), and Zion Congregational (1898). There was also the Anglican Church, which had its initial meeting in 1878 at the Newbridge Inn, until a temporary structure could be opened in 1888—a new building opened 1929.[651]

Newbridge benefitted from the effects of the Revival in 1904–05 with the expansion of the Baptist and Presbyterian churches in particular; the influx of workers to the coal industry also brought a rise in population which became a potential field of evangelism. Despite the success of the chapels, by 1918 a Pentecostal group was in embryonic form within the village. Mercy records how some three thousand people gathered in the open air to listen to the testimony of Pentecost from Crosskeys members; some of those in the audience were eventually converted and joined the chapel at Golden Grove. The Newbridge Pentecostal church began in Griffiths's shop, in Greenfield Terrace. It was to this shop that Mrs Terrell, an elder's wife from the Crosskeys Full Gospel Mission, came to help her sister with the business. Mr Terrell, a man with a passion for personal witness, would often visit the shop and sit talking to the customers about their need of salvation. Sidney Mercy refers to

---

[648] Missen, *Sound of a Going*, 47.

[649] Mercy, 'Pentecost in South Wales'.

[650] Mercy, 'Pentecost in South Wales'. The AoG church in Newbridge is located at Golden Grove.

[651] Temple, Zoar, and Zion are no longer functioning as worshipping communities. The Catholic Church: Our Lady of Peace was built in 1939. Newbridge was also home to a Christadelphian Church between 1923 and 1981.

the founding of the Newbridge assembly when he mentions a significant healing that occurred.[652] Mrs Pearce, a regular visit to Griffiths's shop in Greenfield had a seriously sick daughter who, according to Mercy, was suffering from cancer. Mr Terrell asked if he may be permitted to visit the child and pray for her healing; he did so and she recovered. This incident led to much debate and excitement within the community and Mr Terrell made frequent visits to the Pearce household in order to explain the Bible, preach, witness, promote the Pentecostal doctrines, and pray for others. Over a period of time, a small group started to gather at a house on North Road, the home of Mr and Mrs Pearce.

The belief in divine healing held an important place in the life and theology of the early Pentecostals, and the conviction that the gospel should be presented 'with signs following' is still an integral part of AoG teaching.[653] This was modelled on the account of Acts 3 where the healing of the lame man at the Temple gate provided the opportunity for Peter to preach about Jesus; consequently the Pentecostals saw healing ministry as a 'tool' for evangelism.[654] In order to maintain the progress in the work, Blodwyn Terrell and Ada Mercy of Crosskeys continued to visit Newbridge and build on the foundational ministry of Mr Terrell. These women would preach and testify to the work of God in their lives and eventually laid the foundation for a strong Pentecostal work in the village. The Pearce household was soon too small for the growing band of followers and the meetings were moved to Tynewydd Farm, at the top of High Street. The Pentecostal testimony continued, with people crowding into the kitchen and sitting on the stairs in order to listen to the message. The farm soon became too small to accommodate the enquirers and the need arose to find a permanent place of worship. Mr Fudge, the grocer, offered a room above his warehouse but on hearing more of the Pentecostal teaching, and particularly the emphasis on the Second Coming, he withdrew his offer of help. In a short time, a property became available to rent in Golden Grove. It was a building which had been owned by Oxford University and Llanover Estate but which had been sold to the local Methodist

---

[652] Mercy, 'Pentecost in South Wales'.

[653] Gee, *Trophimus I Have Left Sick*.

[654] David Petts, *Body Builders* (Mattersey: Mattersey Hall, 2002), 149–69 and Petts, *Just a Taste of Heaven*.

Connexion in 1832. Old Zion, as it was known, was no longer in use and from 1923, the 'Second Comers' rented the premises, eventually purchasing the property in 1928 for the sum of £750. The original leaders who signed the deeds were David Beecham (b. 1897), Mr Williams, Harry Parry (b. 1882), Ivor Walters (b. 1893), George Pullen (b. 1889), and A. Leonard Jenkins.[655] On 12 April 1929 John Henry (Harry) Parry registered the building as an official place of worship known as 'The Full Gospel Mission'. A. Leonard Jenkins, an elder from Crosskeys, was invited to be the first Pastor. His duties commenced in an unofficial capacity from 1922 and he served an initial congregation of thirty members whilst continuing his work as a gardener at the 'Lodge' in Crosskeys. He never received a wage from the church and served the growing congregation until 1967. A member of the executive council of AoG GB&I from 1929 until 1957, Leonard Jenkins became known as 'the elder statesman' of AoG in SE Wales.[656]

This chapter has offered the opportunity to trace the development and assess the impact made by the Crosskeys Full Gospel Mission. Despite the scarcity of primary and even secondary sources, enough has been uncovered to agree with Gee's assessment of its importance. The Mercy family, especially Sidney and Tom, were particularly prominent and stand as examples of individuals who were prepared to face any opposition in their stance for the truth they saw as being contained in their expression of Pentecostalism.

The next chapter will reflect on some of the important issues and questions which have arisen throughout this book.

---

[655] As Williams is such a popular name in Wales it is difficult to obtain any specific details about the Mr. Williams who signed the original deeds at Newbridge.

[656] The Newbridge AoG Church is currently (2015) led by Pastor Phillip Evans.

Chapter 6 Reflection: More Work to be Done

Despite the minority status of Pentecostalism in South Wales and elsewhere, the activity of these believers during the early decades of the twentieth century created a vibrant movement which was to become a significant part of Welsh religious history.[657]

As yet there is no definitive work on early Pentecostalism within Wales. It is hoped that this study will in part address that lack. There are a number of histories of the Apostolic Church and biographies of George Jeffreys, founder of Elim; however it would be valuable to compare and contrast these denominations, within their historical Welsh context.[658]

It is not the intention of this chapter to probe all aspects of this work as some subjects such as the Welsh Revival of 1904–05 have received voluminous attention, so too have the origins of AoG GB&I, as well as the generally accepted core distinctive of AoG theology, 'initial evidence'.[659] However an assessment will be made of those questions or even anomalies that surround a small group of Welsh Christians who deserted their traditional denominations in search of what they perceived to be a deeper experience of God.

From a socio-political perspective, there will be a brief analysis of the internationalisation of Welsh society, especially how the industrialisation of SE Wales made it easier for individuals to seek help and support from the American Pentecostals. In addition, there will be an assessment of reasons behind the demise of the influence of Rev. A. A. Boddy in Wales. The impact

---

[657]D. Gareth Evans, *A History of Wales 1906–2000* (Cardiff: University of Wales Press, 2000), 37–66 for a helpful overview of the interaction between religion and social issues. See also Robert Pope, *Seeking God's Kingdom* (Cardiff: University of Wales Press, 1999) and D. Densil Morgan, *The Span of The Cross* (Cardiff: University of Wales Press, 1999), both of which emphasise the complexity of the social, political, and theological situation within Wales between 1900 and 1924. D. Martyn Lloyd-Jones, 'Living The Christian Life - 5, New Developments in the 18th and 19th Century Teaching' in *Living the Christian Life: 1974 Westminster Conference Papers,* (Stoke-on-Trent: Tentmaker, 1974), 82–99, who charts the development of some of the theology that may have contributed to the rise of Pentecostalism in Wales.

[658] T. N. Turnbull, *What God Hath Wrought* (Bradford: Puritan Press, 1959); James Robinson, *Pentecostal Origins* (Milton Keynes: Paternoster, 2005); Des Cartwright, *The Great Evangelists* (Basingstoke: Marshall, Morgan & Scott, 1986).

[659] For example: Noel Gibbard, *Fire on the Altar* (Bridgend: Bryntirion Press, 2005); Donald Gee, *Wind and Flame* (Croydon: AoG, 1967); James D. G. Dunn *Baptism in the Holy Spirit* (Philadelphia: Westminster Press, 1970); and David Petts, *The Holy Spirit an Introduction* (Mattersey: Mattersey Hall, 1998).

of World War I on the development of Pentecostalism at Crosskeys will be further assessed.

Within a theological context, two critical issues central to Crosskeys will be analysed; firstly the importance of eschatology and secondly, an over emphasis on and misunderstanding of the doctrine of divine healing, a subject which has been central to AoG since its inception.[660] Both eschatology and divine healing pre-date the issue of evidential tongues at Crosskeys by at least two years and were foundational within its development. The contention of this present thesis is that the true core of Pentecostalism was a premillennial eschatology which motivated a vigorous missiology.[661] The traditional Welsh denominations subscribed to all of the major evangelical doctrines; however, divine healing and tongues-speaking is what differentiated Pentecostalism from Welsh denominationalism. Eschatology was not new to theological debate; however the emphasis placed upon premillennialism and its application by Pentecostalism was an essential factor in its growth. Another interesting question to explore is whether the doctrinal emphasis on eschatology and healing attracted certain types of people to the proto-AoG groups. Coupled to this is a need to assess how the proto-AoG groups journeyed along the difficult road to theological acceptance within Wales and the wider British context.

The area of accountability and denominationalism will also be examined. In particular why did a relatively healthy group of assemblies in South Wales correspond with American AG in search of support?[662] The Welsh believers were 'ground-breaking' in initiating this correspondence within the context of the formation of AoG GB&I; however, there developed a clear dominance of the English within that denomination. The assembly at Crosskeys is now an Independent Pentecostal Church; this could or should have been the case since

---

[660] Divine Healing was a large part of the ministry of Stephen Jeffreys and Smith Wigglesworth both influential in the establishing of early AoG congregations.

[661] Chris Palmer, 'Mission: The True Pentecostal Heritage as Illustrated in Early British AoG' *JEPTA* 30/2 (2010), 39–50.

[662] See Edith Blumhofer, *Assemblies of God, vol.1*, (Springfield, MO: GPH, 1989), 17–64 who deals with the similar issues in relation to the emergence of American AG.

its inception in 1912, and that denominationalism could or should have either been avoided or at least contained within the confines of AoG W&Mon.[663]

The Internationalisation of Society

The early years of the twentieth century saw prolific advances in the establishing of what we now call globalisation. The world was slowly becoming a smaller place. During this period in the areas of politics, philosophy, science, commerce, and theology the world was in a state of flux.[664] Communications and transport were evolving at a rapid rate so that both national and international travel was becoming easier. This is epitomised by the rise of the international holiday company, Thomas Cook, which commenced British excursions c. 1841 and by the 1860s was offering European holidays. The iconic symbol of travel during this period was the doomed ocean liner RMS Titanic which was launched in April 1912 only to sink on her maiden voyage. Another example of the easing of communications during this period was the invention of Marconi's wireless system which would allow for a speedier accessing of information around the world and in particular between Britain and America. How these developments may have affected the village of Crosskeys is a complex question with no straightforward answer. However, as mentioned in chapter two, one major result was the arrival in the South Wales coal fields of international migrants who brought their own worldview. Trinity Congregational church, Pontywaun, the home church of Sidney Mercy, was opened in order to help accommodate the influx of English speaking workers to the industrial heartland of SE Wales.

It is important to state that it was not a sudden event that led to the opening up of Wales to the outside. The Welsh valley dwellers were gradually exposed to international travellers, preachers, and teachers. They were also not afraid to leave Wales in search of their fortune in the coalfields of America.[665] There is

---

[663] The denominational possibilities are illustrated in the formation of the Apostolic Church under the leadership of D. Williams which was largely a West Wales based phenomenon; see, James E. Worsfold, *The Origins of the Apostolic Church in Great Britain* (Wellington, NZ: Julian Literature Trust, 1991).

[664] In chapter two I deal with the impact of the industrial Revolution and subsequent quest for Welsh coal and steel.

[665] Passage to America had commenced in earnest with the Pilgrim Fathers in 1620; Gwyn Davies, *A Light in the Land* (Bridgend: Bryntirion, 2002), 55–68. John Davies records how Welsh people joined the exodus across the

an unsubstantiated report that Sidney Mercy spent time working in Canada as a young man.[666] Within Christian circles, many international preachers and teachers had been visitors to Britain. For example, Charles Finney visited in the late 1850s and according to Hardman and Jones, Finney's writings on revival had been particularly influential in Wales from the mid-1840s.[667] The impact of Finney is another area that requires further research. Why were many Welsh Christians challenged by his teachings? The excitement and spectacular nature of the reports surrounding Finney's ministry—coupled to his belief in a definite path to revival—may have allowed people to be influenced by his methods and theology.

There was also a significant input from Humphrey Jones who returned from America to the Aberystwyth area in 1858 after tasting the 1858 New York revival.[668] Humphrey Jones had also been influenced by the writings of Finney and proceeded to have a significant influence on the 1859 revival in Wales.[669] There was also the influence of others such as D. L. Moody in 1875, then A. T. Pierson, who was a regular visitor to Keswick in Wales; as was John MacNeil, the international Keswick speaker whose book, *Filled with the Spirit,* was translated into Welsh in 1906 under the title of *Y Bywyd Llawn o'r Ysbryd.*[670] There was also the considerable influence of 'holiness' literature from South Africa particularly from the pen of Andrew Murray;[671] and, as mentioned in

---

Atlantic and in 1795 the cost was £2; John Davies, *A History of Wales* (London: Penguin, 1990), 326. See also D. Gareth Evans, *A History of Wales 1815–1906* (Cardiff: University of Wales Press, 1989), 62–8.

[666] This information was passed to me from an older member of the Crosskeys assembly Mrs. Lorna Smith. However, Paul Mercy does not make mention of this issue.

[667] Keith J. Hardman, *Charles Grandison Finney, 1792–1875* (Darlington: Evangelical Press, 1987); D. Geraint Jones, *Favoured With Frequent Revivals* (Cardiff: Heath Christian Trust, 2001), 39–45 and 102–3. See also Thomas Phillips, *The Welsh Revival: It's Origins and Development* (Edinburgh: Banner of Truth, 1989).

[668] Eifion Evans, *Fire in the Thatch* (Bridgend: Evangelical Press, 1996), 186–205.

[669] Eifion Evans, *Revival comes to Wales: The Stories of the 1859 Revival in Wales* (Bridgend: Evangelical Press, 1959). See also Wesley Duewel, *Revival Fire* (Grand Rapids, MI: Zondervan, 1995), 125–36 and 161–70 who also refers to the influence of Finney.

[670] I have dealt with MacNeil's influence in chapter 3; it is noteworthy that Rees Howells also spent time and was influenced in America; Norman Grubb, *Rees Howells: Intercessor* (Cambridge: Lutterworth Press, 1952).

[671] Andrew Murray, *The Full Blessing of Pentecost* (Plainfield, NJ: Logos, 1974).

chapter 3, W. S. Jones had spent time ministering in America before returning with his message of 'baptism with fire'.[672]

As mentioned in chapter 3 the major international influence at Crosskeys was initially experienced through the Keswick in Wales Conventions; for not only was this the popular pulpit for Welsh Evangelical preachers such as R. B. Jones, it was also an important centre for other British and international figures, such as F. B. Meyer and A. T. Pierson.[673] Sidney Mercy would have been influenced by Keswick in Wales due to his visits to the convention meetings before 1914. It was this that provided the two main theological influences at Crosskeys: firstly, the fullness of the Spirit and secondly, an introduction to teaching on the Second Coming. Jones makes reference to the 1913 Keswick in Wales Convention at which there were present 'many Europeans and Americans'; no doubt bringing their particular denominational theological understanding. It was during the period that Mercy and his fellow 'Second Comers' were regular visitors to Llandrindod.[674] In 1914 twelve of the Crosskeys congregation—almost the entire congregation in those early years—made the trip to Llandrindod. As the exposure to Pentecostalism via the influence of Tom Mercy's visit to London in 1914 and subsequent visits to Sunderland increased, so the Keswick influence dwindled; however it had made a lasting impression.

This openness and willingness to learn from beyond the borders of Wales introduced the Welsh evangelicals to a whole new arena of social, political, and theological teaching. Negatively, this internationalisation allowed for a freer flow of theological ideology which brought liberal theology to many of the churches and chapels in the valleys of Wales.[675] However it also allowed for the influx of biblical teachings such as the 'holiness' teaching which was gathering momentum in the late nineteenth century and which influenced Keswick

---

[672] See Davies, *Light in the Land,* Eifion Evans, *The Welsh Revival* (Bridgend: Bryntirion Press, 1969), 9–21; See Brynmor Pierce Jones, *The King's Champions* (Cwmbran: CLP, 1986) for further details of the travels of some of the evangelical leaders pre 1900.

[673] Morgan, *Span,* 137–44 who links R. B. Jones, Keswick, American Fundamentalism, and Dispensationalist teaching.

[674] Brynmor Pierce Jones, *The Spiritual History of Keswick in Wales* (Cwmbran: CLP, 1989), 24.

[675] See Pope, *Seeking God's Kingdom* and R. Tudur Jones, *Faith and the Crisis of a Nation* (Cardiff: University of Wales Press, 2004) for a wider discussion of the problems facing the Welsh Evangelicals at this time.

teaching, and subsequently the extensive ministry of figures such as R. B. Jones.[676] Other notable figures who visited Wales during the early twentieth century were J. Gresham Machen, R. A. Torrey, and Charles Alexander. From a specifically Pentecostal standpoint, A. A. Boddy, Cecil Polhill, Gerrit Polman, Stephen Jeffreys, Smith Wigglesworth, W. F. P. Burton, Howard Carter, and Donald Gee were also influential.

Travel facilities may have been improving between continents, but in the early twentieth century a visit from Crosskeys to Cardiff was an important event. Miners often took whatever holidays they could afford in Barry Island or Porthcawl, a mere twenty miles from home.[677] It is interesting to discover that Tom Mercy travelled to London to hear about Pentecostalism; still others visited Sunderland, Glossop, and Belfast to attend conventions, and this suggests that they were prepared to travel in order to fulfil their desires for a new experience within their Christian life. This would have demanded sacrificial financial commitments for poorly paid labourers as they searched for a greater understanding and experience of the gospel.

Internationalisation clearly played a crucial role in the emergence of Pentecostalism in SE Wales; mainly in terms of the introduction of the initial evidence doctrine to Britain through some significant international preachers. A distinction must be made between imposition and adoption of this theological position. The Welsh proto-AoG groups welcomed the teaching on initial evidence post-1914, and it is essential not to portray a scene of heavy handed foreign preachers imposing their thinking. The Welsh groups led by Crosskeys openly welcomed Pentecostalism with all of its theological vagaries, questions, and expressions. It was, as stated in chapter four, the visit to Ebbw Vale of American A. H. Post, which acted as the spark to ignite the Pentecostal 'fire in the valleys'. This experience was then nurtured by T. M. Jeffreys, Waunlwyd, band encouraged by the influential ministry of A. A. Boddy. It was not so much Boddy's preaching—for as Wakefield records, Boddy made only

---

[676] See, Jones, *King's Champions,* for an overview of the Welsh preachers of this period.

[677] Barry Island, near Cardiff, was home to a Butlin's holiday camp and Porthcawl is still the site of the large Trecco Bay caravan site. During the summer 'shut down' weeks (last week of July and first week of August) many of the industrial workers took their holidays in these two sites.

three visits to Wales during his ministry (in 1904 to experience the Welsh Revival, in 1909 for the opening night of the first Welsh Pentecostal Conference in Cardiff, and in 1913 for a visit to the Llandrindod Convention).[678] His influence spread despite his lack of physical presence in Wales, through his major publication *Confidence,* which was widely read in some parts of the county, including Wattsville.

However in Crosskeys the focus moved from Boddy to W. F. P. Burton as the 'icon' of Pentecostalism.[679] Garrard correctly suggests that W. F. P. Burton had a wide-ranging impact on emergent Pentecostalism and the suggestion that he openly dismissed Boddy as not being a 'true Pentecostal' may to some extent explain the waning of the latter's popularity in Wales.[680] Boddy's role must be recognised as central to the foundations of Pentecostalism in Britain and Burton's views may have been prejudiced by his suspicion of the Anglican Church.[681] Nevertheless, Boddy's influence in SE Wales weakened following 1914.

It is also interesting that the Sunderland Conventions, which were undoubtedly the 'Mecca' for early Pentecostals, ceased with the outbreak of war in 1914. The focus for the Pentecostals then became the London Conventions under the supervision of Cecil Polhill with Boddy being one of the visiting speakers. Gee comments that these London conventions were gradually losing their Pentecostal nature. He states that in his opinion some meetings were 'almost dreary' and this was in order to appeal to a wider evangelical audience.[682] Boddy's resignation from the PMU Council in 1924 at its amalgamation with AoG further distanced him from the denomination. Wakefield suggests that there was a 'dislike' by Boddy of the absorption of PMU into AoG and that Boddy had a greater affinity with Elim because of his friendship with George Jeffreys.[683] Womersley states that Burton and Boddy

---

[678] Gavin Wakefield, *Alexander Boddy Pentecostal Anglican Pioneer* (London: Paternoster, 2007), 222–28.

[679] See Appendix 8 for a summary of the CEM doctrinal position which summarises Burton's thinking.

[680] David Garrard, 'Burton's Early Years of Ministry and Doctrine under the auspices of the PMU', *JEPTA* 32/1 (2012), 3–14 and David Garrard, 'William F.P. Burton and the Rupture with the PMU', *JEPTA* 33/1 (2013), 14–27.

[681] William K. Kay, 'Sunderland's legacy in new denominations', *JEPTA* 28/2 (2008), 183–99.

[682] Gee, *Wind and Flame,* 111–12. See also Wakefield, *Alexander Boddy,* 197–201 who also highlights this change in emphasis.

[683] Wakefield, *Alexander Boddy,* 207.

were also at loggerheads over the issue of baptism; Boddy held to the sufficiency of sprinkling whereas Burton was a believer in total immersion.[684] This difference further fuelled the concerns which Burton held over the nature of Boddy's particular brand of Pentecostalism. Anderson suggests another possible cause of the schism between Boddy and AoG leaders; namely that the denomination's stance on pacifism which would have been contrary to Boddy's support of the war effort.[685] Wakefield also draws attention to this issue and the effects it may have had upon relationships between Boddy and the Pentecostal denominations.[686] It must be remembered that Howard Carter spent time in prison for his pacifist beliefs and that Donald Gee was forced to carry out farm labouring in order to avoid military conscription.[687]

According to Wakefield, Gee also levelled criticism at Boddy and Polhill for their lack of leadership within British Pentecostalism.[688] With respect to Boddy this criticism was most likely due to his insistence on remaining within Anglicanism, whilst in Polhill's case, Gee doubted his suitability to lead any overtly Pentecostal ministry, considering him a 'poor chairman' who lacked a 'platform personality' and as someone whose approach was more evangelical than Pentecostal.[689] Gee was a classical Pentecostal who promoted initial evidence and the public demonstration of charismatic gifts. Polhill was less convinced of such charismatic expressions and for Gee this was apparent in his handling of Pentecostal conference meetings. Gee relates how he had been asked by Polhill to bring the interpretation to any messages in tongues whilst he was at the London convention meetings. It is therefore apparent that leaders of AoG such as Carter, Gee, and the influential Burton slowly ostracised the aging Boddy from the denomination's development. One can however concur with Kay and Wakefield that Boddy's pivotal role in

---

[684] Harold Womersley, *Wm. F. Burton Congo Pioneer* (Eastbourne: Victory Press, 1973), 32–3.

[685] Allan Anderson, *An Introduction to Pentecostalism* (Cambridge: C.U.P., 2004), 94 and Wakefield, *Alexander Boddy,* 227, who records Boddy's visit to support the troops in June–July 1915.

[686] Wakefield, *Alexander Boddy,* 191–210

[687] John Carter, *Howard Carter Man of the Spirit* (Nottingham: AoG, 1971) and Richard Massey, *Another Springtime* (Guildford: Highland, 1992).

[688] Wakefield, *Alexander Boddy,* 207 & 212 Wakefield also provides some interesting remarks regarding the demise of Boddy, 214–16.

[689] Donald Gee, *These Men I Knew* (Nottingham: AoG, 1980), 73–6.

introducing Pentecostalism to Britain cannot be overstated. Despite his failure to see the whole church renewed by the Holy Spirit and prevent new denominations appearing Boddy must be given a place of honour in the legacy of British Pentecostalism.

Nothing will ever diminish the debt of lasting gratitude which, under God, the Pentecostal Movement in the British Isles owes to Alexander A. Boddy and Cecil Polhill for their devoted leadership during its earliest years.[690] It is a fair assessment that Boddy, supported by Polhill, was the catalyst that led to three major Pentecostal denominations that have continued to function since 1916.[691] And, as has been shown, the Apostolic Church, Elim Church, and the AoG GB&I all began in Wales.

In Crosskeys the rise of the influential W. F. P. Burton requires further attention. If Garrard's assessment of Burton is correct, and his influence in Crosskeys was significant, then it is essential to understand Burton's theology. This will allow for an assessment of any possible agreement between Burton and Crosskeys. W. F. P. Burton can be viewed as a classical British Pentecostal believing in a subsequent or post-conversion baptism of the Holy Spirit with initial evidence, an emphasis on divine healing and an expectation of the imminent premillennial return of Christ.[692] The mixture of these major doctrines was the bedrock upon which the Crosskeys assembly flourished in its early years. Burton's views on eschatology and healing will be assessed in the relevant sections below.

Due largely to the industrial revolution, Welsh society had been in a state of flux for many years. There had been a free flow of people and ideas into Wales which made the importation of differing theological views much easier. This changing emphasis in society benefitted the 'new Pentecostalism' as people became more accepting of different views, practices, and ideologies.

---

[690] Gee, *Wind and Flame*, 132.

[691] The Apostolic Church, Elim and AoG leaders all had contact with Boddy and Sunderland.

[692] Garrard, 'Burton's Early Years of Ministry and Doctrine under the auspices of the PMU'. See also W. F. Burton, *Bible Notes* (Johannesburg, S.A. c. 1962) and W. F. Burton, *Teachings from the Word of God* (Upington, S.A.: Verkrygbaar Van, n.d.).

Theological Reflection: The Second Coming and Divine Healing

Beginning at the End

Pentecostalism has been defined in recent years by the issue of Spirit baptism and glossolalia; however Frank D. Macchia, promotes the view that eschatology is more important to understanding Pentecostal theology than Spirit baptism.[693] This eschatological and pneumatological link is dealt with by Stanley M. Horton who suggests the cross denominational reaction to Spirit baptism was a normal feature of early Pentecostalism.[694] Horton suggests that people were attracted to Pentecostalism from the entire evangelical denominational spectrum in America. This allowed these individuals to bring their denominational understandings in to the development of Pentecostalism and its theology and praxis. This was similarly the case in SE Wales. In Crosskeys, however, the majority of new Pentecostals emerged from the Congregational chapels due to their emphasis on adventism and premillennialism. This focus on premillennialism coupled to the effects of liberal theology within the established denominations may have combined to make separation the only course.

It appears that the emphasis upon the spectacular and the manifestation(s) of Spirit baptism eventually replaced the practical eschatological application of the experience, namely power for service. Both Alan Anderson and Robert Anderson suggest that this shift in emphasis came about due to a fading in the understanding of xenolalia and the imminence of the Second Coming. Hence eschatology was replaced by pneumatology and, in particular, initial evidence as the central theological tenet. It is also apparent that the prosperous Western Pentecostals have, to some extent, lost their desire for the eschatological hope due to the comfort of their earthly existence.[695] However, the central thrust of Pentecostalism, whether focused on eschatology or pneumatology, still remains

---

[693] Frank D. Macchia, *Baptized In The Spirit* (Grand Rapids, MI: Zondervan, 2006), 41. See also Donald Dayton, *The Theological Roots of Pentecostalism* (Metuchen, NJ: Hendrickson, 1987), 143–71; Walter Hollenweger, *The Pentecostals* (London: SCM, 1972), 413–23 and Keith Warrington, *Pentecostal Theology* (London: T&T Clark, 2008), 309–23.

[694] Stanley M. Horton, 'The Holy Spirit and Christ's Coming', *Paraclete*, Fall (1968), 12–16.

[695] Anderson, *Introduction to Pentecostalism*, 219.

the preaching of the four-fold gospel in order to facilitate the experience of conversion. This view could well be illustrated in Crosskeys where the 'second comer' title was the precursor to their Pentecostalism. 'The end of the world is nigh' is a phrase that would have been popular with the majority of early Welsh Pentecostals. The initial events at Wattsville, although fuelled by the afterglow of the Welsh Revival 1904–05, centred upon the preaching on the Second Coming. As mentioned in chapter three, this doctrine was popularised through the initial work of J. N. Darby and later C. I. Schofield. Premillennialism became the accepted position of British AoG following the lead of their American counterparts.[696] Hollenweger provides a broad summary of the main elements of Pentecostal eschatology:

> The consummation of God's plan of salvation will take place in the following stages:
>
> The rapture of the church.
>
> Great tribulation under the Antichrist.
>
> The return of Christ to redeem Israel and to set up the millennial kingdom of peace.
>
> The resurrection of the dead for the last judgment.
>
> The destruction and re-creation of heaven and earth, the new Jerusalem, God is all in all.[697]

Hollenweger provides a helpful framework and it is essential to note that within Pentecostalism(s) there was much debate regarding the exact details of this plan. Commenting on the thoughts of Steven Land, Allan Anderson identifies two reasons why premillennial teaching is important to Pentecostals: firstly, the simple urgency to see 'people saved' and secondly, that this activity would hasten the return of Christ according to Matthew 24:14.[698] The simple desire at the heart of Pentecostal preaching was to 'see their saviour and be with him eternally'. Within the specific context of SE Wales, there was also the

---

[696] See Appendix 6 for the American AG Statement of Faith.

[697] Hollenweger, *Pentecostals*, 415.

[698] Anderson, *Introduction to Pentecostalism*, 218 and Blumhofer, *Assemblies Vol.1*, 22-6.

reality of the hope of eternal deliverance from the harsh pressures of the present life.

It is, however, necessary to briefly trace the development of the eschatological interpretations that eventually led to the rise of Premillennialism and to the influence of the American teachers on the subject.[699] There are three primary millennial views: amillennialism, postmillennialism, and premillennialism and a brief definition of each will allow for a greater understanding of the position adopted by the emergent AoG.[700] Amillennialism popularise by Augustine (354–430 A.D.) denies the literal future kingdom of Christ on earth, believing rather that the present age is the millennium which will culminate in the return of Christ and the inauguration of the new heaven and earth. This has been a popular view due in the main to the simplicity of its approach and the ability to avoid many of the intricate and difficult prophetic scriptures relating to eschatology. Postmillennialism was popularised by Daniel Whitby (1628–1725); his view was of a progression of the church and gospel that would produce the triumph of good over evil and a thousand years of peace and prosperity (the millennium) before Christ returned. However this view of the progression of good floundered on the carnage of two world wars and the ensuing social and political unrest worldwide. Premillennialism is based on a literal interpretation of prophecy that allows for the second advent of Christ to usher in his millennial reign, a view based on Revelation 20. The development of premillennialism and its acceptance by the emergent Pentecostals gave the proto-AoG group at Crosskeys a distinct theological tenet upon which to build their theology and missiology.

Closely linked to the development of premillennialism was that of dispensationalism, as promoted by Darby. This view further suggests that history could be divided into seven eras or dispensations during which periods God deals with humanity in certain ways; the seven dispensations are:

---

[699] Dayton, *Theological Roots,* 143–71.

[700] John F. Walvoord, *Prophecy – 14 Essential Keys to Understanding the Final Drama* (Nashville, TN: Thomas Nelson, 1993. See also Mal Couch, ed., *Dictionary of Premillennial Theology* (Grand Rapids, MI: Kregel, 1996) and Stanley N. Gundry and Darrell L. Bock, eds., *Three Views of the Millennium and Beyond* (Grand Rapids, MI: Zondervan, 1999).

innocence, conscience, civil government, patriarchal rule, Mosaic Law, grace, and the millennium.[701]

As with Blumhofer it is essential to note the influence of Darby and Schofield; however Dayton refers to other important Americans, some of whom influenced Welsh evangelicalism, they being: Finney, Moody, and Pierson. Moody was particularly convinced about the necessity of missionary activity in light of the imminent return of Christ; this position was adopted by the later Pentecostals and Pierson spoke on the subject at the Welsh Keswick.

Dayton provides a helpful overview of the developments within eschatology, tracing the influence of important figures relating to the Pentecostal acceptance of premillennialism. A crucial issue raised by Dayton and Blumhofer is that of the way in which Pentecostals read Scriptures; the emphasis is upon the fulfilment of Old Testament prophecy within the framework of the New Testament and of subsequent experiences of the early twentieth century. As a result much of the Pentecostal method for Scripture reading focused on a futurist interpretation of the Old Testament in light of the anticipation of Pentecost and the return of Christ. The ministry of Henry Allan Ironside (1876–1951) was particularly influential in terms of premillennialism during this period. According to Michael D. Stallard, Ironside's teaching influenced thousands of people in the English speaking world.[702] However, Ironside's thinking was simply continuing the traditions of his predecessor in Chicago, D. L. Moody. Moody was a world-travelled evangelist and teacher who had influence in Britain as well as America.[703] As this teaching began to make inroads into American evangelicalism, so too it crossed the Atlantic and influenced such movements as Keswick and individuals like R. B. Jones, who according to Gibbard, was a particular conduit for the teaching in Wales.[704] This no doubt would have helped some of

---

[701] See Charles C. Ryrie, 'Dispensationalism' in Couch, ed., *Dictionary of Premillennialism*, 93–8.

[702] Michael D. Stallard, 'Ironside, Henry Allan, Eschatology of' in Couch, ed., *Dictionary of Premillennial*, 183–4.

[703] Harold D. Foss, 'Moody, Dwight Lyman', in Couch, ed., *Dictionary of Premillennial*, 272–3 and Stanley N. Gundry, *Love Them In The Life and Theology of D.L. Moody* (Chicago, IL: Moody Press, 1976), 181–99.

[704] Noel Gibbard, *R. B. Jones Gospel Ministry in Turbulent Times* (Bridgend: Bryntirion Press, 2009), 151–6. See also Brynmor Pierce Jones, *The Trials and Triumphs of Mrs. Jessie Penn-Lewis* (North Brunswick, NJ: Bridge-Logos, 1997), 281–90, for the particular influence of American thinking on Penn-Lewis and R. B. Jones at this time.

the industrial workers to accept the hope of eternity in light of the gloom of their present experiences. Gibbard records how Humphrey Jones and others involved in the 1859 Revival in Wales believed in the millennial reign of Christ and that this also influenced the leaders of the 1904–05 Welsh Revival. There is an important link between this doctrine and the ministry of the Keswick in Wales Conventions for as early as 1904 A. T. Pierson addressed the convention on the subject. As Gibbard states:

> A.T. Pierson spoke on the Second Coming of Christ under the following headings: return, reign, refreshing, revival, restitution, regeneration, final redemption and final reconciliation ... the themes of Sonship and of the Second Coming were soon to be very prominent in RB's (Jones) preaching. [705]

Gibbard provides a helpful six point summary of R. B. Jones's teaching on premillennialism; [706] highlighting that perhaps one of the strongest elements was that all believers should live their lives in a holy, morally upright, and spiritual manner in light of the Second Coming. This is something the emergent Pentecostals would have accepted and preached with fervour. Gibbard also refers to Pierson's prophecy that the return of Christ would occur between 1910 and 1915; sadly such predictions of the timing of this divine act have evoked ridicule on such ardent proponents of the doctrine. Jones further records that E. W. Hamilton spoke of 'the little known doctrines of the Second Coming' at the 1906 Keswick event. [707] Premillennialism slowly began to emerge in Wales through the ministry of Keswick and individuals such as R. B. Jones and later became influential at Crosskeys through the leadership of Sidney Mercy, a Keswick devotee. [708] Morgan suggests that premillennialism provided a framework by which preachers could interpret the poor state of church and society in Wales. [709] By the early 1900s the Welsh proto-AoG

---

[705] Gibbard, *R. B. Jones*, 35. See also Gibbard, *Fire on the Altar*, 178–81; Dayton, *Theological Roots*, 162–3 also highlights the prominence of Pierson.

[706] Gibbard, *Fire on the Altar*, 180–1.

[707] Gibbard, *R. B. Jones*, 35 and Jones, *Spiritual History*, 18 and 29. Jones also records that in 1917 the main Bible teacher was Mr. Langton who also spoke on the Second Coming.

[708] See Gundry, ed., *Three Views*, 157–276 for an excellent survey of the developments of Premillennialism.

[709] Morgan, *Span*, 139–40.

adherents were beginning to engage with the theological significance of the turmoil of World War 1, asking whether this was the cataclysmic event that would usher in the Parousia?

Within the context of the rising Pentecostalism it is necessary to trace the premillennial position to some of the American figures such as Charles Parham and William Seymour. Parham supported the premillennial position and passed this teaching on to Seymour; this theological stance was circulated through the *Apostolic Faith* magazine. When recording the theological tenets of that movement in its periodical, the editors write that they believe in:

> The Second Coming of Jesus – The return of Jesus is just as literal as His going away. Acts 1:9–11; John 14:3. There will be two appearances under one coming; first, to catch away His waiting bride (Matt 24:40–44 and 1 Thess 4:16, 17), second to execute judgement upon the ungodly 2 Thess 1:7–10; Jude 14 and 15; Zech 14:3, 4.

The statement of faith continues the eschatological theme by stating:

> The Tribulation – Jesus prophesied a great tribulation such as was not from the beginning of the world. Matt 24:21, 22, 29; Rev 9; Rev 16; Isa 26:20, 21; Mal 4:1
>
> Christ's Millennial Reign is the 1000 years of the literal reign of Jesus on earth. It will be ushered in by the coming of Jesus back to earth with ten thousand of his saints. Jude 14, 15; II Thess1:7–10. During this time the devil will (there is no more wording provided in this phrase?). Hos 2:18; Zech 14:9, 20; Isa2:2–4.[710]

A careful reading of the American Assemblies of God statement of faith reveals close links with that of Seymour's Apostolic Faith Mission.[711] Pentecostal eschatology relies heavily upon a close relationship between the prophecy of Joel and the events of Acts 2.[712] This is significant because the original American AG tenets of faith were supplied to both Welsh and English proto-

---

[710] *Apostolic Faith* on CD. Rom, Number 13, 13.

[711] See Appendix 6. See also E. L. Blumhofer, 'Apostolic Faith Mission (Portland, OR)' in *NIDPCM*, 327 and 'Apostolic Faith Movement, Origins', *NIDPCM*, 327–9 and Blumhofer, *Assemblies Vol.1*, 67–92.

[712] D. J. Wilson, 'Eschatology, Pentecostal Perspectives on' in *NIDPCM*, 601–605.

AoG groups and were used as the basis for the eventual AoG GB&I statement of faith in 1924.

Being ready to 'meet one's maker' was a clarion call from proto-AoG pulpits in the valleys, and although this teaching is not as prevalent today, it still has a foundational position in that denomination. The premillennial development in SE Wales Pentecostalism is apparent in *Confidence* which records a sermon of T. M. Jeffreys entitled, 'The Parousia, Or "Appearing" of The Lord'. In this early Pentecostal based message Jeffreys relates tongues or Latter Rain as an essential aspect of eschatology.[713] A. A. Boddy, as Wakefield suggests, was no theologian; however his various comments, articles, and testimonies recorded in *Confidence* confirm that he supported a premillennialist viewpoint.[714] Boddy had emphasised the return of Christ throughout his ministry; however with his exposure to Pentecostalism he linked the outpouring of the Spirit to the Latter Rain typology. It is of interest to note that at the first Whitsun Convention in Sunderland it was the ministry of two women, Miss Barbour and Miss Sissons (USA) that focused on the 'Near Coming of the Lord'.[715] However Boddy's emphasis upon the imminent Parousia manifested itself in a call to missionary action rather than dwelling on the details of the events leading to the end time. Boddy was adamant that a heightened interest in the return of Christ was a natural result of the Baptism in the Holy Spirit which was in essence 'power for service'.[716] This understanding of Boddy was wholly accepted by the emergent AoG leaders though with time the focus moved away from eschatology and focused on pneumatology. This became linked to a greater pre-occupation with the extraordinary and spectacular rather than a missionary emphasis, a trend which has continued to the present day in some parts of the Charismatic movement.

---

[713] *Confidence,* June 1910, 149–51, the use of the terminology 'latter rain' by Jeffreys is not to be confused with the later Latter Rain Movement which adopted much of the Pentecostal understanding, and grew in the mid twentieth century to become a catalyst for the charismatic movement of the 1970s; see R. M. Riss, 'Latter Rain Movement' in *NIDPCM,* 830–833.

[714] Wakefield, *Alexander Boddy,* 178–181.

[715] This was also the case at Wattsville where the ministry of a young lady was the cause of much debate surrounding the Parousia.

[716] For a helpful overview see James D. Brown, 'The Holy Spirit's Activity in Evangelism', *Paraclete,* Fall (1968), 6–11.

The emphasis upon imminence within AoG circles is further strengthened by Donald Gee writing in the first edition of *Redemption Tidings* on the subject 'Jesus is Coming Again'.[717] In this article, Gee sets down the basis for the expectancy of the return of Christ as being woven into the fabric of the new denomination. Gee begins by stating the centrality of John16:7, stating that the promised Comforter would be sent into the world; he further develops the link between Pentecost and eschatology through offering various Bible verses to support his argument. The reliance upon a link between Joel 2:28–32 and the experience of Acts 2:1–11 is also central to his argument. Gee promoted the belief that the Pentecostal outpourings of the twentieth century heralded the arrival of 'the last days' which produced joyous expectation within AoG churches, and a call for preparation in holiness and mission. Gee records that the doctrine of the Second Coming was not widely taught in British churches and that this emphasis was one of the most significant factors of the new AoG denomination; this was particularly the case in Crosskeys. Such teaching from pioneer British Pentecostals such as Gee and Burton laid the foundations for tenet number 10 in the original AoG GB&I Statement of Faith which states:[718]

> We believe in the premillennial Second Coming of the Lord Jesus Christ Himself is the blessed hope set before all believers. 1 Cor 15:22–24; 1 Thess 4:13–18; 1 Cor 15:51–57.[719]

Glenn Balfour gives a broad overview of Pentecostal eschatology and provides a helpful summary of its main foci which included a belief in imminent futurist eschatology, Premillennialism, and the eschatological significance of the nation of Israel.[720] Balfour's thoughts are particularly significant in relation to the emergence of Pentecostalism in SE Wales where these three areas were particularly prominent.

Premillennialism impacted early AoG adherents on a practical level and especially in their response to, and involvement with, the 'world'. The teaching

---

[717] *Redemption,* July 1924, 9–10.

[718] Burton, *Teachings from the Word of God,* 12–13 and Burton, *Bible Notes,* 22, 34, 83, 86 all of which contain references to the Millennium. It is of interest to note that copies of Burton's handwritten notes were found amongst the papers of former elder and secretary of Crosskeys the late William Davage.

[719] Minutes, 1 February 1924, 3. See also John Carter, *Questions and Answers on Vital Subjects* (n.d.), 17–20.

[720] Glenn Balfour, 'Pentecostal Eschatology Revisited' in *JEPTA* 31/2 (2011), 127–40; cf. Couch, ed., *Dictionary of Premillennial,* 106–9

fostered within Pentecostalism, and in particular the Welsh AoG, was a three pronged public expression of their belief: firstly, calls to holiness in light of the end times; secondly, urgency of gospel presentation; and thirdly, the hope of eternal redemption. Their biblical support is found particularly in 2 Peter 3 and enhanced by Acts 1:8, 1 Corinthians 15, and 1 Thessalonians 4–5. The essence of these scriptures being an emphasis on holiness in life due to the imminent end of the world—this end necessitates a proclamation of the gospel in order to see people won for the Kingdom of God. A very simplistic yet powerful message of salvation by faith in Christ in order to gain heaven and avoid hell was the usual gospel message proclaimed by AoG preachers. Balfour's suggestion of this imminent futurist eschatology leading to a fear of children within Pentecostal families being 'left behind' was in fact a sobering reality. Debates over the sequence of events leading to the rapture and return of Christ were widespread within the local Welsh Assemblies even in the 1970s and 80s; though this is becoming a less prevalent and has been replaced by debates on alcohol, drugs, and sexuality amongst many young Pentecostals. It is possibly more accurate to state that the younger generation in many AoG and other Pentecostal churches should be classed as 'post-pentecostals' as there is largely a departure from teaching on Spirit baptism and charismata and an emphasis on music, singing, and social issues.

The pursuit of holiness caused the AoG adherents to separate themselves from anything they deemed to be 'of the world' and contrary to wholesome biblical living; consequently, they shunned the cinema, public houses, rugby or football matches, theatres, and most forms of entertainment that were not centred on the local church with its meetings, preaching, and seeking after God. It was the norm for meetings to be held daily with some prayer meetings continuing throughout the night; there were also regular rallies held on Saturdays at different locations where the Pentecostal testimony was propounded. To some, the approach of Pentecostals was regarded as being extreme and they were criticised for legalism and narrow-mindedness; however, they were honest in their desire to follow the perceived biblical patterns within their search for holiness. Premillennial eschatology was a major focus of the emerging Pentecostalism in SE Wales.

Premillennialism had been adopted by the new movement due in the main to outside influences which had originated through Darby and Schofield and channelled through America. This eschatological viewpoint led to an ease in accepting the pneumatological idiosyncrasies of Pentecostalism which were based largely upon the 'end-time' prophecy of Joel as supported by Acts 2. Pentecostalism, and in particular proto-AoG, in SE Wales was a pneumatically empowered vehicle of gospel presentation in the light of a belief in the imminence of the return of Christ. On the basis of this evidence it is apparent that Pentecostalism in SE Wales had its foundations in eschatology, not pneumatology; as a result the true heritage of Pentecostalism is mission and not a narrow charismatic elitism focused on an experience based on Acts 1:8 and 2:1–11. For the proto-AoG group at Crosskeys the Return of Christ was the catalyst to establishing a small Gospel Mission; for as Attwood writes:

> Now, the Second Coming was all new to them, and it became the greatest subject of the conversation.[721]

This interest, which could be described almost as an obsession, led the way to separation from their denominations and to the formation of AoG W&Mon then subsequently AoG GB&I. The subsequent history of the Crosskeys assembly has reflected a keen interest in the Parousia; this has manifested itself in a desire to propagate the gospel through both local and in particular overseas mission. This has been particularly reflected in a continued interest in Burton's CEM.

Divine Healing

Donald Dayton suggests that the development of the Divine Healing Movement in America was an essential precursor to the rise of Pentecostalism.[722] Petts further suggests that this concentration on the power of God to heal was a notable feature of emergent Pentecostalism.[723] The link between emergent Pentecostalism and AoG GB&I doctrines on healing are found through the ministry of Boddy, Stephen and George Jeffreys, and proto-

---

[721] Attwood, *How Pentecost*, 1.

[722] Dayton, *Theological Roots*, 115–41. For an alternative view of healing see John F. MacArthur, *Charismatic Chaos* (Grand Rapids, MI: Zondervan, 1992), 237–69.

[723] David Petts, *You'd Better Believe It* (Mattersey: Mattersey Hall, 1999), 107.

AoG leaders such as Burton and Parr. The thoughts of Petts are particularly poignant in relation to the emergence of the Crosskeys assembly. Petts gives an excellent summary of the issues relating to divine healing and, provides sensible answers to the main problems within this area.[724] An emphasis on divine healing was promoted at Crosskeys following the healing of Sidney Mercy under the ministry of Pastor Howton; this personal experience challenged the 'Second Comers' to accept this teaching.[725] This acceptance of the possibility of divine healing would have facilitated an easier acceptance later on of the Pentecostal gifts, since the group was now familiar with God's perceived desire to restore his spiritual gifts to the local church. In order to contextualize this it is necessary to briefly trace the doctrine of divine healing in the years prior to the emergence of Pentecostalism.[726]

The most controversial aspect of this theological tenet was the emergence of 'Healing in the Atonement'; the two major proponents of this teaching being A. B. Simpson (1843–1919) and A. J. Gordon.[727] Petts defines healing in the atonement as:

> The view that Christians may claim healing from sickness on the grounds that Christ has already carried that sickness for them just as he has carried their sins.[728]

The doctrine relies heavily upon the biblical text of Isaiah 53:5. Following the work of Simpson and Gordon it was, according to Dayton, the ministry of John Alexander Dowie (1847–1907) that proved to be the major propagator of the healing doctrine that fed into rising Pentecostalism.[729] Remaining true to his

---

[724] David Petts, *Just a Taste of Heaven* (Mattersey: Mattersey Hall, 2006).

[725] Howton, Richard, *Divine healing and Demon Possession* (London: Ward, Lock & Co. Ltd. 1909), <www.revival-library.org> see also 'Record of the International Conference on Divine Healing and True Holiness', London, June 1 to 5 1885 (London: J. Snow & Co., 1885) available from <www.revival-library.org>

[726] Dayton, *Theological Roots,* and Blumhofer, *Assemblies, vol. 1.*

[727] See C. Nienkirchen, 'Simpson, Albert Benjamin' in *NIDPCM,* 1069–70 and A. J. Gordon, *The Ministry of Healing: Miracles of Cures in All Ages* (n.d. available from Revival Library, Bishop's Waltham).

[728] David Petts, 'Healing and the Atonement', *JEPTA* 12 (1993), 23–7.

[729] Dayton, *Theological Roots,* 136–7; E. L. Blumhofer, 'Dowie, John Alexander' in *NIDPCM,* 586–7 and Hollenweger, *Pentecostals,* 116–22, see also John Alexander Dowie, 'Christ's Method of Healing', *A Voice from Zion* (May 1898) 2/5; John Alexander Dowie, 'What Should a Christian do when sick?' *A Voice from Zion*

Congregationalist roots, Dowie refuted the Pentecostal experience of initial evidence; however his teaching on divine healing was widely respected amongst the emerging Pentecostals.[730] As with eschatology, divine healing was prominent in the thinking of the Pentecostal forefathers, such as Parham and Seymour. Their position was found in the tenets of the Apostolic Faith Mission which states:

> Healing of the Body – Sickness and disease are destroyed through the precious atonement of Jesus (Isa 53:4–5; Matt 8:17; Mark 16:18; Jas 5:14–16). All sickness is the work of the Devil, which Jesus came to destroy (1 John 3:8; Luke 13:16; Acts 10:38). Jesus cast out devils and commissioned His disciples to do the same (Mark 16:17; Luke 10:19; Mark 9:25–26).[731]

Dowie's influence upon Parham and Seymour is highlighted in the tenet of faith recorded above which would be in line with Dowie's thinking. Three figures whose work was significant in this field were the Americans Maria Woodworth-Etter (1844–1924), Carrie Judd Montgomery (1858–1946), and Fred Francis Bosworth (1877–1958).[732] All had been influenced by Simpson and Dowie and then operated within the sphere of the rising Pentecostal movement. F. F. Bosworth was a delegate to the meetings which led to the formation of the American AG in Hot Springs Arkansas in 1914. He too had also been affected by Parham's teaching and experience; however Bosworth resigned from AG in a debate over Initial Evidence in 1918. Healing in the atonement was consequently adopted by the leaders of the embryonic American AG and subsequently crossed the Atlantic in the form of the Statement of Faith sent to Crosskeys in 1921. Much of the AoG basis for healing is based on Isaiah 53:4–5, the disputed text of Mark 16:14–20, James 5:13–18 and 1 Cor 12:9–10.[733] As the original AoG GB&I statement of faith reads we believe in:

(January 1898) 2/1, available from <www.revival-libaray.org> and Donald Dean Smeeton, 'John Alexander Dowie: An Evaluation', *Paraclete* Spring (1981), 27–31.

[730] Smeeton, 'John Alexander Dowie: An Evaluation', 29–30.

[731] *Apostolic Faith*, Number 13, 13. See also Blumhofer, *Assemblies Vol.1*, 67–92.

[732] W. E. Warner, 'Woodworth-Etter, Maria Beulah', in *NIDPCM*, 1211–13; W. E. Warner, 'Montgomery, Carrie Judd' in *NIDPCM*, 904–6 and R. M. Riss, 'Bosworth, Fred Francis', in *NIDPCM*, 439–40.

[733] Petts, *Just a Taste of Heaven* and Hollenweger, *Pentecostals*, 353–76.

> Divine Healing—Deliverance from sickness is provided for in the Atonement Isaiah liii, 1–5; Matt viii, 16–17; Jas v, 13–16.[734]

Prior to its acceptance by AoG GB&I, divine healing was supported by Boddy, Wigglesworth, the Jeffreys brothers, and Burton. It was also central in developments at Crosskeys.

In setting the scene for the impact of divine healing in Britain, we must turn to the 'father of British Pentecostalism,' A. A. Boddy. According to *Confidence,* Boddy had an interest in healing and had been used in this ministry since 1892.[735] In an article entitled 'Anointing with Oil', Boddy sets down his interpretation of the biblical paradigm for healing as based on James 5:13–16 and Mark 16:18; these two biblical references were fundamental to AoG healing beliefs. Boddy disseminated his teaching via the pages of *Confidence* which contained testimonies to God's power to heal; thus introducing more people to the possibility of divine healing. The topic was also the subject of much debate during the Sunderland Conventions where Boddy propounded the increasingly popular view that healing was available through the atonement.[736] High regard was paid by Boddy to the personal experience of his wife Mary who was healed of asthma on 23 February 1899. According to Kay and Wakefield, this personal experience allowed for a more balanced view of healing.[737] Boddy viewed divine healing as a necessary consequence of the Pentecostal outpouring at the beginning of the twentieth century and sensibly believed that healing was not always guaranteed but a present possibility. Wakefield suggests Boddy was kept from the more extreme views on healing by his insistence on basing all belief on Scripture.

As the ministry of Boddy continued, so others became influential in the debates surrounding divine healing. In Wales Jessie Penn-Lewis offered an

---

[734] Appendix 4, Carter, *Questions and Answers,* 13–16. See also Keith Warrington, 'Anointing with Oil and Healing', *JEPTA* (1993) 12, 5–22 and G. Raymond Carlson, 'Anointing with Oil', *Paraclete,* Spring (1969), 15–17.

[735] *Confidence,* April 1922, 21–2. See also Wakefield, *Alexander Boddy,* 172–8 and William K. Kay, *Pentecostals in Britain* (Carlisle: Paternoster, 2000), 82–106.

[736] See David Petts, 'Healing and the Atonement', 23–37.

[737] Kay, *Pentecostals in Britain,* 82 and Wakefield, *Alexander,* 173–4.

opinion on Isaiah 53:4-5.[738] Penn-Lewis was not particularly clear in her thinking on healing, however she did believe that there was a connection between Jesus Christ's sacrificial death and the cure of sickness. This, though, should not lead to an expectation of instant miraculous cures but to an acceptance of God's sovereignty; neither did she believe that sickness was necessarily a result of sin or unbelief. In the present context three significant figures emerged within AoG healing circles, namely Smith Wigglesworth, Stephen Jeffreys, and W. F. P. Burton, each of whom had important roles to play in the development of AoG within SE Wales. However none of these could be claimed by AoG GB&I as its own.

Smith Wigglesworth (1859–1947), the Bradford plumber known as the 'Apostle of Faith', emphasised a ministry of the miraculous; it was in 1907 that he encountered Boddy and the Sunderland phenomenon before subsequently receiving his Pentecostal Spirit baptism.[739] Wigglesworth embarked upon a worldwide itinerant ministry utilising some unorthodox measures and preaching the fact of healing in the atonement. No denomination could claim Wigglesworth for its own; however he worked closely with the emerging AoG and was a popular speaker at Crosskeys.[740] Stephen Jeffreys, brother of the renowned George, was known as the 'Healing Evangelist'.[741] Jeffreys was primarily an evangelist who preached the gospel with a Pentecostal emphasis of baptism in the Holy Spirit with signs following; he believed that healing was available through Christ. His message was, according to Whittaker, one of judgement, the Second Coming and urgency to repent and was often accompanied by signs of healing. As with Wigglesworth, the Welsh people warmed to the ministry of Stephen Jeffreys; he was widely respected—not simply because of the miraculous, but because of his passionate preaching which resulted in many being converted. The third international figure to influence Wales—and in particular Crosskeys—was W. F. P. Burton, who was

---

[738] Jones, *Trials and Triumphs*, 267–80.

[739] Colin Whittaker, *Seven Pentecostal Pioneers* (Basingstoke: Marshalls, 1983), 19–46 and Jack Hywel-Davies, *Baptised By Fire* (London: Hodder and Stoughton, 1987).

[740] For example Wigglesworth visited Crosskeys on 31 July 1933, receiving £6 for his ministry fee.

[741] E. Jeffreys, *Stephen Jeffreys The Beloved Evangelist* (London: Elim, 1946); Whittaker, *Seven Pentecostal*, 47–78; Alfred E. Missen, *The Sound of a Going* (Nottingham: AoG, 1973), 19–23. See also Gee, *Wind and Flame*, 131–49 for his overview of this period of evangelistic fervour and instances of divine healing.

also used in the ministry of healing.[742] Burton's belief is summarised in the statement of faith and practice of the C. E. M. which records a belief in: 'Healing of the physical body provided for in the atonement'.[743] Garrard stresses the important matter of Burton being involved in a healing ministry before his pioneer work in the Congo stating that:

> It is not possible to separate Burton's healing ministry from that of the evangelistic work in which he engaged … Burton indicates that there were a number of dramatic healings taking place.[744]

Burton's evangelistic ministry saw him cover extensive parts of northern England, preaching and being used in the ministry of healing; this was a principle he applied to his own health as well as for the healing of others. During his time in malaria-ridden Africa, Burton initially relied on prayer, not medicine, to maintain or restore his health. However, as Garrard relates, he did change his view on this as so many of his fellow workers died due to the onset of tropical diseases. This change of understanding did not filter through to Crosskeys, however, where according to Gee, people such as Tom Mercy continued to hold extreme views on healing.[745] As mentioned above, Burton held iconic status in Crosskeys where his influence was more important than any other on the formative congregation post-1914. There was a major financial commitment to the work of Burton and the CEM and he and fellow missionaries like Jimmy Salter and Teddy Hodgson were regular preachers at Crosskeys.[746] Hence Burton brought his own brand of staunch Pentecostalism to the Welsh valleys and it became foundational at Crosskeys. In Burton the Crosskeys leadership found a way to formulate their experience into an acceptable doctrine and practice, although this in no way negates the influence of other key figures such as Gee, Carter, Parker, and Horton.[747]

---

[742] Burton, *Bible Notes*, 61; Burton, *Teachings from the Word of God*, 46–7; Whittaker, *Seven Pentecostal*, 146–69; Garrard, 'Burton's Early years of Ministry and Doctrine under the auspices of the PMU'.

[743] Appendix 8.

[744] Garrard, 'Burton's Early Years of Ministry and Doctrine under the auspices of the PMU', 8.

[745] Gee, *These Men I Knew*, 62.

[746] The missionary financial records show monthly insertions of monies sent to CEM until 1968 – the limit of the records I have – the church still supports CEM in its new guise as Central Africa Mission (as of 2012).

[747] Many of these leading figures of AoG were regular preachers at Crosskeys.

If Wigglesworth, Jeffreys, and Burton were the high profile promoters of divine healing, Pastor Richard Howton had a direct impact at Crosskeys through the dramatic healing of Sidney Mercy. Attwood records how Mercy was a frail old man with a severe heart complaint but was miraculously healed and became like a 'new young man'.[748] Howton's healing doctrine resulted from his acceptance that healing was available through the atonement and his position is summarised in the title of his book *Divine Healing and Demon Possession*, in which he relates the onset of sickness to the work of the Devil. Howton writes:

> The doctrine of Divine Healing remains a stubborn truth established in God's Word, and is part of the foundation and superstructure of the New Testament. Its claims do not rest on the honesty of human teachers or leaders, or in the accepted theories of theologians, but *in the redeeming work of the Lord Jesus Christ* [my emphasis].[749]

Howton professed the necessity of a holy life in line with the Keswick model, especially in a person to be used in divine healing. He believed that the abundant life in Christ should lead to believers enjoying both spiritual and physical healing. Sickness, for Howton, was a penalty of sin and a result of the curse of God (Gen 2:17); as such he believed the only way to rectify this was through God's divine remedy of the atoning work of Christ. A major area of concern within this view of the atonement was that as one should expect salvation as an instantaneous event, so too one should expect healing.[750] I concur with Petts that the dependency of supporters upon the text of Isaiah 53:4–5 and relating it to physical rather than spiritual healing (salvation) is the biggest pitfall of this teaching. Although Howton's views are well presented, I see some areas of concern in accepting them.

Firstly he removes the sovereignty of God from all of life's problems and pays no attention to those individuals in the scripture that were not healed—such as Paul, Trophimus, Timothy, and Epaphras—whose inclusion in the canon of

[748] Attwood, *How Pentecost*, 6.

[749] Howton, *Divine Healing*, 64.

[750] Donald Gee, *Trophimus I left Sick* (London: Elim, 1952).

scripture must serve as a counter balance to extreme thinking on healing.[751] Secondly, as he focuses on the Old Testament story of Job, he does not include the fact that Satan only did what God allowed (Job 1:12 and 2:6). A third issue to raise against Howton's view is that within the life of Jesus, people were healed from a variety of diseases which are given a variety of causes; for example Luke 13:16 (cause Satan), Luke 14:1–4 (cause not recorded), Luke 17:11–21 (cause exposure to leprosy) and John 9:1–3 (sin is not the cause of illness). Caution must be taken with Howton's views, since he implies that all sickness is from a demonic source; as a result people can be led into a realm of demonology which can be both harmful and untrue. A balanced view of healing is vital within the church; Christians need to acknowledge the sovereignty of God in all matters of health and well-being in order to cope with their ill-health whilst still enjoying the assurance of salvation. However, the possibility is still that God may heal people of a variety of sickness as recorded in the biblical text and supported throughout church history. The fact remains that Mercy's encounter with Howton allowed him to bring the message of divine healing back to Crosskeys and it became a foundational element in establishing the work.

Due to the potency of his own experience Sidney Mercy included a reference to divine healing in his summary of the doctrinal stance of the Crosskeys Assembly in 1928.[752] As mentioned in chapter five, Mercy records a number of instances of healings of people, crops, and even animals! However the occasions of healing at Crosskeys led to an opportunity to preach the gospel and offer salvation to listeners; this must surely be regarded as the purpose of God's miraculous intervention. Nevertheless this practice led to some unbalanced views on health and sickness; Gee reckoning that it was Tom Mercy's views on divine healing which led to his premature death, for he neglected medical advice and insisted that God's power alone would heal and keep him.[753] Instances of healing presented the Crosskeys fellowship with the

---

[751] It is widely accepted that those mentioned all had some health issues during their ministry. See Gal 4:13; Phil 2:27; 1 Tim 5:23; and 2 Tim 4:20; Petts, *Just a Taste of Heaven*, 172–87.

[752] Mercy, 'Pentecost in South Wales'.

[753] Gee, *These Men I Knew*, 62.

opportunity to propagate the gospel and as a direct result some people were drawn to the Mission hall. [754] If eschatology and divine healing were key issues in the emergence of Pentecostalism in SE Wales, the question must be asked about why people were attracted to this particular expression of Christianity?

Attraction and Growth

An interesting theory relating to the attraction of people to Pentecostalism is supported by John E. Minor in his comparison of emerging Pentecostalism and Primitive Methodism in America. [755] Minor presents some interesting similarities between the constituent members of both these revivalist movements; though he states the differences between their theological positions. Minor suggests that Pentecostalism in America related to a particular type of person, who was excluded from the more traditional denominations due in the main to their educational and social disadvantages. He further suggests that there was a rejection by some of the traditional intellectual and liturgical styles of services in search of a more spontaneous expression of worship. Hollenweger agrees with Minor's assessment, suggesting that the disadvantaged found courage to express themselves in public worship when gathered together with people from similar socio-political backgrounds. [756] This is best illustrated in the role of William J. Seymour, the leader of the Azusa Street Mission; he fought the restrictions of white supremacy in America in order to see the 'colour line' washed away and all classes of people worshipping together. Cox makes some interesting suggestions in respect to the socio-political situation in America, and particularly Los Angeles, in the early twentieth century; a similar view could be held regarding the melting-pot which was Welsh society during the early twentieth century. [757]

Pope makes a more in-depth study regarding the socio-political and theological context of SE Wales. [758] Hollenweger makes reference to Wales and labels it as

---

[754] Attwood, *How Pentecost,* who records some of these miraculous occurrences.

[755] John E. Minor, 'The Mantle of Elijah Nineteenth-century Primitive Methodism and Twentieth-century Pentecostalism', *Proceedings of the Wesley Historical Society,* December (1982) 43, 141–9, available from <www.biblicalstudies.org.uk>

[756] Hollenweger, *Pentecostals,* 457–96.

[757] Harvey Cox, *Fire From Heaven* (London: Cassell, 1996).

[758] Pope, *Seeking God's Kingdom,* 1–105.

being in a 'geographical disadvantage'; his remarks relate to its location in comparison to the rest of Britain and in particular to communication, economics, and language.[759] This 'disadvantaged' state expressed itself powerfully through the Welsh Revival 1904–05 in which the congregations were able to express themselves in a manner intrinsically Welsh. For Hollenweger, this was characterised by much singing, congregational prayer, the decline of the sermon, an emphasis upon the essential ministry of the Spirit and the occasions of *hwyl* which was a particular mid- and late- 19th century Welsh phenomenon associated with the ecstatic oratory of the preacher.[760] In Welsh AoG and Pentecostal situations this would be referred to as knowing or experiencing 'the unction of the Spirit' upon the preacher. Hollenweger's comments interestingly focus upon experience and expression rather than theology and this could link the 'Children of the Revival' with rising Pentecostalism. This would allow for a hypothesis that some of the emerging Welsh Pentecostals were searching for a return to the liberty experienced in the Welsh Revival.

In relation to the spiritual condition of Wales, and in particular some of the leading Nonconformist preachers, Pope suggests that the predominant aim of preaching focused on social issues; and that this was the fruit of liberal theology.[761] With the rise of liberal theology there was a removal by many of the traditional biblical distinctives, such as salvation by grace through faith in Christ alone, which had for decades dominated many of the Welsh churches. Some possible questions can be raised over the cause and effect of Pentecostal 'reaction' to the social gospel: did Pentecostals, whether by default rather than design, offer an alternative to this liberal theology being presented in many Welsh chapels? Hence was this alternative option a reaction against the 'socialising' of the gospel which liberal theology espoused? Pentecostals had a social conscience and identified with the working classes within society; they were not indifferent to community care, compassion, and involvement in

---

[759] Hollenweger, *Pentecostals,* 461.

[760] Cyril G. Williams, *Tongues of the Spirit A Study of Pentecostal Glossolalia and Related Phenomena* (Cardiff: University of Wales Press, 1981).

[761] Pope, *Seeking God's Kingdom,* 105.

society. However, this concern was not fostered by some theologically liberal or socialising context. If there was any unconscious response to the social gospel it was manifested in the Pentecostal view that the answers to moral, social, or global problems were contained within the Bible. Their teaching concerning salvation in Christ alone and appropriated by personal faith focused the Pentecostals on a missiology that confronted personal sin rather than social well-being. The change needed in a person's life was possible through a radical encounter with God; personal conversion leading to a transformation of the individual and consequently society. Pentecostals therefore emphasised a spiritual gospel promoting personal reformation; and were not immediately preoccupied with tackling injustices through social or political measures.

However, it is somewhat superficial to conclude that Pentecostals and evangelicals in traditional churches were merely reacting to a social gospel. The latter was only one significant and radical expression of the liberal theology which was now espoused by many ministers and denominational seminaries. And for many revival converts in the denominations, they did not understand or respond to such content, partly because they may not have understood it and partly because they found it at variance with their own experience and knowledge of Bible teaching. The proto-AoG groups were not so much reacting against liberal theology as they were investigating the new experiences which had led them to Pentecostalism in the first place.

Can Pentecostals also be viewed as offering a 'reformation of evangelicalism' by deserting formal, traditional worship by standing for the truth of scripture and centring on an experiential faith?[762] Pentecostalism emphasised that what individuals needed most of all was salvation and a hope of eternal deliverance. The liberty of worship experienced during the 1904–05 Revival could well have encouraged some to join the proto-AoG groups in SE Wales, especially when under a more cerebral type of liberal preaching church services became somewhat dull and difficult to cope with. Hollenweger suggests that in embryonic Pentecostalism people witnessed and enjoyed a freedom of expression, spectacular healings, and charismatic demonstrations. In this

---

[762] Terry L. Johnson, *The Case for Traditional Protestantism* (Edinburgh: Banner of Truth, 2004).

respect, emotionalism was encouraged and not frowned upon; allowing for what could be labelled as 'escapism' from the reality of life. During the hey-day of the coal and steel industries in Wales people lived in constant fear of death; explosions or flooding underground, uncontainable fires at the blast furnaces, or the outbreak of epidemic disease, were daily realities. The Pentecostals worshipped in a free manner and preached a release from the sufferings of this present world through the hope of eternal redemption which was characterised by the joyous prospect of a soon coming eternal Kingdom of God in which reigned love, peace, and eternal joy; a stark contrast to life in the grime and horror of Industrial Wales.

This book has demonstrated that the eschatological viewpoint which fuelled the missionary nature of Pentecostalism was more important than the supposed 'distinctive' theology of Spirit baptism and initial evidence. Their initial interaction with charismatic issues may have come about merely as a bi-product of the attraction to a form of worship that appealed to the intrinsically 'charismatic' character of the Welsh. As mentioned in chapter five, Crosskeys had a relatively strong group of evangelical churches during this period; however what caused a person to leave these traditional denominations and join Pentecostalism is not as simple to answer. Yet it was the Congregationalists who ejected the 'Second Comers' from their fellowships. It was then a core of Congregationalists that established Crosskeys AoG, due in the main, to a rejection of their emphasis upon premillennial teaching and then later the adoption of Pentecostal teaching. This 'Congregational imbalance' may well explain the reasons behind the form of church government adopted by the group and which may have later influenced the AoG GB&I. It must be highlighted that not all who were dissatisfied with the influx of liberal theology found solace in Pentecostalism. Some moved to other denominational churches where there was a more satisfying ministry or, as often happened, remained where they were and suffered a ministry which they may have been unhappy with because they respected the minister's education and status.[763] Still others

---

[763] Martyn Lloyd-Jones refers to these issues in a lecture presented at The Bala Ministers Conference in 1970; the transcript is to be published as an appendix in Eryl Davies, *The Bala Ministers Conference 1955–2014* (Bridgend: Bryntirion Press, 2014).

were attracted to Gospel Halls or Independent Mission Halls throughout Wales; some of which, such as Crosskeys, developed along Pentecostal lines.[764] The growth of these Gospel Halls and Mission Halls is another area of Welsh religious history that requires further investigation.[765]

A negative aspect of the question of attraction and growth is the impact of 'elitism' within both Pentecostals groups and traditional denominations. In some Pentecostal groups there was an erroneous teaching that people were truly converted only if they had spoken in tongues as evidence of Spirit baptism.[766] Some held a very high view of their theological position and experience though they were not at all self-critical. This could lead to them being seen as narrow-minded and almost cultic in understanding; after all, the apostle Paul had told the Corinthians that not all Christians spoke with tongues.[767] Spirit baptism is not a badge of spiritual superiority rather a means to an end—greater impact in evangelism. From a denominational and evangelical perspective, there was also concern that Pentecostals were unsophisticated, uneducated, and theologically naive. Yet whilst this has some truth, it is not wholly true as we have seen individuals such as Tom Mercy held responsible positions within the industrial community and still later men such as C. L. Parker were Oxford educated and serious theological thinkers. Pentecostals may have been unsophisticated in that they lacked higher education, yet their fervour, zeal, and commitment offered individuals something that the established denominations no longer offered. Although these pioneers were not great theologians and relied too heavily upon experience, they were honest 'reformers' in pursuit of a theological basis upon which to build their mission and later denomination. Despite the lack of theological training they must never be dismissed as inept thinkers with no interest in theology and its development. For they pursued a deeper understanding of their experiences through regular prayer, Bible study and attendance at various Pentecostal Conventions; they also had a deep concern

---

[764] The ministry of D. Martyn Lloyd-Jones at Sandfields Port Talbot stands in stark contrast to the failing branches of the evangelical churches in S. Wales.

[765] Morgan, *Span*, 9–15 for a brief introduction to the smaller evangelical denominations in Wales.

[766] A now deceased member of Crosskeys assembly, Mr. Bill Davage, told me how he recalled this idea being preached in the early days.

[767] 1 Cor 12:30 and 1 Cor 14:5.

for the spiritual well-being of their communities and were committed to proclaiming the 'Full Gospel'.

Morgan and Pope devote much attention to the socio-political situation in Wales, illustrating how Welsh Nonconformity was closely linked to Liberal Party politics.[768] During the nineteenth century, Liberal politics had tended to share the platform with evangelical theology; however, the changes in Welsh politics brought Pentecostalism into contact with socialism. In the early decades of the twentieth-century, the Labour Party was beginning to take a grip on Welsh society; a grip which it has maintained for more than one hundred years.[769] The rise of Labour was also highly influential within the industrial heartland of Wales, the eastern valleys providing a pool of militant miners who accepted the politics of Labour. As Morgan suggests, the people of Wales slowly became more politicised whereas the chapels began to lose their interest in politics.[770] The result of this distancing of politics and religion allowed for a man to vote Labour but still remain within a local Pentecostal church with no fear of recrimination from the minister. In Crosskeys, this issue was particularly important as Tom Mercy served not only as pastor of the Mission but also as Secretary of the local N.U.M. With such a position, Mercy would have faced the probability of confrontation with mine owners and officials. However, Mercy was able to combine 'socialist' based political leanings with a radical expression of evangelical theology; which ironically saw the local miners building the new hall at Gladstone Street during a miners strike in 1933.

Coupled to this political/religious shift was the influence of the Great War 1914–1918; the political parties each took their own stance on the war effort and the Liberals spearheaded by Lloyd George led the call to arms. Although Lloyd George's influence caused many Welshmen to join the armed forces, the rising Labour Party was less supportive of the war effort. Labour's

---

[768] Morgan, *Span;* Pope, *Seeking God's Kingdom* and David Ross, *Wales History Of A Nation* (New Lanark: Geddes & Grosset, 2005), 203–25.

[769] Evans, *History 1906–2000,* 67–110 for a summary of the political manoeuvrings at this time see also Duncan Tanner, Chris Williams and Deian Hopkins, eds., *The Labour Party in Wales 1900–2000* (Cardiff: University of Wales Press, 2000).

[770] Morgan, *Span,* 148–80.

inconsistency over the war helped the Crosskeys miners to remain within the proto-AoG group; they avoided conscription and used their energies to fight for the gospel whilst excavating coal to fire the blast furnaces that produced the hardware for war.[771] The close link of Labour, miners, and emerging Pentecostals would have eased the external pressure upon those Pentecostals to conform to the war effort. This lack of peer or political pressure allowed Pentecostals to remain within the community and supported the development of the congregation; whereas many other chapels that supported the war and Liberal politics lost many of their young men in the trenches of Europe.

A Cry for Help: From Network to Denomination

A major question that has arisen as a result of researching Crosskeys and AoG W&Mon is; why did the group seek denominational status with the American AG? If the group led by the Crosskeys fellowship consisted of spiritually charged individuals, endeavouring to perpetuate the liberty of the Wales Revival with an eschatological focus, why did they not continue in their original AoG W&Mon format and avoid both American and English support?

Gee suggests this 'cry for help' revolved around theological differences and particularly those originating from the proselytising Apostolic Church in Wales. These differences centred upon the role of the Apostle and Prophet within the local assembly and in particular the belief in, and practice of, personal instructive prophecy. However, I suggest that the group of Pentecostal mission halls led by the members of Crosskeys could have remained independent or at least remained as a Welsh denomination. Careful readings of the letters to America from Crosskeys reveal a desire to discover a network of kindred believers, this would also allow for denominational structure and doctrinal conformity. This should not be perceived negatively, however, for it illustrates a concern to provide a doctrinal safety net for a fledgling group with a different approach to worship, experience, and doctrine. On the other hand they could be criticised for seeking a like-minded group and therefore of not being willing to engage with other biblical based evangelicals who would have questioned the Pentecostal aspect of their theology. Their search for such a supportive network led them eventually to the American

---

[771] Evans, *History 1906–2000*, 87.

Assemblies of God which they hoped would serve as a defence against the growing influence of the Apostolic Church in Wales. The cry for help was also possibly a reaction to the liberal theology in denominational churches in Wales which strengthened their determination to uphold orthodox biblical teaching. These men in Crosskeys, who were forced to leave their traditional denominations, could have followed three possible alternative courses.

Firstly, before the influence of Pentecostalism, could they have found a suitable network within Wales? This could have been achieved perhaps by affiliating themselves to chapels where there was a clear biblical ministry unspoilt by liberal theology. A major complication here is that such chapels would have needed to be open to premillennial teaching and the fervent proclamation of the Parousia. There *were* such chapels, but they were limited in number and would have been represented by men such as R. B. Jones and supported by the infrastructure of Keswick in Wales. Jones supported water baptism, holiness of life, and premillennial eschatology which were the foundational tenets at Crosskeys before 1914. However, the issue of divine healing may have been a more difficult tenet with which to have found agreement. For as Gibbard records the ministry of Pastor Howton, with its emphasis upon miraculous manifestations, was viewed with suspicion among many Welsh evangelicals.[772] Secondly, as a local congregation in a small village, they could have remained as an independent mission hall. According to Attwood, there was a sensible approach to 'team ministry' led by Tom Mercy, a man well respected both in Christian circles and in the local industrial community.[773] With time the congregation grew to an estimated one hundred and twenty people and as such would have been capable of surviving both financially and structurally.[774]

If an independent course was not possible at Crosskeys then my third suggestion would have been for AoG W&Mon to have continued its identity as a separate recognised denomination. The formation of AoG GB&I in 1924 saw the coming together of some seventy Pentecostal missions from around Britain and Ireland, half of those being Welsh. With that amount of Pentecostal

---

[772] Gibbard, *R. B. Jones,* 61–2.
[773] Attwood, *How Pentecost.*
[774] Mercy, 'Pentecost in South Wales'.

mission halls within Wales, this would have been adequate to have formed an official denomination, in line with the smaller Apostolic Church. The advantage is that this would have given the group an even stronger Welsh flavour and orientation.

However there is the fact that the proto-AoG group did not have a sufficiently gifted theological leader who could take the reins of such a denomination and see it develop. As the letters to America reveal, there was an adequate internal structure of chairman, secretary, and treasurer; even so, the lack of theological training and insight may have left the group feeling vulnerable to the proselytising Apostolics. If the situation in SE Wales can be summarised as 'an experience in search of a theology', these men led by Tom Mercy were looking to America purely for theological security and recognised ministerial status for their leaders. The urgent request for 'ordination certificates' was made by H. Crook in the letter sent to America on 5 December 1921.[775] Such status was essential if the AoG W&Mon pastors were to avoid the difficult situation of military conscription as encounter by Carter and Gee.[776] This leads to a further question and possibility. If there had been a theologically astute leader within this group, would the AoG W&Mon still exist today? This is only an assumption and may result from a personal issue regarding the overtaking of the Welsh pioneers in the leadership of AoG GB&I by the more theologically aware English leaders. Another possible area of further research concerns how D. P. Williams and George Jeffreys engaged in the inevitable theological debates required to place their respective denominations on secure theological foundations. Further, could such models have been utilised by the AoG W&Mon in their development?

Within the area of networks and denominationalism a major question arises over the status of local AoG churches. The denomination prided itself on the autonomy of local assemblies within a fellowship of like-minded churches. In Crosskeys this form of church governance would have been 'imported' from the Congregational model that was the norm for the majority of the early leaders. However is there any tension between local autonomy and denominational control or central government? According to Gee these issues

[775] Appendix 1.
[776] John Carter, *Howard Carter,* 39–49.

were essential in establishing the AoG GB&I especially in its reaction against both Apostolic and Elim patterns of governance. An examination of the modern AoG GB&I will reveal a move towards a more centralised government led by the National Leadership Team. Further research by the AoG GB&I is required in order to re-examine its origins and ethos in an attempt to recapture the central thrust and purpose of the Fellowship.

As the British AoG denomination developed, one figure emerges as an influence in endeavouring to connect Wales and England, namely, W. F. P. Burton.[777] Burton was already known and revered in SE Wales, and when home on furlough from Congo in 1922 he circulated amongst the emerging independent Pentecostal mission halls and saw, in his opinion, the need to create a denomination. It could be suggested that Burton, an Englishman, had a greater desire for order and organising in contrast to a more typical Welsh style of a more 'free' and spontaneous approach. Burton's influence on SE Wales and the wider British scene was vast; with his precise mind, Burton established a wide network of mission stations and churches in Congo. Burton was a man of vision but also of method and organisation; he conceived a plan of attack for the evangelising of the Central Congo region of Africa which was implemented by a faithful group of missionaries.[778] Following the establishing of a base at Mwanza and seeing his first convert in 1915 by 1960 there were 985 assemblies organised around Burton and a team of missionaries who held regular field council meetings in order to monitor the progress of the CEM.[779] Organisation was something which Burton revelled in and it may be suggested that this structured method is something he encouraged at home during his 1921–22 furlough. Burton's link with the Crosskeys group is heightened by the fact that Tom Mercy served on the Home Reference and Advisory Committee of CEM until his death. Whether Burton influenced the Welsh proto-AoG group to seek organisation is not documented. With the close link between Burton and Mercy there would have been the opportunity for such

---

[777] David J. Garrard, 'W. F. Burton and His Missionary Call', *JEPTA* 32/2 (2012), 237–47.

[778] W. F. Burton, *God Working With Them* (London: Victory Press, 1933).

[779] By 1973, two years following Burton's death, there were some 2100 assemblies in Congo.

organisational issues to have been discussed. Gee summarises Burton's role and influence:

> Mr W. F. P. Burton was home for his first furlough from the Congo in 1922, and his itineraries revealed to him the widespread need and desire. Before returning to the field he used his influence to secure the necessary preliminary steps. [780]

If Gee's assessment is correct and there was a desire for unity, this desire was apparent through the letters to America in SE Wales before 1922, and, if as suggested, Burton was particularly influential in Crosskeys, his guidance may well have been essential in this move towards founding a denomination. [781]

Contemporary Pastoral Implications

Assessing the contemporary pastoral implications and application of this research is a more difficult task; however, I will offer some observations within the context of SE Wales and, in particular, Crosskeys.

Firstly denominational allegiance is not necessary in order to continue a successful local assembly. At Crosskeys the independent status has in no way affected the continuation of the church's witness within the community. However the matter of accountability depends upon spiritually gifted leaders within the assembly who perceive the aims of the gospel as being more important than personal recognition.

Secondly, the theological position of the Pentecostal churches needs to be reassessed in order to ascertain if initial evidence should take as major role as it has previously assumed in the churches' understanding of Spirit baptism. The role of the pastor within the local assembly is no doubt crucial to the resolving of this issue. It may be time for Pentecostals to recover their distinctives of eschatology and missiology, and allow their teaching on Spirit baptism and charismatic issues to be linked more fully with a wide ranging understanding of pneumatology, which promotes the greater work of the Spirit in all areas of a believer's life. This proposal would cause much debate and may require a

---

[780] Gee, *Wind and Flame,* 126. See also Kay, *Inside Story,* 69–83; Kay, *Pentecostals in Britain,* 27–31 and David Allen, *There Is A River* (Tonbridge: Authentic, 2004), 137–40.

[781] I refer to the Letter of 1921 between Crosskeys and America.

change of mind-set from within some Pentecostal training institutions, so that all prospective Pastors may have opportunity to reflect on their traditional understanding of Pentecostal theology.

A final pastoral implication that has arisen is that of attraction. During the early years of Pentecostalism in SE Wales, the close knit nature of society saw men working shoulder to shoulder with Pentecostal believers. This, coupled to spectacular healings, warnings of eternal judgement, and a respect earned by Pentecostals in face of the regular threat of death in industry, saw people attracted to Pentecostal halls. Today society has changed dramatically but Pentecostal assemblies still need to attract people to their meetings and message. There is no simple answer to this dilemma. However, as a pastor now in the same Crosskeys Pentecostal assembly, I recognise the need to be relevant and contemporary but how this is achieved remains an ongoing matter for church leaders in the valleys of SE Wales.

Conclusion

This book has identified a mixture of various theological streams feeding into the emergence of Pentecostalism in SE Wales together with teachings like premillennialism, healing, and Spirit baptism which were supported through a variety of preachers and conventions in Britain. As has been shown Pentecostal theology was, on the whole, imported from America through some significant British and European figures. Figures such as Boddy, Barratt, and T. M. Jeffreys were sowing seeds of Pentecostalism in SE Wales in ground prepared by Congregational church polity, influential ministry from national and international preachers, and the Welsh Keswick. This research reveals that early Welsh Pentecostals were not theological revolutionaries as they accepted the general framework of biblical and Evangelical theology. Nevertheless, they were innovative within the area of pneumatology in accepting teaching from England and America which they wedded with their eschatological urgency and missiological emphasis.[782] It has also been suggested that there were theological tendencies and personality traits that allowed Pentecostalism to flourish in the valleys of SE Wales.

---

[782] Ian Randall, *Evangelical Experiences* (Milton Keynes: Paternoster, 1999), 229.

The Crosskeys proto-AoG group was affected by these streams with the Crosskeys Full Gospel Mission eventually being formed in 1912. This led the way for establishing AoG W&Mon and subsequently AoG GB&I. This group of eager believers were set on encountering God. For them this encounter was fulfilled in the eschatological, missiological and pneumatological paradigm of Pentecostalism.

Chapter 7 Conclusion

Summary of Research

This book has examined the historical context of the emergent Pentecostal movement in SE Wales and in particular that brand of Pentecostalism which emerged in Crosskeys. It has also discussed the sociological, economic, political, and theological context within Wales in the early twentieth century in an attempt to ascertain the degree of influence each had upon the emergent Pentecostal congregations.

It has been suggested that Welsh Pentecostalism was affected by both external and internal streams. The effects of the Azusa Street Revival spread to Europe and beyond through influential figures such as T. B. Barratt and A. H. Post, having an impact in SE Wales. The particular role of the relatively unknown Rev. T. M. Jeffreys, Waunlwyd, was critical in the establishing of Pentecostalism in SE Wales; Jeffreys' association with A. A. Boddy was an important contributory factor. The Welsh Revival 1904–05 is also significant in this period and some early Pentecostals were affected by this phenomenon. That was true for Tom Mercy who was converted during this outbreak of religious fervour.

Two further factors arose from the Welsh Revival, namely, an emphasis on the essential ministry of the Holy Spirit and liberty or informality in worship; both were encouraged in the emerging Pentecostalism. The harsh conditions endured by many workers in industrial Wales disposed some to accept this style of Pentecostal worship more readily and especially the emphasis on the eschatological hope. In the Crosskeys area involvement with the premillennial based Wattsville house group led some to an eventual acceptance of Pentecostal pneumatology. However at Crosskeys initially premillennialism and Pastor Howton's teaching on divine healing proved to be more influential than Initial Evidence. This emphasis on eschatology and healing led to a fervent missiology with a particular focus on Burton's Congo Evangelistic Mission. Those involved at Wattsville, and subsequently Crosskeys, eventually found their theological and experiential fulfilment in the later adopted

Pentecostalism. However, the core teaching of Pentecostalism was imported from America via England.

The most significant aspect of this research has been to ascertain the central role played by what would become the Crosskeys Full Gospel Mission. Sidney and Tom Mercy and their associates proved to be a vital link in the chain of events that led to the formation of AoG GB&I. The particular relevance of the letters to America has not previously been given adequate recognition by scholars studying this developmental period.

This study has sought to redress, describe, and analyse the pivotal role played by this group of proto-AoG figures emerging in Crosskeys and the wider region of SE Wales. These Welsh pioneers must be given due recognition for their role alongside their better known English counterparts, such as J. Nelson Parr, Howard Carter, and Donald Gee. These Welshmen were in the vanguard of promoting Pentecostalism in Wales and continued to have an influence through various positions on the National Executive Council of AoG GB&I.

Future Research

This book has suggested areas in which further research is necessary to understand better the early beginnings and development of Welsh Pentecostalism.

Firstly the relationship between the eschatology of leading figures within Welsh evangelicalism during this period and the emerging Pentecostals requires further attention. In particular, the teaching on premillennialism as advocated by individuals such as R. B. Jones which found sympathy and support in Pentecostalism. Apart from those few affected by the Keswick in Wales Conferences, the link between teachers such as Jones and the early Pentecostals is less obvious and has not been explored academically.

It is necessary to address the rise of the other proto-AoG assemblies within South Wales. As Missen suggests, some forty assemblies owed their origins to the ministry of the Crosskeys assembly. I have discussed the origins of my home assembly at Newbridge but research into the origins and growth of each of these congregations could contribute significantly to our knowledge of early

Welsh Pentecostalism.[783] However this task could prove difficult due to the lack of primary sources and the dearth of sufficiently corroborated material from those who were close to the main characters and events as they unfolded.

The accepted distinctive theological tenet of Pentecostalism, Initial Evidence, also requires further research. The contributions made in recent years within this area of research has been acknowledged.[784] However it is clear that Pentecostalism as a whole and the AoG in particular, should be viewed from their eschatological and missiological foundations rather than their experiential distinctives.[785] If the original Pentecostal understanding of this experience is re emphasised namely, power for service, there could possibly be a resurgence in mission and a desire to see the gospel extended to the 'ends of the earth' before Christ's return.

A further theological consideration arising from this research is the relationship between the rise of Pentecostalism in SE Wales and the presence of liberal theology, especially in the valleys. Pentecostalism has been viewed as a peripheral theological entity but it emerged in Wales during the growing influence of liberal theology and preaching within the traditional Protestant denominations. What, if any, were the links between the emergence of these different theological perspectives? Was Pentecostalism, as I have suggested, more probably an accidental reaction to liberal teaching? It is disappointing that early Pentecostals did not engage with, and record their views on, the emerging liberalism within the denominations. Even Gee, the most prolific of early AoG authors, avoids detailed reference to the subject—preferring to concentrate more on the divergent views of the Apostolic Church; the issue of Ultimate Reconciliation being the only major area of liberalism he deals with. The embryonic Pentecostals concentrated more on the pursuit of their new experience and theology and to a large extent were ignored by the more traditional evangelical denominations in SE Wales.

---

[783] Alfred E. Missen, *The Sound Of A Going* (Nottingham: AoG, 1973), 47.

[784] Gary B. McGee, ed., *Initial Evidence: Historical and Biblical Perspectives on the Pentecostal Doctrine of Spirit Baptism.* (Eugene, OR: Wipf & Stock, 2007) helps to enlarge the debate on tongues.

[785] Chris Palmer, 'Mission: The True Heritage of Pentecostalism as illustrated in Early British AoG Thinking.' *JEPTA* 30/2 (2010), 39–50.

The final, vital area of further research is the so-called 'Post-Pentecostalism'. There has been a move away from the 'classical' understanding of Pentecostal theology and practice within many Pentecostal assemblies in SE Wales. Sustained teaching on the classical Pentecostal understanding of the necessity and purpose of Spirit baptism as related to eschatology and missiology has been lost.[786] The current generation of young Pentecostals are more interested in matters of social concern and entertainment based worship.[787] As a result, the essence and dynamism of the Pentecostal experience has been lost. An engagement with the younger members in Pentecostal churches in Wales, and more widely across Britain, is necessary in order to ascertain their perspectives of their denominational teaching on important spiritual issues. Classical Pentecostalism is currently in danger of being reduced to a category in church history and is being replaced by the Charismatic Renewal and the increasing influence of the Emerging Church.[788] The focus for Pentecostal pastors and leaders ought to be a re-emphasis on the fundamental theological tenets of their denominations—the essential person and work of the Spirit, and a militant missiology fuelled by an expectant eschatology—in order to facilitate spiritual growth for members and congregations.

Personal

On a personal level, this research has stimulated me to be self-critical and to re-examine analytically my theological roots. This journey of discovery has helped me formulate a more balanced understanding of that heritage but also to asses my present theological experience. This greater understanding of early AoG history in SE Wales has already helped me in my ministry, particularly in my pastoral duties at Crosskeys. I have also been able to use my research findings in theological teaching and training, especially through my work with

---

[786] A recent conversation with Phillip Evans, the pastor of the assembly at Newbridge, highlighted the fact that a group of young people from the church spent a week at a large Christian conference because they wanted to find out more about the work of Spirit; I submit that this should have been addressed by the local AoG minister and that hence there is a lack of true teaching on the subject.

[787] I submit this theory due in the main to conversations I have had with young people in SE Wales who are more eager to debate social issues than to engage with biblical theology or doctrine.

[788] Eddie Gibbs and Ryan K. Bolger, *Emerging Churches: Creating Christian Community in Postmodern Cultures* (London: SPCK, 2006).

One Mission Society, a body which has contact with several Bible Colleges worldwide.

This study, therefore, contributes to learning by partly filling a gap in Welsh church history in relation to the Pentecostalism that emerged in SE Wales in the early Twentieth century.

Appendix 1: Correspondence between Hubert Crook of South Wales and E.N. Bell of USA AOG

The following letters were supplied to me by Mr Desmond Cartwright, Elim historian and member of the Donald Gee Archive centre at Mattersey Hall. The condition of some of the letters is poor; however, I have reproduced them here as transcripts of the originals.

Letter Number 1: H. Crook to E.N. Bell

23 Tynewydd Road

Pontnewydd

Nr. Newport

Mon

South Wales

Dec. 5th 1921

Dear Brother in Jesus,

In reply to your kind letter, I wish to offer my personal thanks for your kind and immediate attention to my previous letter Re. "Council".

Also inform you that the representatives of the "Assemblies of God" of Wales and Monmouthshire join me in gratitude to you and your staff for your valuable suggestions and advice respecting the formation of a Council in this part of the Country.

I am also instructed to order at once (thirty-two) copies of your Combined Minutes of the General Council of the Assemblies of God; we want these Minutes for circulation amongst our people here, that they may obtain a thorough knowledge of the Constitution and work of the General Council. Send to the above address.

At our committee meeting on Sat Dec 3rd 1921 we unanimously decided to adopt your Combined Minutes as the basis of a District Council for Wales and Monmouthshire of the General Council of the Assemblies of God in the U.S.A. and hereby make application to be incorporated into your Council as such.

I should like a copy of your Ordination Certificate as issued to ordained and approved Ministers as this matter must be dealt with at once with us here.

Page 2

I shall be very pleased to receive any further information and advice you are able to give, towards making the Council a success.

Pray that the Lord's blessing may be upon us in this important work, and that we may be privileged to experience similar results to those obtained by your Council,

With warmest greetings

Yours in Christ

H. Crook

Enclosed Money Order for

  £1.8.0 Combined Minutes

   7.0 Evangel

  £1.15.0 Total Enclosed.

Letter Number 2: E.N. Bell to H. Crook

Elder H. Crook, Sec.

4 Tynewydd Road

Pontnewydd

Nr. Newport, Mon

South Wales.

December 13, 1921

Dear Brother Crook:-

Thank you for the subscription sent and for your order of Minutes. The Minutes are now in the Press and we expect to be able to mail to you inside of a week.

We are glad to note that you are making progress in the matter of a District Council, and shall be glad to consider your application as soon as we get the customary information. It is customary with us for the Secretary to send Minutes of the meeting in which the District was organized, with the names and addresses of those taking part. The names and addresses are always an important matter, since it shows the person that they are undertaking an enterprise, and gives some basis of judgement for the hope of success. We know not a whit in the way of such recognition, but would be glad to have the Minutes, with the names as above referred to, and then we shall give the matter final consideration.

We are enclosing a copy of our ordination certificate and the annual fellowship certificate which goes with it. We have found conditions changing rapidly, and workers often so quickly changing their views, that this annual check-up required in the fellowship certificate has been found to be very successful in giving a chance to let those drop out who have gone wrong in any way, without the necessity of calling in their fellowship certificate. Unless your ministers are all well settled men of very mature convictions you may find it well to adopt the fellowship idea to go with the credentials, and to be renewed annually. Most full credentials issued direct from this office to the ministers on recommendation of the District Council.

We are sending you, however a copy of the credentials which are issued by the District Councils, also we are sending you a copy of the application blank which this office uses. If we can be of any further service to you we shall be very glad to do so.

Yours in Christ Jesus

ENB.HAS   Chairman

Letter Number 3: H. Crook to E.N. Bell

4 Tynewydd Road

Pontnewydd

Nr. Newport

Mon

Feb 6th 1922

Dear Brother Bell

Thank you very much for the kind attention that you have given to my correspondence relating to matters of a District Council. I am very pleased that you are willing to give our "application for recognition within your Council" your careful consideration. I am therefore sending herewith the necessary information required for that purpose.

Minutes of formation Council

On Saturday Oct 22nd 1921 at a meeting which had been convened by one of the largest Assemblies in Wales and Mon, and to which each Assembly in the District had been invited to send delegates, for the purpose of considering the necessity of UNITY between all the Assemblies; it was unanimously decided that we recognize ourselves as members of HIS BODY and that there be no division as He commanded.

That we recognize ourselves as members of the General Assembly (or Church) of the first born, which are written in heaven, (Heb 12:23) and we do not believe in establishing ourselves into a sect, or separating ourselves from fellowship with other members of the teaching of Christ and the Apostles.

Resolved, that recognising ourselves as a GENERAL DISTRICT COUNCIL of (Spirit Baptized) Saints from local Churches of God in Christ, Assemblies of God, various Apostolic Faith Missions, Full Gospel Pentecostal Missions and all Assemblies of like faith in Great Britain.

Also

That we recognize all the above said Assemblies of various names, and speak to them and refer to them by the general Scriptural name "Assemblies of God".

And recommend that they all recognize themselves by the same name:- "Assembly of God" and adopt it as soon as practicable etc.

Officers

Tom Hicks, 63 Islwyn Road, Wattsville, Crosskeys, Nr. Newport, Mon (CHAIRMAN)

Hubert Crook, 4 Tynewydd Rd, Pontnewydd, Nr. Newport, MON (SECRETARY)

Richard Anthony, 3 Beechwood Avenue, Wattsville, Crosskeys, MON (TREASURER)

EXECUTIVE

William Attwood Risca Road, Crosskeys, Nr. Newport. MON

Tom Mercy 15 Islwyn Rd, Wattsville, Crosskeys, MON

Price Davies Hafod Arthem Farm, St. Illtyds, Aberbeeg, MON.

All the other delegates present at the meeting were Overseers or Elders of the various Assemblies represented.

Kindly send me as soon as possible a copy of the MANUAL as used by the General Council for raising the standard of efficiency in the Ministry, and by the ordinary committee.

Also send sufficient Credentials (Fellowship & Ordination) to supply 50 Ministers; only we would like you to add after, Assemblies of God the words Great Britain for to cover our Council as well. We shall be pleased to remit on receipt of your invoice for these goods.

Yours in Jesus Love, H. Crook.

Letter Number 4: E.N. Bell to H. Crook

Pastor H. Crook,

4 Tynewydd Road,

Pontnewydd,

Nr. Newport, Mon.,

Wales.

March 29th 1922

Dear Brother Crook.

I have just returned from my trip to the western part of the United States and find your good letters on hand which show that you have organized a District Council and are ready for credentials, etc. In reply I would say that we have never gotten out a manual, and for that reason are not able to help you on that line. We can consider the matter of credentials after the matter to be considered below.

We have just received notice from another bunch of good ministers, namely in England, who are planning to come together in what they call a Leaders Conference, and are to hold their meeting during the Swanwick Convention in April. They do not give the exact date, but perhaps you know the date of this convention. The call for such meeting is issued by W. Burton, E. C. Boulton, A. (Howard) Carter, J. Douglas, Geo. Jeffreys, T. H. Jewitt, G. Kingston, Thos. Myerscough, E. W. Moser, J. Tetchner, J & L. Walshaw, E. Blackburn. Correspondence is to be addressed to Pastor E. C. Boulton, 2 May St., Hull, Yorks.

It would seem to us to be much better for all you brethren to be together in one general organisation. We do not know what the brethren will call their meeting, but they have done the same as you have, namely secured the General Council Minutes and other literature as a guide to the deliberations. We are not especially concerned about the name. We suggest for the good of the work in Great Britain that you take up correspondence with these brethren and seek to get together. We are going to write them about you and make the same suggestion to them. We hope that you may all get together on some common basis, and though they may decide to issue their own credentials we could have an understanding whereby there would be mutual fellowship and cooperation just the same, so far as the wide distance would permit. We will await the outcome of this suggestion before taking up the matter of issuing credentials.

We are glad to see the progress that you have made, and we extend hearty love and fellowship in Jesus, and hope that we may be able to serve you further in these matters.

Yours with love in Christ Jesus,

ENB.HAS   Chairman

Appendix 2 Statements of Faith of Apostolic, Elim and AoG Churches

Apostolic Church: Tenets

1. The one true and living God who eternally exists in three persons in unity: Father, Son and Holy Spirit.

2. The inherent corruptness of man through the Fall; The necessity of repentance and regeneration by grace and through faith in Christ alone and the eternal separation from God of the finally unrepentant.

3. The Virgin birth, sinless life, atoning death, triumphant resurrection, ascension and continuing intercession of our Lord Jesus Christ; His Second Coming and millennial reign upon earth.

4. The Justification and sanctification of believers through the finished work of Christ.

5. The baptism of the Holy spirit for believers with supernatural signs, empowering the church for its mission in the world.

6. The gifts of the Holy Spirit for the building up of the Church and ministry to the world.

7. The Sacraments of Baptism by immersion and of the Lord's Supper

8. The divine inspiration and authority of the Holy Scriptures.

9. Christ's leadership of the Church through apostles, prophets, evangelists, pastors, teachers, elders and deacons, for unity, maturity and growth of the church.

10. The security of the believer as he remains in Christ

11. The privilege and responsibility of bringing tithes and offerings to the Lord[789]

---

[789] <www.apostolic-church.org>

Elim Church

1. The Bible. We believe the Bible, as originally given, to be without error, the fully inspired and infallible Word of God and the supreme and final authority in all matters of faith and conduct.

2. The Trinity. We believe that the Godhead exists co-equally and co-eternally in three persons - Father, Son and Holy Spirit - and that these three are one God, sovereign in creation, providence and redemption.

3. The Saviour. We believe in the true and proper deity of our Lord Jesus Christ, in His virgin birth, in His real and complete humanity, in His sinless life, in His authoritative teaching, in His substitutionary and atoning sacrifice through His blood shed, in His bodily resurrection, in His ascension to the right hand of the Father, in His heavenly intercession and His second advent to receive His Church.

4. The Holy Spirit. We believe in the deity of the Holy Spirit who proceeds from the Father and the Son and the necessity of His work in conviction of sin, repentance, regeneration and sanctification, and that the believer is also promised an enduement of power as the gift of Christ through the baptism in the Holy Spirit with signs following. Through this enduement the believer is empowered for fuller participation in the ministry of the Church, its worship, evangelism and service.

5. Mankind. We believe in the universal sinfulness of all men since the Fall, rendering man subject to God's wrath and condemnation.

6. Salvation. We believe in the necessity for salvation of repentance towards God and faith in the Lord Jesus Christ by which the sinner is pardoned and accepted as righteous in God's sight. This justification is imputed by the grace of God because of the atoning work of Christ, is received by faith alone and is evidenced by the Fruit of the Spirit and a holy life.

7. The Church. We believe in the spiritual unity and the priesthood of all believers in Christ and that these comprise the universal Church, the Body of Christ.

8. The Ministry. We believe in the ministries that Christ has set in His Church, namely, apostles, prophets, evangelists, pastors and teachers and in the present operation of the manifold Gifts of the Holy Spirit according to the New Testament.

9. The Ordinances. We believe in the baptism of believers in water in obedience to the command of Christ and the commemoration of Christ's death by the observance of the Lord's Supper until His return.

10. The Commission. We believe that the Gospel embraces the needs of the whole man and that the Church is therefore commissioned to preach the Gospel to the world and to fulfil a ministry of healing and deliverance to the spiritual and physical needs of mankind.

11. The Coming King. We believe in the personal, physical and visible return of the Lord Jesus Christ to reign in power and glory.

12. The Future State. We believe in the resurrection of the dead and in the final judgement of the world, the eternal conscious bliss of the righteous and the eternal conscious punishment of the wicked. [790]

AoG GB&I

1. We believe that the Bible (i.e. the Old and New Testaments excluding the Apocrypha), is the inspired Word of God, the infallible, all sufficient rule for faith and practice. (*2 Tim 3:15–16; 2 Pet 1:21*)

2. We believe in the unity of the One True and Living God who is the Eternal, Self-Existent "I AM", Who has also revealed Himself as One being co-existing in three Persons – Father, Son and Holy Spirit. (*Deut 6:4; Mark 12:29; Matt 28:19; 2 Cor 13:14*)

3. We believe in the Virgin Birth, Sinless Life, Miraculous Ministry, Substitutionary Atoning Death, Bodily Resurrection, Triumphant Ascension and Abiding Intercession of the Lord Jesus Christ and in His personal, visible, bodily return in power and glory as the blessed hope of all believers. (*Isa 7:14; Matt 1:23; Heb 7:26; 1 Pet 2:22; Acts 2:22, 10:38; 2 Cor 5:21; Heb 9:12; Luke*

---

[790] <www.elim.org.uk> I have added numbers for ease of referencing.

24:39; 1 Cor 15:4; Acts 1:9; Eph 4:8–10; Rom 8:34; Heb 7:25; 1 Cor 15:22–24, 51–57; 1 Thess 4:13–18; Rev 20:1–6)

4. We believe in the fall of man, who was created pure and upright, but fell by voluntary transgression. (*Gen 1:26–31, 3:1–7; Rom 5:12–21*)

5. We believe in salvation through faith in Christ, who, according to the Scriptures, died for our sins, was buried and was raised from the dead on the third day, and that through His Blood we have Redemption. (*Tit 2:11, 3:5–7; Rom 10:8–15; 1 Cor 15:3–4)*

This experience is also known as the new birth, and is an instantaneous and complete operation of the Holy Spirit upon initial faith in the Lord Jesus Christ. (*John 3:5–6; James 1:18; 1 Pet 1:23; 1 John 5:1*)

6. We believe that all who have truly repented and believed in Christ as Lord and Saviour are commanded to be baptised by immersion in water. (*Matt 28:19; Acts 10:47–48; Acts 2:38–39*)

7. We believe in the baptism in the Holy Spirit as an enduement of the believer with power for service, the essential, biblical evidence of which is the speaking with other tongues as the Spirit gives utterance. (*Acts 1:4–5, 8, 2:4, 10:44–46, 11:14–16, 19:6*)

8. We believe in the operation of the gifts of the Holy Spirit and the gifts of Christ in the Church today. (*1 Cor 12:4–11, 28; Eph 4:7–16*)

9. We believe in holiness of life and conduct in obedience to the command of God. (*1 Pet 1:14–16; Heb 12:14; 1 Thess 5:23; 1 John 2:6*)

10. We believe that deliverance from sickness, by Divine Healing is provided for in the Atonement. (*Isa 53:4–5; Matt 8:16–17; James 5:13–16*)

11. We believe that all who have truly repented and believe in Christ as Lord and Saviour should regularly participate in Breaking of Bread. (*Luke 22:14–20; 1 Cor 11:20–34*)

10. We believe in the bodily resurrection of all men, the everlasting conscious bliss of all who truly believe in our Lord Jesus Christ and the everlasting

conscious punishment of all whose names are not written in the Book of Life. (*Dan 12:2–3; John 5:28–29; 1 Cor 15:22–24; Matt 25:46; 2 Thess 1:9; Rev 20:10–15*)[791]

---

[791] <www.aog.org.uk> I have added numbers for ease of referencing.

Appendix 3 Important Pentecostal Manifesto

Evangelists, Pastors, and Workers present at the Pentecostal Camp Meeting held at Alliance. Ohio, June 1908, meeting in conference and prayer to consider means to mutually advance the work of God, send greeting:

"Forasmuch as we have heard that certain which went out from us have troubled you, it seemed good to us, and we trust to the Holy Spirit, being assembled with one accord to write you after this manner".

(1) We believe that the formation of any ruling body would not meet the approval of God's baptized people, but that such an affiliation of Pentecostal Missions is desirable as will preserve and increase the tender sweet bond of love and fellowship now existing and guard against abuse of legitimate liberty.

(2) We would urge all those baptized with the Holy Spirit, who believe they are called to be missionaries, either at home or on the foreign field, not to be hasty in going forth, but to tarry until very clearly shown that it is the Lord's time; and that they seek such preparation, both in Bible study and practical work, enabling them to go forth with the necessary equipment, being thus prepared as much as possible.

(3) That workers going out into the field should obtain from their home body papers of recognition and approval, showing that like Peter and John, Paul and Barnabas, they have been sent out by the assembly (Acts 8:14; 13:1–4; 15:22–28).

(4) That Assemblies be exceedingly careful to lay hands suddenly on no man, but follow the example of the early church, as shown in the above passages; that no one be recognized as workers, but those who have shown themselves well-grounded in the truth, in love and in doctrine, and to have received, at least in some measure, suitable gifts and equipment of the Spirit.

(5) Exercising great care and prudence, yet under necessity, to notify one another of those travelling false apostles, who are bringing such injury to the

work of God. (Rom 16:17–18; 2 Cor 11:13; 1 Tim 1:18–20; 1 Cor 5:1 – 2; 2 Pet 2:1–3, 1 John 4:1)[792]

Appendix 4: Original AoG Statement of Faith 1924

A Statement of Fundamental Truths Approved by the General Presbytery of the Assemblies of God of Great Britain & Ireland.

The Scriptures, known as the Bible, are the Inspired Word of God; the infallible and all-sufficient rule for faith, practice and conduct. This Statement of Fundamental Truths is not intended as a creed for the Church, but as a basis of unity for a full Gospel Ministry (1 Cor 1:10), and we do not claim that it contains all truth in the Scriptures.

1. The Bible is the inspired Word of God. (2 Tim 3:15–16; 1 Pet 2:2).

2. The unity of The One True and Living God who is the Eternally self-existent "I AM," Who has also revealed Himself as One Being in Three Persons— Father, Son and Holy Spirit. (Deut 6:4; Mark 12:29; Matt 28:19).

3. The fall of man, who was created pure and upright, but fell by voluntary transgression. (Gen 1:26–31; 3:1–7; Rom 5:12).

4. Salvation through faith in Christ, Who died for our sins according to Scriptures, was buried, but was raised from among the dead on the third clay according to the Scrip lures, and through his Blood we have Redemption. (Tit 2:11; Rom 10:8–15; Tit 3:5–7; 1 Cor 15:34).

5 The baptism by immersion in water is enjoined upon all who have really repented and have truly believed with all their hearts in Christ as Saviour and Lord. (Matt 28:19; Acts 10:47–48; Acts 2:38–39).

6. The baptism in the Holy Spirit, the initial evidence of which is the speaking with other tongues. (Acts 2:4, 10:44–46, 11:14–16, 19:6).

7. Holiness of life and conduct in obedience to the command of God "Be ye holy for I am holy." (1 Pet 1:14–16; Heb 12:14; 1 Thess 5:23; 1 John 2:6; also 1 Cor 13).

8. Divine Healing—Deliverance from sickness is provided for in the Atonement. (Isa 53:5; Matt 8:16–17; Jas 5:13–16).

9. The Breaking of Bread—This is enjoined upon all believers until the Lord comes. (Luke 22:14–20; 1 Cor 11:20–34).

10. The premillennial Second Coming of the Lord Jesus Christ Himself is the blessed hope set before all believers. (1 Cor 15:22–24; 1 Thess 4:13–15; 1 Cor 15:51–57).

11. The everlasting punishment of all who are not written in the Book of Life. (Rev 20:10–15).

12. The Gifts of the Holy Spirit and the offices as recorded in the New Testament. (Eph 4:7–16; 1 Cor 12).[793]

---

[793] *Redemption Tidings*, July 1924, 19.

Appendix 5 Pastors of Crosskeys Pentecostal Church since 1912

Tom Mercy: 1912–1935

Wilfred Mercy: 1935–1968

Joe French: 1968 – [794]

Alfred Hibbert

Joe Ivinson

Edgar Davies: 1982

David Kidd: 1982–1989

David Palmer: 1989–2005

Due to ill health of David Palmer during 2003–2005 the church was also supported in ministry by Ken Campbell.

Phillip Gibson: 2005–2008

Christopher Palmer: 2011–2013

---

[794] Unfortunately due to the loss of the church records for the Crosskeys Assembly it has proved difficult to verify the exact dates that four of the pastors served the congregation; there are also no records at AoG Headquarters.

Appendix 6 Statement of Faith American Assemblies of God

The Bible is our all-sufficient rule for faith and practice. This Statement of Fundamental Truths is intended simply as a basis of fellowship among us (i.e., that we all speak the same thing, 1 Corinthians 1:10; Acts 2:42). The phraseology employed in this statement is not inspired or contended for, but the truth set forth is held to be essential to a full-gospel ministry. No claim is made that it contains all biblical truth, only that it covers our need as to these fundamental doctrines.

1. The Scriptures Inspired

The Scriptures, both the Old and New Testaments, are verbally inspired of God and are the revelation of God to man, the infallible, authoritative rule of faith and conduct (2 Timothy 3:15–17; 1 Thessalonians 2:13; 2 Peter 1:21).

2. The One True God

The one true God has revealed himself as the eternally self-existent "I AM," the Creator of heaven and earth and the Redeemer of mankind. He has further revealed himself as embodying the principles of relationship and association as Father, Son, and Holy Spirit (Deuteronomy 6:4; Isaiah 43:10, 11; Matthew 28:19; Luke 3:22).

THE ADORABLE GODHEAD

(a) Terms Defined

The terms trinity and persons, as related to the godhead, while not found in the Scriptures, are words in harmony with Scripture, whereby we may convey to others our immediate understanding of the doctrine of Christ respecting the Being of God, as distinguished from "gods many and lords many." We therefore may speak with propriety of the Lord our God, who is One Lord, as a Trinity or as one Being of three persons, and still be absolutely scriptural (examples, Matthew 28:19; 2 Corinthians 13:14; John 14:16,17).

(b) Distinction and Relationship in the Godhead

Christ taught a distinction of persons in the godhead which He expressed in specific terms of relationship, as Father, Son, and Holy Spirit, but that this distinction and relationship, as to its mode is inscrutable and incomprehensible, because unexplained (Luke 1:35; 1 Corinthians 1:24; Matthew 11:25–27; 28:19; 2 Corinthians 13:14; 1 John 1:3,4).

(c) Unity of the One Being of Father, Son, and Holy Spirit

Accordingly, therefore, there is that in the Father which constitutes Him the Father and not the Son; there is that in the Son which constitutes Him the Son and not the Father; and there is that in the Holy Spirit which constitutes Him the Holy Spirit and not either the Father or the Son. Wherefore, the Father is the Begetter; the Son is the Begotten; and the Holy Spirit is the One proceeding from the Father and the Son. Therefore, because these three persons in the godhead are in a state of unity, there is but one Lord God Almighty and His name one (John 1:18; 15:26; 17:11, 21; Zechariah 14:9)

(d) Identity and Cooperation in the Godhead

The Father, the Son, and the Holy Spirit are never identical as to person; nor confused as to relation; nor divided in respect to the godhead; nor opposed as to cooperation. The Son is in the Father and the Father is in the Son as to relationship. The Son is with the Father and the Father is with the Son, as to fellowship. The Father is not from the Son, but the Son is from the Father, as to authority. The Holy Spirit is from the Father and the Son proceeding, as to nature, relationship, cooperation, and authority. Hence, no person in the godhead either exists or works separately or independently of the others (John 5:17–30, 32, 37; 8:17, 18).

(e) The Title, Lord Jesus Christ

The appellation Lord Jesus Christ is a proper name. It is never applied in the New Testament either to the Father or to the Holy Spirit. It therefore belongs exclusively to the Son of God (Romans 1:1–3, 7; 2 John 3).

(f) The Lord Jesus Christ, God With Us

The Lord Jesus Christ, as to His divine and eternal nature, is the proper and only Begotten of the Father, but as to His human nature, He is the proper Son of Man. He is, therefore, acknowledged to be both God and man; who because He is God and man, is "Immanuel," God with us (Matthew 1:23; 1 John 4:2, 10, 14; Revelation 1:13, 17).

(g) The Title, Son of God

Since the name Immanuel embraces both God and man, in the one person, our Lord Jesus Christ, it follows that the title Son of God describes His proper deity, and the title Son of Man, His proper humanity. Therefore, the title Son of God belongs to the order of eternity, and the title Son of Man to the order of time (Matthew 1:21–23; 2 John 3; 1 John 3:8; Hebrews 7:3; 1:1–13).

(h) Transgression of the Doctrine of Christ

Wherefore, it is a transgression of the doctrine of Christ to say that Jesus Christ derived the title Son of God solely from the fact of the Incarnation, or because of His relation to the economy of redemption. Therefore, to deny that the Father is a real and eternal Father, and that the Son is a real and eternal Son, is a denial of the distinction and relationship in the Being of God; a denial of the Father and the Son; and a displacement of the truth that Jesus Christ is come in the flesh (2 John 9; John 1:1,2,14,18,29,49; 1 John 2:22,23; 4:1–5; Hebrews 12:2).

(i) Exaltation of Jesus Christ as Lord

The Son of God, our Lord Jesus Christ, having by himself purged our sins, sat down on the right hand of the Majesty on high, angels and principalities and powers having been made subject unto Him. And having been made both Lord and Christ, He sent the Holy Spirit that we, in the name of Jesus, might bow our knees and confess that Jesus Christ is Lord to the glory of God the Father until the end, when the Son shall become subject to the Father that God may be all in all (Hebrews 1:3; 1 Peter 3:22; Acts 2:32–36; Romans 14:11; 1 Corinthians 15:24–28)

(j) Equal Honor to the Father and to the Son

Wherefore, since the Father has delivered all judgment unto the Son, it is not only the express duty of all in heaven and on earth to bow the knee, but it is an unspeakable joy in the Holy Spirit to ascribe unto the Son all the attributes of deity, and to give Him all the honor and the glory contained in all the names and titles of the godhead except those which express relationship (see paragraphs b, c, and d), and thus honor the Son even as we honor the Father (John 5:22,23; 1 Peter 1:8; Revelation 5:6–14; Philippians 2:8, 9; Revelation 7:9, 10; 4:8–11).

3. The Deity of the Lord Jesus Christ

The Lord Jesus Christ is the eternal Son of God. The Scriptures declare:

a. His virgin birth (Matthew 1:23; Luke 1:31, 35).

b. His sinless life (Hebrews 7:26; 1 Peter 2:22).

c. His miracles (Acts 2:22; 10:38).

d. His substitutionary work on the cross (1 Corinthians 15:3; 2 Corinthians 5:21).

e. His bodily resurrection from the dead (Matthew 28:6; Luke 24:39; 1 Corinthians 15:4).

f. His exaltation to the right hand of God (Acts 1:9, 11; 2:33; Philippians 2:9–11; Hebrews 1:3).

4. The Fall of Man

Man was created good and upright; for God said, "Let us make man in our image, after our likeness." However, man by voluntary transgression fell and thereby incurred not only physical death but also spiritual death, which is separation from God (Genesis 1:26, 27; 2:17; 3:6; Romans 5:12–19).

5. The Salvation of Man

Man's only hope of redemption is through the shed blood of Jesus Christ the Son of God.

(a) Conditions to Salvation

Salvation is received through repentance toward God and faith toward the Lord Jesus Christ. By the washing of regeneration and renewing of the Holy Spirit, being justified by grace through faith, man becomes an heir of God according to the hope of eternal life (Luke 24:47; John 3:3; Romans 10:13–15; Ephesians 2:8; Titus 2:11; 3:5–7).

(b) The Evidences of Salvation

The inward evidence of salvation is the direct witness of the Spirit (Romans 8:16). The outward evidence to all men is a life of righteousness and true holiness (Ephesians 4:24; Titus 2:12).

6. The Ordinances of the Church

(a) Baptism in Water

The ordinance of baptism by immersion is commanded in the Scriptures. All who repent and believe on Christ as Savior and Lord are to be baptized. Thus they declare to the world that they have died with Christ and that they also have been raised with Him to walk in newness of life (Matthew 28:19; Mark 16:16; Acts 10:47, 48; Romans 6:4).

(b) Holy Communion

The Lord's Supper, consisting of the elements—bread and the fruit of the vine—is the symbol expressing our sharing the divine nature of our Lord Jesus Christ (2 Peter 1:4); a memorial of His suffering and death (1 Corinthians 11:26); and a prophecy of His Second Coming (1 Corinthians 11:26); and is enjoined on all believers "till He come!"

7. The Baptism in the Holy Spirit

All believers are entitled to and should ardently expect and earnestly seek the promise of the Father, the baptism in the Holy Spirit and fire, according to the command of our Lord Jesus Christ. This was the normal experience of all in the early Christian church. With it comes the enduement of power for life and service, the bestowment of the gifts and their uses in the work of the ministry (Luke 24:49; Acts 1:4,8; 1 Corinthians 12:1–31). This experience is distinct from and subsequent to the experience of the new birth (Acts 8:12–17; 10:44–

46; 11:14–16; 15:7–9). With the baptism in the Holy Spirit come such experiences as an overflowing fullness of the Spirit (John 7:37–39; Acts 4:8), a deepened reverence for God (Acts 2:43; Hebrews 12:28), an intensified consecration to God and dedication to His work (Acts 2:42), and a more active love for Christ, for His Word, and for the lost (Mark 16:20).

8. The Initial Physical Evidence of the Baptism in the Holy Spirit

The baptism of believers in the Holy Spirit is witnessed by the initial physical sign of speaking with other tongues as the Spirit of God gives them utterance (Acts 2:4). The speaking in tongues in this instance is the same in essence as the gift of tongues (1 Corinthians 12:4–10, 28), but different in purpose and use.

9. Sanctification

Sanctification is an act of separation from that which is evil, and of dedication unto God (Romans 12:1–2; 1 Thessalonians 5:23; Hebrews 13:12). Scriptures teach a life of "holiness without which no man shall see the Lord" (Hebrews 12:14). By the power of the Holy Spirit we are able to obey the command: "Be ye holy, for I am holy" (1 Peter 1:15–16).

Sanctification is realized in the believer by recognizing his identification with Christ in His death and resurrection, and by faith reckoning daily upon the fact of that union, and by offering every faculty continually to the dominion of the Holy Spirit (Romans 6:1–11, 13; 8:1–2, 13; Galatians 2:20; Philippians 2:12–13; 1 Peter 1:5).

10. The Church and Its Mission

The Church is the body of Christ, the habitation of God through the Spirit, with divine appointments for the fulfillment of her Great Commission. Each believer, born of the Spirit, is an integral part of the general assembly and church of the firstborn, which are written in heaven (Ephesians 1:22–23; 2:22; Hebrews 12:23).

Since God's purpose concerning man is to seek and to save that which is lost, to be worshiped by man, to build a body of believers in the image of His Son, and to demonstrate His love and compassion for all the world, the priority reason-for-being of the Assemblies of God as part of the Church is:

a. To be an agency of God for evangelizing the world (Acts 1:8; Matthew 28:19–20; Mark 16:15–16).

b. To be a corporate body in which man may worship God (1 Corinthians 12:13).

c. To be a channel of God's purpose to build a body of saints being perfected in the image of His Son (Ephesians 4:11–16; 1 Corinthians 12:28; 14:12).

d. To be a people who demonstrate God's love and compassion for all the world (Psalms 112:9; Galatians 2:10; 6:10; James 1:27).

The Assemblies of God exists expressly to give continuing emphasis to this reason-for-being in the New Testament apostolic pattern by teaching and encouraging believers to be baptized in the Holy Spirit. This experience:

a. Enables them to evangelize in the power of the Spirit with accompanying supernatural signs (Mark 16:15–20; Acts 4:29–31; Hebrews 2:3–4).

b. Adds a necessary dimension to a worshipful relationship with God (1 Corinthians 2:10–16; 1 Corinthians 12–14).

c. Enables them to respond to the full working of the Holy Spirit in expression of fruit and gifts and ministries as in New Testament times for the edifying of the body of Christ and care for the poor and needy of the world (Galatians 5:22–26; Matthew 25:37–40; Galatians 6:10; 1 Corinthians 14:12; Ephesians 4:11–12; 1 Corinthians 12:28; Colossians 1:29).

11. The Ministry

A divinely called and scripturally ordained ministry has been provided by our Lord for the fourfold purpose of leading the Church in: (1) evangelization of the world (Mark 16:15–20), (2) worship of God (John 4:23–24), (3) building a Body of saints being perfected in the image of His Son (Ephesians 4:11, 16), and (4) meeting human need with ministries of love and compassion (Psalms 112:9; Galatians 2:10; 6:10; James 1:27).

12. Divine Healing

Divine healing is an integral part of the gospel. Deliverance from sickness is provided for in the Atonement, and is the privilege of all believers (Isaiah 53:4–5; Matthew 8:16–17; James 5:14–16).

13. The Blessed Hope

The resurrection of those who have fallen asleep in Christ and their translation together with those who are alive and remain unto the coming of the Lord is the imminent and blessed hope of the Church (1 Thessalonians 4:16–17; Romans 8:23; Titus 2:13; 1 Corinthians 15:51 52).

14. The Millennial Reign of Christ

The Second Coming of Christ includes the rapture of the saints, which is our blessed hope, followed by the visible return of Christ with His saints to reign on the earth for one thousand years (Zechariah 14:5; Matthew 24:27, 30; Revelation 1:7; 19:11–14; 20:1–6). This millennial reign will bring the salvation of national Israel (Ezekiel 37:21–22; Zephaniah 3:19–20; Romans 11:26–27) and the establishment of universal peace (Isaiah 11:6–9; Psalm 72:3–8; Micah 4:3–4).

15. The Final Judgment

There will be a final judgment in which the wicked dead will be raised and judged according to their works. Whosoever is not found written in the Book of Life, together with the devil and his angels, the beast and the false prophet, will be consigned to everlasting punishment in the lake which burneth with fire and brimstone, which is the second death (Matthew 25:46; Mark 9:43– 48; Revelation 19:20; 20:11–15; 21:8).

16. The New Heavens and the New Earth

"We, according to His promise, look for new heavens and a new earth, wherein dwelleth righteousness" (2 Peter 3:13; Revelation 21–22).

Appendix 7 Crosskeys Pentecostal Church Constitution 2013

CONTENTS

10.   Members Meetings

    10.1   Annual General Meeting

    10.2   Special Meetings

INTRODUCTION

This constitutional church management document has been prepared and aligned for the purposes of the trust deed of Crosskeys Pentecostal Church which is an independent evangelical fellowship. This document should be read in conjunction with the deed and is subsidiary to the deed. All terms used in this document shall have the meaning attributed to them in the deed.

The name of the church is Crosskeys Pentecostal Church and is presently located at Gladstone Street Crosskeys NP117PA in the County Borough of Caerphilly.

1. Purpose of the church and what we believe

1.1:   The purpose of the church shall be:

(i)   The advancement of the Christian faith by the proclamation of the gospel of God concerning his son Jesus Christ the Lord and the preaching and teaching of the word of God by the church in accordance with its statement of faith.

(ii)   The promotion of the spiritual teaching and the maintenance of the statement and the promotion of religious observances that manifest the statement.

(iii)   The furtherance of the charitable work of the church consistent with the   statement of fundamental truths.

(iv)   Such other charitable purposes as shall further the attainment of the above purpose of the church.

1.2:   The Statement of Faith:

We believe that the scriptures, known as the Bible, are the inspired word of God, the infallible and all sufficient rule for faith, practice and conduct. The following statement of fundamental truths is not intended as a creed for the church, but as a basis of unity for a full gospel ministry (1 Cor 1:10).

(i)   The Bible is the inspired word of God (2 Tim 3:15–16; 2 Peter 1:21).

(ii)   The unity of the one true and living God who is the eternal, self – existent 'I am', who has revealed himself as one being in three persons, Father, Son, and Holy Spirit (Deut 6:4; Mark 12:29; Matt 28: 19).

(iii)   The fall of man, who was created pure and upright, but fell by voluntary transgression (Gen 1:26–31; 3:1–7; Rom 5:12–21).

(iv)   Salvation through faith in Christ, who died for our sins according to the scriptures, was buried, and was raised from the dead on the third day, according to the scriptures, and through his blood we have redemption (Tit 2: 11; 3:5–7; Rom 10:8–15; 1 Cor 15:3–4). This experience is also known as the new birth, and is an instantaneous and complete operation of the Holy Spirit upon initial faith in the Lord Jesus Christ (John 3:5–6; James 1:18; 1 Peter 1:13–23; 1 John 5:1).

(v)   Baptism by immersion in water is enjoined upon all who have really repented and have truly believed with all their hearts in Christ as saviour and lord (Matt 28:19; Acts 10:47–48; Acts 2:38–39).

(vi)   The baptism in the Holy Spirit, the initial evidence of which is the speaking with other tongues as the spirit gives utterance (Acts 2:4; 10:44–46; 11:14–16; 19:6; Isa 8:18).

(vii)   Holiness of life and conduct in obedience to the command of God, "be ye holy for I am holy" (1 Peter 1:14–16; Heb 12:14; 1 Thess 5:23; 1 John 2:6; 1 Cor 13).

(viii) Deliverance from sickness, by divine healing, is provided for in the Atonement (Isa 53:4–5; Matt 8:16–17).

(ix)   Breaking of bread is enjoined upon all believers until the Lord comes (Luke 22:14–20; 1 Cor 11:20–34).

(x)   The premillennial Second Coming of the Lord Jesus Christ is the blessed hope set before all believers (1 Cor 15:22–24, 51–57; 1 Thess 4:13–18).

(xi)   Everlasting punishment is the portion of all who are not written in the Book of life (Rev 20:10–15).

(xii)   The gifts of the Holy Spirit and the offices have been set by God in the church as recorded in the New Testament (1 Cor 12:4–11, 28; Rom 12; Eph 4:7–16).

2. The Church Council

(i)   The management of church affairs shall be vested in the church council and shall consist of the minister(s), elders, deacons, secretary and treasurer. The minimum number on the council shall be three. A quorum shall consist of more than half the number of church council members. All members shall be informed of the dates and time of any meeting at least 48 hours in advance.

(ii)   The officers of the church shall be the chairman, secretary and treasurer. Normally the senior minister at the church shall be the chairman of the church council unless the church council (in the absence of a minister or if the minister declines) shall resolve otherwise. The officers of the church will administer the business of the church and will be responsible to the church council.

(iii)   The church council will meet at regular intervals to manage church affairs. The minimum number of meetings in any one year period will be four.

(iv)   At its meetings the church council shall endeavour to reach a consensus on matters under discussion. In the event of the chairman considering a vote to be necessary on a particular item the chairman shall not have a second casting vote in the event of a deadlock.

(v)   The church council may co-opt other persons to attend and speak at its meetings but such persons shall not vote on any matters.

(vi)   Requests for specific matters to be considered by the church council may be submitted in writing to the church secretary at least one week before a meeting of the church council.

(vii) The church is a registered charity and the church council are the managers of the charity in law with a minimum of three people constituting the members of the church council.

3. Leadership

The leadership and spiritual oversight of the church shall be vested in the appointed minister(s) and elders supported as appropriate by deacons and helps in accordance with scripture.

3.1 Ministers

(i) In order to be appointed, a minister must:

(a) be a committed Christian in agreement with the church statement of faith as contained within the constitution and demonstrating a spiritual life in accordance with the Word of God.

(b) satisfy the eldership requirements of scripture 1 Tim 3:2–7.

(c) be committed to the work and vision of the church

(d) be nominated by a two/thirds majority of the existing church council and confirmed by the church via a two week consultation period.

(ii) By virtue of their appointment, ministers will ...

(a) be entrusted with the spiritual oversight of the church

(b) be responsible jointly or separately for the church's worship, prayer, Bible teaching, ministry, pastoral care and evangelism.

(iii) Any complaint about a minister may be made to a fellow minister or elder and must be confirmed by a witness. The fellow minister or elder will then share the matter at a meeting of all the church council and report back to the complainants on any decisions made.

(iv) A minister may resign at any time by written notice but will normally be expected to serve one month's notice or exceptionally a period to be mutually agreed with the church council.

(v) A minister shall be required to resign from office immediately if.

(a) The minister is found to be living in a manner out of keeping with scriptural requirements, or

(b) The minister no longer accepts the church's statement of faith.

(c) Unanimously requested to do so by the church council on the grounds of gross negligence of the ministerial role.

(vi) It is recognised that on occasions it may be in the best interests of the church to make available residential accommodation for any minister or ministers serving the church. In the event of the church providing such accommodation the same must be provided as against appropriate security documentation to preserve the property of the church.

3.2   Elders

(i) In order to be appointed, an elder must:

(a) be a committed Christian and satisfy the eldership requirements of scripture as set out in 1 Tim 3:2–7 and Titus 1:5–9.

(b) be committed to the work and vision of the church.

(c) be unanimously nominated by the church council and confirmed by the church via a two week consultation period.

(d) accept the church's statement of faith as set out in the constitution.

(ii) By virtue of their appointment, elders will be entrusted with the spiritual oversight of the church

(iii) Any complaint about an elder may be made to a minister or fellow elder and must be confirmed by a witness. The fellow minister or elder will then share the matter at a meeting of the ministers and elders and report back to the complainants on any decision made.

(iv) An elder may resign at any time by written notice but will normally be expected to serve one months' notice or exceptionally a period to be mutually agreed with the church council.

(v) An elder will be required to resign from office immediately if:

(a) The elder is found to be living in a manner out of keeping with the scriptural requirements, or

(b) The elder no longer accepts the church's statement of faith

(c) Unanimously requested to do so by the church council on the grounds of gross negligence of the eldership role.

3.3 Deacons

(i) In order to be appointed, a deacon must:

(a) be a committed Christian and satisfy the requirements of scripture 1 Tim 3:8–13.

(b) accept the church's statement of faith as set out in the constitution.

(c) be committed to the work and vision of the church .

(d) be unanimously nominated by the church council and confirmed by the church via a two week consultation period.

(ii) Any complaint about a deacon may be made to a minister or elder who will then share the matter with the deacon privately or, if necessary, at a meeting of all the ministers and elders and report back to the complainant on any decision made.

(iii) A deacon may resign at any time by written notice but will normally be expected to serve one month's notice or exceptionally a period to be mutually agreed with the church council.

(iv) A deacon will be required to resign immediately if:

(a) The deacon is found to be living in a manner out of keeping with scriptural requirements, or

(b) The deacon no longer accepts the church's statement of faith, or

(c) Unanimously requested to do so by the church council on the grounds of gross negligence of the deacon role.

3.4 Helps

Those appointed by the church council to have responsibility for leading or working in specific areas of the Church's work must:

(a) Be a committed Christian and accept the church's statement of faith as set out in the constitution and be committed to the work and vision of the church.

(b) Exercise their authority under the supervision and authority of the church council subject to the provisions of Section 7.4.

(c) Relinquish their leadership or work if a meeting of all the church council should deem this to be appropriate.

4. Church staff

(i) All appointments to remunerated positions must be agreed by the church council.

(ii) All remunerated staff will be under contract to the church council.

(iii) Remuneration of remunerated staff will be determined by the church council.

5. Remuneration of members of Church council.

In accordance with the provisions of the trust deed (section 12- Application of Funds), The remuneration of any member of the church council for the supply of services and /or employment as a servant of the church shall be determined by the church council provided that:

(i) Such a member of the church council shall not be present at or take part in any discussion relating to such matters except at the invitation of the remaining members of the church council.

(ii) Decisions or resolutions regarding remuneration are unanimously agreed by the remaining members of the church council.

(iii) The number of members of the church council receiving remuneration is not a majority of the church council.

6. Holding trustees

(i) The responsibilities of the holding trustees are set out in the deed.

(ii) The appointment and removal of the holding trustees as is set out in the deed.

(iii) Meetings of the holding trustees shall be chaired by the chairman of the church council.

(iv) The holding trustees may appoint a secretary to keep minutes at their meetings and record all resolutions.

(v) The holding trustees with the prior consent of the church council may appoint one or more of their number to undertake administrative and/or liaison work with professional advisors and other third parties.

(vi) The holding trustees shall meet at least once in every year to hear receive discuss and accept reports and accounts as appropriate.

7. Church officers

The officers of the church shall be the chairman, secretary and treasurer who will administer the business of the church and be responsible to the church council. The duties of the treasurer and the secretary may be altered by the church council by prior written notification and they shall comply with all lawful instructions issued by the church council. All officers will be Christians in good standing and in agreement with the statement of faith of Crosskeys Pentecostal Church.

7.1 Chairman

(i) The chairman of the church council will normally be the senior minister of the church unless the church council (in the absence of a minister or if the minister declines) shall resolve otherwise, the appointment to be reviewed annually.

(ii) The chairman shall:

(a) ensure that all requirements specified in the deed are satisfied.

(b) normally chair all church council and church membership meetings when in attendance.

(c) support the secretary and treasurer in the administration of church business.

7.2 The Secretary

(i) The secretary holds office in accordance with the terms of the deed, the appointment to be reviewed annually.

(ii) The secretary shall:

(a) prepare and keep signed copies of the minutes of members' meetings and church council meetings.

(b) receive and keep certified copies of the minutes of the meetings of the holding trustees and other church departments.

(c) sign on behalf of the church council official documents requiring the signature of the secretary.

(d) maintain the church register of membership.

(e) maintain insurance cover as required by the church council and holding trustees for the church's assets.

(f) act as counter signatory with the treasurer for payments due for goods and services payable by cheque (see 7.3 (ii) (f)).

7.3 Treasurer

(i) The treasurer holds office in accordance with the terms of the deed, the appointment to be reviewed annually.

(ii) The treasurer shall:

(a) receive all income to the church except for that more properly received by other departments.

(b) make all salaries superannuation expenses payments to employees of the church and pay to the Inland Revenue all due income tax and national insurance contributions.

(c) deal with all documentation relating to the Inland Revenue including the annual returns.

(d) deal with all documentation relating to the filing of the annual returns and accounts to the charity commissioners.

(e) maintain a book in which to record all collections - all collections to be counted and signed for by not less than two persons.

(f) make payments due and payable for goods and/or services ordered or purposes previously approved by the church council and other payments without specific authorisation subject to a limit of £200 for any one payment.

(g) keep full records of all income and expenditure and present an annual report to the Annual General Meeting and a quarterly report to the church council.

(h) make arrangements for the banking and investment (subject to appropriate professional advice) of church moneys.

(i) negotiate loans required for the church where approved by the church council.

(j) administer the Deeds of Covenant and Gift Aid Schemes in accordance with the requirements of the Inland Revenue.

7.4 Other Leaders

Any leader of a church department/ministry must be a committed Christian in full agreement with the statement of faith. The responsibilities of other departmental leaders or committees shall be set by the church council at the time of such appointments.

8. Membership

8.1 Basis

(i) Membership shall be open to all who:

(a) by grace have exhibited saving faith in the Lord Jesus Christ and

(b) have been or are willing to be baptised in water,

(c) desire to worship and serve God in the context of the principles set out in this constitution.

(d) be in agreement with the statement of faith of Crosskeys Pentecostal Church.

(e) normally live within reasonable travelling distance of the church.

(f) applications for membership may be made to the church council by persons aged 16 years and over. Young people who have been regular attendees at the main Sunday services during the previous 12 months and who meet all the criteria for membership, shall become members on their 16th birthday unless they indicate otherwise. The church council shall decide upon all applications for membership.

(g) the church council may confer emeritus membership to members of long standing who move away from the church e.g. on retirement. Emeritus members are not entitled to vote at members' meetings.

(iii) A membership list should be kept by the church council to whom prospective members should apply.

8.2 Responsibilities and privileges

(i) Members shall:

(a) take an active part in the work and worship of the church, according to their ability and circumstances.

(b) relate into the church's system of pastoral care.

(c) prayerfully contribute to the unity, encouragement and fellowship of the church.

(d) show a scriptural regard for those in positions of leadership.

(ii) Members shall support the Church by:

(a) regular attendance at services of worship in accordance with Acts 2:42.

(b) regular private prayer for the fellowship and its activities.

(c) considered giving of tithes and offerings in accordance with scriptural principles..

(iii) All members will be entitled to attend at church meetings. Only members of 18 and over will be entitled to vote at church meetings.

(iv) A church meeting may be requested in writing to the Church council if supported by at least 35% of the recorded membership.

9. Discipline and grievance procedures.

(i) It is implicit in membership of the church that members:

(a) are prepared to live by the accepted rules of Christian conduct as ruled upon by the church council. The church council must base its rulings upon Scriptural principles.

(b) accept the government and discipline of the church.

(ii) Church membership may be terminated by the church council for any of the following reasons:

(a) removal from the area as in for a period of six months.

(b) failure to attend the church services for six consecutive months without reasonable cause.

(c) death or presumed death.

(d) misconduct as ruled upon by the church council.

(e) regular attendance at another church.

(f) in the opinion of the church council ceasing to hold and practice the church's Statement of Faith.

(iii) The leadership is responsible for maintaining good discipline within the church for the glory of God and the sake of the testimony. The minister(s), or if this is impracticable due to their absence or personal involvement, a member of the eldership shall investigate any alleged breach of the accepted rules of Christian conduct. Where a breach is substantiated the following disciplinary measures may be imposed:

(a)   private verbal caution

(b)   verbal caution in presence of leadership

(c)   written caution as to future behaviour

(d)   temporary suspension of membership for a limited period involving absence from church activities and business meetings

(e)   removal from office

(f)   permanent revocation of membership

(iv) The making of apologies and/or restitution may also be required. Generally, these will follow the principle that they should be as private or public as the action causing offence. Measures (c)–(f) shall only be imposed after the church council has considered a report on the situation. Before the church council considers the matter the investigating officer shall inform the person of their findings and proposed disciplinary recommendation. The individual shall have the right to make representations in person or writing to the church council when the matter is considered. The decision of the church council shall be final.

(v) In accordance with scriptural requirements it may also be necessary for the leadership to inform the church of a disciplinary measure.

(vi) Notwithstanding the provisions above it will be the leadership's intention to restore and reinstate in a loving and discreet manner. The more severe measures will only be adopted where the greater interests of the church require such a course of action.

(vii) A member with a grievance other than one relating to a disciplinary matter may ask the leadership to investigate the matter. The minister(s) or if this is impracticable due to their absence or personal involvement, a member of the eldership shall investigate the matter. The investigator shall inform interested parties of his findings and any proposed recommendations before reporting to the leadership or if appropriate, the church council. Interested parties may make further representations to the church council. The church council shall then decide on the matter and their decision shall be final.

(viii) Members may make representations in writing to the church council with suggested improvements for the running of the church. At the discretion of the church council, church members may be invited to meet the church council to discuss such matters.

10. Member's meeting

10.1 Annual General Meeting

Meetings of the members of the church shall be held annually in accordance with the trust deed and will receive a report from the church council on the financial position of the church and the current number of members.

10.2 Special Meetings

Special meetings can be called in accordance with section 8.2 para (iv).

END

Appendix 8

The Congo Evangelistic Mission Stands For And Teaches.

1.   The inspiration of the Scriptures.

2.   The Eternal Deity of our Lord Jesus Christ.

3.   The personality of the Holy Spirit.

4.   The entire efficacy of the death and shed blood of our Lord Jesus Christ, for the remission of every sin of every sinner.

5.   The natural depravity of man.

6.   The bodily resurrection and personal coming again of our Lord Jesus Christ.

7.   Justification by faith alone.

8.   A new and holy life as a result of the new birth.

9.   Baptism by immersion, after conversion.

10.   Healing of the physical body provided for in the atonement.

11.   A baptism in the Holy Spirit, as God's enduement with power for service, distinct from and subsequent to conversion: this experience being attested to by praising God in new tongues.

12.   The eternal conscious bliss of the saved and the eternal conscious suffering of the unbeliever.[795]

---

[795] W. F. P. Burton, *God Working With Them* (London: Victory Press, 1933).

Bibliography

Abrams, Minnie F., *The Baptism of the Holy Ghost and Fire* (Kedgaon, India: Pandita Ramabai Mukti Mission, 1905)

Adams, Kevin, *A Diary of Revival: The Outbreak of the 1904 Welsh Awakening* (Farnham: CWR, 2004)

Adams, Kevin and Jones, Emyr, *A Pictorial History of Revival: The Outbreak of the 1904 Welsh Awakening* (Farnham: CWR, 2004)

Allen, David, *Glorious Names Studies on the Person and Work of Christ* (Mattersey: Mattersey Hall, 1999)

————, *Neglected Feast: Rescuing the Breaking of Bread* (Nottingham: New Life Publishing, 2007)

————, *There is a River: A Charismatic Church History in Outline* (Tonbridge: Authentic Media, 2004)

————, *The Unfailing Stream A Charismatic Church History in Outline* (Tonbridge: Sovereign World, 1994)

Anderson, Allan, *An Introduction to Pentecostalism* (Cambridge: C.U.P. 2004)

————, *Spreading Fires: The Missionary Nature of early Pentecostalism.* (London: SCM, 2007)

————, ed., *Studying Global Pentecostalism: Theories and Methods* (London: University of California Press, 2010)

Andrews, E. H., *The Promise of the Spirit* (Welwyn: Evangelical Press, 1982)

Apostolic Church, *Introducing the Apostolic Church: A Manual of Belief, Practice and History* (Penygroes: Apostolic Church, 1988)

Barabas, Steven, *So Great Salvation: The History and Message of the Keswick Convention* (Eugene, OR: Wipf & Stock, 2005)

Barnes, Albert, *1st Corinthians* (London: Blackie, 1847)

Barrett, C. K., *The First Epistle to the Corinthians* (London: A & C Black, 1971)

Bartleman, Frank, *Azusa Street* (Gainesville, FL: Bridge-Logos, 1980)

—————, *Two Years Mission Work in Europe*, Jawbone Digital, n.d. (Frank Bartleman, 1924)

Bebbington, D. W., *Evangelicalism in Modern Britain: A History from the 1730s to the 1980s* (London: Routledge, 1993)

Beeke, Joel, ed., *The Experimental Knowledge of Christ and Additional Sermons of John Elias (1774–1841)* (Grand Rapids, MI: Reformation Heritage Books, 2006)

Berkhof, Louis, *Systematic Theology* (Edinburgh: Banner of Truth, 1958, repr. 1998)

Blumhofer, Edith, *The Assemblies of God: A Popular History* (Springfield, MO: Radiant Books, 1985)

—————, *The Assemblies of God Vol. 1* (Springfield, MO: G.P.H., 1989)

Boddy, A. A., *"Pentecost" at Sunderland: A Vicar's Testimony* (Sunderland: A. A. Boddy, n.d.)

—————, *Pentecost for England, (and other lands) With Signs Following* (Sunderland: Boddy, 1907)

Booth-Clibborn, William, *The Baptism in the Holy Spirit: A Personal Testimony* (Portland, OR: Ryder, 1936)

Boulton, E. C. W., Chris Cartwright, ed., *George Jeffreys – A Ministry of the Miraculous* (Tonbridge: Sovereign World, 1999)

Brand, Chad Owen, ed., *Perspectives on Spirit Baptism* (Nashville, TN: B&H Publishing, 2004)

Brewster, P. S., ed., *Pentecostal Doctrine* (Elim: Grenehurst Press, 1976)

Brown, Paul E., *The Holy Spirit & The Bible* (Fearn: Christian Focus, 2002)

Bruce, F. F., *The Epistle to the Hebrews* (Grand Rapids, MI: Eerdmans, 1990)

Brumbeck, Carl, *What Meaneth This?* (London: Elim, 1946)

Bruner, Frederick Dale, *A Theology of the Holy Spirit* (Grand Rapids, MI: Eerdmans, 1970)

Buchanan, Bob, *Blaenau Gwent Baptist Church: Celebrating 350 years of God's Faithfulness 1660–2010* (Abertillery, 2010)

Burgess, Stanley M., and Gary B. McGee, eds., *Dictionary of Pentecostal and Charismatic Movements* (Grand Rapids, MI: Zondervan, 1988)

—————, ed., and Eduard M. Van Der Mass, assoc. ed., *The New International Dictionary of Pentecostal and Charismatic Movements* (Grand Rapids, MI: Zondervan, 2002)

Burland, Len, *A Historical Tour around Mynyddislwyn Mountain* (Abertillery: Old Bakehouse, 2002)

Burton, W. F. P., *Bible Notes* (Johannesburg: A. G. Fischer, 1962)

—————, *God Working With Them, Being Eighteen Years of Congo Evangelistic Mission History* (London: Victory Press, 1933)

—————, *Teachings From The Word Of God* (Upington, S. Africa: Verkrygbaar Van, n.d.)

Butts, John Hopkin, *A History of Beulah Baptist Chapel Newbridge* (Abertillery: Old Bakehouse, 2010)

Calvin, John, *1 Corinthians* (Grand Rapids, MI: Eerdmans, 1960)

Calvinistic Methodists, *The History, Constitution and Confession of Faith of the Calvinistic Methodists in Wales, Drawn up by Their Own Associated Ministers* (Memphis, TN: General Books, 1827; repr. 2010)

Canty, George, *The Practice of Pentecost* (Basingstoke: Marshalls, 1987)

Carson, D. A., *The Gospel According to John* (Leicester: I.V.P., 1991)

—————, *Showing the Spirit: A Theological Exposition of 1 Corinthians 12–14* (Grand Rapids, MI: Baker, 1987)

Carter, Howard, *Spiritual Gifts and their Operation* (Springfield, MO: GPH, 1968)

Carter, John, *Donald Gee: Pentecostal Statesman* (Nottingham: AoG, 1975)

—————, *A Full Life* (London: Evangel, 1979)

—————, *Howard Carter: Man of the Spirit* (Nottingham: AoG, 1971)

—————, *Questions and Answers on Vital Subjects* (J. Carter: n.d.)

Cartwright, Desmond W., *The Great Evangelists: The Remarkable Lives of George and Stephen Jeffreys* (Basingstoke: Marshall Pickering, 1986)

Chadwick, Samuel, *The Way to Pentecost* (London: Hodder, 1932)

Chivers, Alan, *Coal, Guns and Rugby: A Monmouthshire Memoir* (Usk: Oakwood Press, 2005)

Crouter, Richard, ed., *Friedrich Schleiermacher On Religion* (Cambridge: CUP, 1988)

Collins, Brian, *Crumlin to Pontymister Places of Worship: A Sketchbook History* (Abertillery: Old Bakehouse, 2005)

Cornwell, John, *Collieries of Western Gwent* (Cowbridge: D. Brown & Sons, 1983)

Couch, Mal, ed., *Dictionary of Premillennial Theology* (Grand Rapids, MI: Kregel, 1996)

Cox, Harvey, *Fire from Heaven: The Rise of Pentecostal Spirituality and the Reshaping of Religion in the Twenty-first Century* (London: Cassell, 1996)

Cross, Joseph, *Sermons and Memoirs of Christmas Evans* (Grand Rapids, MI: Kregel, 1986)

Dallimore, Arnold, *The Life of Edward Irving: Forerunner of the Charismatic Movement* (Edinburgh: Banner of Truth, 1983)

Davies, D. Hywel, *The Welsh Nationalist Party 1925–45: A Call to Nationhood* (Cardiff: University of Wales Press, 1983)

Davies, D. P., *Against the Tide: Christianity in Wales on the Threshold of a New Millennium* (Llandysul: Gomer, 1995)

Davies, Eryl, *The Bala Ministers Conference 1955–2014* (Bridgend: Bryntirion Press, 2014)

————, *The Beddgelert Revival* (Bridgend: Bryntirion Press, 2004)

Davies, Gwyn, *A Light in the Land: Christianity in Wales 200–2000* (Bridgend: Bryntirion Press, 2002)

Davies, Horton, *The English Free Churches* (London: O.U.P., 1963)

Davies, John, *A History of Wales* (London: Penguin, 2007)

Davies, Price, *The Beginning of the Pentecostal Movement in the Merthyr Borough* (<www.dustandashes.com>, c. 1960).

Dayton, Donald, *Theological Roots of Pentecostalism* (Metuchen, NJ: Hendrickson, 1987)

Dempster, Murray W., Byron D. Klaus and Douglas Petersen, eds., *The Globalization of Pentecostalism: A Religion Made To Travel* (Oxford: Regnum Books International, 1999)

————, Byron D. Klaus and Douglas Petersen, eds., *Called & Empowered: Global Mission in Pentecostal Perspective* (Peabody, MA: Hendrickson, 1991)

Dodd, A. H., *A Short History of Wales* (London: B.T. Batsford, 1972)

Duewel, Wesley, *Revival Fire* (Grand Rapids, MI: Zondervan, 1995)

Dunn, James D. G., *Baptism In The Holy Spirit* (Philadelphia, PA: Westminster Press, 1970)

Dyer, Helen S., (complier), *Revival In India 1905–1906* (New York, NY: GPH, 1907)

Eaton, Michael A., *Baptism with the Spirit: The Teaching of Dr. Martyn Lloyd-Jones* (Leicester: I.V.P., 1989)

Edwards, Brian H., R*evival! A People Saturated with God* (Darlington: Evangelical Press, 1990)

Edwards, Jonathan, *Jonathan Edwards on Revival* (Edinburgh: Banner Of Truth, 1995)

Evans, D. Gareth, *A History of Wales 1815–1906* (Cardiff: University of Wales Press, 1989)

—————, *A History of Wales 1906–2000* (Cardiff: University of Wales Press, 2000)

Evans, Eifion, *Fire in the Thatch* (Bridgend: Evangelical Press, 1996)

—————, *Revival Comes to Wales: The Story of the 1859 Revival in Wales* (Bridgend: Evangelical Press, 1959, repr. 1995)

—————, *The Welsh Revival of 1904* (Bridgend: Bryntirion Press, 3rd ed. repr. 2004)

Fee, Gordon D., *The First Epistle To The Corinthians* (Grand Rapids, MI: Eerdmans, 1987)

—————, *God's Empowering Presence: The Holy Spirit in the Letters of Paul* (Peabody, MA: Hendrickson, 1994)

—————, *Gospel and Spirit* (Peabody, MA.: Hendrickson, 1991)

Ferguson, Sinclair B., and David F. Wright, eds., *New Dictionary of Theology* (Leicester: IVP, 1988)

Field, Marion, *John Nelson Darby: Prophetic Pioneer* (Godalming: Highland, 2008)

Fielder, Geraint, *Grace, Grit & Gumption: The Exploits of Evangelists John Pugh, Frank and Seth Joshua* (Fearn: Christian Focus, 2004)

Finney, Charles, *Principles of Revival* (Minneapolis, MN: Bethany House, 1987)

—————, *Revivals of Religion* (London: Morgan & Scott, 1910)

—————, *Systematic Theology* (Bloomington, MI: Bethany House, 1994)

Frodsham, Stanley H., *With Signs Following* (Springfield, MO: GPH, 1946)

Gaffin, Richard B. Jr., *Perspectives on Pentecost: New Testament Teaching on the Gifts of the Holy Spirit* (Phillipsburg, NJ: Presbyterian and Reformed Publishing Company, 1979)

Gee, Donald, *Concerning Spiritual Gifts* (Springfield, MO: GPH, 1947)

————, *The Ministry Gifts of Christ* (Springfield, MO: GPH, 1930)

————, *These Men I Knew; Personal Memories of Our Pioneers* (Nottingham: AoG, 1980)

————, *Towards Pentecostal Unity* (Springfield, MO: GPH, 1961)

————, *Trophimus I have left Sick* (London: Elim, 1952)

————, *Why Pentecost?* (London: Victory Press, n.d.)

————, *Wind and Flame* (London: AoG, 1967)

Gee, Henry, and Hardy, William John, *Documents Illustrative of English Church History* (London: Macmillan and Co., 1921)

Gibbard, Noel, *Fire on the Altar: A History and Evaluation of the 1904–05 Revival in Wales* (Bridgend: Bryntirion Press, 2005)

————, *On the Wings of the Dove* (Bridgend: Bryntirion Press, 2002)

————, *R. B. Jones: Gospel Ministry in Turbulent Times* (Bridgend: Bryntirion Press, 2009)

————, *Walter Craddock: 'A New Testament Saint'* (Bridgend: Evangelical Library of Wales, No.4, 1977)

Gibbs, Eddie, and Ryan K. Bolger, *Emerging Churches: Creating Christian Community in Postmodern Cultures* (London: SPCK, 2006)

Gray-Jones, Arthur, *A History of Ebbw Vale* (Rogerstone: Gwent County Council, 1970; 2nd ed. 1992)

Green, Roger Joseph, *The Life and Ministry of William Booth: Founder of the Salvation Army* (Nashville, TN: Abingdon Press, 2005)

Gresham, John L. Jr., *Charles G. Finney's Doctrine of the Baptism of the Holy Spirit* (Peabody, MA: Hendrickson, 1987)

Griffiths, George, *What God hath Wrought: A Brief Account Of The History Of The Tro'r Glein Mission Hall, Cwmtwrch On The Occasion Of Its Half-Century Celebrations* (Cwmtwrch: George Griffiths, 1962)

Grudem, Wayne, ed., *Are Miraculous Gifts for Today?* (Grand Rapids. MI: Zondervan, 1996)

—————, Sy*stematic Theology: An Introduction to Biblical Doctrine* (Leicester: I.V.P., 1994)

Gundry, Stanley N., ed., *Five Views on Sanctification* (Grand Rapids, MI: Zondervan, 1987)

—————, *Love Them In: The Life and Theology of D. L. Moody* (Chicago, IL: Moody Press, 1976)

—————, ed., *Three Views of the Millennium and Beyond* (Grand Rapids, MI: Zondervan, 1999)

Hamilton, James M. Jr., *God's Indwelling Presence: The Holy Spirit in the Old and New Testaments* (Nashville, TN: B&H Academic, 2006)

Hando, Fred. J., *The Pleasant Land of Gwent* (Newport: R.H. Johns, 1944)

Harper, Michael, *As At The Beginning: The Twentieth Century Pentecostal Revival* (London: Hodder and Stoughton, 1965)

Hastings, Adrian, ed., *The Oxford Companion To Christian Thought* (Oxford: O.U.P., 2004)

Hathaway, W. G., *Spiritual Gifts in the Church* (London: Marshall, 1933)

Haykin, Michael A. G., and Kenneth J. Stewart, eds., *The Emergence of Evangelicalism: Exploring Historical Continuities* (Nottingham: I.V.P. 2008)

Hendrickson, William, *New Testament Commentary Romans 9–11* (Edinburgh: Banner of Truth, 1981)

Henry, Matthew, *Matthew Henry's Commentary in One Volume* (London: Marshall, 1960)

Hodge, Charles, *The First Epistle to the Corinthians* (London: Banner of Truth, 1958)

Hodgson, E., *Fishing For Congo Fisher Folk* (London: AoG, 1934)

290

Hoekema, Anthony A., *What About Tongue Speaking?* (Exeter: Paternoster, 1966)

Hollenweger, Walter J., *Pentecostalism Origins and Developments Worldwide* (Peabody, MA: Hendrickson, 1997)

—————, *The Pentecostals* (London: SCM, 1972)

Holman, Bob, *F. B. Meyer,* (Fearn: Christian Focus, 2007)

Hopkins, Mark, *Nonconformity's Romantic Generation: Evangelical and Liberal Theologies in Victorian England* (Milton Keynes: Paternoster, 2004)

Horne, C. Silvester, *A Popular History Of The Free Churches* (London: Congregational Union, 1926)

Horridge, Charlotte, *The Salvation Army: A Pictorial Record* (Godalming: Ammonite Books, 1989)

Horton, Harold, *The Gifts of the Spirit* (Nottingham: AoG, 1934)

Horton, Stanley M., ed., *Systematic Theology* (Springfield, MO: Logion, 1995)

—————, *What The Bible Says About The Holy Spirit* (Springfield, MO: G.P.H., 1995)

Howton, Richard, *Divine healing and Demon Possession* (London: Ward, Lock&Co. Ltd., 1909) <www.revival-library.org>

Hulse, Erroll, *Crisis Experiences* (Haywards Heath: Carey, c. 1984)

Hywel-Davies, Jack, *Baptised By Fire: The Life of Smith Wigglesworth* (London: Hodder, 1987)

Jeffreys, Edward, *Stephen Jeffreys: The Beloved Evangelist* (London: Elim, 1946)

Johnson, Terry L., *The Case For Traditional Protestantism* (Edinburgh: Banner of Truth, 2004)

Jones, Alan Victor, *Risca - Its Industrial and Social Development* (Bognor: New Horizon, 1980)

Jones, Brynmor Pierce, *An Instrument of Revival: The Complete Life of Evan Roberts 1878–1951* (South Plainfield, NJ: Bridge, 1995)

—————, *How Lovely Are Thy Dwellings* (Newport: Wellspring, 1999)

—————, *The King's Champions: Revival and Reaction 1905–1935* (Cwmbran: CLP., 1968; repr. 1986)

—————, *Sowing Beside All Waters* (Cwmbran: Gwent Baptist Association, 1985)

—————, *The Spiritual History of Keswick in Wales 1903–1983* (Cwmbran: CLP, 1989)

—————, *The Trials and Triumphs of Mrs Jessie Penn-Lewis* (North Brunswick, NJ: Bridge-Logos, 1997)

—————, *Voices From the Welsh Revival 1904–1905* (Bridgend: Evangelical Press, 1995)

Jones, D. Geraint, *Favoured With Frequent Revivals: Revivals in Wales 1762–1862* (Cardiff: Heath Christian Trust, 2001)

Jones, John Morgan and William Morgan, *The Calvinistic Methodist Fathers Of Wales Volume 1,* translated by John Aaron (Edinburgh: Banner of Truth, 2008)

—————, and William Morgan, *The Calvinistic Methodist Fathers Of Wales Volume 2,* trans. John Aaron (Edinburgh: Banner of Truth, 2008)

Jones, Peter Morgan, *Hills of Fire and Iron* (Abertillery: Old Bakehouse, 1992)

Jones, R. B., *Rent Heavens* (London: Stanley Martin & Co., 1930)

Jones, R. Tudur, *Congregationalism in Wales* (Cardiff: University of Wales Press, 2004)

—————, *Faith and the Crisis of a Nation Wales 1890–1914,* Robert Pope ed., translated by Sylvia Prys Jones (Cardiff: University of Wales Press, 2004)

Joyner, Rick, *The Power to Change the World The Welsh and Azusa Street Revivals* (Fort Mill, SC: MorningStar, 2006)

292

Karkkainen, Veli-Matti, *Pneumatology* (Grand Rapids, MI: Baker, 2002)

Kay, William K., *Inside Story A History of British Assemblies of God* (Mattersey: Mattersey Hall, 1990)

————, *Pentecostals in Britain* (Carlisle: Paternoster, 2000)

————, *Prophecy!* (Nottingham: Life Stream, 1991)

Knox, R. Buick, *Voices From The Past: History of the English Conference of the Presbyterian Church in Wales, 1889–1939* (Llandyssul: Gomerian Press, 1969)

Kydd, Ronald A. N., *Charismatic Gifts in the Early Church* (Peabody, MA: Hendrickson, 1984)

Lazell, David, *Gypsy From The Forest* (Bridgend: Bryntirion Press, 1997)

Letham, Robert, *The Holy Trinity In Scripture, History, Theology and Worship* (Phillipsburg, NJ: P&R Publishing, 2004)

————, *The Lord's Supper Eternal Word in Broken Bread* (Phillipsburg, NJ: P&R Publishing, 2001)

Lewis, William Henry, *And He Gave Some Apostles* (Bradford: Puritan Books, 1954)

Liardon, Roberts, *The Azusa Street Revival: When The Fire Fell* (Shippensburg, PA: Destiny Image, 2006)

————, (compiler), *Smith Wigglesworth The Complete Collection of His Life Teaching* (Tulsa, OK: Albury, 1996)

Linford, Aaron, *A Course Study on Spiritual Gifts* (London: AoG, 1969)

Llewelyn, Abdiel and Bailey, Dorothy R., *Bethesda, Tydu: A Bicentenary Survey of the History of Bethesda Baptist Church Tydu* (Rogerstone: Bethesda Baptist, 1942; expanded 1984)

Lloyd-Jones, D. Martyn, *Joy Unspeakable: The Baptism with the Holy Spirit*, ed. Christopher Catherwood (Eastbourne: Kingsway, 1984)

Lord, Andrew, *Spirit-Shaped Mission: A Holistic Charismatic Missiology* (Milton Keynes: Paternoster, 2005)

Lowe, Karen, *Carriers of the Fire: The Women of the Welsh Revival 1904/05* (Llanelli: Shedhead Productions, 2004)

McClung, Grant, ed., *Azusa Street and Beyond* (Gainesville, FL: Bridge-Logos, 2006)

McDonnell, Killian and George T. Montague, *Christian Initiation And Baptism In The Holy Spirit* (Collegeville, MI: Liturgical Press, 1991)

McGee, Gary B., ed., *Initial Evidence: Historical and Biblical Perspectives on the Pentecostal Doctrine of Spirit Baptism* (Eugene, OR: Wipf & Stock, 2007)

MacArthur, John F. Jr., *Charismatic Chaos* (Grand Rapids, MI: Zondervan, 1992)

MacNeil, John, *The Spirit-Filled Life Updated Edition,* ed. Avdi Benkefa (Sven Pederson: 2006; first published Australia 1895 <www.fairthings.com>)

Macpherson, Ian, *The Faith Once Delivered* (Milton Keynes: Word, 1988)

Macchia, Frank D., *Baptized in The Spirit: A Global Pentecostal Theology* (Grand Rapids MI: Zondervan, 2006)

Machen, J. Gresham, *Christianity and Liberalism* (Grand Rapids, MI, Eerdmans, 1923)

Madden, Lionel, ed., *Methodism In Wales: A Short History Of The Wesley Tradition* (Llandudno: Methodist Conference, 2003)

Malcomson, Keith, *Pentecostal Pioneers Remembered: British and Irish Pioneers of Pentecost* (Xulon Press: xulonpress.com, 2008)

Marr, Andrew, *The Making of Modern Britain* (London: Macmillan, 2009)

Marshall, I. Howard, *Luke Historian and Theologian* (Exeter: Paternoster, 1979)

Massey, Richard, *Another Springtime: The Life Of Donald Gee Pentecostal Leader and Teacher* (Guildford: Highland, 1992)

Matthews, David, *I Saw the Welsh Revival* (Jasper, AR: End-time Handmaidens, Inc., n.d.)

294

Metcalfe, J. C., *Molded by the Cross: The Biography of Jessie Penn-Lewis* (Fort Washington, PA: CLC, 1997)

Menzies, Robert P., *Empowered for Witness: The Spirit in Luke-Acts* (London: T&T Clark, 2004)

Menzies, William W., and Robert P. Menzies, *Spirit and Power: Foundations of Pentecostal Experience* (Grand Rapids, MI: Zondervan, 2000)

Missen, Alfred F., *The Sound Of A Going* (Nottingham: AoG, 1973)

Morgan, D. Densil, *The Span of the Cross Christian Religion and Society in Wales 1914–2000* (Cardiff: University of Wales Press, 2011)

Morgan, G. Campbell, *The Spirit of God* (London: Westminster City Publishing, n.d.)

Morgan, Kenneth O., *Rebirth of a Nation A History of Modern Wales* (Oxford: O.U.P., 1981)

Murray, Andrew, *The Collected Works of Andrew Murray* (Kindle Edition: 2011, <www.amazon.co.uk>)

————, *The Full Blessing of Pentecost* (Plainfield, NJ: Logos International, 1974)

————, *Divine Healing* (Importantia Publishing: Kindle Edition <www.amazon.co.uk>)

————, *The Spirit of Christ* (London: Marshall, Morgan & Scott, 1963)

Murray, Iain H., *D. Martyn Lloyd-Jones The First Forty Years 1899–1939* (Edinburgh: Banner of Truth Trust, 1982)

Murray, Ian H., *Lloyd-Jones Messenger of Grace* (Edinburgh: Banner of Truth, 2008)

Nee, Watchman, *A Living Sacrifice.* (New York, NY: Christian Fellowship Publishers, 1972)

————, *Spiritual Knowledge* (New York, NY: Christian Fellowship Publishers, 1973)

—————, *The Spiritual Man* (New York, NY: Christian Fellowship Publishers, 1968)

Newport Borough Council, *A History of Newport* (Newport County Council, 1986)

Olford, Stephen F., *Heart-Cry for Revival* (London: Marshall, Morgan & Scott, 1962)

Osborne, Graham O., *A History of Hope Baptist Church Crosskeys* (Abertillery: Old Bakehouse, 2006)

Packer, J. I., *Keep In Step With The Spirit: Finding Fullness In Our Walk With God* (*New Expanded Edition*) (Leicester: I.V.P. 2005)

Parham, Mrs Sarah E., *The Life of Charles Fox Parham: Founder of the Apostolic Faith Movement* (Joplin, MO: Tri-State Publishing, 1930)

Parr, John Nelson, *Incredible* (Fleetwood: John Nelson Parr, 1972)

Pearlman, Myer, *Knowing the Doctrines of the Bible* (Springfield, MO: G.P.H., 1937; 21st printing 1999)

Peel, Albert, *These Hundred Years* (London: Congregational Union, 1931)

Penn-Lewis, Jessie, *The Awakening in Wales* (Fort Washington, PA: CLC, 1993)

—————, with Evan Roberts *War on the Saints* (Burgess Hill: Diggory Press, 2005)

—————, *The Work of the Holy Spirit* (Fort Washington, PA: CLC, 1992)

Penney, John Michael, *The Missionary Emphasis of Lukan Pneumatology*, Journal of Pentecostal Theology Supplement 12 (Sheffield: Sheffield Academic Press, 1997)

Peskett, Howard, and Vinroth Ramachandra, *The Message of Mission* (Leicester: I.V.P., 2003)

Petts, David, *Body Builders: Gifts to Make God's People Grow* (Mattersey: Mattersey Hall, 2002)

—————, *The Dynamic Difference* (Springfield, MO: G.P.H., 1976)

—————, *The Holy Spirit – an Introduction* (Mattersey: Mattersey Hall, 1998)

—————, *Just a Taste of Heaven: a Biblical and Balanced Approach to God's Healing Power* (Mattersey: Mattersey Hall, 2006)

—————, *You'd Better Believe It* (Mattersey: Mattersey Hall, 2005)

Pinnock, Clark H., *Flame of Love: A Theology of The Holy Spirit* (Downers Grove, IL: I.V.P. 1996)

Pollock, John, *The Cambridge Seven* (Fearn: Christian Focus, 2006 repr. 2009)

—————, *John Wesley* (Oxford: Lion, 1989)

—————, *Whitefield: The Evangelist* (Eastbourne: Kingsway, 2000)

—————, *The Keswick Story: The Authorized History of the Keswick Convention – Updated!* (Fort Washington, PA: CLC, 2006)

Pope, Robert, *Building Jerusalem: Nonconformity, Labour and the Social Question in Wales, 1906–1939* (Cardiff: University of Wales Press, 1998)

—————, *Seeking God's Kingdom: The Nonconformist Social Gospel in Wales 1906–1939* (Cardiff: University of Wales Press, 1999)

Randall, Ian M., *Evangelical Experiences: A Study in the Spirituality of English Evangelicalism 1918–1939* (Milton Keynes: Paternoster, 1999)

Rea, John, *The Holy Spirit in the Bible* (London: Marshall, 1990)

Rees, T. Mardy, *Seth and Frank Joshua: The Renowned Evangelists The Story Of Their Wonderful Work* (Wrexham: Principality Press, 1929)

Robeck, Cecil M. Jr., *The Azusa Street Mission and Revival: The Birth of the Global Pentecostal Movement* (Nashville, TN: Nelson, 2006)

Roberts, Dyfed Wyn, ed., *Revival, Renewal and the Holy Spirit* (Milton Keynes: Paternoster, 2009)

Roberts, J. H. A., *A View From The Hill* (Risca: Moriah Baptist Church, c. 1986)

Robinson, James, *Pentecostal Origins: Early Pentecostalism in Ireland in the Context of the British Isles* (Milton Keynes: Paternoster, 2005)

Roderick, A. J., ed., *Wales Through The Ages Volume 2 Modern Wales* (Llandybie: Christopher Davies, 1960)

Ross, David, *Wales: History of a Nation* (New Lanark: Geddes & Grosset, 2008)

Rosser, Rayner, *Collieries of the Sirhowy Valley* (Abertillery: Old Bakehouse, 1996)

Rowe, William A. C., *One Lord One Faith* (Penygroes: Apostolic Publications, 1988)

Salvation Army, *The Salvation Army: Its Origin and Development* (London, Salvationist Publishing and Supplies Limited, 1927; Revised 1945)

Saunders, Raymond, *1884: Memories of Tab. A Brief History of Tabernacle Congregational Chapel Rhiwderin* (Rhiwderin: R. Saunders, 2006)

Scofield, C. I., ed., *The New Scofield Reference Bible* (New York, NY: O.U.P., 1967)

Searby, Peter, *The Chartists in Wales* (Harlow: Longman, 1986)

Seymour, William, *The Azusa Papers* (Kindle Edition: Jawbone Digital, 2012)

Spencer, Colin, *The Lamps Have Gone Out at the Celynen North & Graig Fawr Collieries* (Newbridge: Spencer, n.d.)

Spittler, Russell P., ed., *Perspectives on the New Pentecostalism* (Grand Rapids, MI: Baker, 1976)

Spurgeon, C. H., *Twelve Sermons on the Holy Spirit* (Grand Rapids, MI: Baker, 1973)

Stevenson, Herbert F., ed., *Keswick's Authentic Voice: Sixty-Five Dynamic Addresses Delivered At The Keswick Convention 1875–1957* (London: Marshall, Morgan & Scott, 1959)

Stewart, James A., *Invasion of Wales By The Spirit Through Evan Roberts* (Fort Washington, PA: Christian Literature Crusade, 1963)

Stronstad, Roger, *The Charismatic Theology of St. Luke* (Peabody, MA: Hendrickson, 1984)

Synan, Vinson, *The Holiness-Pentecostal Movement in the United States* (Grand Rapids, MI: Eerdmans, 1977)

—————, *The Holiness-Pentecostal Tradition* (Grand Rapids, MI: Zondervan, 1997)

Tanner, D., C. Williams and D. Hopkins, eds., *The Labour Party in Wales, 1900–2000* (Cardiff: University of Wales Press, 2000)

Taylor, A. J. P., *English History 1914–1945* (London: Book Club Associates, 1977)

Thomas, I. D. E., *God's Harvest: The Nature of True Revival* (Bridgend: Bryntirion Press, 1997)

Thomas, John Christopher, *Toward a Pentecostal Ecclesiology: The Church and the Fivefold Gospel* (Cleveland, TN: CPT Press, 2010)

Thomas, Ralph, *Oakdale – The Model Village* (Blackwood: R. E. Thomas, 2004)

Thompson, Steven, *Unemployment, Poverty and Health in Inter-War South Wales* (Cardiff: University of Wales Press, 2006)

Torrey, R. A., *The Person and Work of the Holy Spirit* (New York, NY: Fleming H. Revell, 1910, Kindle Edition, <www.amazon.co.uk>)

Torrey, R. A., *What the Bible Teaches* (Springdale, PA: Whittaker House, 1998)

Trumbull, Charles Gallaudet, *The Life of C. I. Scofield* (New York, NY: O.U.P., 1920; Digitized version by <www.WholesomeWords.org>)

Turnbull, T. N., *What God Hath Wrought A Short History of the Apostolic Church* (Bradford: Puritan Press, 1959)

Turner, Max, *The Holy Spirit and Spiritual Gifts Then and Now* (London: Paternoster, 2008)

Unger, Merrill F., *New Testament Teaching on Tongues* (Grand Rapids, MI: Kregel, 1971)

Wagner, C. Peter., *Your Spiritual Gifts Can Help Your Church Grow* (Bromley: Marc Europe, 1985)

Wakefield, Gavin, *Alexander Boddy, Pentecostal Anglican Pioneer* (London: Paternoster, 2007)

Walker, Andrew and Kristin Aune, eds., *On Revival: A Critical Examination* (Carlisle: Paternoster, 2003)

Walvoord, John F., *Prophecy- 14 Essential Keys to Understanding the Final Drama* (Nashville, TN: Thomas Nelson, 1993)

Warfield, B. B., *Counterfeit Miracles* (Edinburgh: Banner of Truth, 1972)

—————, *The Person and Work of the Holy Spirit* (Amityville, NY: Calvary Press, 1997)

Warrington, Keith, *Discovering the Holy Spirit in the New Testament* (Peabody, MA: Hendrickson, 2005)

—————, *Healing and Suffering: Biblical and Pastoral Reflections* (Milton Keynes: Paternoster, 2005)

—————, *The Message of the Holy Spirit* (Leicester: IVP, 2009)

—————, ed., *Pentecostal Perspectives* (Carlisle: Paternoster, 1998)

—————, *Pentecostal Theology: A Theology of Encounter* (London: T&T Clark, 2008)

Welch, Tim, *Joseph Smale: God's 'Moses' for Pentecostalism* (Milton Keynes: Paternoster, 2013)

Wesley, John, *The Holy Spirit and Power as paraphrased by Clare Weakley* (Plainfield, NJ: Logos International, 1977)

Whittaker, Colin, *Great Revivals: God's Men and Their Message* (Basingstoke: Marshalls, 1984)

—————, *Seven Pentecostal Pioneers* (Basingstoke: Marshalls, 1983)

Williams, Cyril G., *Tongues Of The Spirit. A Study of Pentecostal Glossolalia and Related Phenomena* (Cardiff: University of Wales Press, 1981)

Williams, David, *A History of Modern Wales* (London: John Murray, 1950)

Williams, Howell, *The Romance Of The Forward Movement Of The Presbyterian Church Of Wales* (Denbigh: Gee & Son, n.d.)

Williams, J. Rodman, *Renewal Theology Systematic Theology from a Charismatic Perspective Three volumes in one* (Grand Rapids, MI: Zondervan, 1996)

Williams, William, *Welsh Calvinistic Methodism A Historical Sketch Of The Presbyterian Church Of Wales. Third ed.* (Bridgend: Bryntirion Press, 1998)

Wilmington Group, *The Great Azusa Street Revival The Life and Sermons of William Seymour* (Fort Lauderdale, FL: Wilmington Publishing, 2006)

Womersley, David and David Garrard, eds., *Into Africa: The Thrilling Story of William Burton and Central African Missions* (Preston: Central Africa Missions, 2005)

Womersley, Harold, *Congo Miracle Fifty Years of God's Working in Congo (Zaire)* (Eastbourne: Victory Press, 1974)

—————, *Wm. F. P. Burton Congo Pioneer* (Eastbourne: Victory Press, 1973)

Worsfold, James E., *The Origins of the Apostolic Church in Great Britain; with a Breviate of its Early Missionary Endeavours* (Wellington: Julian Literature Trust, 1991)

Yong, Amos, *The Spirit Poured Out on All Flesh: Pentecostalism and the Possibility of Global Theology* (Grand Rapids, MI: Baker Academic, 2005)

Journal Articles

Allen, David, 'The Glossolalic Ostrich: Isolationism and Other-worldliness in the British Assemblies of God,' *JEPTA* 13 (1994), pp. 50–62

—————, 'Revival – A Classic Pentecostal View,' *JEPTA* 2 (2007), pp. 118–127

Anderson, Allan, 'Signs and Blunders: Pentecostal Mission Issues at "Home and Abroad" in the Twentieth century,' Henry Martyn seminar 17th Feb. (2000) <www.martynmission.com.ac.uk/BArticles.htm>

Balfour, Glenn, 'Pentecostal Eschatology Revisited,' in *JEPTA* 31/2 (2011), pp. 127–140

Blumhofer, Edith, 'The Welsh Revival 1904–1905,' *Paraclete* 20/3 Summer (1986)

Boulton, E. C. W, 'British Council Now Formed,' *The Pentecostal Evangel* August 5 (1922), p. 9

Brown, James D., 'The Holy Spirit's Activity in Evangelism,' *Paraclete* Winter (1968), pp. 6–11

Bundy, David, 'Spiritual Advice to a Seeker: Letters to T. B. Barratt from Azusa Street 1906,' *Pneuma* Fall (1992) 14/2, pp. 159–70

—————, 'Thomas Ball Barratt: From Methodist to Pentecostal,' *JEPTA* 13 (1994), pp. 19–49

Carlson, G. Raymond, 'Anointing with Oil,' *Paraclete* Spring (1969), pp. 15–17

Cartledge, Mark, 'The Early Pentecostal Theology of *Confidence* Magazine 1908–1926: A Version of the Five-Fold Gospel?' *JEPTA* 28/2 (2008), pp. 117–130

Cartwright, Desmond W., 'From The Backstreets Of Brixton To The Royal Albert Hall: British Pentecostalism 1907–1928,' *EPTA* Leuven Belgium December (1981) <www.smithwigglesworth.com/pensketches/brixton.htm>

—————, 'Everywhere Spoken Against: Opposition to Pentecostalism 1907–1930,' Birmingham: *EPTA* (1984)

Cho, Kyuhyung, 'The Importance of the Welsh Religious Revival in the formation of British Pentecostalism,' *JEPTA* 30/1 (2010), pp. 20–33

Christian Herald Welsh Revival Issue, facsimile edition (CPO: Worthing, 2007)

Dowie, John Alexander, 'Christ's Method of Healing.' *A Voice from Zion* 2/5 May (1898) <www.revival-libary.org>

————, 'What should a Christian do when sick?' *A Voice from Zion* 2/1 January (1898) <www.revival-library.org>

E.P.C.R.A. 'Holiness and Pentecostal Spirituality in Inter-war England'. 125th Meeting of the *Society for Pentecostal Studies and The European Pentecostal and Charismatic Research Association*. Mattersey Hall, Doncaster, England 10–14 July, 1995.

Friesen, Aaron, 'The Called Out of the Called Out: Charles Parham's Doctrine of Spirit Baptism.' *JEPTA* 19/1 (2009), pp. 43–55

Garrard, David J., 'Burton's Early Years of Ministry and Doctrine under the auspices of the PMU,' *JEPTA* 32/1 (2012), pp. 3–14

————, 'W. F. P. Burton and His Missionary Call,' *JEPTA* 32/2 (2012), pp. 237–247

————, 'William F. P. Burton and the Rupture with the PMU.' *JEPTA* 33/1 (2013), pp. 14–27

Gibbard, Noel, 'Evan Roberts: The Post Revival Years, 1906–1951,' *The Journal of Welsh Religious History* 5 (2005), pp. 60–76

Goodwin, Leigh, 'The Pneumatological Motivation and Influences of the Cambridge Seven,' *JEPTA* 30/2 (2010), pp. 21–38

Hathaway, Malcolm R., 'The Role of William Oliver Hutchinson and the Apostolic Faith Church in the formation of British Pentecostal Churches,' *JEPTA* 16 (1996), pp. 40–57

Hocken, Fr. Peter, 'Cecil Polhill – Pentecostal Layman.' *PNEUMA* Fall (1988) 10/2, pp. 116–140

Holdcroft, L. Thomas, 'The Gift of the Gifts of Healing', *Paraclete* Spring (1968), pp. 9–12

Horton, Stanley M., 'The Holy Spirit and Christ's Coming', *Paraclete* Winter (1968), pp. 12–16

Hudson, Neil, 'Dealing with the Fire: Early Pentecostal Responses to the practices of speaking in tongues and spoken prophecy.' *JEPTA* 28/2 (2008), pp. 145–157

————, 'The Earliest Days of British Pentecostalism,' *JEPTA* 21 (2001), pp. 49–67

Hurtado, Larry W., 'Healing and Related Factors,' *Paraclete* Spring (1970), pp. 20–25

Irvin, Dale T., 'Drawing All Together in One Bond of Love: The Ecumenical Vision of William J. Seymour and The Azusa Street Revival.' *Journal of Pentecostal Theology* 6 (1995), pp. 25–53

Karkkainen, Veli-Matti, 'Encountering Christ in the Full Gospel Way: An Incarnational Pentecostal Spirituality.' *JEPTA* 27/1 (2007), pp. 5–19

Kay, Peter, 'The Pentecostal Missionary union and the Fourfold Gospel with Baptism in the Holy Spirit and Speaking in Tongues: A New Power for Missions?' *JEPTA* 19 (1999), pp. 89–104

Kay, William K., 'Approaches to Healing in British Pentecostalism,' *Journal Of Pentecostal Theology* 14 (1999), pp. 113–125

————, 'Sunderland's Legacy in New Denominations,' *JEPTA* 28/2 (2008), pp. 183–199

————, 'Why did the Welsh Revival Stop?' Paper to be presented at the Conference, *Revival, Renewal and the Holy Spirit,* University of Wales Bangor 22–26 June (2004).

Laan, Cornelius van der, 'Alexander Boddy: Anglican Father of Dutch Pentecostalism,' *JEPTA* 31/1 (2011), pp. 93–110

Lloyd-Jones, D. Martyn, 'Living the Christian Life – 5 New Developments in the 18th and 19th Century Teaching.' *Living the Christian Life: 1974 Westminster Conference papers,* Westminster Conference (1974), pp. 82–99

Massey, Richard, D., *A Flirtation with Elim – Donald Gee's Negotiations to join the Elim Pentecostal Alliance in 1923*. Extract from Massey, 'A Sound and Scriptural Union' (PhD, Birmingham, 1987)

Mercy, Sidney, 'Pentecost in South Wales.' *Pentecostal Evangel* June (1928), p. 8 <www.ifphc.org/pdf/PentecostalEvangel/1920-1929/1928/1928_06_16pdf#page8>

The Ocean and National Magazine, March/April (1934).

Olsen, Ted, 'American Pentecost.' *Christian History* 58 vol. 17/2 (1998), pp. 10–17

Orr, J. Edwin, 'The Welsh Revival Goes Worldwide.' *Western Mail*, 9 December 1974

Palmer, Chris, 'Mission: The True Pentecostal Heritage as Illustrated in Early British AoG Thinking,' *JEPTA* 30/2 (2010), pp. 39–50

Petts, David, 'Healing and the Atonement,' *JEPTA* 12 (1993), pp. 23–37

Pope, Robert, 'The Consistency of Faith: Calvinism in Early Twentieth Century Welsh Nonconformity,' *The Welsh Journal of Religious History* 4 (2009), pp. 55–69

—————, 'Demythologising the Evan Roberts Revival, 1904–1905,' *The Journal of Ecclesiastical History* 57/3, pp. 515–534

Powers, Janet Evert, 'Missionary Tongues?' *Journal of Pentecostal Theology* 17 October (2000), pp. 39–55

Randall, Ian M., 'Old Time Power: Relationships between Pentecostalism and Evangelical Spirituality in England.' *PNEUMA* 19/1 Spring (1997), pp. 53–80

Record of the International Conference on Divine Healing and True Holiness, London June 1 to 5 1885; London: John Snow & Co. <www.revival-library.org>

Reiff, Anna C., 'Mining – From Coal to Men.' *The Latter Rain Evangel*, October (1922), pp. 14–16 <www.ifphc.org/pdf/LatterRainEvangel/1920-1929>

Roberts, Evan, 'A Message to the World by Evan Roberts.' *The Story of the Welsh Revival by Eyewitnesses* <www.dustandashes.com>

Simpson, Carl, 'Jonathan Paul and The German Pentecostal Movement – The First Seven Years, 1907–1914,' *JEPTA* 28/2 (2008), pp. 169–182

Smeeton, Donald Dean, 'John Alexander Dowie: An Evaluation.' *Paraclete* Spring (1981), pp. 27–31

Sunday Companion, 8th April, 1961.

Sunday Companion, 15th April, 1961.

Sunday Companion, 22nd April, 1961.

Sunday Companion, 29th April, 1961.

Thomas, John Christopher, 'Healing in the Atonement: A Johannine Perspective,' *Journal of Pentecostal Theology* October (2005) 14/1, pp. 23–39

Tudur, Geraint, 'Evan Roberts and the 1904–05 Revival,' *The Journal of Welsh Religious History* 4 (2004), pp. 80–101

Turner, Christopher, 'A Movement of the Laity: The Welsh Religious Revival of 1904–05', *Historical Journal of the Presbyterian Church of Wales* 34 (2010), pp. 130–160

Usher, John, 'The Significance of Cecil H. Polhill for the development of Early Pentecostalism,' *JEPTA* 29/2 (2009), pp. 36–60

Wacker, Grant, 'Hell Hatched Free Lovism,' *Christian History* 58, 17/2 (1998), pp. 28–31

Wakefield, Gavin, 'The Human Face of Pentecostalism: Why the British Pentecostal Moment began in the Sunderland Parish of the Church of England Vicar Alexander Boddy.' *JEPTA* 28/2 (2008), pp. 158–168

Ward, C. M., 'Healing by the Holy Spirit.' *Paraclete* Spring (1968), pp. 13–15

Warrington, Keith, 'Acts and the Healing Narratives: Why?' *Journal of Pentecostal Theology* 14/2 April (2006), pp. 189–218

—————, 'Anointing with Oil and Healing,' *JEPTA* 12 (1993), pp. 5–22

Williams, Peter Howell, 'Jumpers – Blessed Enthusiasts or Bizarre Episodes?' *Historical Journal of the Presbyterian Church of Wales* 29–30 (2005), pp. 43–72

Dissertations

Allen, David, 'Signs and Wonders: The Origins, Growth, Development and Significance of Assemblies of God in Great Britain and Ireland 1900–1980,' (PhD Diss. University of London: unpublished, 1990)

Dyer, A. E., 'Missionary Vocation: A Study of British Assemblies of God's World Missions 1965–2000,' (PhD Diss. University of Wales, Bangor, unpublished, 2008)

Jones, Brynmor Pierce, 'A Biographical Study of the Rev. R. B. Jones (1869–1933) First Principal of the South Wales Bible Institute with A Critical Survey of Welsh Fundamentalism in the post-revival era (1904–1936)' (Dissertation, May 1996, copy held at WEST library)

Llewellyn, H. B., 'A Study of the History and Thought of the Apostolic Church in Wales in the context of Pentecostalism,' (MPhil. Diss. University of Cardiff, 1997) <www.hollenwegercentre.net/logpubls/apostolic.pdf>

Massey, Richard, 'A Sound and Scriptural Union.' An Examination of the origins of the Assemblies of God in Great Britain and Ireland during the years 1920–25,' (PhD Diss. University of Birmingham, unpublished, 1987)

Prothroe, David, 'An Analysis and Theological Evaluation of Revival and Revivalism in America from 1730–1860,' (PhD Diss. University of North West South Africa, Potchefstroom, 2004)

Unpublished Material

80 Years At Golden Grove 1923–2003: Celebrating 80 Years of Pentecostal testimony at Golden Grove. A brief history of the AoG Chapel Newbridge Gwent, <www.pentecostalchurchnewbridge.co.uk>

Attwood, W. G., *How Pentecost Came To Crosskeys.* c. 1940

A Brief Account of the Inception of the Apostolic Church in the Monmouthshire Valleys. Made available to me by Mr Colin Evans Ebbw Vale.

Barratt, T. B., 'The Gift of Tongues: What is it? Being a reply to Dr. A. C. Dixon,' (sermon preached June 1914), Bishop's Waltham: Revival Library <www.revival-library.org>

Davies, Price, *A Testimony and a brief record of the Beginnings of the Pentecostal Movement in the Merthyr Borough, Bedlinog and the Aberdare Valley.* C.1961, <www.dustandashes.com/624.htm>

Duckpool Road Baptist Church, Newport, South Wales 1875–2000, 125th Anniversary Booklet

Garrard, David J., *The Importance of keeping the Premillennial rider in any statement of Faith regarding the Second Coming of Christ* (2002, available at Mattersey Hall, AoG Headquarters)

Gwynne, M., *The History of Oakdale Presbyterian Church* (M. Gwynne: Oakdale, n.d.)

Hyde, Bob., *Do Pentecostals need to be Premillennial?* A Discussion Paper submitted to the General Council of the Assemblies of God, October 2002.

'The Late Pastor Jacob Purnell's Testimony: The Monmouthshire Valleys', unpublished testimony obtained from Mr. Colin Evans of Abergavenny Apostolic Church.

Tabernacle English Baptist Church, Newbridge 150th Anniversary 1859–2009 Souvenir Brochure celebrating the history of Tabernacle, <www.tabernacle-newbridge.org.uk>

CD. ROM

Cauchi, Tony, *The Apostolic Faith: 1906–1908.* Bishop's Waltham: Revival Library, 2004.

—————, *Confidence Magazine: 1908–1926.* Bishop's Waltham: Revival Library, 2004.

—————, *The Elim Evangel and Foursquare Revivalist: 1919–1934.* Bishop's Waltham: Revival Library, 2004.

—————, *Flames of Fire 1911–1917.* Bishop's Waltham: Revival Library, 2004.

—————, *Life of Faith 1905.* Bishop's Waltham: Revival Library, 2010.

—————, *Pentecost Magazine*. Bishop's Waltham: Revival Library.

—————, *Redemption Tidings 1924–1939: The First Official Magazine of the British Assemblies of God*. Bishop's Waltham: Revival Library, 2005.

—————, *Welsh Revival Library: Centenary Edition 1904–2004*. Bishop's Waltham: Revival Library, 2004.

—————, *The Works of Alexander A. Boddy 1854–1930*. Bishop's Waltham: Revival Library, 2010.

Websites

<www.1911census.co.uk>

<www.anglicanhistory.org.nz>

<www.apostolicarchives.com>

<www.apostolic-church.org>

<http://www.blaenau-gwent.gov.uk/theworks/archive/History%20of%20Ebbw%20Vale%20Steelworks.pdf>

<www.chartists.net>

<www.crosskeys.me.uk/history/pits.htm>

<http://darwin-online.org.uk>

<www.dustandashes.com>

<www.dwlib.co.uk/dwlib/family/index.html>

<www.elim.org.uk>

<www.eptaonline.com>

<http://www.genuki.org.uk/big/wal/Dissent.html>

<www.hollenwegercenter.net>

<www.ifphc.org>

<http://www.historylearningsite.co.uk/BritishElectoral_History1832.htm>

<www.num.org.uk/page/History-NUMHistory>

<www.parliament.uk>

<www.pctii.org>

<www.pentecostalpioneers.org>

<www.revival-library.org>

<http://www.salvationarmy.org/ihq/www_sa.nsf/vw-local/United-Kingdom-with-the-Republic-of-Ireland>

<www.trefeca.org.uk>

<http://www2.salvationarmy.org.uk/history>

<www.smithwigglesworth.com>

<www.watchmannee.org>

<www.WholesomeWords.org >

<www.worldtimelines.org.uk>

SD - #0026 - 270225 - C0 - 229/152/17 - PB - 9781910942314 - Gloss Lamination